Walking Through The Storm

KENNETH J. KENDRA

DEDICATION

For my late mother. She always pushed me to give maximum effort in everything I do, when I knew that minimal effort would be good enough. She inspired me to write this book, even if it was a decade after her passing. In my heart I know she would be proud.

CONTENTS

ACKNOWLEDGMENTS

There are so many people that helped make this book possible. I first need to thank my family. My mother always inspired me to aim high and achieve great things. It was ten years after her death that I reflected on a promise that I made to her about writing a book one day. I hope that she is looking down at me from the heavens proud of what I have now accomplished. To my father who brought me into the world of soccer at age six, traveling around the northeast to watch as many of my games as humanly possible. His passion spurred my love for the beautiful game. My sisters Kimi and Krista have always been supportive of everything I do. Lastly to my brother Kevin, who shares my passion for Liverpool Football Club and was there at the beginning of the Raleigh Red movement in July 2012. I couldn't have done it without any of you.

I need to especially thank my brother-in-law Tom Mullen, the most qualified literature expert I know. We share a love for sport and constantly bounce ideas off each other, most of the time with him being the voice of reason for some ludicrous thought I have. I used to joke with my sister Krista that if they ever get divorced then I may choose to keep him over her. Tom spent countless hours reviewing every chapter despite juggling a new career and youth soccer practices. He offered exceptional advice throughout the project to ensure that the narrative was both fluid and accurate.

As you may have guessed, writing is not my primary source of income. I am lucky enough to have an employer that allows me the flexibility and vacation time to travel as much as I needed to for this book. While I used paid time off for the purposes of traveling to various cities, I sincerely appreciate my managers for giving me the latitude needed for this project.

I want to thank Liverpool Football Club for being the greatest soccer club on the planet. Of course I may be slightly biased in that assessment, but their brand has been a complete joy to follow and I am proud to call myself a Red. So proud that I have the ink on my left ankle to prove it.

North American fans of LFC, there are far too many of you to name individually. Over the past few years I have added many of you to my social network. When I shared this idea to travel the continent throughout the season to watch LFC matches live at various pubs, I received numerous invitations far and wide. Unfortunately there are many more pubs than there are matches which I could afford to travel. I did the best I could to visit as many possible given my time and budget constraints, but many great places had to be passed over. Perhaps I can add a second and third story to this narrative in the future and include the neglected establishments and great fans in the process.

KENNETH J. KENDRA

As one of the founding fathers of Raleigh's official LFC supporters club, I want to thank my fellow organizational committee members that have helped make the Raleigh Reds probably the greatest club on the planet. Colin Russell, Sean Dotzauer, and Dan Franklin have done a tremendous job with our little group. We couldn't have achieved so much in a short period of time without you.

I would be remised if I didn't also acknowledge Darren Bridger and Mike Ruiz, owners of the London Bridge Pub, for ensuring the doors to their pub are open for every LFC match including those early Sunday kickoffs. For that matter I would like to thank all of the pub owners that open their doors for Liverpool supporters everywhere.

Every time I go to the pub, whether it be in Raleigh or elsewhere, I see old friends and meet new ones in the process. Many have found their way into this story, but sadly there are too many to include everyone and keep this book at a reasonable size. If you were excluded from these pages, I humbly apologize. Rest assured it was not intentional.

During the season I was lucky enough to meet Austin Long, a soccer podcaster living in Atlanta. He invited me on his *Soccer Nomad* podcast to discuss this project a few times. Even though Austin is a Manchester United supporter, I owe him a debt of gratitude for his efforts to plug this book.

Thank you to Barry McCabe for creating the book cover design exactly as I had envisioned it. The aspiring graphic designer from Dublin, Ireland is the son of Noel McCabe, who you will read about throughout the book. I am proud to have your work grace the cover of my first book.

I would also like to give a special thank you to contemporary romance novelist Judy Kentrus. Through a mutual friend we were connected and she helped guide me through the administrative process of self-publishing a book. She also introduced me to Arran McNicol, who masterfully edited this transcript despite the numerous grammatical errors that I threw his way.

Last but certainly not least, I need to thank my beautiful wife Tori. She has been there supporting this project from the beginning. While she shares my love for travel, she could only join me on a few of my trips. I wish that she could've been with me every step of the way on this journey. While I was off visiting pubs and watching Liverpool, she stayed home to tend to our home and take care of our dog Dakota. She is the true rock in my foundation and I don't know that I could have done this without her. I am the luckiest man to have her as my partner in life.

1 - BEFORE THE STORM

Three of my favorite hobbies in the world are traveling, drinking beers in pubs, and watching Liverpool Football Club. The accessibility of the sport coupled with social media make it possible for me to combine all three into a single project. Why not travel the country throughout the season watching Liverpool matches, sharing pints with Reds fans in their home pubs? With four different competitions, the season inevitably feels like a roller-coaster ride of emotions. One week Liverpool will defeat one of the best teams in England with beautiful precision and ease. The next week they'll sloppily lose at home to a club that ends up getting relegated. It's maddening. Merriam-Webster defines the word "tempestuous" as being full of strong emotions, such as anger or excitement. The secondary definition is relating to, or resembling a tempest; "stormy" or "turbulent" are synonyms. I can think of no better way to describe the feeling of supporting Liverpool Football Club. There will be turbulent moments. The club will anger you. They will baffle you. But then there will be a moment they shine with invincibility and the best players on the planet couldn't defeat them.

The season is like a storm, unpredictable in nature. The globalization of the sport has pushed this storm beyond Merseyside and England. All around the world there are fans that go to great extremes to watch a Liverpool match. When our team is victorious, an entire global family rejoices together in celebration. When they lose, we collectively console each other until the next match.

A great example of what I'm talking about was in the spring of 2014. I remember that day like it was yesterday. It was April 27, 2014, and Liverpool were hosting Chelsea with only three matches remaining in the season. Leading up to that moment, Liverpool had won eleven straight league matches and hadn't lost in sixteen. The team was seemingly scoring goals at will, destined to break all sorts of offensive records. Three games

1

were left in the season and the Reds controlled their destiny. Win them all, and Liverpool would be league champions for the first time in twenty-four years. The last team to defeat Liverpool in the league was this same Chelsea squad back on December 29, and now they were coming to Anfield trying to thwart our title hunt. The Blues were no longer in league title contention, so there was reason to believe they'd field a slightly weakened roster. All signs were pointing to a Liverpool victory, followed soon after by Steven Gerrard hoisting his first and only Premier League trophy. Then it happened. The slip. Just before halftime, one of the greatest players to ever don the Liverpool jersey had lost his footing with no support behind him. The ball trickled slowly away from him, leaving Chelsea's Demba Ba free to head toward goal with only the keeper to stop him. He easily scored in front of a shocked home crowd. There was still time for Liverpool to come back in the second half, but it just wasn't their day. For forty-five minutes the Reds attacked the bunkered Chelsea defense, but couldn't break through. The final whistle blew with Liverpool defeated. Just like that, the dream was over.

I remember that day well. I sat at the bar watching with the rest of my friends, about a hundred Raleigh-based Liverpool supporters packed inside the London Bridge Pub. We all support Liverpool, and, to a certain extent, we expect disappointment. Never before could I recall being so optimistic about winning the league title. Adult males were shedding tears at the pub. The entire Liverpool community felt numb. This was our Bill Buckner moment. To have that title so close to our grasp was difficult, but to lose it on a dreadful mistake by your most recognized player was incorrigible. It was a stark reminder that no matter how blue the sky may look, there is always a storm somewhere beyond the horizon ready to unleash its fury. But as our anthem dictates, we never have face it on our own. We remind each other to "hold your head up high" because we "never walk alone."

****

Soccer fans are a unique breed. I had little choice but to become a fan, thrown into the gauntlet of the sport at the age of six. I continued playing through high school, college, and beyond in the men's adult league of New Orleans. As a twenty-something playing on the fields of Lafreniere Park, I would become great friends with expatriates and young professionals that simply loved the sport. Often times we would play long, hard matches, putting our aging muscles to the test, then retire to a local pub to recover with a pint. Back then the European leagues weren't as accessible as they are today, but you could still watch a match if you found a pub that would pay for the satellite feed. Fans would pile into the pub because it was their only option if they wanted to watch their favorite club play on television.

As cable television boomed with new niche channels being created on a weekly basis, it was inevitable that soccer popularity would boom. Often on a Saturday morning I would be bored and flip through the channels, eventually finding a European league match on some random channel. Sitting on a couch with a cup of coffee watching the match still paled in comparison to sitting at the bar with a pint of Guinness amongst a dozen like-minded fans. It was simply preferable to be at the pub with your mates on match day.

Soccer pubs started popping up all across America, soon followed by the supporters clubs. Fans of a particular team would learn that their compatriots would congregate at a particular tavern for every match, so they would join the party. Popularity of social media made it even easier for these clubs to grow their fan base, connecting with other clubs across the country.

It didn't take long for the football organizations to notice the impact of the sport's popularity growth. The globalization of soccer was an opportunity for each club to capitalize on growing their own particular brand. Liverpool Football Club established guidelines to become an official supporters club. These guidelines weren't terribly strict, but sufficient enough to protect the integrity of the club. Over time the network would grow to over two hundred clubs throughout more than fifty different countries. North America alone had thirty-seven such clubs at the start of this season. Each year the list grows as unofficial clubs strive to gain approval through the parent club. When a Liverpool supporter travels to a city away from home, it's safe to say that they'll be able to find a nearby pub to watch a match with other Reds. It's what we call being part of the "LFC Family."

Members of the Official Liverpool Supporters Club (OLSC) in Raleigh meet for all matches at the London Bridge Pub. There is simply no better place to watch soccer matches in the North Carolina capital. Darren Bridger is a lifelong Liverpool supporter raised in London, having moved to America in the early 1990s. He started out as a barman working at the Hibernian Pub nearby, and became one of the more popular bartenders in town. Mike Ruiz was a regular patron there and became friends with Darren, whose loyalty to Liverpool spread like a virus. It didn't take long to infect Mike, who would arrange his schedule to ensure he could watch the Reds with his favorite bartender. On the morning of May 25, 2005, Mike was scheduled to have surgery to repair a ruptured Achilles heel tendon. His girlfriend picked him up at the hospital and drove him straight to the Hibernian to watch Liverpool play in the Champions League final with his foot propped up on a barstool. With his good friend serving him pints from behind the bar, they watched Liverpool win their fifth European Cup with a dramatic come-from-behind victory over AC Milan in the Champions

League Final played in Istanbul.

In early 2012, the two friends ventured into business together, acquiring the space that now holds the London Bridge Pub in downtown Raleigh. The dimly lit pub is just what you would expect for a British pub. As you walk inside, you feel almost as though you've teleported across the pond without clearing customs. The Union Jack flies proudly behind the bar, while autographed jerseys of Liverpool legends Steven Gerrard, Jamie Carragher, and Xabi Alonso hang on the wall neatly amongst a myriad of other soccer-centric memorabilia (including a David Beckham England national team jersey). Scarves from many different clubs are mounted near the ceiling, including the local professional team the Carolina RailHawks. What may have started out as a Liverpool pub quickly became recognized as simply a great place to watch soccer.

The taps are filled with the imported beers that you would expect to see if you were in England. If you want a pint of Bud Light on draught, take a walk to one of the other watering holes in the neighborhood. Brands like Guinness, Boddingtons, and Stella Artois dominate the taps at the London Bridge Pub.

I first met Darren only a few months after they opened the London Bridge Pub. It was July 25, 2012. My brother Kevin and I had traveled up to Boston to watch a preseason friendly match. We acquired prime real estate with a window table in the An Tua Nua pub only a short walk from Fenway Park. As luck would have it, a group of guys sat at the table next to us and we started a conversation. It turned out that Darren was part of this crew, along with Raleigh-based yoga instructor Colin Russell.

Together we drank many pints and talked about Liverpool. Eventually the pub was filled to capacity, with a long waiting list to get inside. We remarked about how impressive it was that OLSC Boston organized these great events. The support was staggering. Wouldn't it be great to have this sort of atmosphere for Liverpool in Raleigh? It may have been the Stella talking, but Darren offered up his newly opened London Bridge Pub as a meeting place for every match. Colin created a Facebook page, and LFC Raleigh was born. I remember that day like it was yesterday. Well, I remember most of that day.

****

Fans choose to root for a particular sports team for many different reasons. It's the history and fanfare that binds them together. If you're a fan of the University of Alabama and you see someone wearing their colors walking down the sidewalk, all you need to do is say "Roll Tide!" to identify yourself as a fellow fan. New Orleans Saints fans will tell you "Who Dat!" if you are wearing the black-and-gold fleur-de-lis as your colors. If a Liverpool fan spots you sporting the Liverbird crest, you might hear them call out "You'll never walk alone!" It's a reference to the official Liverpool anthem sung before and after every match. It's a song about solidarity and faith, whose lyrics couldn't be more appropriate for a suffering sports fan base that's been found desperately wanting.

The song was written for the 1945 Rodgers and Hammerstein musical Carousel. Liverpool musicians Gerry and the Pacemakers recorded a version of the song in 1963 and presented LFC manager Bill Shankly with a copy. According to one of the players, "Shanks was in awe of what he had heard…" and adopted the single as their club anthem. They started playing the song at every home match as thousands of fans would sing along. It quickly became an Anfield tradition. The club immortalized the song by placing the words "You'll Never Walk Alone" on top of the new Shankly Gates unveiled on August 2, 1982, which eventually became part of the club crest that you see today.

To be a Liverpool fan in this era, you really must live by the words of that anthem. The club has been marred with the events that occurred at Hillsborough Stadium in 1989, where ninety-six supporters lost their lives attending a match. The initial blame for these deaths was placed squarely on Liverpool supporters themselves, causing great grief for the families of the deceased. Seemingly unable to help those families desperately fighting for justice, the song is a constant reminder that they are not alone in the fight. As the families "walk through the storm" in search of justice, at the end will be the "golden sky" of redemption.

In 2005 the club had overachieved in the Champions League and earned a berth in the finals against Italian giants AC Milan. The match was held in Istanbul, Turkey, where thousands of Liverpool supporters traveled to watch the beloved Reds attempt to win the club's fifth European Cup. I watched the match from The Grasshopper, an Irish soccer pub in Morristown, New Jersey. My fiancée thought I was out running errands, which was partially true. I had already stopped at the store in town before kickoff.

The match started dubiously when Paolo Maldini scored in the opening minute to give the Italians the early lead. That lead was tripled by Hernan Crespo just before halftime with a pair of goals. With Liverpool trailing 3-0 at halftime, many neutrals considered the match over. I had half a mind to leave The Grasshopper and finish the tasks I had set out to do that day, but the optimist in my mind told me to stay and have another pint.

When the teams returned to the pitch after the break, something magical happened inside Ataturk Olympic Stadium. Thousands of Liverpool fans in attendance started serenading their beloved club, singing "You'll Never Walk Alone" at the top of their lungs. It was a moment that could only be described as surreal. Within fifteen minutes of restarting the play, Xabi

Alonso slammed home the equalizer that put Liverpool back in the match. The game would ultimately be decided on penalties. When Jerzy Dudek saved that final kick to win the cup, the moment was immortalized. I'll never forget the smile on Steven Gerrard's face as he hoisted the cup over his head with red confetti raining from the skies above. Players would later claim that hearing Liverpool fans sing that song inspired them. It pushed them to drive harder than ever, ultimately to victory. It simply added to the legend of "You'll Never Walk Alone."

****

Much had transpired since that abysmal Chelsea match was played in April 2014. Liverpool ended up finishing a respectable second place in the league to Manchester City, and were rewarded with a return to Europe's Champions League. Everyone wondered whether manager Brendan Rodgers could replicate the fantastic season or if it simply was a fluke to have nearly won the league title. Top goal-scorer Luis Suarez left the club for Barcelona before the season, while his striking partner Daniel Sturridge suffered through an injury-plagued campaign. The club were embarrassed to exit the Champions League despite being placed in a relatively easy group. Midway through the season, Gerrard announced he would not re-sign with the club instead choosing to ply his trade in America. The team limped into a sixth-place league finish, despite losing 6-1 at Stoke City on the final match of the season. There were very few positive moments to celebrate. How could one team look so good one season and so dismal the next? Everyone was ready to hit the reset button and start over with a new season.

2 - STOKED TO START A NEW SEASON

Sunday, August 9
London Bridge Pub, Raleigh, NC
Premier League match #1 (at Stoke City)

It was August and that moment had finally arrived. Twenty teams were about to embark on a nine-month journey called the Premier League season. For one very brief moment, all twenty teams were tied for first place. The dawn of a new season brings hope and optimism for everyone. Surely this would be our year, thought every fan of the sport.

The first match of the new season would be at Stoke City. I had been looking forward to this match ever since the schedule was released in the summer. While the first game of the season is always a new dawn for every club, this particular match carried added significance. The last time that Liverpool played a competitive match, they'd tasted bitter defeat with a 6-1 road defeat at Stoke. It was a unique opportunity for Liverpool to kick-start the campaign while simultaneously exorcising the demons that closed out the previous one.

Kickoff for the Stoke City match went off sharply at eleven a.m. on a Sunday. North Carolina law prohibits the sale of alcohol before noon on Sunday, but that didn't stop the fans from packing the pub just before kickoff. Even though I love to watch the matches at the pub with my fellow supporters, it's still about an hour drive from my home in Chatham County. My presence at the pub on match day is practically an all-day event when you take the commute into consideration. A Liverpool win on opening day guaranteed it would be an all-day event. My wife Victoria, known to most of the Raleigh Reds as Tori, has embraced Liverpool fandom through me, and she agreed to drive me downtown for the match.

We arrived about twenty minutes before kickoff and the pub was already buzzing after West Ham United had defeated Arsenal 2-0 in the early match. Many pundits were picking Arsenal as a contender to win the league, and deservedly so. They had finished in the top four of the final league standings for so many years. An early loss at home was unexpected for Arsenal, and a good way to start the day for Liverpool fans.

Success for Liverpool this season hinged on finishing in the top four, thus qualifying for the lucrative Champions League. To achieve that goal, they'd have to leapfrog over one of the established top teams. Manchester United, Manchester City, and defending champions Chelsea are all clubs with deeper pockets than Liverpool, and Arsenal always seems to find their way near the top when the dust settles. Even though this was just the first of thirty-eight matches to be played over the next nine months, it was a golden opportunity for the Reds to gain some ground on a club that could be fighting for a coveted spot in the Champions League.

About an hour before every match kicks off, the lineups are released to the public. It was widely speculated all week that Dejan Lovren would get the call as central defender, and this did not sit well with most Liverpool supporters. The Croatian defender was brought in from Southampton before last season, and his performance had not yet met expectations. I had high hopes for Lovren and expected that he could fill the void that Jamie Carragher's retirement had created not long before. His first season as a Red was woeful by any standard, yet he remained part of Brendan Rodgers' plan for this season.

One of the last season's bright spots was the play of French defender Mamadou Sakho, brought in from the most dominating club in France. The former Paris-St. Germain defender played strong defensively down the stretch a year ago. Most supporters, including myself, believed that Sakho had earned the right to be named starting central defender alongside Martin Skrtel. When the roster was announced with Lovren starting over Sakho, most fans were livid. It turned out that Sakho was left off the squad due to the birth of his child. Most fans were still distraught that Rodgers preferred Lovren over Sakho, and I couldn't honestly say that I blamed them. We wouldn't be fans if we didn't have opinions about our beloved club. If you were to ask a dozen fans about who they would start, you'd likely get close to a dozen different lineups. Even still, I'd bet money that not a single supporter would've selected Lovren to be in their starting eleven for the first match. I thought the criticism of the Croatian had been over the top. Complaining about Lovren had become the easy thing to do, because you knew that everyone else would agree with you. People have every right to form their own opinion about a player, but I wasn't willing to write him off just yet. I believed that he could still come good for the club, regardless of how he had performed in his first season.

Rodgers set up the defense with Lovren and Skrtel in the middle,

Nathaniel Clyne on the right, and eighteen-year-old Joe Gomez on the left. Clyne was the obvious choice. He is a solid defender that likes to push forward on the attack, a quality Rodgers clearly preferred. He was one of the best defenders in the league last season at Southampton, and Liverpool paid good money to acquire his rights in the offseason. Of course, the same comment could have been said about Lovren a year ago, and that didn't exactly pan out for the club. Surely lightning wouldn't strike twice, would it? Joe Gomez was the more surprising selection at this stage. Signed from Charlton Athletic on June 20 earlier that summer, he was more thought to be a player for the future more than the present. He'd impressed in the preseason and earned a spot on this team. I wasn't sure if his inclusion against Stoke City was more of a reward for a stellar preseason, an indictment of Alberto Moreno (who was identified as the most likely starting left back heading into this season), or simply a tactical move by Rodgers to solidify the back line against a difficult opponent on the road. Moreno had developed the reputation of being a marauding-style defender, making many attacking runs on the flank, but his defensive skills somewhat came into question last season and he could be considered a liability. Going on the road to play against a club that just defeated you 6-1 in the most recent competitive fixture may have played into the tactical decision. Gomez should provide better coverage defensively than Moreno. Even though he was only eighteen years old, his size was more imposing than Moreno.

The midfield was no surprise, with newly named captain Jordan Henderson in the middle. James Milner joined him in the center. Milner was a veteran coming over from Manchester City, and his experience was so valued by Rodgers that he was quickly named vice-captain by the gaffer. During preseason, Milner and Henderson formed a nice partnership that would hopefully carry forward to the regular season. Jordon Ibe and Adam Lallana covered the outside of the midfield, while Phillippe Coutinho and Christian Benteke were called upon to round out the attack.

Earlier in the week I had blogged about the importance of winning this opening match, the first time I'd considered any season-opener a must-win for Liverpool. Truth be told, I don't like to use the phrase "must-win" for any match at any part of the season. But when you consider the way that the "football gods" (a.k.a. the Football Association) had set the season up for Liverpool, you can see how this game was a real opportunity to kick-start the season.

Liverpool is entered in four different competitions played concurrently. With their sixth-place finish in last year's league table, they'd earned a berth in the Europa League. There are also two domestic cup competitions, with the League Cup (also known as the Capital One Cup through corporate sponsorship) and the FA Cup. As a result, the fixture list tends to get congested throughout the year. Both Europa League and Capital One Cup started with midweek matches after the September international break ,and the FA Cup wouldn't start until January. For such a long season, it's hard to comprehend the importance of these early fixtures. A stretch of four games is over ten percent of the entire season, which doesn't sound like much. Clearly a poor start can be overcome as the season progresses. Once that first international break was over and the players returned to Melwood, they faced the daunting task of going to Old Trafford to play hated rival Manchester United. Underperforming in the first four matches would do nothing for the confidence of the team or supporters. Once they returned to action, Liverpool would play seven matches in only twenty-three days before the second international break in early October. That was followed with a stretch that included away fixtures at Chelsea, Tottenham, and Manchester City. Underperform in the first four games, and you'd likely see the end of Brendan Rodgers' employment at Liverpool Football Club before January. No pressure.

The first half was a rather dull affair. Neither team really played particularly well. Ultimately it was a series of mistakes made by the Liverpool defense that gave Stoke City the only really good chance of the half. As Gomez was beaten on our left flank, Lovren shifted over to support and was beaten to the touchline. A dangerous cross was played into the box, where it was met by Slovakian defender Martin Skrtel, who did well to get his boot on the ball and disrupt the play. Unfortunately, he couldn't clear the ball out of danger, and it landed at the feet of Glen Johnson with an open shot on goal from about twelve yards out.

Having just left Liverpool in the summer, Johnson was going to be one of the focal points for this match. Six years earlier, Liverpool had signed the English defender away from Portsmouth, and he became a fixture in the starting lineup, lauded for his ability to push into the attack, but his defensive play was frequently in question. Slowly fans started to turn against him, giving him new nicknames to voice their displeasure. From "John Glenson" to the Raleigh favorite "Glen Fecking Johnson," it was clear that no one was disappointed that he didn't sign a new contract with the club last summer. After six decent years at Liverpool, Johnson joined Stoke City on a free transfer, which set up another great storyline for opening weekend. In the days leading up to the match, he was quoted in the media with some less-than-kind remarks about his former club. So when the ball landed at his feet uncontested only twelve yards from goal, you could feel the change in air pressure as Liverpool fans collectively held their breath. Thankfully his shot sailed over the crossbar in what proved to be his best clearance for Liverpool in years.

Charlie Adam was another former Liverpool player who played for the club in the 2011-12 season. The Scottish midfielder looks more like he would be tending bar at your favorite Glaswegian watering hole than a professional footballer. A hard-nosed player whose most infamous moment for the club came in that season's League Cup final at Wembley Stadium when his penalty kick in the shootout launched into orbit and probably still hasn't landed. He joined Stoke City after one season with Liverpool and settled in with the mid-table club. If Liverpool were to lose this match, one would think that it would be a result of some ridiculously bad karma involving Johnson or Adam.

The whistle blew, mercifully ending a boring first half of football, and both teams retreated to the locker room. For the barflies hanging inside the London Bridge Pub that morning, it also meant time to start the countdown to noon.

North Carolina's "blue laws" prevent establishments from the sale of alcoholic beverages before noon on Sunday. With an eleven a.m. local kickoff time, forty-five minutes of drab football was followed by fifteen minutes of non-alcoholic frustration. Dozens of fans lined up to the bar hoping to get their pint orders registered as the three bartenders patiently watched the clock.

There are many fine bartenders at the London Bridge Pub. I can't comment about their mixology skills or how well they can deliver beverages to the patrons, but each has earned my respect with one simple trait: the ability to recognize when I need my next pint of Guinness and have my next one at the ready. Most of these bartenders are new soccer fans and for obvious reasons choose to support Liverpool as it is the best way to increase their gratuity. For the purposes of this narrative, I will collectively refer to all of these servers as "Sam."

Through Sam, I had prearranged pints of Guinness for myself and my friends. They were being crafted well in advance of the ensuing rush at noon. This is one moment that having the right friends in the right places is well worth it. While most of the patrons waited for their first pint to be served, we were enjoying our libations mere seconds after the clock struck noon.

The only Liverpool player not having a good game was Adam Lallana. Playing on the left side, he looked lost at times, and the attack seemed to stagnate whenever he got possession. He seemed to be lost out there with the ball, and every promising attack in the first half seemed to end with Lallana losing possession. It was no surprise to anyone at the pub to see promising German youngster Emre Can sub in for Lallana in the sixty-third minute. Almost instantly that change impacted the flow. Can was able to manage the middle of the park with him imposing play, allowing Milner and Henderson to push forward into the attack. It seemed like the game plan all along was to keep the match 0-0 through the first sixty minutes, and then try to steal the victory at the end. If that truly was the strategy intended by

Rodgers from the outset, it was genius.

As the clock continued to work its way to the end of the match, nerves started becoming more noticeable. This match was a tale of two halves, both on the pitch and at the pub. The first half was relatively quiet, with about a hundred Raleigh Reds focused on the closest television screen. Once it became legal for the bartenders to start passing out the pints, the supporters slowly started increasing their volume. With every possession of the ball and every pint consumed, the frustration became more noticeable. The tension was palpable. The focus was never stronger. As the final moments of the match ticked down, the only question would be if we'd see an explosion of joy or a deflation of esteem. We found out in the eight-sixth minute.

The play started innocently enough, with Lovren having possession in the middle of the pitch. Making the simple pass, he sent the ball to his left, where Gomez waited. Stoke City pressured the eighteen-year-old, who spotted Coutinho running toward him and calling for the ball. The pass was made as a Stoke defender challenged. In a brilliant display of body position and ball control, Coutinho shielded the defender while simultaneously possessing the ball with advancing movement. It was only a brief moment, but as it turned out, it was the most important moment of the match. In that instant, Coutinho had beaten his man with space to run forward.

Liverpool fans have become accustomed to seeing Coutinho gain possession like this and running with the ball. It's why he's been called our "little Brazilian magician," and he's been doing it for years. Last season he appeared to unleash a new weapon to his arsenal with his right foot from twenty yards out. Perhaps he'd always had this weapon at his disposal and never needed it with the likes of Luis Suarez and Daniel Sturridge on the pitch, but last February we saw how lethal that outside shot could be. In a matter of weeks, he scored game-winning goals against Southampton, Manchester City, and Bolton Wanderers. Each goal was a thing of beauty from outside the penalty area, rocketing past a diving goalkeeper who had no chance to stop it. Fans became so accustomed to seeing this that it became expected. It was no surprise to me to hear someone yell "SHOOT IT!" as Coutinho dribbled up the field.

With the Stoke City defenders back-pedaling and Roberto Firmino drawing attention away from the ball with his movement to the right, Coutinho looked up to see an alley of light toward the back of the net. At that moment, you could see the Liverpool fans at the Britannia Stadium begin to stand in unison, anticipating what everyone watching around the globe knew was coming. From twenty-five yards out in the middle of the field, Coutinho unleashed a missile that Stoke City goalkeeper Jack Butland could barely manage to get a fingertip on. As the ball crashed into the back netting, an entire world of Liverpool supporters erupted in celebration. 1-0 to Liverpool.

After hugging my friends and high-fiving as many supporters as I could possibly reach, my heart finally settled down and I could catch my breath long enough to order another pint of Guinness. By the time Sam could get that glass of liquid gold to my hands, the final whistle had blown. It may not have been a must-win game, but I'd be damned if they didn't just pull it off.

A tradition at most every LFC pub around the world immediately following every match is the ceremonious playing of "You'll Never Walk Alone." Over a hundred gleeful supporters raised their scarves and hands, singing at the top of their lungs in unison with Gerry and the Pacemakers. It happens after every match at London Bridge Pub regardless of the result, but after a dramatic win like we'd just experienced, it becomes something special.

After such a tense match, many Raleigh Reds hung around to savor the moment and enjoy another pint. For most of us, it was a reunion. The last time Liverpool played on the big screen at London Bridge Pub was three months prior. No one wanted to leave. We embraced old friends and high-fived new ones. To open the season with three points on the road in such a manner was immense. We ordered another round.

After big wins, pints turn to shots, and shots turn to cab rides home. Certain regulars have been known to request certain songs on the jukebox, which turn into some of the best impromptu group songs you've ever heard. At least they sound great to those drinking, maybe not so much to the sober patrons. One such classic singalong at the London Bridge Pub has become Foreigner's "I Want to Know What Love Is," where grown men over the age of thirty tend to form a group hug while singing the chorus. It surprised no one when that song started playing on the stereo. We all embraced and sang along.

Most people know the chorus. It's the iconic moment of that song that gets most of our hearts pumping. As I mentioned earlier in this chapter, I spent a good portion of the match keying on the defense. I thought the back line played as well as I had seen a Liverpool defense play since Rafael Benitez was at the helm. Maybe it was the Guinness talking, but in particular I felt that Dejan Lovren had earned the honors to be called Man of the Match. Because of that, I couldn't resist changing the chorus as the entire pub sang in near unison: "*I wanna know what LOVREN is?*"

Thankfully, Tori drove me home that day.

3 - MONDAY NIGHT FOOTBALL

Monday, August 17
London Bridge Pub
Premier League match #2 (vs. Bournemouth)

Most Americans know that Monday Night Football is nothing more than a money grab for the National Football League and the television networks that invest so much money into the sport. It should be no surprise that when Sky Television acquired the rights to broadcast the new Premier League for the 1992-93 season that they introduced the same concept to English soccer. On August 17, 1992, Manchester City played Queens Park Rangers in front of a nationwide British audience. The rest, as they say, is history.

For North American supporters, Monday night football in the Premier League sucks in almost every possible way. Kickoff is three p.m. EST on a day when most Americans are still climbing their way out of their weekend hangover. For a big match, fans will come up with a great excuse to get out of work early. Others figure out how to stream the match live on their work computer or personal hand-held device. Personally I don't mind the weekday match, as my occupation in sales allows me certain flexibility to dictate a schedule that works for me. If I need to have a meeting in downtown Raleigh, Monday at three p.m. on match day is as good a day as any.

Most Raleigh Reds aren't as fortunate as me, so when the TV schedule updated to put Liverpool on consecutive Mondays for the second and third matches of the season, there was a collective groan across North America. Liverpool's home opener would be on Monday August 10 against newly promoted AFC Bournemouth. A week later they would travel to the Emirates for their first big test against Arsenal. Most Raleigh Reds would save their work excuse for next Monday's Arsenal match, so it was no surprise to see a much smaller crowd at the pub for the home opener.

Even though OLSC Raleigh hasn't been in existence for a terribly long time, I can safely give the title of most passionate Raleigh Red to co-founder Colin Russell. If you ever watch a match at the London Bridge Pub and you hear a particularly lanky guy voicing his opinion, you know Colin. By day he is a personal trainer and yoga instructor, with his own studio in the affluent suburb of Cary, so he has some flexibility to work his schedule in order to attend most midweek matches. Living in a downtown condominium within walking distance to the pub helps. Colin inherited his love for Liverpool from his Irish grandparents, and even maintains an Irish passport. Even though he was born in Ohio and moved to Raleigh from Boston, Colin displays strong allegiance to the Irish national team as well. I give Colin tons of credit for helping grow the OLSC Raleigh organization, as he runs all social media activities for the club. More often than not he is the first person I see when I walk into the pub for a midweek match. This day was no different.

Colin and I exchanged pleasantries as the teams made their way onto the pitch. NBC Sports does a great job broadcasting the pre-match singing of "You'll Never Walk Alone" before most home matches, and it always fills my heart with pride to witness it. Even though we all expected a win, you could sense the nerves among the supporters milling about in the pub. Sam was tending the bar and studiously poured me a pint of Guinness, which was in hand just before kickoff. Personally I give myself a two-pint limit when I don't have my lovely wife to taxi me home. One pint of Guinness to nurse for the first half, one pint for the second half. It's a winning formula for midweek matches when I have to drive the sixty minutes through Raleigh rush-hour traffic to get home.

AFC Bournemouth is a great story. In February 2008, Bournemouth was forced into administration, suffering a ten-point deduction that ultimately had them relegated to the fourth tier of English Football known as League Two. They had debts of around £4 million and almost went out of business completely. Former player Eddie Howe took over as manager, and at the ripe age of thirty-one led the Cherries on an impressive run back up the food chain that is English football.

One of the great things about this sport is the concept of relegation and promotion. Most Americans take some time to grasp this concept, but when they understand the implications, they seem to appreciate it. Teams can't tank the end of the season, trading away their stars for hot prospects while positioning themselves for a top draft pick. Only in American sports is there a system that penalizes the fans while rewarding the ownership like that. While many clubs in the Premier League desperately work to remain in the top tier, the opportunity exists for smaller clubs like AFC Bournemouth to put together a few good years and find themselves amongst the juggernauts of English football. As champions of the Coca-Cola Championship (the tier just below the Premier League), AFC Bournemouth had earned the privilege to play in England's top level of professional football for the first time in their history.

Bournemouth were not strangers to playing football against Liverpool. Just last year in the quarterfinals of the League Cup, they'd fought hard in a 3-1 defeat. They had scored ninety-eight goals in forty-six league games the season playing in the championship before promotion. This club knew how to put the ball in the back of the net. No one expected them to come to Anfield on the second week of the season and play defensively, trying to steal a result from the Reds. They came to play.

Brendan Rodgers decided against changing his starting lineup for this match, and why should he? The defense was solid, and you could expect they would be tested again. For the opening minutes, Bournemouth took control and played brilliant football. Liverpool was second best in the opening minutes. I don't know if it was Liverpool's hangover from the great result at Stoke, or Bournemouth's refusal to be intimidated in the great cathedral of Anfield Stadium. Whatever the reason, the Cherries looked like a team to contend on that day.

When Bournemouth earned a corner kick in the fifth minute, most Liverpool fans were still in shock at the poor start to the game. I had just received my first pint of Guinness when Bournemouth's Tommy Elphick headed the ball past a flailing Simon Mignolet into the back of the net. What just happened? 1-0 to Bournemouth? Everyone at the pub certainly thought so. To quote some of my favorite Irish friends, I simply screamed "JAY-SUS!" Strangely, though, the scoreboard never changed, and still read 0-0 when we finally saw referee Craig Pawson signaling for a foul. Elphick had appeared to pull down Lovren with his arms in order to free up some space. It was a decision that would later be debated by pundits, some thinking Liverpool was fortunate to get that call. I thought it was a clear foul, in that Elphick never got his head to the ball if he didn't pull down Lovren. Thankfully, the ref agreed with me.

The fact that Bournemouth put the ball into Liverpool's net seemed to be a bit of a wakeup call for the Reds. Minutes later, it was as if someone switched the light on, and the team started to play as you would expect. Several times they attacked and looked certain to take the lead, only to have the play unravel when the last touch failed or the Bournemouth defense tightened up. Finally, Liverpool caught the break they needed. I'm not talking about the fact that Simon Francis conceded the corner kick to Liverpool in the twenty-sixth minute. Of course I am talking about the lineman not raising his flag for offside after Christian Benteke put the ball in the back of the net for Liverpool.

Replays confirmed what we all know to be the case now. The goal should've been disallowed. When Jordan Henderson played the ball across the pitch from the left side, Coutinho was clearly standing in an offside position. If he did nothing, the play was good. But instinctively Coutinho turned toward the ball and made a play on it. He missed it completely, but it fell to Benteke, who was making a run to the far post and put it in the net in front of the home stands known as "the Kop."

A year ago, the offside rule stated that Coutinho would've been onside because he didn't actually impact the movement of the ball. Clearly you could see that his actions forced Bournemouth goalkeeper Artur Boruc into holding his ground on the chance that Coutinho deflected the ball toward the net. This offseason the offside rule was adjusted such that any player in an offside position that makes a movement toward the ball is judged to be offside even if he doesn't affect the ball itself. Clearly this was the case, and the referees missed it. Benteke put the finishing touches on the play and opened up his Liverpool account in front of tens of thousands of adoring fans.

This play would become a major talking point for the rest of the week. It should've been a moot point, because Liverpool missed numerous great scoring chances throughout the rest of the match. To be fair, it looked like it could've been three or four goals to the good for the Reds while the defense remained stalwart.

Pundits continued to rave about the luck that Liverpool got against the newly promoted Cherries. Bournemouth were disallowed a goal that should've counted while Liverpool scored a goal that shouldn't have. I constantly felt the need to remind people that every action of a match causes a reaction. Had the referee not whistled for that foul or had the linesman correctly flagged Coutinho for offside, the game would've played out differently. For most of the second half, Bournemouth was outmatched. If Liverpool needed a goal to earn the victory, maybe Rodgers would've given forwards Danny Ings or Divock Origi their debut for Liverpool instead of putting defensive-minded Alberto Moreno in the game for Coutinho in the eighty-first minute. You simply can't negate a play in the middle of the game and say that the result should've been different. Clearly the better team won the game.

As Pawson blew the final whistle, everyone at the pub was relieved to see that Liverpool earned the three points. A second straight 1-0 victory was still a victory, and the Reds had opened the 2015-16 season with six points of a possible six. Personally I was more relieved when bartender Sam reminded me that Monday was pint night at London Bridge Pub. The damage for my two pints of Guinness? Seven bucks. I gave him $10 and told him to keep the change. See you next Monday, Sam.

4 - ARSED

Monday, August 24
London Bridge Pub
Premier League match #3 (at Arsenal)

No disrespect to Stoke City or AFC Bournemouth, but when I saw that our third fixture was away at the Emirates Stadium against Arsenal Football Club, I made a mental note to keep that date open. I love watching Liverpool at the pub amongst friends, but there's just something special when the opponent is one of the top clubs fighting you for a Champions League spot.

When you walk into London Bridge Pub, there is no hiding the Liverpool allegiances of both ownership and employees. Despite that fact, it never ceases to amaze how many Arsenal fans choose to watch matches at this pub. The Triangle Gooners (Raleigh's official Arsenal supporters club) have their own home pub in Durham, yet some will come to London Bridge Pub anyway. One time I asked a London expatriate and diehard Gooner why he didn't watch the matches at the Durham pub. He replied, "Over there the fans watch the game and then go home. They are Arsenal fans, but not football fans. You could have the two best teams playing after the Arsenal match is over, but the fans leave and the televisions go straight to college football. At London Bridge Pub, they get it. Everyone here is a fan. I just prefer hanging out here." He got no argument from me.

Once again the brilliant minds that manipulate the schedule had decided that this match was perfect for their Monday Night Football of the week. While I have no problem getting to the pub for the match, I know that some of my fellow Raleigh Reds can't get away from the office for a weekday afternoon kickoff, and it usually detracts from the atmosphere. There were more supporters present at the pub than I expected, as apparently many dentists in town were booked with "three p.m. appointments."

That Monday afternoon was particularly dreary in Raleigh. The skies were gray, darkening every minute. I concluded my business for the afternoon and started on my way. Walking through the parking lot felt like being at a movie theater just before the main feature, lights dimming as the cool air rushed across my body. A storm was coming and I was leaving at the right time.

Driving to the pub from my office normally takes about fifteen to twenty minutes, but this day was considerably slower as I safely navigated the monsoon that decided to park itself on Raleigh. Eventually I worked my way far enough away from the storm that I got to downtown Raleigh with no evidence of rain anywhere in sight. I could actually park the car and walk to the pub without getting wet.

I know it's silly to be superstitious, but sometimes I can't help myself. There's a beer commercial that emphasizes the ridiculous superstitions that sports fans deploy in an effort to will their team to victory with the tagline "it's only weird if it doesn't work." I sat at the stoplight at the intersection of Blount and Hargett Streets waiting for the light to turn green. To the left is Moore Square Park and a line of empty street parking spots. It's my preferred place to park during midweek matches because of the quick, convenient exit out of downtown on to the interstate for my trip home. As I pulled the car over, a thought came to mind. Exactly one week prior I had parked in spot #178 and Liverpool somehow pulled off the fortunate win. At that moment I realized the car was in spot #177. I knew I had to move it back one space to keep the mojo that worked so well the week before. It's only weird if it doesn't work, right?

I walked into the pub to be greeted by my good friends, most importantly Sam, who immediately started drawing the pint of black gold that I craved. As I waited for the libation to be properly poured, I walked over to greet my good friend Sean Dotzauer, who was frantically typing away on his laptop. The gift of free wireless Internet provided at the pub allows some the freedom to continue the workday while watching the match. As a banker, Sean frequently takes advantage of this opportunity. He'll even wear a Liverpool jersey under his dress shirt and tie at work just so he can easily change into match attire at the pub.

Sean first picked up his love for the sport with the 2006 World Cup in Germany. He was visiting San Diego for a wedding at the time, and he spent most mornings watching matches on the television. After the World Cup was over, he started watching the Premier League and decided to pick a favorite team. He asked his colleagues for advice, and got friendly solicitations from Manchester United, Arsenal, and Chelsea fans. He wanted to be different and initially chose Watford because they had

American Jay Demerit on their roster. Demerit was also from Sean's home state of Wisconsin, so he focused his support on the Hornets. After announcing this decision to his colleagues, Sean was quickly advised to change allegiances to a team that wouldn't get relegated after a few seasons. It was sage advice. Because he was working on his MBA through online correspondence courses with the University of Liverpool, he started looking at the Reds. The parallels with his beloved Green Bay Packers started taking shape. He learned about the great history of the club. They still played matches in an old, legendary stadium. When he told his colleagues about leaning his support toward Liverpool, they all shuddered in disapproval. That was the final affirmation that Sean needed to become a Red forever.

Sean was one of the first Raleigh Reds that I met after moving here in 2007. It was the inaugural Europa League final, being held in May 2010, and the surprising English squad Fulham were playing Atletico Madrid for the cup. Fulham is not a club one would expect to see in a European competition representing England, let alone make it to the final game of the entire tournament. They were gaining popularity here because they employed American players like Brian McBride and Clint Dempsey. Atletico Madrid defeated Liverpool in the semifinals to get to that game, so this was a competition that piqued my interest. I met Sean at an Irish pub called Trali not far from my office. We struck up a conversation and learned that we both supported Liverpool. It wasn't until years later that we met for the second time during a regular season Liverpool match at the London Bridge Pub.

Sitting next to Sean at the table was Colin Russell, who once again worked his schedule accordingly to ensure attendance at the pub. Colin was a bit more nervous than last Monday, and rightfully so. Arsenal was a much stronger squad than Bournemouth, and Liverpool hadn't looked convincing against the newly promoted team. Lineups were announced an hour before kickoff, and Rodgers looked to deploy a more defensive posture for this match.

"Lucas back in the team," I said to Colin as we shook hands. The Brazilian midfielder had been rumored to be transferred out to Italy before the transfer window closed at the end of August. He nearly was shipped off in the previous January transfer window, if you believe the rumors.

"Yup. Not having Hendo is going to kill us," he replied, referring to the recent foot injury that captain Jordan Henderson incurred the week before. I feared that he may have been right.

Despite the lack of goals scored in the first two matches, Liverpool had controlled the center of the pitch for the most part. James Milner was acquired on a free transfer from Manchester City, and his partnership with Jordan Henderson seemed to be quite effective early in the season.

Henderson picked up a knock and had to be subbed off against Bournemouth. It was a disappointing revelation for a player that was on the pitch for over ninety-five percent of Liverpool's league minutes a season ago. Current prognosis on this injury was that he would be out at least through the September international break. As a result, Rodgers recalled Brazilian Lucas Leiva into the starting squad.

Lucas Leiva has had quite an enigmatic career for Liverpool. Signed from Gremio in the Brazilian league at the age of twenty, the defensive midfielder came to Merseyside with high expectations. In his first season with the club, he became the first Brazilian to ever net a goal for Liverpool, with a nice, curling twenty-five-yard shot in the FA Cup only weeks after his twenty-first birthday. Defensive midfielders aren't supposed to score a lot of goals, but somehow I felt like he should've done better than six goals in 275 appearances for the club. Part of the problem for Lucas had as much to do with managerial instability as anything else. Signed by Rafa Benitez, he endured the reigns of Roy Hodgson, Kenny Dalglish, and now Brendan Rodgers. Each manager had differing ideas on how to use Lucas, but all knew that he was asset worth keeping in the squad. Now twenty-eight years old, he was clearly on the backside of his career and looking to maximize his playing time. Supposedly he was on the way to Serie A in the last January transfer window, but a deal never materialized. As this current window looked to close in less than a week, rumors persisted about another move to Serie A. Regardless, he was still under contract to Liverpool for the moment, and his services were required to shore up the squad against Arsenal.

There was a nervous excitement amongst the crowd, from both Liverpool and Arsenal fans. The ratio was about three to one in favor of Liverpool fans; Gooners clearly are the bravest to invade the London Bridge Pub. I had my pint in hand as the game kicked off.

Liverpool took early control of the game. Arsenal was without two of their better defenders (Per Mertesacker and Laurent Koscielny) due to injury, so one would think Liverpool should be able to capitalize. Coutinho nearly scored in the third minute as his shot ricocheted off the crossbar. Arsenal hit back with their own attack as Santi Cazorla found a streaking Aaron Ramsey on the left side. Ramsey's strike found its way past Simon Mignolet into the back of the Liverpool net, only to be ruled offside. Replays would show that it may have been the wrong decision, and for the second straight game the Reds were the beneficiary of some dubious refereeing. The score remained 0-0.

After the linesman waved his flag to call offside on the Ramsey shot, Arsenal seemed to get even more frustrated. They flailed across the pitch like an impetuous child, still fuming at the denial of a goal. Liverpool gained confidence, stringing passes and making positive play into the Arsenal half of the field. I was growing more confident with each passing minute in the first half. Surely Liverpool was going to break through soon.

Just as Liverpool acquired this newfound confidence, an ominous black cloud hovered over downtown Raleigh. The same rainstorm that I had escaped in Morrisville followed me to the hub of Oak City, ready to wreak havoc on any innocent bystander walking outside. No big deal, as we were safely tucked under the roof of the pub. That is until Sam reminded me of one disturbing fact: "We have satellite television and the signal will be sketchy at best." In the immortal words of Homer Simpson, "D'oh!"

Thinking on his feet, pub owner Darren Bridger came up with an immediate solution. Last summer they'd secured the acquisition of the Royal James pub next door. Just before the Premier League started, they knocked down a wall and had been preparing for the eventual expansion, doubling their existing tavern footprint. Even more salient at the time was the fact that the Royal James had cable and Darren hadn't yet combined the accounts. Cable wouldn't be affected by the storm clouds like satellite television. The Royal James was probably eighty percent ready for occupation, close enough to relocate the eighty or so patrons who were focused on this match.

I found a seat at the empty bar with a perfect view of the match on the small television behind the bar. The majority of the supporters found seats in front of the six-foot projector screen that Darren was able to stream the match on. The place erupted in the thirty-ninth minute when Firmino sent a dangerous cross from the left, which Christian Benteke redirected toward the corner from about four yards out. Only the outstretched arms of a perfectly positioned Petr Cech was able to knock the ball wide. For a split second, the entire pub thought it was about to be 1-0 to Liverpool.

At this stage in the game, both sets of fans were ready to accept a 0-0 halftime score. Before the match had even started, I remarked to another supporter that we needed to go into the second half 0-0, allowing Rodgers to make the offensive adjustments necessary in the final twenty-five minutes to try and steal a win like we did at Stoke two weeks prior. So when the clock hit the forty-fifth minute and Coutinho found possession of the ball down the left side, I didn't think twice. Surely Arsenal wouldn't be able to regain possession and counterattack before the end of the half. Just blow the whistle and let's go to halftime. But in that moment something happened that reminded us all why he's our little Brazilian magician. It was a move we are accustomed to seeing the greatest players like Lionel Messi make, and I can't even describe its beauty adequately enough in words. Arsenal right back Hector Bellerin was left looking for his jockstrap on the deck as Coutinho fired his trademark curling right-footed shot toward the far post. Once again Cech found himself tested, and again he answered. Diving to his left, he got the most miniscule amount of his fingertip on the ball required to push it off the side post and safely away from the net. It took multiple television replays to convince me that he had actually touched the ball, but full credit to the Czech Republic goalkeeper for making a second ridiculously world-beating save to keep his clean sheet intact.

The rains were coming down in Raleigh at halftime. I used the time to sprint down the sidewalk to my car so I could refill the parking meter at spot #178. I was only twenty minutes short until free parking kicked in at five p.m., but knowing my luck, the refusal to put a quarter in the meter to cover those twenty minutes would almost certainly result in a parking ticket costing me much more. I returned to the pub quite wet, but ready for my second pint. Sam was ready to serve it to me.

At this point, the satellite feed had returned at the London Bridge Pub. Yet many fans remained in the Royal James. I was quite content to remain at the bar watching the satellite feed amongst a much smaller crowd. That was, until I discovered the other advantage of having cable over satellite. As I enjoyed the first sips of my Guinness, the crowd next door erupted with a chorus of sighs. I looked at the television in front of me to see an Arsenal player dribbling forward. A few seconds later, he sent a cross into the box that Olivier Giroud couldn't connect on. It was at that time that I realized the cable feed had about a ten-second head start on the satellite feed. Well, that wasn't going to work. How I could enjoy the match knowing that every close play or goal would be anticipated by a loud, rambunctious crowd next door? I had to return to the Royal James, and I did so immediately.

Arsenal clearly had the better of the play in the second half, and it was quite evident that Liverpool were hanging on for the draw. I'm not sure if Arsene Wenger had masterfully changed his tactics as much as some of the key Liverpool contributors were simply running out of gas. Regardless of the situation, Arsenal threatened often. Giroud twice had shots in the sixty-eighth and seventieth minutes from well inside the box that Mignolet was able to parry away to safety. Soon thereafter, Ramsey fired a shot in the seventy-second minute destined for the top right corner, but Mignolet was able to make the save again. The second half started to take the appearance of a carbon copy of the first half, only this time with the home team dominating play, looking for the victory. I was convinced the Gooners would break through, just as strongly as I knew Liverpool would do so in the first half. It was a Charles Dickens type of match, a tale of two halves. Thankfully, the Reds were able to hold on. The final whistle blew, 0-0. For the first time since I could remember, Liverpool had opened the season with three straight clean sheets and sat comfortably near the top of the table.

Arsenal match postscript: I had made plans to meet with a good friend after the match over by N.C. State. Phillip Cheeseman was the food and beverage manager for a new hotel scheduled to open later that fall, and we agreed to meet for drinks and dinner after the match. We were having a drink at a nearby tavern discussing dining options and decided to return to the downtown area for dinner. I asked my friend if he had ever been to the London Bridge Pub, and he replied that he had not. Since we were planning to eat at a restaurant on the next block, I convinced him to join me for a pint there. Most supporters had already gone home. It was a Monday night, after all. But there were a few Arsenal fans hanging around, singing songs and drinking more pints of brew. Pub co-owner Mike Ruiz had joined in their post-match festivities. I had a smile on my face as I thought, *I wonder if there is anyone still hanging around the Gooner pub in Durham drinking and singing*. I was pretty sure I already knew the answer.

****

Seven points out of nine was exactly where I wanted to be at this point in the season. One more match to get through before the dreaded September international break. West Ham United came to Anfield, where they hadn't won a match since 1962. Coming off an impressive result at Arsenal, this was a match that needed to be won. The Hammers posed an interesting challenge, with Slaven Bilic replacing the affable Sam Allardyce at the helm. The last time Bilic led a team against Liverpool was in Istanbul, Turkey, as Besitkas eliminated the Reds from last year's Europa League competition. A well-respected manager, Bilic would not easily be outcoached. Even so, the talent gap between the clubs coupled with the home support at Anfield Stadium should be enough for a Liverpool victory.

On the morning of August 29, 2015, my good friend Noel McCabe and I had the opportunity to play golf at an exclusive private course in Pinehurst. Noel is a die-hard Liverpool fan from Dublin who only moved over to North Carolina a few years ago. As much as we wanted to watch the match, this golf invitation was something that you didn't turn down lightly. We could always watch the replay of the match on DVR.

The weather was gorgeous, and the golf was spectacular. It wasn't until we cleared off the seventh green that I realized the match was probably close to halftime. I pulled my phone out to check the score as my foursome approached the next tee. It's quite rare that I curse out on the golf course, so everyone knew something was wrong when I blurted out, "FUCK!"

"What's up?" Noel asked.

"2-0 to West Ham just before halftime" I replied.

Noel simply hung his head before proceeding to shank his tee shot into the woods. Any chance of playing decent golf went down the toilet at that point. We got to the next hole, and this time it was me approaching the tee box when Noel looked up from his phone. "Coutinho just got sent off. We're screwed."

Liverpool has several rivals in the league. Everyone knows how we hate Manchester United, and true Liverpudlians despise cross-town club Everton. West Ham holds a special place for Noel, as that's the club his mother supports. He was not a happy man.

As we periodically checked our phones in between each hole, we hoped to see that Liverpool score increase from zero. It never happened, and eventually we saw the score go final as the Reds dropped their first match of the season 3-0. Surely it wasn't time to hit the panic button yet. Rodgers would have two weeks with most of the roster at Melwood to prepare for the next match, a huge trip to Old Trafford to meet Manchester United.

The result certainly put a damper on an otherwise great day with a great friend. We got home later that night, still wondering how that result could've happened. I looked at the DVR and simply couldn't muster the strength to watch the replay. With the click of a button on the remote control, the match disappeared from my DVR forever. I was sure I'd get enough feedback from hearing everyone else bitch about what went wrong later in the week. Every great team will lose games at home throughout the season. Just a few weeks earlier that same West Ham United went to the Emirates and defeated Arsenal 2-0. While everyone expected the Gunners to compete for a top four spot at the end of the season, we could only muster a draw against them. Perhaps we weren't giving West Ham enough credit. Surely one home loss to a decent team didn't mean it was time to hit the panic button just yet. In two weeks Liverpool would have a chance to redeem this result with a good effort against Manchester United. And they had two weeks to get ready for it.

****

As it pertains to an entire soccer season, "the Storm" is a complicated conglomeration of four different competitions. Throughout the year I expect to experience many ups and downs for each individual match, but in order to accurately portray the status of Liverpool Football Club, you need to review the status of each competition at various random times throughout the season.

PREMIER LEAGUE STANDINGS (through 4 of 38 matches):
After four matches played, Liverpool sit in seventh place in the league, tied with Manchester United and Arsenal on seven points, only one point from third place. Manchester City sit alone in first place having won all four matches played this season.

EUROPA LEAGUE:
Liverpool qualified for the Europa League by finishing sixth place in last

year's league table. Liverpool join Tottenham as the only two English clubs participating in the group stage. West Ham United and Southampton had earned entry into the competition, but both lost in the summer qualifying rounds and failed to make it the group stage.

There are forty-eight teams that play in the Europa League Group Stage, with the clubs drawn into twelve groups of four teams. Each club will play six matches (three home and three away) in round-robin format. Liverpool were drawn into a group with Rubin Kazan (Russia), FC Sion (Switzerland), and Bordeaux (France). This competition will begin with first matches to be played in September.

LEAGUE CUP:

This tournament is a knockout-style random draw amongst the ninety-two clubs currently participating in the Football League, comprised of the top four divisions in English football. In an effort to increase revenue, this tournament has been sponsored every year since 1980. It has been known as the Milk Cup, the Coca-Cola Cup, the Worthington Cup, the Carling Cup, and now the Capital One Cup. For the purposes of consistency in this book, I will refer to this tournament as simply the League Cup.

All Premier League teams gain a first-round bye, and Liverpool earned a second-round bye due to their qualification to this year's Europa League competition. In the third round of competition, only thirty-two clubs remain alive. Liverpool have been randomly selected to play Carlisle United at home in September to begin this competition.

FOOTBALL ASSOCIATION (FA) CUP:

This tournament is another knockout-style random draw amongst any club officially registered with the English Football Association, including amateur teams. This is the oldest running soccer competition in the world, with this season's competition being the 135th tournament in its history. There were 736 teams entered in this competition with numerous play-in games already in progress. At this stage in the tournament only 392 clubs remain. These early stages of the competition are referred to as qualifying rounds, which run through mid-October. Premier League clubs get automatic byes to the third round of the competition, when only sixty-four clubs remain. Liverpool will learn their eventual opponent in this competition in early December, with the match to be scheduled on the weekend of January 9, 2016.

5 - BEGINNING OF THE END

Saturday, September 12
London Bridge Pub
Premier League match #5 (at Manchester United)

As soon as the upcoming schedule is released every summer, I search for that first Manchester United match and make sure that it gets circled on my calendar. This derby is one of the fiercest rivalries in the sport, as both clubs have a long, storied history. They are the two most decorated football clubs in the country, and their fans particularly dislike one another. This mutual vitriol may be magnified across the pond, but American fans have started to accept the gravity of this rivalry. When I am oftentimes asked the question who my second favorite club is, the answer is simply "whoever is playing Manchester United."

This season's first derby match was scheduled for September 12, when Liverpool went to Old Trafford. The middle of September carries a special place in my heart. Ten years earlier, I married my best friend and the love of my life on September 10, 2005. Forty-three years earlier my mother brought me into this world on September 15, 1972. So when my wife asked me what I wanted to do on this special weekend, my answer was simple. I want to be at the pub watching Liverpool play Manchester United with the rest of the Raleigh Reds. She understood. It helped that we celebrated our tenth anniversary earlier in the year with a week in Hawaii, but she knew the importance this match carried.

Every year FIFA designates certain weekends that all countries leave open on the fixture calendar so various international competitions can be played. These international breaks can be brutal. When the national team calls up a player, they have no choice but to travel and play for their country. I'm torn about these breaks, because I appreciate seeing

Liverpool's finest players suit up for their country, while simultaneously feeling terrified that they'll get a season-ending injury.

During last season's first international break, Daniel Sturridge suffered an injury while training for England. It would be the first of many setbacks during an injury-plagued season where he would play in only eighteen of fifty-eight club matches. Also injured during that same break were Joe Allen (who tweaked his knee as Wales defeated Andorra in a European Championship qualifier) and Emre Can (who turned his ankle badly in an 8-1 victory for the German under-23 national team). The training ground at Melwood looked more like a MASH unit than a football club last September. Rodgers failed to get the results and ended up digging a hole that proved to be too big. I'm not saying that these injuries were to blame for last season's misery, but they certainly didn't help the situation.

Once again Liverpool entered this break with some optimism. The primary goal was to keep the players fit. Mission accomplished. There could be no excuses this season. While Sturridge was still not a hundred percent fit to play following the hip surgery that ended his season last May, everyone else was ready. The ingredients for a good result were present. Liverpool had a strong squad rested, practicing for two weeks with a game plan in mind. While Phillippe Coutinho would be ineligible due to his suspension from the previous game, Liverpool still had some firepower with Roberto Firmino and Christian Benteke. And the defense still managed to keep three clean sheets in four matches to start the season, so there was reason to have hope.

Saturday at twelve thirty p.m. is the perfect kickoff time for a match. It gives you the opportunity to sleep late to start the weekend, get some breakfast, and then head into downtown Raleigh. Every time Liverpool and Manchester United play, it's a big match. This match was especially important for both clubs, so early in the season. The teams both came in with identical records, both suffering disappointing losses before the break. The pub was going to be packed.

****

The sport of soccer in North America has taken a meteoric rise in popularity the last decade. When Fox Soccer Channel became a staple for most cable outlets, accessibility to the sport increased exponentially. Twenty years ago, the majority of the sport's fan base was expatriates that brought their support with them from their homeland. Their allegiances were developed long before they became residents here. Through the power of technology, they would have access to watch their favorite German, Spanish, Italian, or English clubs. It was all available to follow through satellite television and the Internet.

Most North Americans didn't have loyalties when they became fans of the sport. For a long time, soccer was given a bum rap in this country. Every four years the World Cup would arrive in the summer, a time where the sport of soccer had little competition from other sports. The American media took notice and started to focus on the largest sporting event on the planet. The U.S. men's national team had great success in 2002, reaching the quarterfinals before losing to Germany 1-0. American fans also started to take notice. Despite some xenophobic sports talk show hosts trashing the game, many people recognized the beauty of the game. They could see that an entire match was played interruption free, and only a short intermission would break up the two halves. Ninety minutes of action were played in less than two hours. Contrast that to an American football game, where sixty minutes of action (most of which is played as teams huddle up to pick a play) takes over three hours, and some fans started gravitating over to the "beautiful game." With multiple television outlets covering the sport, North Americans started taking notice that the world's most popular sport was being played more than just during a six-week stretch every four years. Club loyalties would follow.

Naturally, the Barclays Premier League would be the biggest beneficiary of the North American sleeping giant. There was no language barrier, and many of the Americans that played in the World Cup earned their paycheck in England. It was a natural fit, so it made sense when NBC paid $250 million for the exclusive broadcast rights to the league starting with the 2013-14 season. The number of quality teams in the league made it ever more intriguing for North Americans. Chelsea, Arsenal, Manchester United, Liverpool, and Manchester City were all clubs that had won either domestic or European league titles in the past decade, so they would naturally become fan favorites of newly christened American fans. Everton, Stoke City, and Fulham were lesser-known clubs that garnered attention due to the fact that the employed some American players. Tottenham, Newcastle, and West Ham are clubs that typically finish in the upper tier of the league standings, but I can't think of any earthly reason why an American with no known allegiances would actually choose to root for them. Yet they all have strong American fan bases.

One of my good friends became a passionate supporter recently, and somehow selected Chelsea as his club. While I consider it a personal failure that I couldn't bring him to the Liverpool camp, he simply reminded me of the Nick Hornby quote from *Fever Pitch*: "more often than not, you don't choose who you root for, the club chooses you." I'm not so sure how true that is for everyone else, but it certainly rings true with me. My first exposure to Liverpool was hearing about how the great Kevin Keegan would lead the mighty Reds to victory. I liked his initials, which sounds like a relatively stupid thing to say, but made perfect sense to kid playing under-

12 travel team soccer in upstate New York. I chose to wear the number 11 for my jersey when I played high school soccer, not to honor a great player like most kids do, rather because K is the eleventh letter in the alphabet. And then my love for the band Pink Floyd cemented my soccer-rooting interests. Their relatively obscure song "Fearless" off the 1972 album *Meddle* struck a chord with me. I never liked being told that I couldn't do particular things as a kid, so the opening lyrics became words to live by. It starts off with someone challenging the singer to climb a steep hill. Instead of tackling that task right away, the singer suggests exercising patience waiting for the optimal moment. When you persevere and reach the peak of that hill, savor the moment. Look down on those doubters and smile at the victory of completing their challenge.

As the song fades toward its conclusion, you can hear the sounds of fans singing at a soccer match. As you listen more closely, you start to recognize these fans are singing the chorus of "You'll Never Walk Alone," and it was quite possibly the most beautiful sound I'd ever heard put to music. It took a little research, but I soon discovered that these were Liverpool fans singing to their beloved club after a hard-fought match. As a player, it made me want to be on that pitch getting serenaded. As a fan, it made me want to be there singing in unison with thousands of others. It helped that Kevin Keegan once played for the mighty Reds, but it was far more important that Pink Floyd saw fit to put their anthem on the track. I always assumed that the members of old psychedelic band were Liverpool fans, but it was later revealed that songwriter Roger Waters is an Arsenal fan and simply admired the way Liverpool fans sang that song on match day. I decided that if it was good enough for Roger Waters and Pink Floyd, it was good enough for me.

Every American has a story for why they end up rooting for a particular club. The stories range from wild and surreal to the extremely basic. Even my college teammate Matt White, born and raised in the suburbs of Cleveland, had a reason for picking Manchester United as his club. As he explained to me, "I simply was tired of rooting for Cleveland teams that always lose and ultimately disappoint, so I wanted to pick a winner." While I can't endorse anyone choosing to throw their allegiance behind our biggest rival, I can't really argue with Matt's rationale. It also helps confirm why many people consider most Manchester United fans to be "glory hunters."

From a global perspective, international soccer is the most capitalist professional sports in existence. Every American sports league carries some form of economic restrictions on teams preventing the rich from getting richer. The NFL, NBA, NHL, and Major League Soccer all carry a salary cap in an effort to keep team spending equitable. Major League Baseball has no salary cap, but they do carry some limitations with a luxury tax. Despite their efforts to level the playing field, the lack of a salary cap in baseball allows a team like the New York Yankees to bring in the best players to assemble the best team that money can buy. The existence of a playoff system is the only thing giving fans of poorer baseball teams any hope of a championship. The Kansas City Royals finished the season with the fourth best regular season record in baseball in 2015, but they'll always be remembered as the World Series champions. When one-third of the entire league gets into the knockout round of Major League Baseball's postseason, it gives fans many reasons to hope in October.

With only farcical economic restrictions in place to help level the playing field, the competitive imbalance for Europe's top football clubs like Real Madrid and Manchester United is staggering. According to the published annual reports for the 2013-14 season, Manchester United made over £433 million in revenue. That easily leads the Premier League, with second-place Manchester City making about £86 million less. Liverpool finished in fifth place with £256 million, or about sixty percent of what United earned that season. With so much more money to spend on talent, a club like Manchester United ought to be near the top of the table every season. So when new fans gravitate to this sport and they inevitably pick a team to support, I am curious to know why they pick United. Choosing to root for Real Madrid or Manchester United without any geographical or family connection is like choosing to root for the Internal Revenue Service when your friends get audited.

****

The Premier League couldn't have asked for a better script to this match. Even though the season was barely ten percent completed, both teams craved the result as if the season was riding on it. A win for either team would put the rest of the league on notice while earning the much-desired bragging rights over their hated rivals. There was little doubt why the television networks picked this match for English prime time.

With a plethora of matches that kicked off earlier that morning, the pub was already nearly full. It was a gorgeous Carolina summer Saturday afternoon, yet most people were inside the pub watching one of the eight televisions that grace the walls. Occasionally a few fans would cheer in the background, clearly celebrating a moment of a match that I wasn't watching. Tori and I arrived about forty-five minutes before kickoff and found a location in the back corner. Sam saw me coming in and started pulling two pints of Guinness for us.

To say the pub was packed by kickoff would be an understatement. During the World Cup in the summer of 2014, the London Bridge Pub was the place to be for every match. They were forced to set up a bouncer just to ensure their capacity didn't exceed the fire marshal's limit. The number of patrons awaiting the Manchester United vs. Liverpool match reminded me of those World Cup matches. It was electric and vibrant, and the majority of people were rooting for Liverpool. Despite being the richest club in England, with one of the largest fan followings in the sport, Manchester United doesn't have a strong supporter's club organization. If you scour the Internet, you may find some Manchester United pubs in the larger cities, but to my knowledge there isn't one in Raleigh. Some of their supporters braved the hostile environment and watched at the London Bridge Pub, but I would say they were outnumbered by a ratio of ten to one.

While Liverpool fans claim "You'll Never Walk Alone" as their anthem, Manchester United fans put their own words to "The Battle Hymn of the Republic," with a chorus line that goes "Glory, glory Man United!" Liverpool fans like to parody that song with a version whose chorus instead goes "Who the fuck are Man United?" Casey Peterson was one of the younger Raleigh Reds in attendance, and he got the chants started moments before kickoff. Most of the crowd gleefully joined in. Casey played soccer as a child in the suburbs of Raleigh and first started to appreciate Liverpool when he saw former striker Peter Crouch do the robot dance as his goal celebration. He started following the club, learning about the great history and players, falling in love with how the fans serenaded the players with "You'll Never Walk Alone" at every match. As I settled into position in time for kickoff, I noticed Casey start singing a song that everyone knew would end with most fans screaming at the top of their lungs, "Who the fuck are Man United?"

The match kicked off promptly at twelve thirty p.m. as I started to consume my first pint of Guinness. It was a nerve-racking start to the match, and neither team looked all that great. Both teams struggled to gain any rhythm on the attack, yet Liverpool seemed the shakiest in the back. Rodgers went with four defenders, with Clyne, Lovren, Skrtel and Gomez in the back, and further solidified the defense with Lucas and Emre Can in the midfield. United capitalized in the midfield and controlled the middle third of the pitch. It was frustrating to see them attack with possession while Liverpool desperately tried to defend. There were moments of anxiety, including some shaky distribution from Mignolet, but they survived the first forty-five minutes as the clubs went into halftime tied 0-0.

Rodgers made no adjustments at halftime, and to be frank, I didn't expect him to do so. I was sure he was willing to go back to Merseyside with a 0-0 draw and call the result a success. Louis van Gaal, also under fire from the United faithful after a road loss at Swansea City the week before, took off Memphis Depay for the more experienced Ashley Young. It was a move that would pay dividends in only four minutes.

United gained possession and Young collected the ball on the left side. He made a nice move to get past Clyne, who thought his best option was to foul Young just before he could take the ball into the box and play a dangerous ball into the area. Young's momentum after the foul took him to the ground inside the box as United fans pleaded for a penalty. It was correctly called outside the box, but the foul earned Clyne a yellow card. As players collected inside the area expecting a dangerous cross, Juan Mata calmly played a ground pass to a streaking, unmarked Daley Blind at the edge of the area. Blind one-timed a left footer into the back of the net for the game's first goal. There was nothing Mignolet could do to prevent the goal, and United had the lead they craved. The small pocket of United fans quietly celebrated the lead with a cheer that was easily muffled by the collective groan of Liverpool supporters.

For the next few minutes, Liverpool looked tired and a bit shell-shocked. A change was needed, and Jordon Ibe came on to replace Firmino in the sixty-fifth minute. Some fans were vocally upset at the decision to take Firmino off, since he appeared to be one of the few offensive threats Liverpool had on the pitch. The move appeared to be more a matter of fitness than tactics, which was somewhat understandable while simultaneously frustrating. With both Europa League and League Cup starting in the coming weeks, the schedule was about to get congested. The assumption was that Ibe could be a change of pace on the attack as well. It didn't seem to matter, as United continued to dominate possession in the midfield. It doesn't do your offense any good if you can't get the ball to your attacking players in positions where they can do some damage.

United continued to press, and they got the cushion they needed when Joe Gomez made an ill-timed tackle on Ander Herrera for a penalty, which he calmly put in the back of the net in the seventieth minute to give United a 2-0 lead. This time the small pocket of United fans added a few more decibels to their celebration, while Liverpool fans could only stare at the screen in silent despair.

Minutes continued to click off the clock and the match looked hopeless for Liverpool. For all intents and purposes, United deserved this victory. They were clearly the better team on that day. As much as I hate to admit it, that was the truth. Liverpool seemed to pick up the play at times, but they never really mustered anything that resembled a decent scoring chance until the eighty-fourth minute on a corner kick. It's ironic to consider any Liverpool corner kick a decent scoring chance when you think about their anemic record scoring from set pieces recently. Every time Liverpool needed a goal and pressed on the attack, a resulting corner kick seemed as threatening as an opposing goal kick. Why bother?

The ball was played into the box as expected, and United failed to clear the ball from danger. Jordon Ibe found himself with possession on the right side near the touchline, and attempted to cross the ball. Daley Blind got his head on the ball to deflect the path, but not enough, as it held close to its original course. The play seemed to move in slow motion. Numerous United defenders crowded the box, blocking most pathways to the goal as Christian Benteke positioned himself to attempt the nearly impossible bicycle kick. My initial thought was, *Great... Another wasted opportunity.*

With near perfection, Benteke turned his body counterclockwise and sent a rocket with his lethal right foot toward the target. The armada of United defenders stood motionless in awe, unable to do anything as the ball careened into the back of the net. Nearly a hundred Liverpool supporters at London Bridge Pub erupted as if Bill Shankly himself had emerged from the dead to announce his return to lead the club. To call it Goal of the Week wouldn't do this strike proper justice. It clearly was a Goal of the Month candidate, and just might get consideration for Goal of the Year. If teams could get bonus style points from an independent panel of judges, Liverpool would've taken the lead on that goal. Sadly, the rules only allowed credit for one goal, and the mighty Reds still trailed 2-1. All of a sudden, there was hope. Only six minutes plus stoppage time remained, but we had hope.

After high-fiving many of my friends in the pub, I looked over to the small pocket of United supporters that had been quite boisterous earlier. I couldn't really see their teeth, as they were all biting off their fingernails. I've always thought that the 2-0 lead is the hardest to maintain if you let your opponent get that first goal. I was feeling confident. We were going to nick a late equalizer and break their hearts. My gut told me so. Sadly, my gut was wrong.

As quickly as Liverpool halved their deficit with the Benteke strike, United retaliated to restore order. Newly acquired French teenager Tony Martial made his Manchester United debut and received the ball deep in the Liverpool end, juking around a hapless Martin Skrtel to get an uncontested shot on goal. Once again Mignolet was powerless to stop the ball from entering the net, and the United two-goal margin was restored. Collectively the Liverpool fans at the pub deflated like a tire running over a bed of nails. When the final whistle blew with Manchester United winning 3-1, you could feel the relief released from the small pocket of United fans.

To say that the Liverpool faithful were disappointed was as unjust as saying Christian Benteke scored a "nice goal." *Gutted* was a more appropriate adjective to describe the emotions in the pub. All signs indicated that Liverpool could possibly pull off the upset were present, but they simply didn't deliver. Some fans blamed the manager for his tactics; others blamed the players for failing to show up. No one wanted to admit that United were simply the better team on that particular day. As I thought back to the goals that Liverpool conceded, one thought crossed my mind.

Each of the three goals could've been prevented had a particular defender simply done their job better. Had Clyne not let Ashley Young beat him early in the second half, he wouldn't have needed to commit the foul that led to the first foal. Had Gomez held his ground and not made a hasty tackle, Herrera never would've gone down for a penalty. Had Skrtel not fallen for the simple fakes of a teenaged French striker making his United debut, they never conceded the late third goal. One player that hadn't made a goal-conceding mistake was Dejan Lovren, the defender that no one wanted to see in the starting lineup to being with.

Before the match began, every Liverpool fan was hoping for a win, but would've been happy with a draw. Losing on the road to United is never good, but it has never meant the season was over. Yet this result seemed to change everyone's attitude altogether. Rodgers suddenly was "over his head" and needed to go. A year ago Liverpool went to Old Trafford and lost 3-0 in December. The result was just as devastating, but the team generated some great scoring chances. David de Gea simply played out of his mind, making incredible save after incredible save. On paper, it was a bigger defeat. Yet the fans took solace out of some wonderful football that created great scoring opportunities, so there were some positives to take away from that match. On this day, a singular incredible effort from Christian Benteke made this result look marginally better, but not a single Liverpool fan would admit that it was a better result.

As the few Manchester United fans in attendance continued their celebrations, the commentary from the pundits on the television faded away in favor of the Gerry and the Pacemakers. Win, lose, or draw, the pub almost always plays "You'll Never Walk Alone" to show support for our club. Perhaps one of the hardest things to do is sing our anthem after a difficult loss, but seeing my friends join in helps ease the pain, if only for a moment.

With some incredibly difficult matches coming down the stretch, the club had better deliver something positive in the near future. If they couldn't do that, then this loss to Manchester United could likely become the moment that would mark the "beginning of the end" to Rodgers' tenure as manager of Liverpool Football Club.

6 – WE DON'T DO EASY

Thursday, September 17
London Bridge Pub
Europa League match #1 (at Bordeaux)

Following the tough loss to bitter rival Manchester United, there was much speculation in the press about Brendan Rodgers being in the hot seat. One of the local Liverpool papers held a fan poll that revealed over ninety percent wanted Rodgers out. Questions were being raised about his preferred choice of formation, selecting Dejan Lovren over Mamadou Sakho at center-back, and using attacking players Danny Ings and Roberto Firmino on the wings, where they would be called upon to defend more than they were used to. The upcoming run of fixtures would be a chance for him to right the ship and get Liverpool back on track.

The match at Old Trafford was the first game of seven to be played over a twenty-three-day stretch before the next international break in October. September marks the beginning of the Europa League, something Liverpool has become quite accustomed to participating in. Europa League was a fine competition when it started out as the UEFA Cup, a knockout competition for Europe's not-quite-great-but-still-good-enough clubs that weren't fortunate enough to make Champions League. Greed ultimately won out over practicality. UEFA abandoned the simple knockout style tournament in 2004 and introduced a group stage format like in the Champions League. The end result is the Europa League. While I'm sure it's nice to reward a small farm village club that managed to overcome the odds and finish third place in the Dutch league, few soccer neutrals care enough to pay attention. Most challenging is the fact that six more fixtures are added to congest the fall schedule, including three away trips to the faraway lands of continental Europe. This year, Liverpool got placed into a group that included Russia's Rubin Kazan, FC Sion from Switzerland, and the French club Bordeaux. The first match was played in Bordeaux on the Thursday following the United loss.

It's understandably easy to ignore the Europa League. Games are played on Thursday afternoons against teams that sound like they are named after a Russian Jewish magician. Clearly we would prefer to play in the Champions League against the legendary clubs across Europe, but for me I am happy to see Liverpool play as often as possible. With Rodgers maintaining the core players in the first five league matches, I speculated that we would see some new faces on the pitch for Liverpool in this match at Bordeaux.

Both Jordan Henderson and James Milner had picked up injuries in the last match and would not be available. Henderson picked up a serious foot injury and was expected to be out for a lengthy spell. He was sent over to America to see a specialist. As a result, eighteen-year-old local boy Jordan Rossiter got the call to start in the central midfield. Rossiter was born in Liverpool and joined the youth club at the age of six. He progressed through the academy and earned his way to a professional contract with Liverpool. Last season he made his senior club debut in the League Cup against Middlesbrough, scoring on a twenty-yard strike in the tenth minute. The last local boy to come through the academy to make an impact was Steven Gerrard. As one local legend departed Merseyside, could we be seeing the start of the next one?

The roster was filled with newcomers and reserve players. Included among those making the trip to France were some kids that had never graced the pitch for Liverpool before. Nineteen-year-olds Connor Randall, Daniel Cleary, and Cameron Brannagan, and eighteen-year-old Pedro Chirivella all traveled and earned a spot on the bench against Bordeaux. Factor in starters Joe Gomez (eighteen), Jordon Ibe (nineteen), and Divock Origi (twenty) for a very young squad playing against Bordeaux.

Rodgers mixed up the starting roster, bringing Sakho back into the fold at central defense. A lot of fans were ecstatic at this piece of news, because it meant Lovren wouldn't be playing. The decision didn't surprise me. Sakho himself was a regular on the French national team, so it made perfect sense to play him in his home country. He was also given the captain's armband for the match.

Most midweek fixtures bring in the same crowd to the pub. Fans that have flexibility in their work schedule tend to be the ones you see on a Thursday afternoon at three p.m., especially when Liverpool are expected to play a reserve squad against a team with players no one has heard of. As a salesperson covering the Carolinas, I am expected to spend a lot of time on the road visiting clients. For midweek matches it makes sense for me to schedule one thirty p.m. work meetings at a client site located a short drive to the pub, so I almost always do. It also helps to have great bosses that don't micromanage and allow me this work flexibility. For that I am extremely grateful.

Jeff Carroll is one supporter that is nearly always at the bar before I get to a midweek match. As a warehouse distribution manager and driver, Jeff is afforded the luxury of a flexible work schedule during midweek matches as well. Jeff is an interesting case study for reasons why American fans select their club. He played soccer in high school, but like most American players, he took a hiatus from the sport for years until he caught the bug again during the 2010 World Cup. He considered himself a casual fan of the sport and didn't feel the need to throw his support toward one club. He always maintained a giant man-crush for NBA star LeBron James, so his mind started to change when, as part of a partnership deal with FSG to gain international representation for LeBron's efforts to expand his personal brand globally, he was given a minority stake in Liverpool Football Club.

Jeff started watching the Premier League with more interest, and he noticed Liverpool had recently spent a lot of money to acquire a player that shared his surname. Andy Carroll was brought in from Newcastle United near the end of the January 2011 transfer window for a fee of £35 million, at the time the highest amount paid for a British footballer. While ultimately considered to be one of the biggest transfer busts in recent memory, the jury was still out when Jeff picked Liverpool as his favorite club. To this day Jeff remains the only person I have ever met that openly admits that Andy Carroll was the reason he supported Liverpool.

Jeff found out about OLSC Raleigh through social media, but it wasn't until spring of 2014 that he first came to the pub to watch a match. During the incredible run at the end of the 2013-14 season, Jeff decided that the match against bitter rival Manchester United would be a good virgin visit to the London Bridge Pub. It was there that he ran into an old friend and high school soccer teammate who, unbeknownst to him, was also a Raleigh Red. He's been a regular ever since.

The former teammate that he met at the pub was Ty Harrell, former North Carolina state assemblyman. Ty is the most affable and optimistic human being that I have ever met. No longer serving as an elected official in the state government, Ty now runs a mortgage brokerage firm in Raleigh. When he was a sophomore in the late eighties, a new kid moved into his neighborhood from Liverpool and joined his high school soccer team. This new friend was a huge Liverpool fan, and they would watch VHS tapes of old matches together on weekend sleepovers. Back then the club had numerous stars as one of the most dominant teams in the game, but it was John Barnes that caught his attention. Immediately attracted to the fact that both were players of color in a sport dominated by whites, Ty related to the former Liverpool legend. Barnes played the sport with speed and strength, enduring a period when racism was both prevalent and tolerated in the league. Barnes would be jeered and taunted, yet he always handled each situation with the utmost dignity. Ty respected that and looked to him as a role model. It cemented his love for Liverpool.

I walked into the pub, acknowledging some of the regular midweek patrons as I walked to the rear of the pub, where Jeff was standing. Sam was already pouring my first pint before I got there. Even though it was the first European match of the season for Liverpool, the pub didn't have as many fans as I expected. It was a decent crowd, but paled in comparison to what was seen a year earlier during our return to the Champions League. It's the trickle-down economics of failing to maintain top-four status in the Premier League. Not only does the club suffer financially, but so do the Liverpool fan pubs.

Bordeaux controlled most of the first half, getting some of the better scoring chances. It was some of the most boring action that I had seen in a professional soccer match. Bordeaux had only one win in the French Ligue Un, sitting mid-table, while Liverpool's mixed bag of experience and youth struggled to do anything when they gained possession. Kolo Toure made short work of his season debut for the Reds, injuring himself in the early minutes. Rodgers replaced him with Pedro Chirivella, the young Spanish kid from Valencia we'd acquired in 2013. It was an opportunity to get my first look at another potential prospect Liverpool had waiting in the wings.

Liverpool picked up the play in the second half, and I must admit that the youthful exuberance of Rossiter and Chirivella had much to do with their improved play. Perhaps their familiarity with each other on the reserve squad helped create the cohesion. It didn't take long for Liverpool to break the ice. Adam Lallana scored the first goal of the match with a deft curling ball inside the right post in the sixty-first minute. It was a well-deserved goal, and Bordeaux looked like they were ready to cave. As the match entered the final ten minutes, Rodgers decided to give young Cameron Brannagan his debut, replacing Rossiter.

The few patrons at the pub were happy with how the match played out. Getting a road win is always a great feat, but to get it with the bulk of your reserves is even better. When Bordeaux striker Jussie found the back of the net late in the game to draw level, I actually found myself cursing. The lads deserved better, and it was a shame they didn't earn all three points. When the final whistle blew, I could only shake my head.

Of the four teams in group play of the Europa League, the top two advance to the knockout stage. When UEFA decided to give the winners an automatic berth to the next Champions League, it added to the significance of the competition. Drawing your away matches in this competition is a great result, because it prevents the opponent from earning three points at home. It's easy to say that Liverpool should be favorites to advance out of the group stage, but if they didn't, it would likely be at the benefit of Bordeaux. This result wasn't the end of the world for Liverpool. It just felt that way. Dropping points in the final minutes of the match sucks, even in the Europa League. It only fueled more speculation on the future of Rodgers as head coach. A few sources started identifying potential replacements, including such high-profile names as Carlo Ancelotti and Jürgen Klopp. I wasn't ready to jump on the "Rodgers out" bandwagon just yet. There was still time to recover from this mediocrity.

****

Part of the problem with playing in the Europa League is the next fixture on the schedule in the league gets moved to Sunday so that players are given adequate rest from the Thursday matches. It's always a difficult draw to get a crowd at the pub on a Sunday morning because of the archaic laws preventing the sale of alcohol until noon. Not that any of that mattered to me, since I had weekend plans with the wife. Instead of figuring out where I would watch the Norwich City match on Sunday at eleven a.m., I was enjoying a nice brunch with my wife in Asheville.

Liverpool have had a great history against Norwich City, winning five and drawing one in six matches since Norwich returned to the top flight in 2011 (side note: Norwich did get relegated after the 2013-14 season, but returned after one short year in the championship). Liverpool scored five goals in three of those six encounters, and three goals in two others. The only scar was a 1-1 draw played at Anfield on October 22, 2011. The common denominator in those six matches is that Luis Suarez starred in all of them, scoring multiple hat tricks. That shouldn't really matter, though, because surely Liverpool was expected to win its home games against newly promoted clubs. Now that Daniel Sturridge had returned from his extended injury, it should be a cakewalk.

I watched the replay of the match on my DVR, and I was excited to see Benteke starting up top with Sturridge. Could this become the dynamic duo of striker partners that we'd been craving since Suarez left to Barcelona? There really wasn't much to write about in that first half, and I found myself fast-forwarding through much of the play. I wasn't expecting Sturridge to play the full ninety minutes, having come back from a long injury spell. When Danny Ings came on as a second-half substitute, I assumed it would be for Sturridge. I was surprised to see Benteke getting yanked due to injury.

It didn't take long for Ings to make his mark, scoring off a nice pass from Alberto Moreno in the forty-eighth minute to open his Liverpool account. 1-0 to Liverpool. Danny Ings was one of many incoming signings this transfer season, and actually the subject of some controversy. Ings made his mark with Burnley in the 2014-15 season, scoring eleven league goals in thirty-five appearances for a club getting relegated. He was rumored to be moving last January as his contract with the club expired at the end of the season, but Burnley kept him through the spring, hoping that his talents would keep them from the bottom three league positions. It didn't work. As the season wound down, Ings was linked with a move to Anfield. Even though he would be out of contract, Liverpool would be forced to pay a developmental fee to Burnley, since he was still under the age of twenty-four and a homegrown player. The two clubs couldn't agree to terms, so the actual fee would be determined by an independent arbitrating tribunal. Someone would quip that "the best Ings in life are free, plus a tribunal fee."

Norwich equalized in the sixty-first minute off a corner kick. As Mignolet flapped about at the cross, Russell Martin calmly flicked home the tying goal. It prompted the Norwich fans to playfully serenade Brendan Rodgers with "you're getting sacked in the morning!" I couldn't believe what I was seeing, and the final whistle blew with Liverpool being held to a draw. This was the same club that we'd outscored 22-6 in the last six matches. This was the same club that only recently got promoted from the championship. Here they were holding our mighty Reds to a draw at Anfield. This was simply unacceptable, and a manager change would be justifiable.

****

Midweek saw what should've been another "easy" fixture for Liverpool as they entered the League Cup, a competition created to give another domestic knockout competition for all ninety-two clubs in the top four divisions of English football. First held in the 1960-61 season, the Football League Cup was created in an effort to make up for lost revenue when the league was expected to lose fixtures due to reorganization. At the time there were strong tensions between the Football League and Football Association, so the tournament was introduced in an attempt to create excitement in a sport that was losing spectators in large quantities. Aston Villa won the inaugural competition with a 3-2 victory over Rotherdam United. Liverpool has won this competition a record eight times (only Chelsea and Aston Villa have won as many as five). With the majority of matches being played in the fall, the bigger clubs involved in European competitions tend to take this competition less seriously, and end up playing younger reserve players in the early stages. For this reason, many fans prefer to call it the "Mickey Mouse Cup." It's still a tournament rewarded with silverware that goes on the trophy shelf, and the winner earns an automatic spot in next year's Europa League competition. For the vast majority of clubs, this is their best shot at glory.

The first round of the tournament involves the seventy-two clubs not playing in the top flight of the Premier League. The thirty-six winners from those first-round matches played in early August advance to the next round. At this stage all Premier League clubs not involved in the European leagues get placed into the random bracket. Since Liverpool would be playing in the Europa League, they would not enter the competition until the third round, with only thirty-one other clubs remaining. The random draw had mighty Carlisle United traveling to Merseyside for a test against Liverpool.

Carlisle United is small club with a big history, based in the small town of the same name situated in the northwest part of England, not far from the Scottish border. The club was formed in 1904, only twelve years after Liverpool Football Club separated from Everton. The Cumbrians, as they are nicknamed, made it to England's top flight in the 1974-75 season and earned the distinction of being the least populated city to ever have a club play in the highest division. Forty-one years later, they sit mid-table in the fourth tier of English football. If you ranked all clubs top to bottom on the professional football ladder, Carlisle United was ranked about eightieth in the entire competition. They would be playing away to a club ranked seventh.

Domestic cup competitions are a great way to get reserve players some action, and I was expecting to see many new faces in the Liverpool starting lineup. One player making his debut would be backup goalkeeper Adam Bogdan. Acquired in the offseason on a free transfer from Bolton Wanderers, the twenty-eight-year-old Hungarian was brought in to be Simon Mignolet's primary backup for the season. Playing a weaker League Two club was a perfect time to give Mignolet a break from the action. I expected to see more of the reserves get a start, but when I saw the starting field players, I was shocked to see none. Lovren, Can, Skrtel, Clyne, Milner, Moreno, Allen, Firmino, Lallana, and Ings made up the roster. Each one of those players had already played significant minutes for the first team, so clearly this game should be a cakewalk.

I was a little busy that week, so instead of getting down to the pub, I decided to follow the game online. From my office I saw the video replay of Danny Ings twenty-third-minute header that gave Liverpool a 1-0 lead, and assumed that the slaughter was on. Or was it? Derek Asamoah would equalize for the Cumbrians in the thirty-fifth minute. Surely the Reds would come through in the second half and distance themselves from this lower-league club. I left work to begin my evening commute home with the match still in question. Imagine my surprise when I got home and checked the Internet to see Liverpool advancing through a penalty shootout.

The more that I read about the match, the clearer it became that Carlisle bunkered their defense like a Jose Mourinho bus stop in an effort to keep the match level. The tactic nearly worked. Liverpool had been struggling to find goals all season long, scoring only five times in seven matches before this game. Breaking down a stingy defense had proven to be a developing issue this season, and Carlisle were able to withstand the pressure for the final forty-five minutes plus thirty minutes of extra time.

Liverpool was victorious through the penalty shootout, and advanced to the next round. It couldn't have been pretty, and clearly the tide of opinion had turned against Brendan Rodgers. Not only were the results not acceptable, but the play wasn't pretty either. It would be one thing to say a team is unlucky, but far too few scoring chances were being created against clubs that had no business competing with Liverpool. Even though the club advanced in the competition, fans weren't buying into this smokescreen. The holes hadn't been plugged and the ship continued to sink.

****

After the match with Carlisle United, it was revealed that Dejan Lovren would be sidelined for about two months with a serious ankle ligament injury. This news didn't disappoint most fans, as his play was below expectation since being acquired from Southampton the previous summer. Under normal circumstances, that bit of news would've been the headline of the sports pages during the week. Instead there was a quote from a German paper where Jürgen Klopp indicated he would like to coach in the English Premier League. "Come and get me" was the direct translation. Klopp was previously the manager for German powerhouse Borussia Dortmund, leading that club to two Bundesliga titles despite being seriously out-funded by his German rival Bayern Munich. He was the dream manager for most Liverpool fans, and this recent headline continued to fuel speculation about Brendan Rodgers' job.

So far this had been an extremely disappointing month for Liverpool. The loss at Old Trafford began a string of dismal results and the club supporters were growing weary of the mediocrity. The final match of the month was at home against Aston Villa, a perfect opportunity for the club to turn it around and wake everyone up from this September slumber.

Danny Ings made the starting team again, and he was quickly endearing himself to Liverpool fans. I was delighted to see him in the lineup. Would Rodgers play him up front as a second striker with Sturridge? Or would he play him out of position on the right wing, like he did against Manchester United? With Coutinho, Lucas, Moreno, and Milner starting in the midfield, my thought was that the gaffer would yield to his stubbornness and stick Ings back in a five-man midfield, leaving Sturridge all alone up top. That was exactly what happened.

I drove to the pub for this Saturday morning match. I didn't expect to see too many regulars, so I was pleasantly surprised when I saw about forty Raleigh Reds milling about the pub before kickoff. The team hadn't been playing inspiring football since the loss to Manchester United, but most of us weren't giving up. One of these supporters was Chris Valentine, a graduate of West Point originally from the nearby city of Rocky Mount. While serving in the U.S. Army, Chris was stationed in Germany, where he picked up his love for the sport. He would join his fellow soldiers on the occasional day trip to a match, and simply fell in love with Liverpool because they were the dominant English team at the time. It helped that the club had some great Irish players like Ronnie Whelan and John Aldridge, as Chris loves everything about Ireland. It was his first match at the pub, so I bought him a pint of Guinness to celebrate the reunion.

The game kicked off as the first sips of Guinness calmed the nerves. This was a critically important game for Liverpool. On paper the results to date hadn't been all that bad. But while the results may not have been bad, the play had been. The train was showing signs of derailment and needed to get firmly back on track. Three points at home against Aston Villa was required.

With barely a minute on the clock, Philippe Coutinho fed the ball to vice-captain Milner, who was standing on the edge of the penalty area. Villa gave Milner far too much room to receive the ball. His first touch wasn't the greatest, but he looked to shoot on target with his right foot. When he saw that lane closed down by the Villa defense, he quickly switched feet to drill home with his weaker left. It was a great goal to open his Liverpool account.

Liverpool thoroughly dominated the first half, and had it not been for American goalkeeper Brad Guzan, the Reds could've made the match academic after forty-five minutes. Their inability to finish kept the lead at one goal as the teams went into the locker room.

It was a good feeling watching the lads respond with solid play and carry a lead into halftime. But they also had a lead against Carlisle and Bordeaux, and let those weaker sides back into the match. Clearly we needed a second goal.

The second half started with more Liverpool domination. When it comes to making tactical substitutions, I subscribe to the thought that one should wait until the sixtieth minute before making a change. If you don't make a change at halftime, then you need to give the starters about fifteen minutes to get back into the groove. As Liverpool pressed for a second goal, the clock approached that sixtieth minute. My first thought was to get Sturridge off the pitch. It wasn't like he was ineffective, but his recent injury log gave me concern when he was playing late in a match that Liverpool look certain to win. "Time to bring on Origi for Sturridge," I said to someone. A minute later, we watched Milner deftly lob the ball over the left side of the defense to a streaking Sturridge. With his preferred left foot, the shot was one-timed to the far post as a helpless Guzan watched the ball hit the side netting. "Maybe keep on Sturridge for a few more minutes," I said. 2-0 to Liverpool. Breathe. Raleigh Reds rejoiced at the pub, singing songs serenading the great striker. We barely stopped high-fiving each other before Villa's Rudy Gestede fired home his own far-post gem to cut the deficit to one. Immediate disbelief overcame us. Here we go again.

Less than a minute after that goal was scored, Sturridge got another nifty back-heel pass from Philippe Coutinho on a give-and-go. Moving to his right, Sturridge slotted home his second goal calmly with his right foot and the two-goal cushion was restored. Breathe again.

Without time to relax on this lead, Rudy Gestede felt the need to increase my anxiety level with a brilliant header goal in the seventy-first minute. It would've been harsh to blame anyone for that goal as the cross came in from the left to a leaping Gestede who powered it past Mignolet. The goal prompted me to scream, "For fuck's sake, can we just once get an easy win?" That goal made the score 3-2 in favor of Liverpool with too much time remaining. As I was beginning to learn, we don't do easy.

The minutes ticked toward the end and Villa looked gassed. It appeared to me that any equalizing goal would likely be at the hands a gross Liverpool error. Thankfully, that never happened. Sturridge had two more chances to complete his hat trick, but he had to settle for the brace. The final whistle blew, and Liverpool earned the three points that were required. If Liverpool couldn't manage to win at home by more than one goal against teams that were always fighting relegation, then I might have to look into more comprehensive medical coverage because my heart wouldn't survive. It wasn't pretty, but we got the result. Breathe at last.

7 - LOS ANGELES

Thursday, October 1
Joxer Daly's, Los Angeles, CA
Europa League match #2 (vs. FC Sion)

Living on the East Coast, one would think there are more convenient locations to make my first away pub visit than Los Angeles. It made sense to try to and coordinate pub visits with other planned excursions. When I was directed to attend a trade show in Anaheim in late September, it gave me the opportunity to watch Liverpool's Europa League clash with FC Sion with the OLSC Los Angeles crew.

Normal kickoff times for midweek matches make for a good way to end your day on the East Coast, but local time in California was noon, a perfect time to spend your lunch. I wasn't expecting a large crowd for this particular match. While it is still a European competition, a lot of people can't be bothered to adjust their schedules for the Europa League. The opponents are far less glamorous, and as seen the week before against Bordeaux, the roster is usually filled with reserve players. None of that bothers me, as I simply appreciate every opportunity to watch and support the Reds.

The OLSC Los Angeles crew is run by Brian Montano. I first met Brian in New York during the 2014 preseason tour, when the club invited all OLSC branch leadership to meet and discuss issues through a focus group session. He carries a remarkable resemblance to Philippe Coutinho, in my opinion, both in size and appearance. When I learned of this work trip to Southern California, I immediately reached out to Brian to arrange this visit.

Brian became a Liverpool fan because of Michael Owen, a similar story told by many others as the Premier League gained popularity at the turn of the century. He'd been coordinating the Los Angeles chapter for many years, but they only officially became chartered in 2012. Originally known as LFC California, they absorbed many other cities in their early years. Doing so gave all of the Southern Californians the benefits that come with being an official branch. As both the sport and Liverpool grew in popularity, they have been able to spawn new official clubs in the area. Now there are official branches in Orange County, San Diego, and San Francisco, but it all started with the crew in Los Angeles, and they meet for all matches at a Culver City tavern called Joxer Daly's.

Other than being a bar when soccer fans like to congregate, I had no clue to what to expect walking to this bar. The décor inside clearly identified with the Emerald Isle, so it had to be considered an Irish bar. What about the name? Most Irish pubs are easily sniffed out by name, but what of Joxer Daly? I consider myself somewhat well versed in the lingo of Irish drinking establishments, but this one had me baffled. I had to research the significance of the pub name. As it turned out, Irish playwright Sean O'Casey wrote a play called *Juno and the Paycock*. The play was set in the tumultuous times just before Ireland seceded from the United Kingdom in 1919. Joxer Daly was a character in that play and had been described as an amiable drinker typically ingratiating himself to whomever he was with, even if it meant contradicting himself as soon as he moved to converse with another patron. He avoided working at all costs, instead spending his time drinking and consorting with his mates. Sounds like the type of guy I would want to hang out with. It also sounds like the perfect name for an Irish pub.

There weren't any Liverpool fans in the bar when I walked into Joxer Daly's, but a few Celtic fans wandered in from the back entrance. The beautiful thing about Europa League match day is the multitude of games scheduled simultaneously, and the Scottish champions were scheduled to play Turkish giants Fenerbahce at the same time Liverpool were to kick off. Wouldn't you know that the Celtic Supporters Club of Los Angeles also calls this pub their home? With plenty of televisions and space, there would be room for everyone.

Brian was one of the first Reds to walk in the pub, taking an extended lunch break from his job. We greeted each other with a firm handshake and grabbed a pint. The match would begin soon, and slowly his crew started making their way inside.

Joxer Daly's wasn't the original home for OLSC Los Angeles, Brian explained to me. They used to go to another nearby pub owned by an actual Scouser from Liverpool, but according to Brian, the pub owner was fearful of being labeled "just a Liverpool pub" by other fans. He didn't want to lose the potential business from other supporters, so by mutual consent, they parted ways with the pub and found a new home.

I grew up in a small town, what we used to call the suburb of a wannabe city in upstate New York. I wasn't exposed to the crime and violence that others experience in a more urban environment like Los Angeles. When Brian told me how the pub owner made sure that police presence was nearby whenever Liverpool faced a major rival, I was quite surprised. He pointed across the street to a parking lot, explaining how just two weeks earlier there were cops in waiting as Liverpool played Manchester United. The pub owner knew that United fans would show up to watch the match and talk shit to their rivals, and he was smart to have law enforcement on standby. It wasn't long before then that some Chelsea fans found their way to Joxer's for one of their matches. Slightly dissatisfied with a Chelsea defeat, they ended up tossing tables inside, causing a major ruckus. One of the patrons went to his car to retrieve his gun to protect his friends just in case, insurance that thankfully wasn't needed. I was assured that was the rare circumstance, and I was never worried. While Los Angeles is known for a diverse population, I wasn't expecting a large Swiss contingent to show up and start shit at this match.

The game kicked off promptly at noon local time, and so I grabbed a seat at the table and started watching. Brian introduced me to Debbie Devlin, a Liverpool-born fan who had moved to the area twenty-three years ago. Debbie is an integral part to their supporters club, and she was simply amazed at how much fan support the club could generate from so far away. When I asked her what she was hoping for this season, her answer startled me. "I just want Rodgers out," she stated emphatically. "This team just doesn't play like the Liverpool teams I grew up watching, and I blame him. He's run off our best players. Legends. And now we have this shit to watch. He needs to go."

Don't sugarcoat it, Debbie. Tell me how you really feel. I appreciated her honesty, and I certainly understood her cynicism. I couldn't really blame her, either. While the results had been decent, I couldn't really see where this club was headed. It was the world's worst hangover, lasting sixteen months since the Reds nearly won the league.

Playing at home, Rodgers decided to give some of the regular starters a rest and gave some of the squad players a run-out. Kolo Toure, Jordan Rossiter, and Divock Origi all returned to the starting lineup for this match. Sion may have finished high enough in the Swiss Super League to earn entry to this competition, but their current form was not much to speak of, sitting mid-table in their domestic league. Their club chairman earlier called the players out in the media for their disappointing play. Theoretically Liverpool reserves should have no trouble winning this match at Anfield.

It didn't take long for Liverpool to put the ball in the net, as Adam Lallana showed some individual brilliance to give the Reds a 1-0 lead in the fourth minute. Finally, it looked like Liverpool would be able to break through with some offense. The team played with flair and made their opponent's defense look like a pub team on their own extended hangover.

In the fourteenth minute, Clyne played a nice ball over to Origi, who then back-heeled it past the Swiss defense into the box on the attack. His left-footed shot was headed on target, but deflected across the goalmouth by the central sweeper. Jordon Ibe tracked the ball down on the left side and turned toward goal. He sent a right-footed shot from a difficult angle toward the target, but that also was easily saved by the goalkeeper. At any moment it would seem Liverpool would open the floodgates and turn the rout on. Or so it would seem.

Against the run of play, Sion would equalize in the seventeenth minute when Xavier Kouassi gained possession in the midfield and launched an arcing pass over the left side of Liverpool's defense. Ghanaian striker Ebenezer Assifuah, loosely marked by Joe Gomez, calmly chested the long pass perfectly to his feet before one-timing the ball past a helpless Simon Mignolet. The goal was probably undeserved, all things considered, but you had to tip your cap at the individual brilliance from the young kid.

The game continued with more Liverpool dominance in possession, but nothing to show for it on the scoreboard. Sion were happy to sit back and let the anemic midfield led by Joe Allen fail to penetrate into the final third. Watching on television, it looked more like an FA Cup game where the local pub team got to travel to the large stadium to play against their heroes. Sion looked more like a League Two side than they did a top team in any continental European league. Yet the halftime whistle blew with the score tied at 1-1.

I worked my way back to the bar at halftime and ordered another pint of Guinness. It was there I met James Jonathan Rodriguez and his four-year old daughter Stella, both wearing this year's red home kit. James is a local employment recruiter that can afford to take afternoons off, and he loves nothing more than spending time with his daughter. When I asked him why he started supporting Liverpool, he had the most honest reply I had ever heard: "I had always loved watching soccer, so one day my wife got me a Liverpool jersey as a present. She picked it out because she liked the look of the jersey better than anything else in the store."

I'd like to say that Rodgers had one of those inspirational talks at halftime, motivating his players to step up and give the home crowd something to cheer for. Instead it was Didier Thorot that seemed to kick his Sion team into a new gear. Rodgers made a single substitution at halftime (Moreno on for Clyne), but it would seem that was mostly to protect Clyne, who had already played all but ninety minutes of Liverpool's first nine games. When I read that fact, it made me wonder why Moreno didn't play in his place from the start. It was just one of many recent Rodgers decisions that made fans scratch their heads. Rodgers brought on Coutinho in the sixty-first minute hoping that the Brazilian magician would once again bail him out, but this tactic also failed to deliver.

As the minutes ticked off the clock and it became clear the 1-1 score line would end up being final, I saw something that I can't honestly say I had seen before. Liverpool fans headed for the exits before the final whistle blew. When you consider that local time was nearly ten p.m. on a school night, I couldn't say that I blamed them. It was the biggest indictment of Brendan Rodgers that I had yet seen. The squad that he had assembled was more than capable of beating Sion. We all knew it. I didn't care if the team "showed great character" or "was extremely unlucky to not have scored a second goal." All too often those were comments Rodgers would share with the media in his post-match press conference. I looked over at Debbie and shook my head.

"Utter shit," she said to me. I could only nod in agreement. As I waited for my next pint of Guinness to be poured, it occurred to me that there were two possible ways to judge Brendan Rodgers as a manager. Either he was too incompetent to motivate the talent and make the necessary tactical adjustments to be a successful manager at Liverpool (in which case he should be sacked), or he happened to be the unluckiest bastard that caused his best players to get injured while unable to hold a one-goal lead (in which case he should also be sacked). The ironic thing was that these results were hardly debilitating to the season so far. There was still time for it to be saved.

Looking at my watch, I noticed that I had about six hours to kill before hopping the red-eye back to Raleigh. I met a few more of the L.A. supporters and moved the party to the outside patio. The weather was typical for Southern California, eighty degrees and sunny without a cloud in the sky. I looked at the weather app on my phone to see Hurricane Joaquin approaching the Carolina coast, bringing buckets of rain with him, validating this decision to spend my final six hours in L.A. enjoying my Guinness on the outdoor patio.

James and Stella joined us on the patio. I spent most of the afternoon calling him Joe, and he was kind enough to not correct the consistent error. It wasn't until the end of the afternoon that we friended each other on Facebook and I noticed that his name wasn't actually Joe. The funny thing is his Facebook profile calls him James Jonothan Rodriguez, and I'm not really sure if he goes by James or Jonothan now. I spent the whole time calling him Joe. To make matters worse, we were joined on the patio by Jesus Rodriguez (no relation), a full-time college student that had the afternoon off. You can't make this up. Too many Js for me.

Jesus is a young, striking lad, who was wearing a long-sleeved flannel shirt over top of the red LFC kit and a Dodgers cap on his head. Jesus was born in Mexico and spent his childhood days loving soccer. His father got him a soccer magazine subscription in 2005, and it came with a full-size poster celebrating Liverpool's Champions League victory over Milan. Not knowing any better, he hung that poster on his bedroom wall, marking the day that Liverpool entered his heart for eternity.

The final member of the patio party was Devon Escudero, another young Hispanic fan who fell in love with the club after seeing the fans sing "You'll Never Walk Alone" on television about twelve years ago. He adored the ideology of the club, and the 2005 Miracle at Istanbul cemented his allegiance to Liverpool.

The four of us took the end table on the patio lamenting over another subpar performance. Most of the conversation dealt with the employment status of Brendan Rodgers. Devon couldn't get past the success from two seasons prior and wanted to keep Rodgers at the helm. Jesus was somewhat undecided, although he did concede that a change could do the team some good. I still couldn't get past how poor the team performances appeared. The results weren't terrible, but for the money invested, the team was clearly underperforming. I always thought that a midseason change in leadership reeked of desperation. Having already decided to invest time writing this book over the course of the next eight months, my own personal desperation was starting to set in. I needed something to get excited about again. The current regime was losing me.

Jesus returned home to get some studying in, and James Jonothan Joe finished his beer. Stella spent most of her patio time running around like a four-year old girl should. She was tired and it was time for them to head home. We said our goodbyes before he poignantly pointed out, "It could be worse. We could be Chelsea fans."

The sun continued to beat down as Devon and I ordered another beer and I started to wonder if I needed to get some sunblock. We bonded well during this time, the two lone Liverpool fans still at the pub. As a marketing consultant running his own firm, he simply made the command decision not to return to the office. It was a tremendously hospitable sacrifice on his part, because he insisted that Joxer's had the best chicken wings in town, and I needed to make sure that I ordered them correctly. He got no argument from me. I love chicken wings.

I checked my phone to see that it was five o'clock and we were still enjoying the great outdoors. The pub had previously been quiet, but began to fill up once again with the evening crowd. My first thought was happy hour, but then I noticed a large number of patrons wearing Pittsburgh Steelers jerseys inside. When you're sitting in the California sunshine, it's easy to forget that your world is three hours behind the East Coast. The NFL's Thursday night game was about to kick off while most Californians were leaving the office.

We returned to the inside of the pub for dinner. Devon didn't lie about the wings. They were tasty, and a much-appreciated meal before heading to the airport. Most of the conversation had drifted away from Liverpool as we got to know one another on more personal terms. I empathized with his current long-distance relationship, a girlfriend that lived in Montreal. We talked about business, politics, and the weather. It seemed that we'd exhausted the discussion about Liverpool, but that was fine with me. The match concluded six hours earlier, and there I was still engaged in conversation with my new friend.

When I first made the decision to write this book, I was excited about the prospect of travel. I was thrilled to have the opportunity to go out and watch Liverpool play with other fans. In my position as president of the OLSC chapter in Raleigh, I have met some great supporters across the country, including Brian Montano. While I am friendly with them all, I can't really call them "friends," as I know little about their personal lives. Visiting my first away pub in Los Angeles, I learned the true value of this project would not be the experience of seeing new places. It would be turning good acquaintances into great friends.

8 - RODGERS OUT

Saturday, October 3
Camp Kendra, Silk Hope, NC
Premier League match #8 (at Everton)

Earlier I mentioned the first two phases of the Liverpool season as defined by the international breaks. The first phase of the season was the opening four fixtures of the Premier League, where Liverpool opened strongly with seven points in the first three matches, including a road draw at Arsenal. As disappointing as the 3-0 home loss to West Ham United was to close out that phase, I kept reminding myself that it wasn't a complete disaster. The second phase of the fixture list would be the true test for this club. Seven matches over twenty-three days across three separate competitions, including away trips to our two biggest rivals in Manchester United and Everton. For me this was always going to be the defining stretch of games for Liverpool. Success in September would go a long way, while failure could be our death knell. Just how you differentiated between success and failure was unknown.

I've already documented the miserable display of football played at Old Trafford. It wasn't the loss that bothered fans as much it was the lack of effort and tactical mediocrity. Not much changed through the next five fixtures. A single one-goal win at home against a relegation-battling Aston Villa would be the only bright spot amongst a litany of draws, and even that light was lacking serious magnitude. It would seem the only possible way to right this ship would be to head across Stanley Park and get a dominating victory at Goodison Park against Everton. To be fair, Liverpool were still alive in all three competitions that had commenced, and we had only lost once through this difficult stretch of games. Rumors of a Rodgers sacking were gaining momentum, so this had to be considered a must-win game for him.

Whenever Liverpool and Everton play each other at Merseyside, you can almost guarantee an early kickoff. Authorities prefer to minimize the amount of time locals can spend enjoying pints at their local pub before walking into the ground. With Liverpool's involvement in the Europa League on the Thursday prior to this match, it wasn't surprising to see this match moved to the eight thirty a.m. Sunday kickoff time. For me, this start time presented a dilemma. I strongly prefer watching the derby matches with my mates at the pub, but the current form of the club left me with little confidence, and I was still feeling the slight effects of jet lag, having returned from California a few days earlier. It didn't help that the entire state of North Carolina was under a flood warning from Hurricane Joaquin all weekend long. I would end up watching this match on my couch.

With both Ings and Sturridge in the starting lineup, I was hopeful the club would spend most of the game attacking their rivals. Unfortunately, it appeared that the midfield would be the missing link for the Reds, as they just couldn't put together any positive play. Everton didn't impress much either, as the first forty minutes passed without much damage. Emre Can showed some emotion in the thirty-fifth minute, getting into a needless scuffle with Ross Barkley as he tried delaying the play after committing an innocuous foul. He deserved a yellow card, but Barkley's inability to let it slide got him in the book as well. As a fan it is frustrating to see the better players booked for what appears to be a needless sin, but now both players would have to be on their best behavior.

Neither club deserved a lead, but Liverpool were seemingly gifted their lead when Everton failed to clear a simple Milner corner kick. At five feet eight, Danny Ings has to be one of the smaller strikers in the game, yet if you leave him unmarked four yards from the goal line on a corner kick he'll easily be able to head the ball in the net. That was precisely what he did, and the Reds took an undeserved 1-0 lead.

As per the recent norm, it was a lead that Liverpool would fail to keep. In four of the previous five matches, Liverpool took a 1-0 lead before eventually yielding an equalizer. It only took Everton three minutes to continue that trend.

Spaniard Gerard Deulofeu played a dangerous cross from Everton's right flank, which Emre Can tried to blast clear of danger. Instead of sending the ball far and wide, Can rocketed it straight into Martin Skrtel as the ball deflected straight to Romelo Lukaku's feet. A simple shot past Mignolet leveled the score just before the half. It was disappointing and deflating, but hardly unexpected given the way things had gone this season.

The late goal seemed to buoy confidence for the Toffees, as they dominated most of the second half. Mignolet was called upon to make some key saves as Liverpool's midfield continued to get owned by their opponent. Every time someone would gain possession, it would seem their only outlet was to send a long, hopeful ball to a lonely Ings. There was a small glimmer of hope late in the match as Sturridge found his way clear toward goal against the run of play, but Everton's Ramiro Funes Mori was able to intercept the ball with his outstretched leg. The final whistle blew on what had to be called a fortunate 1-1 result for Liverpool.

For the fifth time in this stretch of seven matches, Liverpool had wasted a lead and ended ninety minutes of football deadlocked with their opponents. If that alone wasn't enough to draw concern, consider those five clubs were Bordeaux (a mid-table French club), Norwich City (recently promoted from the championship), Carlisle United (a mid-table League Two club), FC Sion (a mid-table Swiss club with the quality of a League Two club), and Everton. It was that realization that soon fired me up. I got off the couch within minutes of the final whistle and started to pen my thoughts for a new blog entry.

Enough was enough. The season was quickly getting derailed as they entered the October international break. You could argue that Liverpool was still technically alive in all three competitions, but something was clearly off. It had already been documented that the club had heavily invested in new talent. On paper, these teams had no business getting results against Liverpool. Yet they did. As much as I wanted the Brendan Rodgers Experiment to work, it was clear to me that it had failed.

I spent the new two hours typing my blog that the time was right for a change. I had jumped onboard the "Rodgers out" train. He had lost all support and it was time for him to go. The club would have two weeks off for the international break, plenty of time to bring in new management and inject some life into the club before it was too late. I wanted to collect some raw data to justify my opinion, so I jumped on the Internet. Apparently John Henry didn't need my opinion to get to the same conclusion. Only a few hours after the match concluded, Liverpool announced that Brendan Rodgers was relieved of his duties.

As a sports fan, it is always easy to blame the coach for a team's failure. It comes with the territory. As much as they get credit for success, they need to be blamed for failure. I always try to be pragmatic when discussing the future of your team's head coach. Change in leadership midseason seems desperate and rarely works out. Typically, the move doesn't involve an upgrade in quality. We would soon learn that this wasn't the typical situation, as Jürgen Klopp would be named the next Liverpool manager within a few days.

Before we move forward with the new regime, I feel like it's important to address the three full seasons with Brendan Rodgers at the helm. At the time of his hire, Liverpool was not considered a top club. Only a few years prior to his arrival, the club itself was in dire financial straits, nearing bankruptcy. In October 2010, only days before the banks were looking to send the club into administration, John Henry and his Fenway Sports Group took control. Roy Hodgson was the manager at the time, and it was clear that the club had suffered serious damage that would take a major effort to fix. Hodgson was let go in January as the legendary Kenny Dalglish came back from retirement to help the rebuilding efforts.

Dalglish served admirably, leading the club to the League Cup trophy in 2012. Uruguayan striker Luis Suarez was quickly becoming the best striker in the English game, and Steven Gerrard was...well, he was still Steven Gerrard. While Dalglish was clearly ready to remain as manager, FSG decided it was time to start fresh with the young Northern Irishman, and brought Rodgers over from Swansea City.

As a fan, I was excited about the prospects of a fresh face. Swansea City looked to be a promising club on the up, and Rodgers had to be a key cog in that success. Neutral skeptics pointed to his unimpressive résumé, but I always defaulted to the fact that every great manager had to start somewhere. Even Sir Alex Ferguson nearly got the sack for Manchester United before his career began. I never thought Rodgers could become the next Sir Alex, but as a fan, I could dream.

While his first season at the helm was disappointing, there was much promise heading into the 2013-14 season. Without the extra football of European competition to worry about, the squad didn't need much depth to compete domestically. On Christmas Day, Liverpool sat on top of the standings. Almost overnight, it felt great to be a Liverpool supporter again. So much so that I joined six of my mates on my first trip to see the Reds play in person.

Two years earlier I had met Bernie Allen at a pub next to Fenway Park on the same day that I met Colin Russell and Darren Bridger. Bernie is a season ticket holder that lives a short walk from the ground, and he worked out a deal to get us all tickets in the Kop to watch Arsenal play the mighty Reds. It was a storybook match that couldn't have been scripted better. Two early Martin Skrtel goals had the Gooners reeling, and before twenty minutes had passed, the Reds were up 4-0. They eventually won that match 5-1, and followed that with an epic 3-2 victory against Fulham at Craven Cottage with a late Gerrard penalty. It was a week that I'll never forget, as the club went through the spring playing quality football that I had never seen them play in my life.

We all know how that season ended, but finally it seemed Liverpool was back where they belonged: amongst the elite of English football clubs. Clearly Rodgers had to be credited with this return to glory. Sure, you could point out the monstrous season that Luis Suarez had, scoring goals seemingly at will. He won the Golden Boot as leading goal scorer by a mile, despite serving an eight-game suspension and not taking a single penalty kick. He had become a household name and one of the top players in the world. And he played for Liverpool.

Unfortunately, even that didn't last long, as he parlayed that success into a large contract upgrade with Spanish giants Barcelona that summer. Still, I wasn't worried, because Rodgers had proven he could manage a top club at a top level. What I didn't know at the time was that while Rodgers was a great manager with great players, he was a mediocre manager with less-than-great players. The 2014-15 season was clearly a disappointment. Placed into a relatively easy Champions League group, the squad failed to advance to the knockout stage. Injuries forced some younger players into vital roles that they simply couldn't deliver. Yet that following spring, the club managed to wiggle its way back into the discussion for a top-four finish. Coutinho stepped up with highlight-worthy goals to beat both Manchester City and Southampton, and we were squarely on the heels of Manchester United for fourth place.

It was another opportunity for Rodgers to show us greatness, yet without the star power of a guy like Suarez, the team failed to deliver. They faded out with difficult losses to teams that had no business competing with Liverpool. I had already decided that change was needed. Rodgers had done little to show me he was the man for the future of the club. Once the season was over, I was on the "Rodgers out" bandwagon, ready for a new regime.

Whenever a team changes its leadership, it is critical that they identify the right successor. If you can't get an upgrade, then maybe the time isn't right. It's a point that I addressed in my blog post "Should He Stay or Should He Go" back on May 2, 2015.

I'm still not sure what FSG will do about Rodgers, but let's say for a moment that changes are coming. Who can they get? Many people are enthralled at the prospect of bringing Jürgen Klopp to Merseyside, as he's already announced his intention to leave Dortmund after the season. Should we be excited? The numbers will tell the story. When you look at this résumé, the first thing that I notice in his fifteen-year management career is that he's managed exactly two clubs. From 2001-08 he led FC Mainz before taking over Borussia Dortmund from 2008-2015. That shows loyalty and dedication, something Liverpool desperately need. What about the results? Prior to taking over at Dortmund, the German club had league finishes of sixth, seventh, seventh, ninth, and thirteenth. Then they hired Klopp, and in his first two years at the club he led them to sixth- and fifth-place finishes. After that, the unthinkable happened. He won the Bundesliga in 2010-11. Look at it a different way. In only three years, he took a team that was fighting off relegation to a league championship. It clearly has to be a fluke, right? Wrong. He repeated the feat the very next season. Two more second-place finishes and a spot in the 2013 Champions League final followed those two Bundesliga crowns. That's an impressive résumé.

Clearly Klopp knows how to win, but how does his club wage bill compare to the rest of the league? To be fair, the club plays in a stadium which seats over eighty thousand supporters (the most in Germany). According to figures obtained from their official accounts, Bayern Munich routinely pay their players more than twice what Dortmund has been paying. The figures in the below chart only go up to the 2010-11 season, which happens to be the first time Klopp led Dortmund to the crown. And then he did it again. Without wasting any more of your time, I think I can rest my case that Jürgen Klopp would be the right hire.

I don't consider myself a great prognosticator. Hiring Klopp was clearly the right call if you could pull it off. He was widely considered one of the top managers in the world, and his history of revitalizing franchises made him the perfect appointment for Liverpool.

In the moments after Rodgers was fired, the entire world of Liverpool supporters exhaled. In the moments after Klopp was hired, that world rejoiced. Imagine being that person in a long-term relationship with an average-looking significant other that continued to treat you like shit. No matter how many times your friends tell you to get out, you simply justify the mediocrity of that relationship. Finally, when enough becomes enough, you get the courage to dump your lover and move on with your life. Days later, you meet the most beautiful creature you've ever seen and you ask them out on a date. Your courage is rewarded and the new story begins. Now, instead of whispering behind your back laughing at your misery, your friends look at you with admiration and jealousy. They wish they were you. They wish Klopp would come manage their club.

In all of my years following sport, I can honestly say that I've never seen a transformation of attitude like Liverpool supporters experienced. The season had been lost; the fans were despondent. Hanging out with mates remained the primary motivation to go to the pub, while watching Liverpool became secondary. Suddenly the nightmares turned into dreams. A ball hadn't even been kicked on the pitch, and now we thought we were top-four contenders again. Some respectable podcasters I listen to went as far to say we could even win the league this year. It was remarkable.

When you consider all that had happened to this point, you could understand the optimism. Even though we were mid-table in the league, Chelsea was worse. In eleven matches under Rodgers, we'd only lost two to clubs that are currently sitting near the top of the table. While we hadn't won any Europa League matches yet, we hadn't lost yet either. We were still alive in the League Cup as well. Despite feeling like the season was already lost, the arrival of one man had completely revitalized our dreams. I couldn't wait to get to the pub to join my mates as we joyfully sing again. It was good to be a Liverpool supporter once more. We went again, and not soon enough.

9 - WILLKOMMEN, HERR KLOPP

Saturday, October 17
Camp Kendra
Premier League match #9 (at Tottenham)

Liverpool's first match under Jürgen Klopp would be a tough test in North London at White Hart Lane against Tottenham Hotspur. Spurs are one of those clubs that always compete with Liverpool for a spot in European football. Their first match of the season was a 1-0 loss at home to Manchester United, but they hadn't been beaten in the league since. Their last home match was an impressive 4-1 thrashing against league leaders Manchester City, so they were in great form. Getting a result wouldn't be an easy task for the Reds, but this was the start of a new era. Klopp would at least have some training time with the club for a week before kickoff.

Before he could even assess the talent pool at the club, Klopp was hit with some difficult news. Young defender Joe Gomez suffered an anterior cruciate ligament (ACL) injury while playing for England's U-21 squad against Kazakhstan, and it would later be learned that he required season-ending knee surgery. Gomez had impressed early in the season under Rodgers, but the inexperienced defender was never expected to be a long-term contributor in this campaign. Liverpool had some depth in the defense, so it was hardly time to hit the panic button.

Young Jordan Rossiter was the next casualty of the recent international break when he strained his hamstring while playing for England's U-19 team. The impact of this injury would not likely affect the first team talent level, as he was still a developing talent, but it was the nature of the injury that disturbed. With three matches in five short days, Rossiter played the full ninety minutes, running the midfield in each. It seemed excessive, and the club was not happy about it.

Lightning would strike again on the first training session under Klopp. Danny Ings would injure his ACL at Melwood, and it would appear he would be sidelined for the rest of the season with the same injury as Gomez. Ings was a solid number three striker behind Benteke and Sturridge, and he had already scored some goals while those guys recovered from their own injuries. Losing Danny Ings would be a much bigger setback than Gomez or Rossiter.

Matters went from bad to worse when it was revealed that Daniel Sturridge had suffered another injury setback in training only a few days before the Spurs match. Four players, each of whom had started at least one match for the Liverpool first team this season, would see significant time in the physio room instead of training under their new manager. It was as though the football gods couldn't allow Liverpool fans to get too much joy with acquiring a top manager. They had to even out our emotions with all of these injuries.

Despite all of these setbacks, Liverpool was still able to field a strong squad against Spurs. Only young striker Divock Origi looked somewhat out of place starting his first ever Premier League match. This was his opportunity to prove he belonged on a top club in the best league on the planet.

I was feeling a bit under the weather, so I decided to stay at home and watch this match from my couch. Straight from the kickoff, you could see Liverpool playing with more energy. The players may have been the same, but there was a renewed intensity that I hadn't seen from the squad in a long time. For the first twenty minutes, Tottenham played like the superior club, but they simply couldn't do anything against the tightened Liverpool defense. In fact, it was the Reds that nearly went on top when Origi hit the crossbar during a corner kick set piece.

Liverpool finally caught their stride later in the first half and seemed to match the play of Spurs. I'd love to sit here and tell you that the first match under Klopp was a thrill ride, but truth be told, there is not much to report. Simon Mignolet was brilliant throughout the match, making key saves, and the defense looked stout. It was only one match, but you could sense that Mamadou Sakho had gained the most confidence with Klopp calling the shots. Under Rodgers, he was often benched in favor of Dejan Lovren, who was still recovering from an ankle injury. Sakho's dominant play was encouraging and you could argue he deserved man-of-the-match honors this night.

One of the trademark traits for a Jürgen Klopp team was the pressing style where players harass the opponent until they would regain possession. "Gegenpress" is a term that came into the sport a few years earlier, loosely translated from German to English as "press against." It wasn't necessarily a change in formation that would be most notable under Klopp, rather the work level of the players without possession as they "Gegenpressed" their way on the pitch.

When the final whistle blew, Liverpool earned another important road point with the 0-0 draw. Clearly not an exciting match for the neutral observer, but it was a step up in class for those that followed the Reds. Only recently had people been tracking running stats in these matches, and it should be noted that Liverpool were the first Premier League club to outdistance Spurs in any match. The "Gegenpress" appeared to have paid dividends. Maybe there was something to be said having a world-class manager leading your club after all.

****

Klopp didn't have long to work with the squad before his next match, as Thursday afternoon Liverpool would welcome Rubin Kazan for a Europa League clash. The Russian club had a decent European track record, with some success in Champions League, so this would not be an easy match. Klopp made it known that he intended to take this competition seriously, so he selected a strong starting lineup for this difficult test. The only change to the Liverpool roster was having Joe Allen in defensive midfield over Lucas Leiva. Rubin Kazan was not off to a great start in the Russian Premier League, but their squad had some talent and they were always going to be a tough opponent.

The Russians took the lead in the fifteenth minute with a play that eerily reminded me of the last goal conceded at home in this competition. Defender Oleg Kuzmin sent a long ball from near midfield over the Liverpool defense to Marko Devic, who brought the ball down with his left shoulder and one-timed it past Mignolet. Much like the goal against Sion, this one came against the run of play. There was still plenty of time to recover, and this was not the same club from a month ago.

Fittingly it would be Liverpool's only German starter that would get Klopp his first goal. Emre Can received the ball on the left side and pushed it past Kuzmin, who clumsily took down the German midfielder. It was a clear yellow card and an easy call for the official, but the fact that Kuzmin had been booked earlier in the half meant he saw the red card. Not only would Liverpool get a dangerous free kick, but they would play with a man advantage for the rest of the match. Coutinho sent the free kick deep into the box, where Origi was able to head the ball across the goalmouth. Can lost his mark in the play and slammed the ball into the back of the net from a yard out. The score was tied 1-1, and the stadium went ballistic. The Reds were back! Cameras quickly shifted to the Liverpool manager, whose enthusiastic goal celebrations have been well documented in the past. His first goal celebration as Liverpool manager did not disappoint.

With the extra player, Liverpool continued to dominate play. You could clearly see the shift in tactics from the Russian team as they sat back, bunkering the defense in hopes of keeping the score tied. The move worked, as the Reds simply lacked enough creativity on the attack to score the game winner. It was a problem that everyone could see under Rodgers when the club played inferior opposition. They simply hadn't had enough time under Klopp to overcome this offensive ineptitude. The match ended 1-1, and the Reds drew their third straight Europa League match.

Liverpool was still in a good spot to advance to the knockout stage of the competition. Two of their final three matches would be on the road, including a long five-hour flight to Kazan in the deep nether regions of Russia. It was not going to be an easy road for the Reds, but qualification to the final thirty-two would be critical for the psyche of the squad. Some people would argue that a club doesn't need another distraction, but I contend the opposite. I refuse to believe in the silver lining that comes whenever your team is eliminated from a competition. With more games comes more experience and improved chemistry. The knockout rounds for the Europa League would not be played until mid-February—plenty of time for Liverpool to get healthy and possibly bring in January reinforcements. Squad depth should not be a concern, and nor should player fatigue. Since the light at the end of this Europa League tunnel was automatic entry into next year's Champions League, it was imperative that Liverpool put in the effort. Considering the teams standing between the Reds and advancement, it would be an embarrassment if they failed.

****

Two matches into the Klopp era and the club had not won or lost under new management. Everyone knew that his impact would take some time, but you still anticipated what that first victory would taste like. The next match would be Klopp's first home league match, against Southampton. Kickoff would be at twelve fifteen p.m., ideal for a Sunday match. Pints could be legally consumed from the outset. While I had every intention of joining my mates at the pub, I was still feeling the effects from a stomach bug I had caught before the Tottenham match, and felt like it was in everyone's best interest for me to remain at home.

Liverpool was still without striker Daniel Sturridge, but Christian Benteke was fit enough after his most recent hamstring injury to be named a substitute. Young Divock Origi would get another Premier League start.

Southampton came out wearing this ugly green kit with a navy-blue diagonal stripe, which honestly looked like something the Seattle Sounders would wear in Major League Soccer. I could only hope their quality of their play would resemble an American club, because that would likely mean a Liverpool victory.

The first half was relatively uneventful, neither team mustering a great opportunity. The match seemed destined to be one of those occasional drab nil-nil draws. Both teams pressed throughout the first forty-five minutes, but it seemed like the similar tactics were nullifying progress for both clubs.

Klopp could see that Origi was overmatched against the stellar Southampton defense, so he made the change to bring on Benteke at halftime. His impact was evident from the time play resumed, but still the Reds couldn't make the breakthrough. Liverpool retained possession more than sixty percent of the time, yet it was the Saints that were generating the most dangerous opportunities. Southampton's Sadio Mane broke free on a counterattack down the right flank into the penalty box, but the Senegalese striker was caught from behind Alberto Moreno, who perfectly timed his tackle and cleared away the danger.

Sensing the need for more attacking options, Klopp changed up the midfield, with Roberto Firmino coming on for Adam Lallana in the sixty-seventh minute. Play continued with much of the same Liverpool possession and no real scoring opportunities to show for it. Then James Milner got the ball in the seventy-seventh minute on the far right touchline and sent a forty-yard cross into the box. Benteke saw it coming and positioned himself alongside the defense. He leapt from the penalty spot with perfect timing and powerfully headed the ball into the upper right corner of the goal. Goalkeeper Maarten Stekelenburg had no chance to make the save. It was sort of goal that you dream about as a child: a head ball with power past a diving goalkeeper in front of thousands of adoring fans. Benteke had only been a Liverpool player for a few months yet had already found the penchant for scoring the most impressive, artistic goals. Liverpool finally had their lead. Surely Klopp would have his first league victory now. Or would he?

Fans were still reveling about the incredible goal that Benteke had scored when Milner needlessly fouled Ryan Bertrand about fifty yards away from goal in the eighty-fifth minute. It wasn't necessarily the manner in which Milner committed the foul that was annoying, as Liverpool were pressing late in the match to try and regain possession. Bertrand took a pass and was headed back away from the Liverpool goal when Milner clumsily charged in with too much momentum. It was an easy call for the ref, who quickly displayed the yellow card to Milner. That would be his fifth yellow card of the season, meaning the vice-captain would have to sit out the midweek League Cup match against Bournemouth.

James Ward-Prowse took the free kick and sent the ball down the middle, where Jose Fonte flicked the ball with his head. Bertrand was loosely marked by Lucas Leiva as the ball headed to the far post, and the Southampton defender was able to arc a head ball cross over the Liverpool defense to the opposite post. It was difficult to tell from the camera angle, but the shot from Bertrand may have gone in the goal on its own. It didn't matter, as Milner left Mane unmarked on the play, and he was able to net the easiest goal he'll likely score in his career. The game was deadlocked once again. Liverpool fans were stunned. Just as quickly as Milner was looking to be one of the heroes with his fantastic assist on Benteke's goal, he became the goat. Not only for the needless foul so far from goal, but for not marking the eventual goal scorer on a continuation play.

Liverpool ended up with one last-gasp effort in the final seconds, but Benteke whiffed on his volley attempt. The ref blew his whistle as Southampton escaped with a point. I couldn't really say that the result was unjust, because neither team really looked that much superior to the other. Liverpool did maintain sixty-one percent of the possession and outshot the Saints 15-8, but both teams looked fairly equal, and the point was earned for the away team. Klopp was still undefeated, but his first win would have to wait.

****

The fourth round of the League Cup was next on the fixture list, and Liverpool would be faced with another home match against AFC Bournemouth. There was much speculation as to what sort of lineup Klopp would go with for this contest. Klopp had previously stated his intention to take all competitions seriously, but the growing list of injuries was becoming a concern, and players needed some rest. Young reserve players Connor Randall, Cameron Brannagan, and Joao Carlos Teixeira all started for the Reds in this match.

Even though Liverpool were fielding a team that included many reserves, Bournemouth also were fielding a weakened roster. Success for the Cherries this season would not likely come with a deep cup run, rather survival from relegation. On paper it would seem Liverpool would still remain favorites to win.

The one player that I was keen to see on the pitch was Teixeira, the Portuguese twenty-two-year-old midfielder signed from Sporting Lisbon in January 2012. He was thought to be a promising talent that never seemed to get a chance under Brendan Rodgers. He'd only played about ten minutes for Liverpool's first team in his career, coming on as an eighty-second-minute substitute against Fulham on February 12, 2014. That match was one of the two Liverpool matches that I'd seen live when five of my fellow Raleigh Reds and I journeyed across the pond to watch the team that season. As I recall, Teixeira nearly scored a nifty goal late at the goal that we were sitting behind. He never saw the pitch for the first team after that match. He was sent to Brighton and Hove Albion on loan for the 2014-15 season, where he impressed before breaking his leg to end the season. If Teixeira was going to have a career for Liverpool, time was running out.

Liverpool came out firing and looked to be the dominant team. Needing to improve his match fitness, Roberto Firmino got the start in midfield, and he was lauded as the classiest player on the pitch. In the seventeenth minute, Firmino slid a perfectly timed pass to the charging Teixeira, who tried a clever back-heel shot on target. The ball got past Bournemouth goalkeeper Adam Federici, but not defender Adam Smith, who was able to weakly clear it off the line. Nathaniel Clyne followed the play up well, and collected the weak clearance. He fired it into the net for his first Liverpool goal, and the Reds took an early 1-0 lead.

Recent history had given reason for anxiety when Liverpool held a 1-0 lead late in the match, but on this day the defense would hold firm. Neither team could generate any offense, but Liverpool didn't need to. The full-time result was official, and Klopp had earned his first Liverpool victory with a 1-0 score line.

While the first victory under Klopp was somewhat underwhelming, it was at least something that we didn't have to worry about any longer. Kolo Toure became the next injury casualty when he strained a hamstring in the thirty-third minute of play. It was expected that he wouldn't return until December. Difficult away fixtures waited in the coming weeks (Chelsea and Manchester City). Klopp would surely be tested soon. He hadn't had the luxury of a fully fit squad yet, but Jordan Henderson and Daniel Sturridge would be back in the near future. It would be interesting to see how he incorporated the added depth into the squad rotation.

10 - BOONE

Saturday, October 31
Blue Ridge Mountains near Boone, NC
Premier League match #11 (at Chelsea)

With his first win under his belt, Klopp could finally direct his attention back to the league with his first big test. The Reds would travel to London and face the defending league champions Chelsea Football Club. As Liverpool traveled to Stamford Bridge for the early Saturday morning match, I was faced with my own personal travel dilemma. Long before the schedule was released, Tori and I had agreed to join our friends in the Blue Ridge Mountains of western North Carolina for a weekend getaway. The nearest OSLC chapter was located too far away to drive, so I was forced to improvise.

A quick Google search of "soccer pubs near me" revealed a quaint establishment called the Boone Saloon, advertised as "Boone's only soccer pub." If I was going to get to a pub to watch this match, it would appear that would be my only hope. I was encouraged to see the pub's official logo, a clear copycat image of the Liverpool crest with the words "You'll Never Drink Alone" emblazoned on the gates above the shield. Clearly the owner was a Red.

Even though their website claimed the establishment opened at eleven a.m. on Saturdays, I called a few days in advance, hoping to convince pub owner Stephen "Skip" Sinanian to open the doors early and watch the match with me. We spoke at length on the phone, but ultimately my efforts were unsuccessful. He simply couldn't justify opening the pub early when few people would show up for the matches. Boone was still a town of only eighteen thousand residents, not including students attending Appalachian State University, so they had a much smaller pool of soccer fans to support a pub's early opening. While I would have to find other arrangements to watch the Chelsea match, Skip invited me to join him for "the best brunch in Boone" when they opened at noon on Sunday.

We arrived at the mountain cabin late at night, and I was immediately relieved when I saw their satellite TV package included NBC Sports. No need to venture off to watch this critical match. I would end up watching from the cozy confines of our mountain cabin 3600 feet above sea level.

Chelsea always represents an interesting fixture for the Reds. Before Russian billionaire Roman Abramovich acquired over ninety percent of the shares in August of 2003, they had only been crowned league champions once before in their ninety-eight years of existence (in the 1954-55 season). After delisting the club from the AIM stock exchange, Abramovich took on responsibility for the club's debt of £80 million, quickly paying most of it off. He then invested heavily into the club, acquiring talent to both play and manage. Specifically, he brought in Portuguese manager Jose Mourinho from Porto after he guided them to the 2003 Champions League title. In his first season as Chelsea manager, the club set a record with ninety-five points out of a possible 114, and won the league easily. Then he won the league again the following year. Soon the honeymoon was over, and the two massive personalities of Abramovich and Mourinho started to clash. It was eerily similar to the situation that the Dallas Cowboys faced in the early nineties, when Jerry Jones and Jimmy Johnson parted ways after winning two Super Bowls. In September of 2007, Mourinho resigned from Chelsea Football Club.

Over the course of the next six years, Chelsea went on to win one more league title with Carlo Ancelotti at the helm. Meanwhile, Mourinho was off winning more honors on the continent with Inter Milan and then Real Madrid. A few seasons of failure for both Mourinho and Abramovich preceded them from rekindling their partnership. The two egos were able to see past their previous transgressions, and Mourinho returned to manage Chelsea before the 2013-14 season. Chelsea won the league in his second season back.

Chelsea and Liverpool fans quickly learned to dislike one another. It really is an intriguing dynamic. Situated in West London, Chelsea's only geographical rivals are Fulham and Queens Park Rangers, but neither of those teams are consistently good enough to stay in the top flight. Arsenal are the only other title contender based in the capital city, but they have one of the game's longest rivalries with Tottenham. No one really cared to think about Chelsea before they were acquired by the bottomless Russian wallet.

This new rivalry probably started after Chelsea won their first league title under Mourinho. Liverpool had won the league eighteen times, the most of any club at the time. Chelsea had won two. It's why Liverpool fans started singing how "Chelsea FC ain't got no history!" Even though the Blues supporters could enjoy winning the league in 2005, they had to endure Liverpool fans one-upping them with their own miracle in Istanbul a few weeks later. Many Chelsea fans believed that they were robbed when Luis Garcia's "ghost goal" eliminated them from that competition only a month earlier. Let's forget the fact that Chelsea's Peter Cech clearly fouled Milan Baros in the box and should've been sent off. If you were to believe Chelsea fans, Garcia's toe poke never crossed the goal line, and Chelsea was effectively screwed by the ref. Mourinho confirmed that sentiment, so it had to be true. Liverpool advanced to the Champions League final 1-0 on aggregate. A few weeks later, Chelsea were celebrating their first league title in fifty years, only to be upstaged by Liverpool's fifth European Cup at the Miracle of Istanbul. Tensions between the two clubs would increase in 2008 when Liverpool defeated Chelsea at Stamford Bridge to end their eight-six-match home unbeaten streak, a record for top-flight English football clubs. Then came the 2013-14 season, when Liverpool controlled their own destiny, needing only to win their final three games to claim their nineteenth league title. Chelsea came to Anfield with a weakened squad, Gerrard slipped, and Chelsea fans took great pleasure in seeing the Reds fail to claim the title.

These two clubs had developed an infant rivalry that was amongst the most heated in all of England. In only a short few years, Liverpool and Chelsea fans learned to develop a mutual hatred of each other. One set of supporters calls their team the Reds. Another set calls their team the Blues. Enough said.

Even though Chelsea was defending champion, they were off to a hellish start. Coming into this match, they had only amassed eleven points in eleven matches, and were sitting alone in fifteenth place. Almost a third through the campaign and it would appear as though the Blues were in a relegation battle, not a title defense.

Stamford Bridge was normally considered a fortress that no visiting team expected to leave victorious under Mourinho. Before this season started, he had managed Chelsea ninety-eight times in league fixtures at the West London stadium. He was victorious seventy-six times, with an additional twenty-one draws. The only loss Mourinho suffered was against Sunderland in March of 2014. Despite that amazing winning percentage, both Crystal Palace and Southampton were victorious at Stamford Bridge earlier this season. This Chelsea team was loaded with talent, and everyone expected them to claw their way back into the fight before the season ended. Liverpool fans could only hope their rejuvenated squad would be able to capitalize and keep Chelsea fans hearing the blues.

Jürgen Klopp had only faced Mourinho a few times before, most recently as manager of Borussia Dortmund in the 2012-13 Champions League semifinals. Mourinho was in charge of famed Real Madrid and perhaps the most expensive squad ever assembled. Dortmund defeated Madrid in that competition, a result which many believe led to Mourinho's dismissal.

Only one change from the previous league match against Southampton was made, with Klopp replacing Divock Origi with Brazilian Roberto Firmino. It would be a risky move, but the good chemistry obtained from playing Firmino alongside countryman Phil Coutinho would hopefully counter the fact that Liverpool would have no true striker on the pitch. Mourinho tried to shake things up a bit, leaving both Cesc Fabregas and Nemanja Matic on the bench.

I refreshed my cup of coffee and found my way to the couch in time for kickoff. I was worried that the Klopp Effect would not be strong enough to overcome the talented Chelsea squad. My worries were confirmed in the opening minutes.

Less than three minutes had passed when Chelsea gained possession along the right side of our defense. Eden Hazard passed calmly to Cesar Azpilicueta, who sent the ball to the dangerous Diego Costa. Costa held the ball nicely as Nathaniel Clyne defended for Liverpool. Azpilicueta made an overlapping run, which was met by a nifty Costa back-heel pass. He easily beat the lunging James Milner forcing Martin Skrtel to charge across and defend. As Chelsea's Spanish defender made his way to the touchline, he cut the ball back to his favored right foot and sent a dangerous cross into the box. Alberto Moreno stood waiting in position to clear the ball out as Ramires rushed onto the ball uncontested for an easy header into the back of the net. Mignolet had no chance, and Chelsea was up 1-0. Had it not been the fact that others were still sleeping in the cabin, I'm pretty sure I would've yelled out a rather loud curse that would've echoed long across the valley floor.

Liverpool looked stunned. Here we go again, was the only thought that could come across my mind. I was praying that it wouldn't get out of hand too early. Klopp was urging the team to keep their heads up, but the play on the pitch wasn't reflective of his efforts. They weren't pressing like they had in the past, and Chelsea maintained possession all across the pitch. Lucas Leiva was forced to foul Willian in a dangerous spot about twenty-five yards from goal, the first of numerous fouls he would commit. Known for his incredible free kick ability that rivaled David Beckham, Willian arced the ball over the Liverpool wall to the far post. Chelsea's talismanic captain John Terry got his head on the ball and sent the ball across the goalmouth to John Obi Mikel. His touch wasn't the greatest, and the ball went wide for a Liverpool goal kick. It truly was a shocking miss that should've put the Blues up 2-0 after six minutes. Thankfully for Liverpool, he wasn't a natural goal scorer, with only a single goal in his storied career for Chelsea.

Stamford Bridge was buzzing, and I felt like I needed a pint to calm my nerves. You could hear over forty thousand Chelsea supporters singing at the top of their lungs about the now-infamous Steven Gerrard slip in the April 2014 encounter at Anfield that ultimately cost Liverpool a chance to win the league. Liverpool fans would serenade their long-time hero (sung to the tune of "Que Sera, Sera"):

"Steven Gerrard, Gerrard
He'll pass the ball forty yards…"

After watching Gerrard slip at midfield, allowing Demba Ba to break free uncontested to score the goal that would sink Liverpool's 2013-14 title dreams, Chelsea fans created their own version:

"Steven Gerrard, Gerrard
He'll slip on his fucking arse…"

Did I mention that Chelsea and Liverpool fans hate each other now?

Forty minutes had passed, and it was clear to me that Liverpool had had the better of the play. It was almost like the early goal was a blessing in disguise. It caused Mourinho to change his tactic and sit back, allowing Liverpool to gain their rhythm.

Chelsea were happy to focus on the counterattack. Late in the first half, Willian sent a long ball to a surging Costa, who just couldn't seem to get to it on time. Skrtel sprinted over to cover the play, and he inadvertently sent an elbow across the Spaniard's head. Costa fell down holding his head, trying to convince referee Mark Clattenburg that the Slovakian deserved a yellow card for a flagrant foul. It didn't work. These two players had quite the history, despite only playing against each other a few years. In last year's League Cup semifinals, Costa intentionally stomped on Skrtel's ankle in an effort to injure him. It was initially missed by the referees, and ultimately Costa was banned three matches for that incident. Skrtel and Costa then crossed paths with an altercation while playing for their respective national teams in a European Championship qualifier that same year. This wasn't the first time they had clashed, and it appeared that it would not be the last.

The end of the first half was near. Despite being dominated by the away side, Chelsea held on to that 1-0 lead. Mourinho stood up and headed toward the tunnel as the fourth official signified that a minimum of two minutes of stoppage time would be added. The key word in that phrase that often gets overlooked is the word "minimum." One minute and fifty-nine seconds does not get you to the minimum of two minutes.

I've often been asked why the sport handles clock management this way. Decades ago the referee would keep track of time on a wristwatch. If a team scored a goal and started to celebrate, the ref could simply stop the clock manually at his discretion. If a player got significantly injured, he would stop the clock again if he wanted to. Demand for the sport to be broadcast through mass media continued to grow, but the lack of knowing how much time remained made it difficult to follow on television. Networks began to start a clock from the opening kickoff and just let it run. There was no way to know when the referee would stop the clock for any reason, so the networks never stopped their clock. It wasn't perfect, but at least you had an idea when the final whistle was near. In an effort to be more transparent, FIFA started having the fourth official display how many minutes would be added so that everyone had a better idea of when the match would end. It would come to be known as "stoppage time."

When the fourth official holds the sign up that simply reads "2," that indicates a minimum of two minutes will be added. Most often the time goes over because the referee will let the team with possession complete their attack before stopping play. In this particular situation, Mamadou Sakho regained possession at midfield just as the stoppage time clock reached two minutes. He passed the ball forward to Coutinho as Liverpool pressed to attack. Coutinho sent the ball to Emre Can, who sent it over to Alberto Moreno. Chelsea deflected the next pass over to Lucas Leiva, who sent the ball wide to the right flank for James Milner. Two minutes and fifteen seconds of stoppage time had passed at this point, and Liverpool was still working the attack. It would've been harsh for Clattenburg to whistle the half over.

Milner then confidently passed the ball to Firmino in the penalty box. The Brazilian looked to turn, but instead passed back to Coutinho, who was just outside the box. Coutinho juked past the defending Ramires and moved the ball to his left, where he curled the ball past John Terry's outstretched leg and a diving Begovic for the equalizing goal. The clock read 47:24 when the ball rattled the back of the net, twenty-four seconds past the minimum of two minutes. I mention all of this because the goal would be disputed by Chelsea fans as unfair, yet all indications show that Clattenburg was right to allow Liverpool to complete its attack. If Chelsea fans wanted the half to be over, perhaps their defense should've pressed harder to regain possession. Television cameras caught an obviously annoyed Mourinho storm down the tunnel into the locker room. Seeing his reaction put a smile on my face.

The goal was a relief for all Liverpool fans. Their club had dominated play the entire half with sixty-five percent of the possession, outshooting Chelsea 7-1. Liverpool's lack of scoring had been well documented, so it was critical to get on the board and tie the match before half. "This goal changes everything," said NBC Sports analyst Robbie Mustoe, and he was absolutely right.

During the halftime break I grabbed some quick breakfast in the cabin, and my friend Steve joined me for the second half. Steve is a young kid from Southern Virginia and not a huge fan of the sport, but he could tell this match was important based on my reactions, so he was curious to watch. His alternative was to spend the next forty-five minutes in the kitchen as two chatty girlfriends talked about nothing he wanted to talk about. I was happy to have someone to talk with, even if it meant I had to explain a few rules along the way.

The second half kicked off with no changes made by either team. The late goal must've infuriated Mourinho, and you could see the fire in the Chelsea players as play resumed. Oscar made a nice move past Sakho in the opening minute, but Skrtel rushed over to clear the ball wide. Just get past the first few minutes and settle in, I thought. Liverpool was the better team on this day, and patience could get us the victory.

Thirteen minutes into the second half and Mourinho made the first change, bringing nineteen-year-old Brazilian Kenedy onto the pitch. The promising young attacker could pose problems for Liverpool's defense. Interestingly enough, Mourinho took off Belgian stud Eden Hazard with the substitution. He may not have been having his best match, but Hazard is one of the best midfielders on the planet. It was possible that he'd picked up a slight injury that no one knew about. Nonetheless, I was not going to complain, especially after Kenedy sent his first shot well wide of the goal only seconds after getting on the pitch. Hazard would've put the ball on target and tested Mignolet.

Moments later the ball was played toward the midfield line as Skrtel and Costa tussled for possession. They both jumped in the air, contesting a header. Both players fell toward the ground, with Costa landing on top of Skrtel. It would appear that Costa followed through with his right leg, kicking Skrtel in the chest with his cleats. Replays confirmed the malicious maneuver, which could've resulted in a straight red card for the Spaniard had it been seen by the ref. Not only did Costa have a history with Skrtel, but he had a track record of antagonizing opponents into dumb retaliatory fouls which get them sent off. It had happened earlier this season against Arsenal's Gabriel in the Blues' 2-0 victory at Stamford Bridge, a play that later saw Costa himself suspended for his role in the fracas. Skrtel was keen not to react. Costa immediately put on the innocent look once he realized he was not getting to Skrtel, and Clattenburg did nothing. With the benefit of instant replay, the commentators were quick to comment on the violent nature of Costa's foul, and since no card was issued, it was assumed that the ref simply missed it. Retroactive punishment just may have been in Costa's future.

The intensity of the match picked up after a close call for Lucas Leiva that nearly resulted in his second yellow card. Both teams picked up their aggressiveness, hungrily looking for victory. Many matches are won between the sixty-fifth and seventy-fifth minutes as fatigue begins to settle in. This match was no different. After one Liverpool attack, Willian gained possession in the seventieth minute and looked to counter. Moreno did well to track back on his left sided to pressure the Chelsea attacker, as Skrtel was well positioned to thwart the counter. Liverpool regained control through the midfield, but Lucas was stripped of the ball by Oscar in a nice tackle. Oscar looked up and noticed Simon Mignolet standing on the edge of the penalty box eighteen yards from goal. The Brazilian didn't hesitate, and sent the ball toward goal from forty-five yards away. The ball floated toward the open net as the entire stadium gasped for what could be an incredible goal. Tracking back to his line, Mignolet leapt and was able to deflect the ball to the side for a Chelsea corner kick. Oscar only needed a little more oomph on the ball to give the Blues the lead.

Liverpool regained possession, this time with Sakho collecting the ball near midfield. The Frenchman launched a high ball down the right side. Benteke easily won the header and directed it laterally over to Coutinho's left foot. A simple touch to his right sent Gary Cahill in the wrong direction, leaving a small opening toward the net for Coutinho. He shot the ball toward target, taking a slight deflection off John Terry and past the diving Begovic for his second goal of the game. Complete elation ensued as Coutinho sprinted toward the Liverpool fans with his trademark knee slide to the corner flag. He must've traveled twenty yards on his knees before the rest of the team could catch him and join the celebration. Liverpool got the deserved 2-1 lead with Coutinho's second goal of the match, the first time the Brazilian had scored a brace in his Liverpool career.

The final nail was driven into Chelsea's coffin in the eight-second minute on a play that began with a simple Mignolet goal kick. Benteke won another header at midfield, and Ibe ran onto the ball down the right side. He sent the ball across to a streaking Adam Lallana, who expertly dummied the ball to fake out the defense. Staying with the play, Benteke found the ball just inside the box. He made a few simple touches to keep possession before striking an authoritative shot to the far post and in the net. Liverpool 3, Chelsea 1. This time the team celebration carried to the edge of the Liverpool fans, clearly elated with what they had just witnessed. Chelsea fans were seen leaving the pitch in disgust as Liverpool fans serenaded Mourinho, "You're getting sacked in the morning!"

The final whistle blew. I sat on the couch somewhat still unsure of what just happened, and Steve said to me, "I never knew soccer could be so exciting." I couldn't argue. To be fair, it was a particularly great game to see. My only regret was that I wasn't at the pub to enjoy it with my mates.

The next day we trekked into town to visit Skip at the Boone Saloon. The bar is what you would expect from a college town establishment, with a long bar running the length of the building. In the back left was a large space with some pool tables and a CD jukebox, where some students were queueing up their favorite tunes. About a dozen people were in seats eating breakfast, while others filled up the few tables in the front of the saloon. We grabbed a window seat with a perfect view of people wandering the sidewalks in downtown Boone.

Skip served me a pint and we sat down to talk about the match. We lamented over the fact that he couldn't justify opening early so that we could've watched the Liverpool victory together. Skip informed me that Boone was slowly building a fan base for the sport over time. During the last World Cup, his bar was the busiest spot in the county. But there just wasn't enough interest from fans to get up early on a Saturday morning and trek down to the pub to watch a match. Saturday mornings in the fall were reserved for Appalachian State football preparations, and most of the student population were still sleeping after a long Friday night by the time the Liverpool match kicked off. I could see exactly where he was coming from, although he was hopeful that would change in February once football season was over, and suggested the possibility of opening the pub early when a big rivalry match was scheduled for the early Saturday kickoff.

Originally from California, Skip moved to the Atlanta area before finally settling in the North Carolina mountains. He opened the saloon in February 2004 as an adult safe haven away from the college students that dominated the town when school was in session. When they first opened the bar, Boone was a dry town that couldn't serve hard liquor. He fought hard to get that rule overturned in the summer of 2008. We shared some good laughs as I enjoyed the best Sunday brunch in town. It didn't disappoint. He gave me a Boone Saloon T-shirt with the "You'll Never Drink Alone" slogan on it, and in return I handed him the OLSC Raleigh scarf that I brought along. As we said goodbye, I assured him that I would return to watch a Liverpool match live in his pub. He promised there would be a good crowd and that our scarf would proudly hang on the pub wall. I had no doubt.

11 - STILL ALIVE AND KICKING

Thursday, November 5
London Bridge Pub
Europa League match #4 (at Rubin Kazan)

Liverpool didn't have long to celebrate the momentous victory at Stamford Bridge. The longest road trip of the regular season awaited with a trip to Kazan in the Republic of Tatarstan, Russia. Situated about five hundred miles east of Moscow on the banks of the Volga River, Kazan would be about a five-hour flight for the club. Having fans attend the match would be even more challenging, as the tourist visas for anyone visiting Russia were quite difficult to obtain.

At this stage in the competition, the club was hoping to have a nice cushion, allowing them to send a team of reserves to the remote Russian outpost. With only three points in the first three matches, it was crucial to try and go for the win in Russia, and Klopp was forced to bring a strong squad to face Rubin Kazan.

Kickoff was set for one p.m. EST, so I considered this an "extended working lunch." I would likely head back to the office after the match, which meant I wouldn't be drinking any pints. I wasn't alone, as most of the patrons planned to head back to the office following the match. Only a few people were enjoying a tasty libation from the bar.

Rubin Arena had been recently renovated in advance of the 2018 World Cup hosted by Russia, so the facility was top-notch. Unfortunately, the pitch looked a bit sloppy, as it was recently re-established after the stadium hosted the World Swimming Championships in July. They had to dig up the playing surface and build two swimming pools on it before reversing the process to restore football activity. It was easy to spot the turf deficiencies on high-definition television.

The first half passed with not much to report, but Liverpool appeared to be the most dangerous team. Just before halftime, Liverpool attacked with a few passes that resulted in a fine Roberto Firmino shot toward goal. Sergey Ryzhikov stuck out his left hand to stop the ball from going in the back of the net, and the Russians momentarily survived.

The second half was all Liverpool, although nothing got registered on the scoreboard until the fifty-second minute. Nathaniel Clyne got possession and found Firmino coming back to the ball. The Brazilian flicked the pass to Jordon Ibe, who streaked down the right flank with pace. Ibe split two defenders and carried the ball into the box, where he saw daylight between himself and the target. He fired a low, hard shot to the Russian keeper's right, and the ball ricocheted off the post into the back of the net, giving Liverpool the deserved 1-0 lead.

The rest of the second half passed with little flair. There was a nice attempt by James Milner later in the half, but it was easily saved by the goalkeeper. The pub was relatively quiet throughout the match, possibly due to the lack of booze consumed per capita. I'm not entirely sure if there is a scientific correlation, but there would appear to be a relation between overall pub noise level and average blood-alcohol content of the supporters. Yet despite this fact, there was nice applause coming when the final whistle blew to confirm Liverpool's 1-0 victory.

Four matches into the Europa League competition and Liverpool controlled their own destiny. Two matches remained, with the next match at home on Thanksgiving Day against Bordeaux. A victory in that match would cement Liverpool's advancement to the knockout stage. More importantly, the team appeared to be building some confidence. After drawing his first three matches as Liverpool manager, Klopp had now won three in a row. One match remained before the year's final international break. It was a home match against Crystal Palace, a match that Liverpool would expect to win on most days. I was a little concerned about the fact that Klopp brought a strong club to Kazan. The charter flight wouldn't land at John Lennon Airport in Liverpool until early Friday morning, leaving the club little time to recover and prepare for the Crystal Palace match. For now, I wasn't going to worry about it, as Klopp clearly had the ship righted and heading in the right direction.

****

When my wife decided she wanted to run her first marathon, I didn't think twice about supporting her. Having run the race myself in 2004, I understood the time commitment it requires. What I didn't count on was the fact that I would probably need to be there for her when the time came to run the event. She decided to run the Outer Banks marathon on the

North Carolina coast. Unfortunately for me, the start time of the race conflicted with Liverpool's Sunday kickoff against Crystal Palace. Thanks to NBC Sports and their Live Extra app on my iPhone, I would be able to watch parts of the match as I followed Tori around the marathon trail.

James Milner was added to the Liverpool MASH unit, having suffered a hamstring injury against Rubin Kazan, so Lucas Leiva was given the armband for the second time in his career. Much of the talk leading up to the match surrounded the return of Steven Gerrard to the area. With his MLS season completed, he had reportedly reached out to Jürgen Klopp about joining the club for some training sessions in his offseason. Media outlets took these discussions to the extreme, and some were reporting the possibility of the legend coming back on loan in January. These rumors were quickly dispelled by both Klopp and Gerrard himself, but the former captain took the time to get a great seat for this match.

The weather looked abysmal, even from the small view I had on my iPhone. Sloppy conditions can sometimes equalize the play, and Crystal Palace seemed to take advantage, getting the better of play early in the match. Liverpool appeared unsettled, perhaps still fatigued after coming home from Russia a few days earlier. Maybe the Rodgers Effect was still curtailing my confidence, but I was getting an uneasy feeling as the first half progressed.

Those feelings would be confirmed in the twentieth minute when Wilfried Zaha collected the ball near the corner of the penalty box. He sent the ball into the area, where five Liverpool defenders were waiting to halt the attack. Emre Can stuck out his foot to block the pass, but his touch lacked conviction and rebounded toward Yannick Bolasie. Lucas was trying to defend, but the Crystal Palace striker easily muscled past him and received the deflection. Martin Skrtel moved to get in the way, but Bolasie fired a shot to the right corner past Simon Mignolet, giving the visitors a 1-0 lead.

Judging from the overall play early on, the goal was probably deserved. At the same time, it was sort of unlucky for Liverpool. The play started with a deflection from Alberto Moreno that found its way to open space that Zaha could exploit. The former Manchester United player sent in a cross that worked its way through a charging Mamadou Sakho. Bolasie's shot could've easily been deflected by Skrtel as well. Liverpool looked to have the play well defended, but sometimes the ball just doesn't bounce in your favor.

Play continued innocuously in the thirty-fourth minute, when Sakho looked to head a ball at midfield on defense, but he appeared to have hyperextended his right knee when landing on the soft turf. There was little pressure from Palace at the time, but Sakho appeared to be seriously injured. Dejan Lovren readied himself for the game, to the dismay of the home crowd, but Sakho tried to forge ahead. Liverpool fans rejoiced and began chanting his name. He clearly looked less than a hundred percent, hobbling around and nearly giving away a second goal. His weak pass out of the defense was intercepted by Palace, and Bakary Sako eventually launched a long shot into the net. The play was rightfully ruled offside, and it was clear that Sakho's day was done. Lovren replaced him after that play.

Liverpool would tie the score in the forty-first minute on a nice team play. Jordon Ibe collected a pass just outside the penalty box. Under pressure from three defenders, Ibe somehow found Nathaniel Clyne running down the right flank unmarked. Clyne sent the low cross into the box, where Lallana was able to get a slight deflection to Coutinho, who calmly slotted the ball into the net to tie the score.

Liverpool continued to press in the final minutes of the first half. Twice they earned corner kicks that were well taken, both times met by Lovren with headers on target. Both times the ball was saved at the line. Had one of those gone in the net, Liverpool would've had the momentum on their side for the second half. They didn't, and the teams were level at 1-1 when play resumed.

The second half had a more vibrant look, with Liverpool creating numerous chances. Benteke failed to connect on an open header six yards out. Lallana had a free shot that was deflected over the crossbar by Hennessey. Ibe had a dangerous counterattack thwarted by the recovering Palace defense. Certainly Liverpool would take the lead soon enough, right?

About ten minutes from the full-time whistle and I had to stop watching the game. Tori was nearing the end of her first marathon, and it was vitally important for me to be there taking pictures. Having seen the way that the second half was playing out, I was pretty confident that Liverpool would get a result. It wasn't until an hour later, when I'd settled into the local brewery to have a celebratory pint with the wife, that I saw the final score. Crystal Palace 2, Liverpool 1. What happened?

I later watched the replay of the match to see Scott Dann's goal off the corner kick. It was a well-taken header that was initially saved by Mignolet, but the rebound went straight back to Dann, whose second effort would not miss the net. Dann did a good job getting away from his mark on the play, and I could only question why the six-four defender was being marked by the five-ten Roberto Firmino. I was sure this would be something that Klopp would discuss in training during the off week.

The final whistle blew and Liverpool had lost its first match with Klopp at the helm. It was a bitter pill to swallow, knowing that our next match was two weeks away against Manchester City. Much like the West Ham match in August, Liverpool went into an international break suffering a bad home defeat after a successive run of good results. Much like that West Ham game, I let other obligations take precedence over watching the match live with mates at the pub. I'd like to think that this fact was pure coincidence, but I was just superstitious enough to make every effort to avoid a similar fate in the future. The wife would just have to plan her next marathon more carefully.

****

Heading to the final international break of the calendar year, Manchester City and Arsenal were tied atop the table on twenty-six points in twelve matches. The big surprise was Leicester City sitting in third place only a point behind the leaders. They were relegated the previous season, so no one expected to see them near the top of table. Manchester United held fourth place. Liverpool sat in tenth position with only seventeen points from a possible thirty-six. It was hard not to notice the gap created by the missed opportunity against Crystal Palace. Had the club been able to hold serve, Liverpool would only be four points behind Manchester United for that coveted last Champions League spot. There was still a lot of football to be played, with over two-thirds of the fixtures remaining.

The win in Russia put Liverpool in great position to advance in the Europa League, and they would travel to Southampton in a few weeks to play in the League Cup quarterfinals. We were still alive and kicking in all four competitions this season.

12 - MIAMI

Saturday, November 2t
Fox and Hounds, Oakland Park, FL
Premier League match #13 (at Manchester City)

I first met Roy Yates in Boston during Liverpool's 2012 preseason tour. I was just one of hundreds of LFC supporters enjoying pre-match pints at the pub near Fenway Park when Roy introduced himself as the guy who runs the "Reds in America" newsletter. Our friendship was solidified through Facebook, and we reconnected during the 2014 preseason tour matches in New York and Charlotte. In fact, it was Roy that arranged our transportation to Yankee Stadium via the open roof of a double-decker bus. I'll never forget the moment the bus drove through Times Square with us serenading hundreds of confused tourists with Liverpool songs. Roy was also responsible for helping OLSC Raleigh plan its first Liverpool Legend party in April of 2013. He called me up informing me that former goalkeeper Bruce Grobbelaar was coming to Raleigh as assistant coach of the Ottawa Fury, who was scheduled to play our local club the Carolina RailHawks in the North American Soccer League season opener. Roy arranged to have Bruce visit our pub for the night prior to the match, a wildly successful evening for the Raleigh Reds. Roy does so much for all American LFC supporters that it was a no-brainer for me to travel to South Florida and meet him for some pints during the Manchester City match.

South Florida is flooded with retired expatriates living out their golden years, and as a result there are pockets of supporters across the region watching at numerous pubs. Even though there was a decent contingent watching at a Fado's Irish pub closer to my Miami Beach hotel, I chose to drive north to Oakland Park and watch at the Fox and Hounds.

With all due respect to Chelsea Football Club, I viewed this match as the first true test for Jürgen Klopp as Liverpool boss. Man City were coming into the game at the top of the table, having outscored their opponents 26-9 through only twelve matches. To make matters worse was the entire Raheem Sterling saga that Liverpool fans had endured throughout the summer.

Sterling was a good player for Liverpool, but in my opinion he never distinguished himself as a great one. The loss of Luis Suarez in the summer of 2014, coupled with Daniel Sturridge's injury-plagued season, left a giant void in the Liverpool attack. It was a hole that Sterling needed to fill for the Reds to have a successful season. Too often I watched the youngster miss glorious scoring chances that world-class talents always finish.

As the 2014-15 season neared its conclusion, it became clear that the twenty-year-old wanted an upgrade that he didn't see coming at Anfield. I didn't begrudge the kid for wanting a better paycheck playing for a more successful club, but the manner in which it happened left a bitter taste in everyone's mouth. I could write an entire chapter alone on how Sterling's agent Aidy Ward seriously mishandled the move, but instead I'll simply comment how badly charred that bridge he took out of town must look. It would take a cold day in hell to see Sterling welcomed back to Anfield anytime soon.

My friends were tossing around score predictions via text message. My first prediction was "1-0 to Liverpool on a Sterling own goal." I didn't know of a single Liverpool supporter that wouldn't have signed up for that glorious result. I was hoping for a draw, or anything else, as long as Sterling wasn't on the score sheet.

I drove up to the Fox and Hounds from my Miami Beach hotel and struggled to located the pub at first. I initially confused the pub with the more popular franchise known as the Fox and Hound Sports Tavern. With dozens of locations across the continent, I had been to a few of these upscale bars, typically located in a giant shopping area. As I wandered around North Dixie Highway in the Fort Lauderdale area, I saw nothing that resembled a mega-shopping complex with hundreds of parking spaces. On my third pass of the address according to my GPS, I started thinking about giving up. It was then that I noticed the England flag on the wall of a relatively nondescript building. The slightly overweight balding middle-aged man smoking a cigarette by the front door confirmed that I'd found the right place. There weren't much room available for cars in front of the pub, but luckily there was an open space.

As soon as you step inside the pub, you can tell immediately that it's authentically British. The dimly lit bar was partially illuminated from the various television screens, while a group of guys in the corner were throwing darts while drinking their lagers. To the left of the entrance hung a large-screen projector blasting images of football on a blank wall as about a dozen Celtic supporters watched their beloved club in the Scottish league. To my right I witnessed small groups of fans all watching their favorite English clubs on one the pub's half-dozen monitors. It was exactly the type of place where a British expatriate would feel right at home, except with much better weather outside.

I'd arrived with enough time to grab a proper English breakfast as the earlier ten a.m. matches concluded. Wearing my red 2012-13 Martin Skrtel jersey, I grabbed a seat at the bar and started watching the Chelsea-Norwich match. I ordered a pint of Guinness and thought it was a little odd that the bartender served it to me in a regular Heineken pint glass. Apparently this British pub couldn't care less about such a blasphemous presentation of the Irish black gold.

Across the bar I noticed a Chelsea fan that strikingly resembled that club's legend Frank Lampard. He was sitting by himself and had apparently been consuming pints since the morning's first match started three hours earlier. We made eye contact, and when he noticed my red Liverpool shirt, he simply shook his head in disapproval. He watched the match as I patiently waited for my food, occasionally bitching out loud about Chelsea's poor play. When he realized that no one in particular was listening, he looked over at me as if I would somehow agree with his assessment. I simply laughed and nodded at Not-Frank-Lampard, which was enough vindication in his mind. After a particular poor attempt on target by Diego Costa, he pointed to the Chelsea patch on his jersey and said to me, "I'm embarrassed to wear this badge!" I didn't argue with him as he consumed another pint.

Late in the second half of that match, as Diego Costa scored to give the Blues a 1-0 victory, Not-Frank-Lampard announced to the rest of the patrons, "About fucking time!" Before the final whistle blew, an inebriated Not-Frank-Lampard soon disappeared, to the delight of everyone else, including the other Chelsea fans watching nearby. I heard the bartender mumble concern about whether or not he drove home.

For a relatively small pub, there was a good crowd. A table of Arsenal fans was watching their club lose to West Bromwich Albion, and I took particular delight witnessing their dismay when Santi Cazorla's penalty kick soared over the crossbar late in that match to preserve the loss. To their left was a table of Evertonians watching the Toffees defeat Aston Villa 4-0. Slowly but surely, the Liverpool fans made their way to the pub. I relocated from the bar to an open table and waited nervously for the start of the match.

Roy arrived a few minutes before kickoff, and as expected, he had plenty of friends to greet before seeing me at the table. There were about forty Liverpool fans tucked into the right side of the pub. I would've thought that such a large contingency of supporters would justify putting the game on the big screen where Celtic were playing earlier, but the El Clasico rivalry match of Real Madrid vs. Barcelona was being played at the same time. We had plenty of televisions on our side of the bar, so there was no complaints from us.

Eventually Roy made his way over to our table and sat down. We had a nervous chat about the match and caught up. The big news before the match was the announcement that Sergio Aguero was available for Manchester City and in the starting lineup, but both of Liverpool's star strikers Benteke and Sturridge would be on the bench. I thought it was a risky move not to start an out-and-out striker, instead playing Roberto Firmino as a "false number nine" alongside countryman Phillippe Coutinho. The two paired well together for the Brazilian national team this summer, and with City's defense weakened by the injury to Vincent Kompany, there was reason for hope.

The funny thing about playing away against one of the league leaders is that you tend to temper your expectations about the result. If you end up losing, you can shake it off with the old "we weren't supposed to get a result in their house." But if you do snatch a result, like we had three weeks earlier at Stamford Bridge, then it feels like that moment you discover a twenty-dollar bill in the coat pocket. There are few better feelings than unexpected joy. Not even the most avid Liverpool supporter would tell you that they expected what we were about to witness in the upcoming ninety minutes of football. If they do, they are lying.

The game kicked off to a raucous capacity crowd at Etihad Stadium. Both teams shared some decent possession early, but the fun began in the seventh minute of play after City's goalkeeper Joe Hart collected the ball. He distributed the ball to Bacary Sagna, who quickly tried to move the ball up field. Coutinho caught him from behind and dispossessed the French defender with a nice, legal tackle. Expecting the referee to blow his whistle, Sagna wildly waved his arms in disgust. Meanwhile, Coutinho found Firmino running down the left side. Roy jumped out of his chair, yelling, "ATTACK! ATTACK!" as Firmino looked toward goal. Hart came off his line, but Firmino perhaps felt the angle wasn't optimal, so he attempted a pass back to Coutinho. With Hart moving to his left, City defender Eliaquim Mangala stuck out his leg to intercept the pass. The ball ricocheted off his leg into the open net. It went down as an own goal for the Frenchman, but replays confirmed to me that Coutinho would've had an open shot on target had Mangala not intervened. The pub erupted as Liverpool took the early lead.

After a round of high fives, the fans made their way back to their positions. One of the Everton fans piped up: "Lucky goal. If you score nine more goals then you can call yourselves the best club on Merseyside!" He was obviously referring to being tied with Everton on points on the table, but well below their superior goal difference over the Reds.

Without missing a beat, Roy brilliantly replied, "And if I had two assholes, I'd be in the fucking circus." Everyone had a good laugh and went back to watching the match. Roy grabbed me a second pint of Guinness from the bar, this time poured in a Carlsberg tall pilsner glass. Surely I couldn't let such apathy go unnoticed, but since Carlsberg had been a long-time shirt sponsor for Liverpool, I decided to ignore this blatant indiscretion.

It didn't take long for Man City for respond. They quickly regained control of the possession and moved forward on the attack. In the ninth minute of play, Sterling found himself with the ball in the corner of the box. Former Man City midfielder James Milner dispossessed him from behind, causing Sterling to fall to the turf. The partisan crowd at the stadium stood up, pleading for a penalty to be called, as did Sterling. We simply laughed at the former Liverpool kid begging the ref for a call. Roy took it a bit further that most of us at the pub, loudly proclaiming, "GET UP, YOU FUCKING CUNT!"

I forget that words often carry different magnitudes of discomfort, depending on where someone was raised. Having met numerous people from Great Britain and Ireland over the years, they don't think twice when they hear someone using that word. However, American males have been well trained not to utter that word, as it is one of the ugliest things you could call a woman. Sensing my discomfort with his choice of language, Roy winked and continued, "You can put that quote in your book if you like."

Twenty minutes of the match had passed, with Man City still controlling the possession battle rather handily. We all worried about the offensive talent that Manuel Pellegrino had assembled for Man City, knowing that they could strike back in an instant. It looked like Liverpool was concerned as well, and I was afraid that they would bunker up defensively, trying to maintain the lead. Klopp noticed this as well, yelling to Firmino to stay up higher on the pitch. Normally Firmino would be playing more of a midfield role, but as a "false nine," he needed to stay in a more advanced position to stretch the defense and provide a deep outlet for when Liverpool regained possession.

It was fortuitous that he did in the twenty-second minute of play, because Milner regained possession and sent the ball toward Firmino. Man City had only three defenders back at the time, with Mangala and Martin Demichelis fumbling about in the back. The ball was pushed to the left, where Firmino chased Aleksandar Kolarov for possession. The Serbian was no match, as Firmino took the ball toward goal. All three defenders began to chase down Firmino while Coutinho followed behind unmarked. There was nothing Joe Hart could do when Coutinho calmly one-touched the perfect pass into the back of the net. It was a goal "made in Brazil," according to Arlo White from NBC Sports, and suddenly Liverpool was beating the league leaders 2-0.

Bedlam ensued. While the players chased after Coutinho to embrace him in the corner of the pitch, dozens of Liverpool supporters in the South Florida pub were already embracing in a group hug. My heart was racing a mile a minute. Once again we settled back to reality, hardly believing what we were witnessing.

As expected, Man City regained control and tried to work the ball around into the Liverpool defensive third. I was still trying to catch my breath in the thirty-first minute with City attacking. There was a noticeable step-up in play from the home team. Roy wasn't worried, saying, "We'll catch them with a quick counterattack."

Kolarov got the ball for Man City and attempted a cross that was blocked by Martin Skrtel. I noticed all ten Liverpool field players back in their defensive third when Milner found himself with the ball. He escaped the play with a nice give-and-go pass through Firmino, and just like Roy predicted, the counterattack ensued.

Milner must've run forty yards with the ball down the right flank before passing to a wide-open Coutinho in the middle of the pitch. Coutinho fired a shot easily saved by Hart, who decided to parry the ball to his right into safety. Alberto Moreno collected the ball in the corner as Man City quickly retreated to defend. Moreno got the ball back to Coutino, who passed over to Emre Can. The German midfielder started heading away from goal, looking for an outlet. He caught a glimpse of Firmino charging forward unmarked, and with his back heel, Can returned the pass to Coutinho. Only Joe Hart stood between the two Brazilians and a third Liverpool goal, but Firmino's run had put him into an offside position. Coutinho moved toward the English goalkeeper, allowing Firmino to step back onside before receiving a perfect lateral pass that eluded Hart. It was the simplest of goals in the end, and Firmino's first as a Red.

Everyone stood around, not sure what to do. The play had happened so fast that Firmino looked to be offside in real time. I assumed the goal would be denied by the assistant referee. Even Firmino wasn't sure if the goal was going to count, because he was looking around at the refs as well. There was no call made, and replays confirmed that it was the correct decision to allow the goal. It was the most delayed celebration to a goal that I can recall. Our boys had just walked into the league leader's house and gone up 3-0 in the first half. What was happening here?

Man City must've been as shocked as we were. Firmino nearly added another goal in the thirty-fourth minute when he broke free on goal via another beautiful pass from Coutinho. Hart made a nice save to keep Liverpool's fourth goal off the board. A minute later, Coutinho played a lovely pass over the defense to Firmino again, whose shot this time ventured just wide.

The minutes ticked down as we waited for halftime. A team like Man City had enough talent to erase a three-goal deficit, so I held my breath every time the ball ended up in our defensive third. *Just keep a clean sheet until halftime*, I kept telling myself, but my worst fears were realized in the forty-third minute. Skrtel's attempted long ball was hit too low and blocked by Kolarov's head, ending up straight at the feet of Sergio Aguero. The Argentine took a few steps with the ball and showed the world exactly why he is still one of the best strikers on the planet. From twenty-five yards out, the right-footed shot caromed off the side net for Man City's first goal. Simon Mignolet had no chance to make a save.

The whistle blew for halftime with Liverpool leading 3-1. Any Liverpool fan would've signed up for that lead before kickoff, I assure you. The only thing going through my mind was how it easily could've been 5-1. Surely the contest was still in question, but I couldn't think of a more devastating way to lose if somehow Man City were to figure it out and get the win.

Halftime meant it was time for another beer. Earlier in the match I had been introduced to Jim Nicholson, a former policeman from Belfast, Northern Ireland. Jim was an extremely nice old gentleman that had moved to the States in 1996. His American journeys took him to Colorado, then Minneapolis, where he'd helped start their OLSC branch a few years ago. He retired to Naples in 2012, where he lives today. I thought that I had it rough with an hour's drive to the London Bridge Pub for matches. Jim drives almost two hours each way across Alligator Alley to watch the match at the Fox and Hounds. Jim was kind enough to put this beer on his tab. I refrained from complaining that this time the Guinness was presented to me in a Newcastle goblet. Really? Three pints of Guinness each served in a different style glass labeled with a different brand of beer? Now they were just getting silly.

Following a quick trip to the urinal and a look over to see Barcelona beating Real Madrid in the El Clasico, I was back at the table for the second half. Pelligrini made the decision to bring on Fernandinho for Yaya Toure, a move that perplexed me at first. Admittedly, I don't watch a ton of Man City games, but Toure always seemed to be the player that scared me the most with his combination of size and ability. I was glad to see him come off the pitch at halftime.

The second half carried much of the same vibe as the first half. Man City controlled possession while Liverpool defended and waited for the right moment to counter. We nervously watched, hoping to see Liverpool do what they hadn't done all season: score a fourth goal. It nearly came in the fifty-ninth minute when Emre Can sent Firmino clear in on goal, but once again Hart was up to the task with a nice kick save. Three minutes later, Firmino found Coutinho with a nice pass that Coutinho put in the back of the net, but the play was rightfully ruled offside. Defensively Liverpool's back four were holding firm, and the Brazilian connection were creating some great opportunities. As long as the defense could continue its form, confidence would continue to build.

Catastrophe was nearly realized in the sixty-fourth minute when Milner tried to keep possession with a weak back pass to Mignolet. Sterling anticipated the play well, collecting the free ball and moving in uncontested as the Belgian goalkeeper approached eight yards off his line. Speaking for the entire pub, I mumbled, "Not fucking Sterling!" Thankfully, it was a difficult angle and would've required an extremely precise shot, so he laid the ball back to Aguero, who sent a weak shot toward goal from fifteen yards out. The pass from Sterling only took a split second, but it was enough time for Mignolet to retreat toward goal, make the diving save, and preserve the two-goal lead.

I breathed another sigh of relief a minute later when Aguero was substituted. I had completely forgotten his lack of fitness due to recent injury, so it was a pleasure watching him trot off the pitch. Man City were infinitely less likely to score without him.

When the clock turned over past the eightieth minute, the tension started to disappear. You could sense victory was in our grasp. Even though Man City continued to attack, it just didn't seem likely that City would break through the Liverpool defense to notch another goal.

Late in the match, Liverpool earned a corner kick. It was taken by Adam Lallana as he sent the ball toward the penalty spot. Benteke got his head on it, but the ball deflected toward Skrtel. You could see it develop as if it were playing in slow motion. Skrtel turned on a dime and volleyed the ball with extreme authority. Hart must've felt like a lonely soldier at war when the ball whizzed past his flailing body into the back of the net. As the Slovakian and his teammates celebrated in front of the traveling Liverpool supporters, scores of Man City supporters exited the stadium. Game, set, and match.

The final whistle blew and the pints continued to flow. With such a great crowd, the bartender must've surely appreciated a Liverpool win as much as we did. As the Liverpool fans at the pub gleefully mingled, I met another Scouse expatriate named David Cruice. I immediately liked him, since he bought me a pint. I was so ecstatic at the result that I don't even recall what type of glass she poured it in. That's old news. David moved to the States in 1990 and now works for a real estate investment firm in town, but like most everyone else that I met, was born and raised across the River Mersey in Birkenhead.

I was quickly introduced to Rob Danenberger, who had just recently moved to the area from Charleston after retiring from the Navy. Rob served twenty years as a nuclear engineer in the Navy, so I bought him a pint in gratitude. Rob was an active member of the South Carolina chapter, so we quickly started telling stories about our common friends with OLSC South Carolina.

Craig Posner joined the conversation along with a few others. Craig is a young lad that recently graduated from law school, passing the bar exam not long ago. Of the dozen or so people that I met on this great day, Craig had the luxury of being the only one actually born in the state of Florida. He handed me his business card and said with a straight face, "If you ever need a lawyer in town, give me a call." No offense, Craig, but I hope that I don't ever need your services.

Another young fan milling about was Jarrod Dinwoodie, a network systems administrator living in Portland, Oregon. Jarrod was originally from the area and attended Florida Atlantic University. He became a regular at the Fox and Hounds during Liverpool matches and was back in town visiting family.

As the afternoon wound down, people slowly made their escape back to the real world. I had met some great people and connected with most of them through social media, and I felt confident that we would stay in touch.

I knew that I should probably get back to my Miami Beach hotel, but I just didn't want to leave the euphoria that was still lingering around in the pub. Neither did Roy. We both wanted the party to continue, but knew that it would have to end sometime. "You can come back to this pub to watch Liverpool anytime you like," Roy said to me as we prepare to bid farewell.

With a wink and a smile, I replied, "I just might."

13 - GIVING THANKS

Thursday, November 26
Camp Kendra
Premier League match #5 (vs. Bordeaux)

One of my favorite holidays of the year is Thanksgiving. Every year we celebrate this day with neighbors and friends, and sometimes the occasional family member makes the trek. I pull out the turkey fryer while the wife coordinates the rest of the meal with those attending. Most Americans enjoy watching American football on the television in the afternoon. This year there would be a different sort of football in the Kendra house, as Liverpool hosted French club Bordeaux.

This was an important fixture, as a Liverpool victory would clinch their advancement to the knockout stage of the Europa League. It was not a match to be taken lightly. In honor of our opponent, I opened a bottle of a fine red wine from the Bordeaux region of France to enjoy with my turkey dinner. Normally I would drink a fine white wine with turkey, but Bordeaux is better known for their reds. It was a successful turkey dinner, and I had barely had finished my last bite of pumpkin pie when the match came on the television. I poured myself another glass of Bordeaux wine and retired to the couch.

Bordeaux wasn't playing the best of football, sitting mid-table of the French Ligue Un, so everyone was expecting a victory at Anfield. The first ten minutes of the match showed little spark from either team, and the tryptophan was beginning to kick-start the heavy eyelids. I might've even dozed off a bit before some excitement in the Liverpool end in the thirty-second minute. Simon Mignolet had possession of the ball but couldn't decide what to do with it. He held the ball for a long time before Israeli referee Alon Yefet whistled to call delay of game. It's a rare call that is usually only seen on the amateur level, if at all, but it was the correct decision, as Mignolet held possession for twenty-two seconds, unable to decide how to dispatch the ball. The result was an indirect free kick for Bordeaux about fourteen yards from goal. Every Liverpool player got behind the ball, but it didn't matter, as Henri Saivet fired the ball into the top left corner of the net to give Bordeaux the 1-0 lead.

Liverpool would equalize a few minutes later with a dubious penalty call following a hopeful James Milner cross. The ball was sent in from the left touchline toward Benteke, who was seemingly brought down by defender Ludovic Sane, thus impeding his attempt to get on the end of the cross. There was definitely contact on the shoulder by the defender, but Benteke went down far too easily. To make matters worse for Bordeaux, there was simply no chance that Benteke would get to the ball, and it would've been an easy play for goalkeeper Cedric Carrasso. Yefet didn't hesitate to whistle for the penalty, which Milner easily slotted into the net to tie the score 1-1.

The final seconds of the first half were dwindling as I got off the couch to refill my glass of wine, when Benteke put the Reds up with a brilliant goal of his own. Nathaniel Clyne sent a cross from the right side toward the Belgian attacker, who deftly brought the ball down with his foot in a perfect position. With a quick step he fired a laser beam past a diving Carrasso just before halftime. It may not have been as impressive as his late strike against Manchester United in September, but it was certainly a magnificent goal.

I managed to keep myself awake for the entire second half, despite the lack of action displayed on the pitch. Liverpool had some decent chances, but Bordeaux were simply outclassed for the final forty-five minutes and the match ended 2-1. Mission accomplished. Liverpool was through the next round of the Europa League with one more match to play in the group stage.

****

The next match was held three days later at home against Swansea City. It was another Sunday morning match for the Reds, but as the four-day holiday weekend came to a close, I decided to trek down to the pub to watch with my friends.

There was a decent crowd at the pub despite it being a holiday weekend. We were all expecting some continued good play after watching Liverpool win both matches since the last international break. The big news was the return of Jordan Henderson to the squad following a fifteen-match absence with his heel injury. Our captain was named to the bench, and we were all hopeful that he'd make a cameo appearance. Daniel Sturridge was still unfit, which caused great concern for everyone, dominating the pre-match conversation in the pub.

Swansea City was a disappointing squad thus far, having won only one match all season long. Unfortunately, Liverpool continued to look woeful in the attacking third. It had all the makings of a drab nil-nil draw that added fuel to the fire for those that consider soccer such a boring sport. The first half of play didn't help.

The real highlight in the pub was every time Mignolet got possession with his hands. Colin and Sean created their own cheer that they derived from childhood. While playing two-hand touch American football, most rules stipulated that you couldn't rush the quarterback until after a predetermined number of seconds. When the ball was hiked by the offense, one defender would stand at the line counting out loud, "One Mississippi, two Mississippi, three Mississippi..." until reaching some predetermined magic number. At the time, the defender would rush in to try and sack the quarterback. Colin and Sean took this idea to the next level at the pub. Every time our Belgian keeper had the ball in his hands, they would start counting, "One Mignolet, two Mignolet, three Mignolet..." until he got rid of the ball. They were clearly and cleverly mocking the goalkeeper's ridiculous blunder against Bordeaux, and it made me chuckle every time.

Liverpool would eventually get the only goal of the game when Jordon Ibe's cross struck Neil Taylor's arm inside the box. Initially referee Anthony Taylor didn't appear to call the infringement, but his sideline assistant flagged for the call and the penalty was given. Once again James Milner stepped up and shot into the upper roof netting to give the Reds the 1-0 victory. It was another one of those ugly wins against a stingy defense, but still an important three points.

****

Liverpool had won all three matches since the last international break concluded over two weeks ago. For the fourth time in less than two weeks, Liverpool had a game to play. Next up on the schedule was the League Cup quarterfinal against Southampton. Everyone expected Klopp would give players a rest while giving others a chance to shine. For Daniel Sturridge it was his opportunity to shake off the rust, and I expected to see Jordan Henderson get a run-out as well. I thought Portuguese midfielder Joao Carlos Teixeira would get another chance after a solid game in the previous victory against Bournemouth, but an hour before kickoff I saw the team sheet and noted that he didn't even make the bench.

Not only had Klopp decided to shake up the roster, it would appear he was looking to shake up the formation a bit as well. Both Sturridge and Divock Origi were named starters up front, indicating a 4-4-2 lineup was likely. Joe Allen was added to the midfield to replace James Milner, and former Southampton captain Adam Lallana was a decent bet to get the start as well. Emre Can was probably the most surprising start for me, not because he was unworthy, but because the kid needed a break sometime. He'd started all but four Liverpool matches so far, and came on as a substitute in three of the other four. I believed that he had earned a break, but Klopp kept his countryman in the side. Lucas Leiva returned to the lineup after serving his suspension for accumulating too many yellow cards, and he completed the midfield. The defense was relatively set. The only change in the back four would be young Connor Randall starting at right back in place of Nathaniel Clyne, who had played every LFC minute this season minus three halves of football. Klopp agreed it was time for Clyne to get a rest.

Southampton fielded a very strong roster, possibly their best eleven. Dutch manager Ronald Koeman sensed an opportunity playing at home against an inexperienced and rusty lineup. The other three semifinalists advanced the day before, as Manchester City, Everton and Stoke City would fill out the bracket. A home win against a weakened Liverpool team and Koeman would earn a good chance to win the club's first major trophy since winning this competition in 1979.

I walk into the pub a few minutes before kickoff, knowing that many folks of the regular crowd wouldn't be in attendance. Mike was at the front door talking to a vendor, and was quick to greet me, as I noticed Sean taking off his dress shirt in the back of the pub. Proper work attire for the banker was shirt and tie, but Sean often would see fit to use his white LFC home kit as an undershirt, making it easy to get match ready after a tough day at the office. Jeff Carroll was sitting at one of the tables, but I almost didn't recognize him without a Liverpool hat and proper game-day attire. Cara Dempster, in her final year at law school, became a pub regular at midweek fixtures due to her class schedule, and that was fine with us. Her husband Evan is also a regular Raleigh Red, but he is a school teacher and can't attend most midweek matches. There were a few other stragglers, but for the most part it was a lighter roster at the pub. I rolled up to the bar next to Sean and waited for Sam to serve my first pint.

The game kicked off with Liverpool moving backward, hoping to set up possession. Southampton earned a throw-in at midfield, and Serbian Dusan Tadic found himself with the ball on the left flank just outside the box. Tadic laid the ball off to Ryan Bertrand, who crossed over to an unmarked Sadio Mane for an easy header into the corner. I hadn't really savored my first sip of Guinness and the Saints were up 1-0 only forty-one seconds into the match. Replays confirmed what I initially thought, as Alberto Moreno was caught ball-watching on the play. It was the second goal Mane had scored against Liverpool this season and was simply too easy.

Four minutes later, Tadic found himself with the ball in the left corner of the attack. It looked like a planned tactic from Koeman to have the

Saints attacking the inexperienced twenty-year-old Randall on defense. Tadic sent a long right-footed cross to a wide-open Victor Wanyama, who fiercely headed his shot straight at Bogdan for a simple save. Sean looked over at me and said, "Should be 2-0 right now."

I nodded in acknowledgement. "This could get ugly."

Thankfully, the team settled in a little, although Liverpool was still losing the battle against the charged Southampton midfield. The Saints had a few more chances but couldn't get the ball on target before Randall started a counterattack from the right side with a quick throw-in to Divock Origi, who confidently passed the ball across midfield to Joe Allen. The Welshmen one-timed a perfectly sent ball forty yards over the Southampton defense to Sturridge, whose rusty first touch seemed to let him down. Sturridge retrieved the ball inside the box, with two Southampton defenders setting position to block any effort. It wouldn't be enough, as Sturridge fired his strong left-footed shot from a difficult angle to the far post and into the net. All square at 1-1—we could breathe a little easier. I felt that Southampton had the better of the play up until that point, and Liverpool had never really threatened the net. It was their first real shot on target, but the pure quality of the Liverpool striker was enough to equalize the match.

After a round of high fives from the small pub crowd, Darren Bridger walked in with a smile. Today was his day to drop off his daughter with her mother, so he'd missed the first part of the match. He grabbed his pint of Stella Artois just in time to join our celebration.

Only four minutes had passed when Lallana regained possession in the midfield and touched over to Emre Can. The German moved the ball into open space on his left with a clever back heel before using the outside of his right foot to arc a pass over the Southampton defender Cedric Soares. Sturridge timed his run perfectly to remain onside, and volleyed the ball past Martin Stekelenburg to give Liverpool the 2-1 lead. It didn't matter that the pub wasn't nearly as full as during a big weekend match—the loud eruption from the few supporters in the pub was enough to wake Rip Van Winkle from his slumber. It was pure class, as Darren referred to that goal as "better than sex." No comment.

The first half looked about done when Liverpool earned a corner kick that Lallana took from the right side. The out-swinging ball skimmed off the head of Daniel Sturridge and seemed destined for safety when Alberto Moreno first-timed a rocket with his left foot from twenty-five yards out through the defense and into the goal. It was a great strike by the Spaniard, who would later be credited with the assist after replays confirmed that Origi got a slight touch on the ball before sending it in the net. We didn't care who got credit for the goal; the pub jubilantly celebrated a 3-1 lead going into halftime.

The intermission gave me just enough time to pay the parking meter, check my work emails, and grab a quick bathroom break. It also gave me enough time to reflect on the fact that this was Klopp's eleventh game as Liverpool boss, the same number of games that Rodgers had in charge of the club this season. The squad led by Rodgers had only scored eleven goals in those matches, only once scoring more than one goal in the same game. Klopp's team had netted eighteen goals thus far with one more half of football still to be played, scoring multiple goals in four of their eleven games to date. Two years earlier, Rodgers' system was credited with generating more goals than any other club in Premier League history, yet the manner in which these guys were scoring under Klopp had me wondering how much was the system and how much was the talent?

The first fifteen minutes of the second half were relatively uneventful, with no substitutions being made by either squad. Jordon Ibe was the first substitution, coming on for Sturridge, who'd put in an extremely solid shift. Early in the match we were joking about hoping he simply didn't get injured, but the skill of his first two goals reminded us all of how valuable he was to this club.

It didn't take Ibe long to put his mark on the match. Southampton had possession in Liverpool's end when the midfield press paid off, and they regained the ball. Allen sent the ball to the right flank as Ibe held possession, looking for the right pass. It wasn't long ago when Ibe would take the ball and try to beat a few defenders one versus one down the flank. I wasn't sure if he was being instructed differently by the coaching staff or was simply maturing as a player. Either way, his smart play allowed him to play a forward ball to Origi on the right side of the box. As Origi ran onto the ball and moved to strike it with his right foot, my first thought was, Why not? It wasn't a great angle, and you'd have to call it a low-percentage shot. But there wasn't a single Liverpool player close to him, with six Southampton players retreating to help on defense. With a 3-1 lead in your back pocket, Origi had nothing to lose. He blasted another rocket that skimmed the crossbar on its way past Stekelenburg and into the back net. 4-1 to Liverpool as Origi celebrated in front of thousands of traveling supporters. Surely our ticket to the semifinals was punched now.

Only five minutes after the Origi wonder strike, the Liverpool youngsters attacked the left side again. In the seventy-third minute, Origi maintained possession on the left side, this time back-heeling the pass to an overlapping Moreno. The Spaniard moved toward goal and immediately spotted Ibe sitting at the top of the box. Moreno sent the ball across where Ibe chested the ball to his right and volleys into the net for Liverpool's fifth goal. It was yet another beauty that deserved to make the highlight reels. This wasn't Barcelona in disguise, was it?

Even more satisfying than the brilliance of the Ibe goal was the chant heard coming from Liverpool fans immediately after. Earlier in the match, both Dejan Lovren and Adam Lallana were consistently booed and jeered by Southampton supporters. It was only a few years earlier that the two players laced up for Southampton, and many fans felt betrayed when they signed for Liverpool. The boos were loud and evident in the first twenty minutes of the match with Southampton leading 1-0. Sixty minutes later, the only sounds I could hear from the stands were Liverpool fans singing, "He's leading 5-1. He's leading 5-1! ADAM LALLANA! He's leading 5-1!"

The cherry on top for Liverpool came in the eighty-sixth minute, when substitute Brad Smith took the ball from the left side and crossed the ball into the box from the touchline. Once again the young Belgian striker found himself loosely marked and able to charge the ball for an easy shot on target. It would be Origi's first ever hat trick for Liverpool and the second of his young career. The cross from Smith was sublime, and again it looked as though Liverpool had generated a goal from nowhere. The sixth goal of the night closed the book on Southampton as Liverpool would advance to the semifinals with a 6-1 road win.

As the pub crowd started to dissipate and head home for the evening, Sean and I went over the remarkable evening. Normally I set myself a two-beer limit for midweek matches, but something told me it would be okay to remain at the pub a bit longer this evening. Darren and Mike joined us at the bar, and we could only shake our heads in disbelief. We recounted the night and eventually loudly cheered when it was announced that our semifinal opponent would be Stoke City (and not Manchester City). I would've preferred to see a Merseyside derby in the semis.

I have one final note to mention about this match. Much had been said about Liverpool's transfer committee looking to acquire young talent and groom them for the future of the club. The final four goals of this match could be summarized thus:

• Divock Origi (twenty years old) scored on an Alberto Moreno (twenty-three) assist
  • Origi scored on a Jordon Ibe (nineteen) assist
  • Ibe scored on a Moreno assist
  • Origi scored on a Brad Smith (twenty-one) assist

Looked like this club may have a bright future.

14 - RICHMOND

Sunday, December 6
Penny Lane Pub, Richmond, VA
Premier League match #15 (at Newcastle)

People have asked me what it means to be an official LFC supporters club (OLSC). If you look on their website, the club will explain several reasons that this program exists. The primary reason is obviously to represent the club in local regions around the world, primarily by bringing local fans of the club together while providing high-quality services and events for branch members. The benefits include access to match tickets and discounts on club merchandise. Members of OLSC Raleigh won't typically take advantage of these benefits, so why bother going through the arduous process? For us it was all about recognition. Having the club recognize the passion exuded from a group of fans in one of the smaller markets of America filled us with great pride.

The primary requirement to qualify as an OLSC is to have a minimum of fifty local members, at least fifteen of which must also be registered members of Liverpool Football Club as well. There are other requirements, such as establishing an organizational committee, drafting bylaws, and having an annual general meeting open to all members. After meeting these requirements, you submit an application to the club for review. These are typically due in August, reviewed by the club, and successful new chapters are announced in October. The 2015 list included a new branch in Richmond, Virginia. Richmond is a short drive from Raleigh, so I simply knew that I had to go visit their pub for a match.

Richmond and Raleigh share several similarities. Both are state capitals of Southern states and both cities have populations of around one million (although Raleigh needs to include the Durham and Chapel Hill cities to get near that mark). Both cities are dwarfed by larger metropolitan areas within two hours' drive away (Washington and Charlotte) with multiple sports teams to entertain the locals. It's almost as though both Raleigh and Richmond are the redheaded stepchildren of their respective states.

I was initially intrigued to discover that Richmond now had an official club, mostly because I was completely unaware that they had such a significant fan base. OLSC Raleigh is one of the newer branches in North America, but I'd connected with leadership from chapters all across the southeast United States and had never heard anyone mention a group in Richmond. The wife and I have good friends living just outside Richmond, so we planned a trip to visit them one weekend where Liverpool had a Sunday match. I reached out to Ryan Drake, the president of OLSC Richmond, and scheduled a visit to the Penny Lane Pub.

There was much to be excited about as a Liverpool fan. The club had won four straight matches, including impressive away wins at Manchester City (4-1) and Southampton (6-1). The Reds were sitting seventh on the table and climbing. A victory would move them into a tie for fifth place with Tottenham, only three points shy of a Champions League spot. Newcastle United was fighting to get out of the relegation zone, as they sat in nineteenth place before the match started. Matches in the Premier League are never easy, especially on the road to places like St. James Park, but there was good reason to be confident heading into this match.

The Penny Lane Pub is located in the heart of downtown Richmond. As we walked around town before the match, the downtown area looked exactly as you would think, with large multistory buildings, one-way streets, and a myriad of parking meters. It was easy to spot the pub from the road, as it was the only building with British and football flags hanging from the second-story balcony. We walked into what appeared to be an enclosed courtyard with a nice garden room. I noticed a door leading into a dark, dungeon-like space with low ceilings and hundreds of scarves nailed to the crossbeams above me. Once inside, I saw a long bar with multiple taps of beer and numerous old pictures from Liverpool and England hanging on the wall. I knew this was the right spot.

Ryan was waiting for me upon arrival, having saved a prime seat for me in the corner. A large Tottenham flag hung below the large television by our table. I looked over at Ryan, who quickly explained that the Penny Lane was also home to a few other supporters clubs in Richmond. I guessed that was understandable for a small town, but it didn't mean I had to like it. "Can't you at least take down that flag for our match?" I asked. A shrug told me that I wasn't the first person to inquire and get denied.

The waiter came up to me and asked me if I wanted a drink. Since the match was on a Sunday morning, I figured that a pint of Guinness would be out of the question. I was about to order a cup of coffee when I saw a pint of golden elixir sitting in front of Ryan's friend. How could that be? "Can you drink beer legally on Sunday?" I asked the server.

"Of course, why wouldn't you?" he replied.

I looked at the clock, confirming that it was still before noon. I actually forgot that our short drive up I-95 took me into the state of Virginia. It was the best news I had gotten all day. "Never mind," I gleefully answered, "give me a pint of Guinness, please."

Ryan is a younger local, born and raised in the area. He graduated from James Madison University in 2002, the same institution that gave my sister and brother-in-law their degrees about a decade earlier. Small world, isn't it? He's a certified financial planner with his own business, which makes it easy for him to plan his week around LFC matches. Surprisingly, though, he admitted to have been following the club only since the remarkable 2013-14 season.

How did a relatively new fan to the sport and club become the guy that undertook the time-consuming task of becoming an official LFC supporters club? "Because no one else would do the work," he replied. It was an answer that hit close to home and gave me another reason to appreciate this chapter. The club will often talk about being in the Liverpool family. I was starting to look at the newly formed OLSC Richmond as though they were my little brother in that family. We are similar in so many ways, with OLSC Raleigh only a few years older.

Ryan's good friend Scott Keel was sitting next to him at the table. Scott is a pediatrician in town, but spent about ten years living in Europe and had no choice but to fall in love with the sport. All of his European friends were Liverpool supporters, so Scott succumbed to peer pressure and went along with the Reds.

Scott brought Ryan to the Penny Lane one day during the eleven-game winning streak in the 2013-14 season. Ryan saw the passion and exuberance emanating from the Liverpool supporters. It was a wonderful new experience. At that moment, the club gained another fan.

We were joined at the table by two other men wearing Liverpool red kits. I was introduced to Joey Cothran, a bartender turned insurance salesman. Joey fell in love with the sport during the France 1998 World Cup. He was watching England play Argentina in the first knockout stage of the tournament when a then-eighteen-year-old Michael Owen scored one of the most magnificent goals in English history. Owen took possession near midfield and ran past defenders Roberto Ayala and Jose Chamot before firing a shot in the left corner past Carlos Roa to give England a 2-1 lead. It was the sort of play from which legends are born.

The other man sitting near us was Jimmy Sprawls, another Richmond native. Jimmy played youth soccer in the developmental leagues and had the opportunity to play in an international tournament held in Dallas in the mid-1990s. The best team at that tournament was from the Liverpool academy, and that was enough to seal his rooting interests as a Red. It is unclear if he got to see a young Steven Gerrard, Jamie Carragher, or even Michael Owen play in Dallas, but he'd like to think so. It'd be tough to imagine any team would be able to compete against those kids.

The match kicked off as I took a sip from my pint of Guinness, smiling at the fact that my Raleigh Red brethren back at the London Bridge Pub had another hour to wait before consuming their first libation. Liverpool's recent form had me thinking that there could be a surge of support at the pubs, and I was hoping for a good crowd at the Penny Lane. They didn't disappoint, as fans continued to pour into the tiny basement tavern even after kickoff.

The Reds came out strong, forcing three corner kicks in the opening few minutes, but failed to capitalize. Newcastle settled into a rhythm and held their own, but still they were clearly being outmatched by the visiting Reds. Christian Benteke missed an early chance when Dejan Lovren headed a corner kick toward the target, and you could sense the frustration from the bar as a distant fan hollered out in disgust. I wasn't worried, because Newcastle weren't showing much offensively. Even a 0-0 draw wouldn't be the worst result.

Halftime came with the score knotted, so I took a brief walk around the pub. At first glance the Penny Lane looks like a quaint and cozy pub, but walk around and you'll notice other rooms that provide a capacity larger than expected. There must've been fifty LFC supporters hanging around waiting for the second half, yet I had no clue where any of them had come from. The table we sat at was sheltered from the main entrance, but it was also possible that many supporters refused to watch a television with a large Tottenham banner hanging below it.

After using the bathroom, I returned to the table with another pint of Guinness. A young lad had taken a seat at the table engaged in conversation with Ryan. I wasn't completely convinced that this guy was of legal drinking age, but I certainly didn't care. He introduced himself as Walker, and he worked in the kitchen of a local downtown restaurant. He explained that he came to most weekend matches since he mostly worked in the evening. During weekday matches when he was at the restaurant, he would change all of the restaurant televisions to the Liverpool match and then hide the remote controls from the servers. On his breaks, he would step out to the lounge to watch a few minutes and a patron would ask him to change the channel. "Sorry," he would reply, "I just work in the kitchen. You'll have to ask the manager." Brilliant move. Well played, son.

The second half started off similarly to the first, with Liverpool taking charge from the outset. They controlled possession but never threatened the target. Fifteen minutes into the half, Klopp made a decisive change, taking off Christian Benteke and Roberto Firmino in favor of Adam Lallana and Daniel Sturridge. I was somewhat surprised that Sturridge didn't get the start. He'd scored two great goals in sixty minutes in their 6-1 thrashing at Southampton a few days earlier. I was confident that this substitution would pay off. Only a few minutes later, a Liverpool player hit the ball into the back of the net. Unfortunately, that player was Martin Skrtel, who deflected Georginio Wijnaldum's shot past Simon Mignolet for an own goal. The home team took an undeserved lead, and the pub went silent.

Despite the setback, there was plenty of time for Liverpool to equalize. The goal seemed to deflate the team and make the club look like a ship lost at sea. My immediate thought was to bring on Jordan Henderson. The squad needed their captain to kick their ass into gear, but Klopp thought differently. Instead he brought on the red-hot Divock Origi in the seventy-fifth minute to pair up front with Sturridge. It was clearly an attacking move to bring on a second striker, a move many fans had begged Brendan Rodgers to make a long time ago. Combined, the two strikers had put five goals past Southampton, so who was I to argue the tactical change?

Liverpool failed to generate any legitimate scoring chances in the final minutes, and Wijnaldum sealed the match in stoppage time with a counterattacking goal to give Newcastle the 2-0 victory. It's never easy to win a road match in the Premier League, but this defeat was difficult to swallow. The club appeared to be making strides up the ladder and had just stumbled down a few without cause. The roller-coaster ride continued.

We sat around the table in disbelief when the pub owner made his way over the table after the match was over and offered a pint on the house. The old man was wearing the classic white Carlsberg away kit that Liverpool wore in the 2007-08 season, with an apron tied around his waist. Clearly past the age that most workers start collecting retirement checks, Terry O'Neill had already put in a full shift serving breakfast to his patrons before Sunday midday. The former Liverpool man wouldn't have it any other way.

In the 1950s, air travel was still a luxury that a lot of people couldn't afford, so boat transport remained a popular option amongst travelers that needed to cross the Atlantic Ocean. Terry worked on one of these ships that once docked in New York Harbor in the summer of 1958. During Terry's time off on the shore, a man approached him and some friends with an offer to work in the kitchen at the Four Seasons hotel. The Englishmen discussed this opportunity amongst themselves before collectively making the bold decision to jump ship.

For years Terry worked as an illegal immigrant in various roles of the restaurant industry before finding his way to the Richmond area to settle down. He got married, started a family, and opened his own place in 1979. He named it the Penny Lane Pub in honor of his hometown of Liverpool.

Most people recognize "Penny Lane" as a song by the Beatles, but few realize that it is an actual place where John Lennon and Paul McCartney would meet to catch a bus into the center of the city. Terry tried to make the pub as Liverpool-centric as he could. Even the front page of the menu reveals the pub slogan to be "Liverpool without the airfare!"

These days he runs the pub with the help of his son Terence, who was wearing one of those navy-blue shirts with red lettering in the same fancy font as the Boston Red Sox uniform, except this shirt read "LIVERPOOL" instead. Terry sat down at our table with his plate of pancakes and started telling stories. I asked for another pint of Guinness and eagerly listened. Terry began telling stories that had us all glued to our seats.

The pub relocated to its current location in 2003, but the same artifacts hang around the pub. He refuses to take anything down, as he admits that most of what you can see was donated by other patrons. "As soon as I take something down to make room, the guy that gave me the item would walk in and ask where it was. I don't want to upset anyone, so I just find room somewhere," admitted Terry.

One time Terry was asked by someone why he opened up a British pub instead of an Irish pub, since the latter seemed to be more popular amongst Americans. "If I want to turn this into an Irish pub, I just take down that picture of the queen and put up a picture of Kevin Barry," claimed Terry. We all laughed at the time, but I had to later look up who Kevin Barry was. He was an eighteen-year-old Irish medical student executed in 1920 by the British for his role in an operation that killed three British soldiers. His execution outraged the Irish further and helped precipitate the most violent time during the Irish War of Independence, culminating with Bloody Sunday only a few weeks later. Terry's comment made a lot more sense to me with that knowledge.

We sat around the table listening to Terry tell stories from the past, and consumed more Guinness. From tales of glory on the parks of suburbia to finally gaining his citizenship decades after first jumping ship to work hospitality as an illegal immigrant, it was perhaps the most silent I had ever been at a table drinking pints of Guinness. His stories didn't need any interjection from me, anyway.

Truly a wonderful experience, and I was glad to have made the three-hour road trip north to Richmond for this match. The Penny Lane Pub is a Richmond institution, and LFC are lucky to have one of its own running the place. Football fans from all over town eventually make their way to the Penny Lane, and the mere fact that the affable Scouser running the joint roots for LFC has turned countless Richmond neutrals into Reds fans themselves. Richmond may not be a town with a great soccer history, but thanks to Terry and the Penny Lane Pub, they are holding their own.

15 - HOLIDAY PARTY DRAMA

Sunday, December 13
London Bridge Pub
Premier League match #16 (vs. West Bromwich Albion)

Following the abysmal defeat at Newcastle, the club traveled to Switzerland for their final Europa League group stage match. Having already secured advancement to the knockout round with the Thanksgiving Day victory over Bordeaux, a road win or draw at FC Sion would secure first place in the group. This was important to ensure earning a top seed when the knockout stage matches were drawn. If FC Sion could pull off the victory, they would top the group and Liverpool would have a much more difficult match in the first knockout match. It was little surprising to see Klopp bring such a strong roster.

Whenever you get to a match where both teams would be happy with a tie, you typically don't get a very exciting match. I went to the pub on that Thursday afternoon, and only a handful of Raleigh Reds were in attendance. Even the hardcore regulars didn't see fit to rearrange their normal work schedule for this match. They were right to do so, as I sat at the bar watching one of the drabbest 0-0 matches in recent memory. I can't recall a single great scoring chance for either team. It was the sort of match that gives the sport a bad reputation, but the end result suited both teams. Liverpool won the group with a final record of two wins and four draws, while FC Sion advanced to the knockout stage for the first time since the competition introduced group stage play. Mission accomplished for both clubs on the day.

****

One of my favorite matches of the season is during the month of December leading up to the holidays, when LFC Raleigh decides to have its annual holiday party. At the time the London Bridge Pub didn't have a kitchen, so the idea came about to have a potluck lunch where members would bring their favorite dishes and goodies. We obtained signed memorabilia and goodies to raffle off and raise money for Jamie Carragher's charitable foundation. Regular members brought their families to the pub on a Sunday morning, enjoying a variety of delicacies, including meat pies, scouse stew, and scotch eggs, among others. We would watch our favorite club, enjoy some great food, and afterward some lucky fans would win cool stuff.

The first LFC Raleigh holiday party was the year prior, and wildly successful. Liverpool hosted Arsenal in what turned out to be an epic match. Martin Skrtel took a stud to the skull, which opened a gash on his bald head. He had it stapled shut and wrapped, then returned to the pitch to head in the equalizer in the final seconds off a corner kick. The 2-2 draw as a catalyst for a great run of games that brought the Reds back into contention for a Champions League spot. The turnout at the pub that day was phenomenal, and the club raised $1400 for Jamie Carragher's 23 Foundation. This year Liverpool would host West Bromwich Albion with hopes of erasing the most recent results from the memory bank.

The wife and I arrived at the pub about thirty minutes before kickoff, as I wanted to make sure that the facilities were set up for the potluck lunch. Residual patrons that arrived early enough to watch Arsenal defeat Aston Villa 2-0 in the early match were still milling about the pub. Looking to the back, I noticed Mike Ruiz setting up a table for the many delicious dishes on the way. I was happy to see everything on track as the pub started to fill up with Raleigh Reds carrying in Crock-Pots of warm goodness and Tupperware containers of calories.

Stephen White was the first person I noticed bringing in food. Even though Stephen was raised in upstate New York near the Canadian border, he was actually born in England and recalls picking Liverpool as his club of choice during his childhood years. His parents immigrated to America, but his love for Liverpool never waned. We shared a common friend who attended his high school up until their senior year. This friend moved four hours away to my high school for his final year. We have Facebook to thank for making that connection. Stephen was bringing some jalapeno-bacon deviled eggs for the potluck, and I made a mental note to grab some later.

The pub started filling up quickly as many Raleigh Reds brought in delicious goods for the potluck lunch. I made sure to hide the raffle prizes to be given away after the match, and started vocally advertising the upcoming raffle.

While it is nice to have the social aspect to these events, there still was a football match to be played, and Liverpool needed to bounce back from their recent form. The loss at Newcastle was shocking, but could be easily forgotten with a win today. Many fans were discussing the golden opportunity presented after Bournemouth defeated Manchester United 2-1 the day before. I shy away from discussing other clubs and their results. "Table watching" is where fans closely watch the results of their league rivals, and something that can be very maddening if you're not careful. Just because Manchester United dropped points to a newly promoted club doesn't make Liverpool's current task any more or less vital.

Philippe Coutinho was finally fit, and returned to the starting lineup after a bum hamstring sidelined him for six matches. Christian Benteke also appeared to be back at full strength again. West Bromwich Albion were coached by Tony Pulis, a notoriously defensive-minded coach that wasn't afraid of "parking the bus" to ensure a result. As he often admits, his job is to not to play beautiful football, rather to keep his club from getting relegated. Liverpool had shown some challenges breaking down a bunkered defense, but finally it appeared as though the tools were in place to try.

The Reds got the lead with a superb team goal in the twenty-first minute. The play started off with a goal kick from Simon Mignolet, which was received at midfield by Coutinho. West Brom had nine players retreating to the bunkered defense as Liverpool gladly kept possession. Passing back and forth across the pitch well into the West Brom end, Liverpool made twenty-one successful passes touched by nine different players. Coutinho got the ball about forty yards from the goal. As soon as he turned to strike a long pass, Jordan Henderson sprinted toward the goal. There was no defender watching him at the time, thus no defender to pick him up. Coutinho's pass soared over the defense toward the far post, where Adam Lallana found himself with a chance to play the ball off his head. Noticing Henderson unmarked and running dangerously in the box, Lallana headed an easy pass laterally across the six-yard box, where Henderson one-timed it past Myhill for the game's opening goal.

Our joy was relatively short-lived, as West Brom equalized in the thirtieth minute off a comical corner kick. Chris Brunt whipped in the ball around six yards from the goal. Not known as being a strong keeper in the air, Mignolet looked unsure of his decision to come off his line. He flailed at the ball, trying to punch it to safety, but missed completely. Like in a pinball machine, the ball bounced around a few players before landing at the feet of Craig Dawson, who fired it toward the goal. The shot deflected off Mignolet before magically finding its way through six other Liverpool defenders into the back of the net. West Brom had their equalizer off a set piece, quickly becoming the easiest way to get a goal against Liverpool.

Another set piece almost gave West Brom the lead just before halftime, when the Baggies were given another free kick about forty yards from goal. The ball was sent dangerously in the box to find three different West Brom players ahead of any Liverpool defender. Jonas Olsson stuck out his foot to easily redirect the ball into the back of the net. The entire pub sat stunned as the West Brom players crowded around the Swedish defender to celebrate the goal. As NBC Sports played back the replay, it was clear that all three West Brom players mistimed their runs and were offside. Olsson looked over to see there was no initial flag from the linesman, so he must've assumed that he timed his run perfectly, and began to celebrate with his teammates by the corner flag. It appeared as though referee Craig Pawson had gotten some words in his earpiece, so he went over to consult with linesman Roger West. They spoke about the play, and forty seconds after the ball entered the net, they whistled the play dead for offside. It was a contentious moment that infuriated Tony Pulis, but in the end the referees got the call correct.

The pub breathed a sigh of relief, many people confused at what had just occurred. Personally, I initially thought that the referee saw a replay on the big screen inside the stadium and used that knowledge to get the call right. It was the most bizarre moment I can recall in any Liverpool match, and maybe a good example why instant replay could work in this sport. Nonetheless, the match went to halftime knotted at 1-1.

I looked around the pub at the break and estimated about a hundred LFC fans in attendance. It was easily the largest crowd I had seen there since the Manchester United derby match three months earlier. Many people used this break in the match to sample the wonderful foods donated for the potluck lunch. My personal favorite was the scotch egg that Darren Bridger brought in. It was a hard-boiled egg surrounded by sausage and coated with bread crumbs before getting deep-fried. My digestive system might eventually disagree, but what's not to like about that tasty goodness?

I was still worried about the match. That late goal may have been correctly disallowed, but it still was scored off another set piece, which was quickly becoming our Achilles heel. The easy solution is to stop giving away free kicks in your defensive end, but that's more difficult to achieve in reality. The assumption was that Pulis would be happy with a draw and continue to deploy a bunkered defense. It would take another magnificent play to get the second goal needed to win the match.

Play resumed as fans began to find their space for the second half. I returned to the corner of the bar where I had sat for the entire first half. Normally I find myself changing positions often as I nervously watch the match. If it doesn't look like the Reds are playing well in one position, I move to another part of the bar to watch at another television. It drives some people crazy, but I can't help it. For this match I was forced to remain in one spot, as I was selling raffle tickets for the prizes to be given away after the match. It was a challenge, but I somehow powered through it.

As West Brom started mounting an attack that was ultimately thwarted by Dejan Lovren, I shouted at the top of my lungs, "That's why he's the Croatian Sensation!" Colin Russell still distrusts the defender and is usually voicing this opinion at the pub, so I rather enjoy countering with some loud accolades when he does something well. It is always good for a few laughs and helps break the tension for the moment, but in the back of my head I know how much that annoys Colin. So I continue to do it throughout every match. As Liverpool would maintain possession trying to find a way forward, I would shout, "Get the ball to Lovren!! All goals start with Lovren!"

Later in the first half, West Brom earned a corner kick, which made everyone uneasy, given our history of conceding goals on set pieces. This time Brunt sent this ball in dangerously toward the goal as Olsson leapt to flick the ball in the net just off the near post. On the replay it looked as though no Liverpool player was protecting that near post. I wasn't sure if that was by design or a missed mark, but the lack of a defensive presence at the near post made it an easy goal for Olsson. Just like that, the Baggies took a 2-1 lead. Unlike with their first goal, this time I had a pint of Guinness to help drown the sorrow. Yet again a goal scored against Liverpool off a set piece! For the third time in the match, the ball had found its way into the back of the net following a West Brom free kick. Thankfully, only two of them counted on the scoreboard.

Surely it was going to be a challenge to equalize now, as Pulis continued to fortify the defense. Klopp had just brought on Jordon Ibe to replace a winded Coutinho and had two more subs at his disposal. Perhaps it was time to bring fresh legs to help with the full-court press on the attack. "I'd look to bring on Origi," I said to Dan Franklin, who was sitting next to me.

Dan is one of the original Raleigh Reds that helped form our club in 2012. During his college days Dan spent time abroad in England and quickly acquired a love for the sport. He loved the way Michael Owen and Steven Gerrard played for England in the 1998 and 2002 World Cups, and adopted Liverpool as his club. The Premier League wasn't televised very much over here back then, but he was able to follow the Reds when they played in the Champions League. Winning the 2005 Champions League Final helped cement his loyalty. Dan and I became good friends in 2014 when a group of Raleigh Reds traveled to Liverpool for a few matches. We shared a hotel room in London for a few days of the trip. One night his snoring was so obscene that I couldn't get to sleep without the assistance of some music to drown out the sound. The next morning, he apologized because he'd woken up in the middle of night to see me sleeping away as Pink Floyd's *Dark Side of the Moon* blared loudly through my ear buds. He astutely concluded that his snoring was keeping me awake.

"Origi for whom?" Dan asked me. My gut instinct was to see off a midfielder like Lallana, but I wasn't sure. I just knew we needed another striker up front. As I pondered the thought of who to bring on the pitch, I looked up to see Lovren lying on the pitch writhing in pain. He was holding his knee, and the first thought was a possible lengthy injury spell. The television crew got a close-up of the injury, and blood gushed from just below the knee. A few people gasped, as it was clear Lovren would not be able to continue. It took about five minutes, but eventually the medics had him on the stretcher and took him into the locker room. They had even provided an oxygen mask to help keep him from shock. The fans at Anfield gave a standing ovation for the Croatian, which was nice to see for a player that seemed to be reviled a year earlier.

We looked on the television screen to see Klopp giving some last-second instructions to young Divock Origi, apparently coming on to replace the injured Lovren. Dan smiled at me with a nod and said, "Good call."

Almost immediately after the restart, Lallana had the best chance to equalize, getting the ball on a strange breakaway to goal. Unmarked from the left side, Lallana tried to slot the ball past Boaz Myhill, but the goalkeeper saved it nicely with his feet. If an entire pub could curse in unison, then that would've been the moment.

Liverpool continued to press in the final minutes as the clock approached ninety minutes. We knew there would be extensive time added after the Lovren injury, so no one was surprised to see eight additional minutes. Still dominating possession, the Reds continued to press forward. Six minutes into stoppage time, the ball was cleared to the midfield line. Henderson took possession and passed to his left, where Origi got the ball. He beat his man with the ball before clearly getting fouled about thirty-five yards out. Instead of going down to get the call, the Belgian got up and continued forward on the play. At the time it was a questionable decision, because it would seem we would be more likely to score off our own set piece then through the regular run of play. Nonetheless, the ref gave the universal signal to "play on" as Origi continued his forward run.

You could feel the buildup in the pub. It was like watching a balloon continue to fill up with air, just waiting to burst. Origi now looked to move forward into a scoring position, and the entire pub got ready to erupt. When it became evident that he was going to fire from long-range, I heard Colin shout, "NO!" My gut instinct agreed with him.

Origi let loose from twenty-five yards out and somehow found its way into the back of the net. Replays confirmed that the shot had deflected off a West Brom defender, rendering Myhill useless. Just like that, the game was tied in the unlikeliest way. I wasn't complaining. "YES!" came the collective shouts from behind me, most likely including Colin.

I was running around the pub, embracing total strangers and high-fiving friends. My heart was racing as though I had just sprinted a few hundred yards. There was pure joy throughout the pub, yet we had only equalized the match. One of my friends found his way over to me with a smile. "I guess you were right."

I looked at him curiously and asked, "What do you mean?"

"All goals go through Lovren, right?" he replied. "If he doesn't get hurt, then Origi doesn't get subbed on. So technically we can thank Lovren for that goal." I laughed and sat back down to try and catch my breath.

Replays showed Klopp waving his arms, trying to get the fans excited. Earlier in the season, Klopp had been critical of the fans for leaving early due to lack of faith, but not this time. Klopp continued to incite the crowd, and had to be cautioned by the referee. We laughed watching the replay of this moment as Klopp nodded to Pawson in acknowledgement, telling him, "I'm okay." Then he turned back to the stands and waved his arms up one final time. Anfield was louder than it had been in some time.

What a moment that was to witness, but there was still time to snatch a winner. West Brom was clearly reeling from the late goal, and the Reds could press for all three points. Play resumed moments later with a few more Liverpool attacks, but nothing seriously threatened the goal, and the final whistle blew. Both teams looked knackered, but the 2-2 result seemed just. Personally, I was happy to get some sort of result. As the players congratulated each other on the field, television coverage remained on Klopp gathering his team. All eleven players walked over to the Kop with Klopp, hands held together they bowed as though just performing the final scene of a stage play. The only things missing were the roses being thrown at the lead actor and actress. It was Klopp's way of thanking the fans for keeping their faith in the club, not to make that early exit, and they were being rewarded with a dramatic finish.

At the pub, we were getting ready to raffle off some fantastic prizes. Not a single person had left, as we were all still celebrating the drama. The feeling of being at the pub when Liverpool scores a late meaningful goal is difficult to describe. It happened in the opening match at Stoke City, and it's something I hope you get to experience in your lifetime. I soon realized the eerie parallel from the previous year's holiday party, when Liverpool scored an equalizer in stoppage time to snatch a 2-2 draw against Arsenal.

While the result wasn't exactly what we'd envisioned before the match began, it was not surprising, given the inconsistency Liverpool had produced recently. With Klopp at the helm, I felt like we could defeat any opponent on any given day. Unfortunately, the lingering effects of previous regimes left us feeling that we could also lose to any club as well. The roller-coaster ride continued.

16 - ATLANTA

Sunday, December 20
Meehan's Public House, Atlanta, GA
Premier League match #17 (at Watford)

If there is one simple analogy to describe a group of soccer supporters, it would be that of a family. The parents of this family are the club, and they dictate the behavior of the supporters based on its actions and performance on the pitch. As supporters we are the children, blindly following the parent wherever they take us. A few weeks earlier, I'd met with the guys at OLSC Richmond and called them our "little brother." Using a similar reasoning, I would consider the OLSC Atlanta crew as our big brother.

In October 2013 I had accepted the responsibility to obtain official status for LFC Raleigh with the club using their guidelines. At first glance, it appeared to be a daunting task. The club had recently announced that LFC Atlanta had earned their official status, and with family in the area, I decided to make a trip down to the Georgia capital city. It was Saturday December 5, 2013, and Liverpool was playing West Ham United. I convinced my sister Krista and her husband Tom Mullen, both Liverpool fans as well, to join me at Meehan's Public House for the ten a.m. Saturday kickoff.

Even though Tom married into our family, he has become a great friend of mine that shares a deep passion for sports and statistical analysis, specifically as it relates to gambling. Neither one of us spend a lot of money gambling on sports, but we do try to use statistics in an effort to gain an advantage against the house, looking for consistent winning strategies. The fact that we haven't quit our day jobs yet is proof of our success in this venture, but it helps us keep in contact through email as we theorize a new statistical strategy.

Tom grew up in Virginia Beach, and one of his best friends played soccer as a child. His mother was from England and supported Liverpool, and she used to give them both Liverpool trading cards to play with. It was during a time when soccer popularity waned after the collapse of the original North American Soccer League, so there was absolutely no exposure to the sport on television. But his best friend played soccer and he liked Liverpool, so that was enough for Tom. Years later, he met my sister at James Madison University and they eventually got married. When we discovered our shared support for Liverpool Football Club, it helped cement a bond with my brother-in-law. I used to joke with my sister that if she ever got divorced, then I was keeping him in the family. As Krista started taking an interest in the sport, she learned that her two brothers and husband all rooted for Liverpool, so it was a no-brainer for her. Their two sons Matthew and Andrew never really had a choice. The Mullen household became part of the Liverpool family.

My primary agenda was to watch the match at another LFC-friendly pub, but while there I also hoped to get an introduction to Jamie Harrison, one of the founding members of OLSC Atlanta that was ultimately responsible for getting that club their official status. He had already been down the path that I was embarking on for LFC Raleigh at the time, and I wanted to solicit any support that I could get.

Knowing that we would be having some drinks throughout the match, we decided to take the MARTA commuter train into downtown Atlanta from the suburbs. Located in the heart of downtown, Meehan's Public House is a short block from the station. We arrived early at the pub and grabbed a table against the back wall, which seemed ideal. Meehan's is a proper Irish sports bar, with large-screen televisions throughout the establishment. No matter what table you find, there will be a clear view to the main event somewhere in the bar. We started the day with pints of Guinness and watched the OLSC Atlanta crew slowly fill up the joint.

At some point during the match, I looked around for someone that had the appearance of Jamie Harrison's Facebook profile picture. When he walked by our table, I stopped him to introduce myself. Jamie joined us at the table as the Liverpool match played on. He was excited to learn that a group in Raleigh was striving for official club status, much like he had recently obtained for Atlanta. I ordered him a pint of Guinness, and he slowly introduced me to some of the other original members of their club. It turned out that Jamie and Stuart Brennan were the two original Atlanta Kopites who found each other at the same pub watching Liverpool back around 2007. Both Jamie and Stuart hail from the Liverpool area and are lifelong fans of the club. It was just the two of them at first, but word spread quickly and they slowly grew in numbers to where now they have hundreds of supporters that proudly have joined OLSC Atlanta.

It's difficult to tell exactly when that day turned downhill, but my guess would be when Krista looked at a sign behind the bar, which read, "Today's Special: Jell-O Shots for $3." Oh boy, I thought, this could get interesting.

The match ended with Liverpool defeating West Ham 4-1, prompting a lot of songs to be boomed across the pub. My personal favorite was when Jamie and Stuart climbed up on one of the tables, holding up their LFC Atlanta banner, to start the crowd with a version of the anti-Chelsea song: "FUCK OFF, Chelsea FC! You ain't got no history! Five European Cups and eighteen leagues! That's what we call HISTORY!"

As some of the supporters we'd met that morning departed, I noticed that the bar was actually filling to capacity. A table of four men sat next to us wearing University of Missouri shirts, and it occurred to us that the Southeastern Conference college football championship game was being held later that afternoon in the nearby Georgia Dome. Over sixty thousand fans were coming downtown to watch Missouri play Auburn in the region's biggest college football game of the year. These guys had no idea about soccer or how popular a sport it actually was, but when they learned that we had been there drinking since before the kickoff, they were impressed. Krista got them each a $3 Jell-O shot, and at that moment they became Liverpool fans for life.

The morning was winding down and we were getting ready to order some lunch. I had already ordered some fried pickles as a snack, but now it was time for a heartier meal. Jamie returned to our table and convinced us to delay our lunch plans, as he was leading a group of LFC fans to another pub. Apparently Manchester United had lost their match and Jamie wanted to go visit their home pub to rub it in. Why not?

We got the check from the server and immediately inventoried what we'd consumed in the three short hours of our morning:

- Thirteen pints of Guinness
- Twenty-two Jell-O shots
- One Harp Shandy
- One fried pickles

Tom got our server's attention and showed him the bill. "There must be some mistake," he said. The waiter looked over the bill, trying to figure out what he had gotten wrong. Tom smiled slyly and added, "We didn't drink any damn shandy!" I thought Jamie must've snuck that order in when I was at the bathroom or something. We had a small chuckle and gladly paid the bill.

Later that afternoon, we found ourselves at Fado's Irish Pub in midtown Atlanta, home of the Manchester United supporter's club. There were a few Mancs hanging around the pub watching the late match, and Jamie was quick to start singing some Liverpool chants. At first I was a little concerned about a possible fracas ensuing, but it turned out that most of the supporters clubs in Atlanta are all friendly with each other, and no one seemed to mind. In fact, the camaraderie amongst competing clubs is so strong in Atlanta that big matches are often watched by both clubs at the home pub of the team hosting the match. When Tottenham and Liverpool play at White Hart Lane, the OLSC Atlanta crew will march through downtown Atlanta from Meehan's Public House to the home pub of the Atlanta Spurs, another Meehan's pub located at nearby Atlantic Station.

Later in 2014, as we worked toward becoming an official LFC supporters club, I would get the occasional text from Jamie about our progress. I wasn't really sure what he was doing at the time, but a lot of these texts would come through my phone about the same time bars were closing all across the Eastern time zone. Even more bizarre was the fact that I was awake to reply to each one of them. Jamie put in a good word with the club on our behalf and helped me put together a great application. When I got the call to approve our application later that May, I had Jamie to thank for the assist.

Later that summer, we were reunited for another weekend of shenanigans when Liverpool came to Charlotte as part of their summer preseason tour. Together with OLSC Atlanta, we set up multiple joint parties at various establishments before and after the match. It solidified a bond between our two clubs, and I'll always be grateful to both Jamie and Stuart for their help in getting OLSC Raleigh to where we are today. I consider them my big brother, always ready to give us a hand.

****

Returning to Meehan's as part of this journey was an absolute no-brainer. I timed the visit around the holidays, as it would help punch the family ticket at the same time. Unlike my first visit to Meehan's, this was a Sunday morning match, and Georgia has blue laws just as strict as North Carolina. There would be no pints of Guinness or Jell-O shots for this match.

At one point, OLSC Atlanta tried locking the front door to the pub on Sunday morning, saying that they were "closed for a private party." Members would enter the pub through the back entrance adjacent to the Westin hotel. It worked for a short time, but then one day a non-member walked in and asked the manager how they were able to legally bypass the state's blue law. When he was told that they were closed for a private party, the question was asked: "If it's so private, then how did I get in?" That was the end of Sunday morning libations during LFC matches at Meehan's.

Prior to my arrival, I had been notified by my friends that neither Jamie nor Stuart were going to be in town. Jamie had moved to the country of Colombia, while Stuart was off on his own holiday, visiting family back in England. They left me in the very capable hands of Michael Crump, who was waiting for us with his son Gavin when we arrived. The match was slated for an early eight thirty a.m. kickoff on the Sunday before Christmas, so not exactly prime conditions for good attendance. Still, the fans were piling into the pub just before the match kicked off. I ordered a cup of coffee and got settled into my seat.

Watford was a recently promoted club returning to the Premier League for the first time since the 2006-07 campaign, and are more known as the club once owned by Sir Elton John in the 1970s. Looking at their starting lineup, I was unfamiliar with most of their players. Former Tottenham goalkeeper Heurelho Gomes was the only player that I had recognized. Liverpool's recent form had shown a propensity for them to play down to the skill level of their opponent. The recent loss at Newcastle (nineteenth place at the time) and come-from-behind draw against West Bromwich Albion (thirteenth place at the time) was not considered good form. I was surprised to learn that Watford were actually *ahead* of Liverpool on the table, sitting at seventh place, with one more point than Liverpool. They weren't exactly a bottom-feeder.

The big news of the morning was how Simon Mignolet had failed a fitness test on the weekend, so backup goalkeeper Adam Bogdan would be called into duty for his first Premier League start with Liverpool. It would prove to be an important factor early in the match. The other question mark on defense was the return of Mamadou Sakho, who had been sidelined with a knee injury for many weeks. The timing of his return was great, after Dejan Lovren was stitched up the match before. His prognosis was more promising, with a return likely after sitting out this match. I was initially concerned that Sakho might be a bit rusty, but he'd been rock solid before his injury, so I was hoping for the best.

The game kicked off with Watford gaining possession early. They earned a corner kick in the third minute of play, which was taken by Ben Watson. He played the ball inside the six-yard box, and it should've been an easy catch for the Hungarian stopper. Bogdan fumbled the first ball, which hit straight down on the ground. Surrounded by a group of Watford attackers, Bogdan reached to recover and got both hands on the ball at the same time that Chelsea loan Nathan Ake kicked upward. Replays would confirm Bogdan appeared to have control of the ball when Ake kicked it free, a clear violation of the rules, but referee Mark Clattenburg didn't agree, and let play continue. Ake pounced on the loose ball, giving Watford the early 1-0 lead.

People were still making their way into the pub. When they looked at the score, there was instant disbelief. Ross Sloop walked in with his brother

Scott, who was in town from Nashville. I had met Ross during the Charlotte weekend in August of 2014, so it was good to see a friendly face. After a quick greeting, he asked me what happened on the goals. "Another corner kick goal conceded," I replied. It was all that needed to be said.

Play continued as Liverpool tried to build up some momentum, but there was a lack of cohesion that was evident after that first goal. Watford fans were singing in the stands, enjoying the early lead, and their joy escalated even further in the fifteenth minute when Nigerian striker Odion Ighalo raced onto a nice through ball played by Troy Deeney. He only had to beat Martin Skrtel to get on target, and fired a low shot past Bogdan into the far post, netting from a tight angle. I'd barely had time to put cream in my coffee before Liverpool was trailing 2-0.

The pub was silent in disbelief when a loud man sitting out the bar shouted, "For fuck's sake, they are playing like Sunday League Football!" I assumed that he meant the traditional form of adult recreational soccer for amateurs like me, because that was exactly how I would've described Liverpool's first half. That comment came from Raj Patel, a forty-five-year old IT sales representative from England. Raj was born in the Midlands, but moved all around the English country before relocating to Atlanta in 1998. He picked Liverpool as his favorite club in the seventies because they wore all red, including shorts and socks. Red was his favorite color growing up, but he didn't like how Arsenal had white sleeves and Manchester United wore white shorts. Liverpool was a hundred percent red from neck to toe, so that was all he needed to be a Red himself.

The first half was winding to a close when Skrtel fell awkwardly on his back. When Skrtel stays down for an injury, it means it's legitimate. The Slovakian defender is one of the few players I've ever seen get his head stapled shut so he could continue playing. Skrtel remained down with what appeared to be another hamstring injury. Already down 2-0 on the road, Klopp elected the dramatic swap of replacing Skrtel with striker Divock Origi. I liked the move at the time because the club needed something to jump-start the anemic offense. Origi didn't have enough time to make an impact before the break, so the clubs went in at halftime with Watford leading 2-0.

Whenever I travel to another pub, I like to use the halftime break to introduce myself to the local supporters and hopefully meet new friends. In Atlanta I had already known most of the people there from my first visit in December 2013 and the Charlotte preseason match in August 2014. Adam Wright is one such individual that I consider a good friend, so much so that I invited him to drive up and stay at my house when his beloved dog passed away earlier in the year. He nearly took me up on my offer before deciding last minute to change plans and visit his brother instead. It had been over a year since we saw each other, so we hugged and spent some time catching up.

Adam is a typical single guy that puts his soccer club before his relationships. I respect that very much. He moved to the area from St. Louis with his family in 1996. He learned that his grandfather served in England during World War II and became friends with many Liverpool supporters during that time. During the Champions League final in 2005, he happened to be visiting a girlfriend that was living in Nashville at the time. They went a local bar and he noticed Liverpool was playing AC Milan. Admittedly, he wasn't a big fan at the time, but many Liverpool fans were at that bar watching the match, and he knew that was his grandfather's team. His girlfriend didn't appreciate the lack of attention, so she tried to get him to leave. He handed her some cash and told her to "catch a cab," and that he'd meet her back at the apartment. Liverpool was losing 0-3 at the time, so I can imagine the girlfriend was not at all happy. When Xabi Alonso scored in the sixtieth minute to tie the match 3-3, someone called his girlfriend to tell her about it. She grabbed another cab back to the bar, where Adam was found still watching the match. She needed even more cash to pay that particular cab, which Adam reluctantly gave her. Needless to say, that relationship didn't work out, and he remains single today. He makes certain that any new girlfriend is well aware that Liverpool will always come first, which, in his words, is probably why he's still single.

I also took some time to talk with Brandon Ivey, another Atlanta regular. Brandon and I share another passion when it comes to Liverpool, a passion to try and quantify as much as possible into simple statistics. Brandon would always share great statistical insight on the OLSC Atlanta Facebook page, which probably looks like Greek to most fans, but I always appreciated the articles that he would post. It's the sort of connection that only guys with degrees in a math-related discipline can appreciate.

It was apparent that Klopp had taken advantage of the break to get his team on the same page. While the Reds took control of the match in the second half, they simply couldn't break down the Watford defense. I couldn't help but feel like one Liverpool goal would be enough to spark the club back into the match, but they simply couldn't find a way to get the ball past Gomes. The fate of the match was sealed in the eighty-fifth once Ighalo headed home a fine goal on the counterattack. Down by three goals to none, there was no coming back for Liverpool.

After the final whistle, the guys gathered around the pub to discuss the debacle. I looked over to Raj, shaking my head in disgust. "Utter crap," I told him.

"Calling that crap is a direct insult to crap itself," he countered. "I don't know want to call that."

Raj seemed to have the pulse of the pub with those comments. To make matters worse, we couldn't even get a proper pint to drown out our sorrows. It was barely past ten a.m. on a Sunday. Michael Crump came back over to thank me for stopping at the pub on my tour, and presented me with a beautiful gift. OLSC Atlanta had mini-flasks made with their official logo on one side, but Michael had one specially engraved with my name to document this visit. It was a sincere gesture, and I was only disappointed that the flask contained no alcohol.

After the game, we watched the post-match interviews. I was happy to see that Bogdan accepted responsibility for the first goal. While it could be argued that the play should've been whistled once Ake kicked the ball out of his hand, Bogdan simply stated, "If I catch the first ball, there is no second." Truer words could not have been spoken under those circumstances.

Klopp was also honest and frank in his post-match interview. It was clearly a disappointing result, and he was upset. The defense looked shaky, with Sakho looking extremely rusty all match. Post-match pundits were giving Sakho an abysmal three out of ten possible rating points, unheard of for the French defender. With Skrtel destined to be sidelined for a period, Liverpool was slated to face surprise league leaders Leicester City in the next match. These guys had scored in all seventeen league matches played to date, so if the Liverpool defense couldn't figure something out in a few short days, then it could get ugly. I was hopeful that Lovren would be ready to return, or else it would time for Kolo Toure to step back into the mix.

I said goodbye to my many friends from Atlanta and headed back to my sister's house north of the city. It was a disappointing result to be sure, but I am always happy to return to Meehan's whenever in town for a Liverpool match. You couldn't meet a more hospitable group of guys. As I shook hands with Michael Crump, I was happy to tell him, "See you soon," and know that it was the truth.

17 - NY KOPITES

Saturday, December 26
The Boot Room, New York, NY
Premier League match #18 (vs. Leicester City)

The day after Christmas is traditionally known as Boxing Day in the United Kingdom. Because servants would spend their Christmas days working for their employers, they would celebrate the holiday on the following day. As a gesture of thanks for their efforts, the employer would often gift a "Christmas box" of money and presents to their servants as they delayed their holidays by a day. While the day itself has morphed into a bank holiday celebrated mostly by discount shopping for bargain hunters, the Premier League has its own tradition of gifting football fans with a full day of matches to enjoy on their day off work.

When I made the decision to write this book, the first date on the calendar to get assigned a city was Boxing Day. Every year my Christmas holiday is spent with family in the New York City area, so it was a no-brainer planning to watch Liverpool host Leicester City at one of the numerous LFC pubs around the Big Apple.

With over eight million residents, New York is easily the largest city in the country. One would logically presume that they have the largest base of Liverpool supporters as well. The official supporters club formed during the 1995-96 season and quickly became the first OLSC in North America. They also have the largest following. Their primary home pub for all matches is the 11th Street Bar, located in the lower East Village. I had the pleasure of visiting this pub when Liverpool came to the city on their 2014 summer preseason tour. With less than a thousand square feet of space, it's not the largest pub in the city, but it has the tremendous atmosphere that you would expect in a tavern in the hip neighborhood. The club has recently joined up with The Grafton, another local watering hole a short block away. If supporters fail to get a good seat at the 11th Street Bar, they can walk over to The Grafton.

New York is much more than just the island of Manhattan, so over time the club has extended its reach to the other boroughs and surrounding suburbs. They now list official pubs in Brooklyn (The Monro), Queens (The Ceili House), Long Island (Prost Grill and Garten in Garden City), and even New Jersey (The Cottage Bar in Teaneck). With so many options available, it's an embarrassment of riches for members of the OLSC New York. Yet for simple logistical reasons, I chose to watch the Leicester City match at none of those official pubs.

The Irish-American Bar sits in the basement of one of the large buildings located in the city's Financial District. Owned by lifelong Liverpool supporter Brian McLaughlin, he named this watering hole after the famous McHale's Irish-American Bar located on Lime Street in Liverpool. The original Irish-American Bar opened in 1830, but it acquired its connection to the states during the first world war when the American servicemen stationed in Liverpool began frequenting the tavern. For that reason they started calling it the "American Bar." After the war it was acquired by former boxing promoter and Irishman Terry McHale, which is where the Irish-American connection originated. Brian had decided to honor this famous downtown Liverpool establishment by using the same name for his bar located on John Street just a few blocks from the 9/11 Memorial and Museum is located.

New York's Irish-American Bar has a separate room dedicated to Liverpool Football Club called the Boot Room located adjacent to the main room of the tavern. Originally intended to be a simple game room for his patrons, Brian eventually turned it into Liverpool fan's dream cave. Supporters clubs from all across the world have donated scarves, which now hang in the Boot Room in addition to the numerous club memorabilia that Brian has acquired over the years. In fact, an LFC Raleigh scarf hangs above a mirror engraved with the words "You'll Never Walk Alone." Since New York isn't exactly the easiest city for driving and parking, it made sense for me to take the ferry over from my in-laws' home on Staten Island and walk to the Irish-American Bar from the ferry terminal.

I walked into the Boot Room about fifteen minutes before kickoff and found a spot at the bar. I barely had time to get settled into my seat before a young bartender welcomed me with a smile. In a subtle Irish accent, he asked, "Pint of Guinness, mate?" I had to do a double take to make sure it wasn't one of the fine bartenders from the London Bridge Pub. How could they know my drink of choice so quickly, I wondered. I wanted to blurt out a sarcastic response, but I was dumbfounded and could only nod and reply, "Sounds good." In retrospect, it was probably a safe guess. As it turned out, my arrival was anticipated. Tales of my journey had made its way to Brian, who ensured that I was given a proper welcome upon arrival.

Riain Clifford was working the bar that morning, and he's lifelong Liverpool supporter from Dublin, having moved to New York about five years ago. As I looked around the magnificent shrine to the club, he pointed over to where the LFC Raleigh scarf hung. As he served my pint, he commented, "You're a bit early; most of the guys will show up just before kickoff." Already I knew it was going to be a good day.

The NYC Kopites are a club of Liverpool fans that somehow found each other over the years. Much like many of the supporters I have met across the country, most of the NYC Kopites are expatriates that have relocated to New York for work. I've asked why they don't join the crowd at the 11th Street Bar, and the most common reason is that it gets too crowded during matches. Being a member of the OLSC comes with many benefits, including access to tickets to visit Anfield for a live match. Many expatriates have other means to acquire match tickets when they return to England, so they don't see much advantage to joining the OLSC. Instead of making plans to get to the pub early enough to get a good seat, the NYC Kopites prefer to watch Liverpool with other fans in a less crowded environment.

It was still a few minutes before kickoff as other fans started wandering into the Boot Room. Riain called me over to the other side of the bar, where two regulars sat dressed in their Liverpool kits. I grabbed my things and moved over next to Greg Hardin and Vikas Bhatia, who were already discussing the difficult test ahead of the Reds.

Without question, Leicester City was the talk of the Premier League. The newly promoted club had spent the previous season fighting relegation. They won three of their final four matches to stay in the top flight, and everyone expected a similar battle for survival would ensue this season. Through journeyman striker Jamie Vardy and Algerian midfielder Riyad Mahrez, the Foxes had scored in every Premier League match of the season to date, and found themselves at the top of the table on Christmas Day. It was such a statistical improbability that one betting parlor paid a thousand to one odds for Leicester City to be leading the league on Christmas Day. It turned out to be a very happy Christmas for one fan that collected £5000 on that wager.

Earlier in the season, Vardy had established a new league record, scoring in eleven straight matches. The team had scored in every league match so far, with thirty-seven goals scored in total, and Liverpool would be without Martin Skrtel to injury. Having only earned one point in the three most recent league matches against Newcastle, West Bromwich Albion, and Watford did not give us much confidence heading into this match.

Klopp went with a slightly more attacking approach, leaving Lucas out of the starting eleven in place of a lone striker. Interestingly enough, he picked Divock Origi to play that role instead of Christian Benteke. This past summer the club had spent more money to acquire Benteke than any other player in its history, yet he would have to watch his younger countryman start in his place.

Both Greg Hardin and Vikas Bhatia were nervously making their match predictions when I interrupted their conversation. Greg lives in the Bronx, working web design from home as his day job, while Vikas runs his own IT consulting firm in the city. The two fans represent both sides of the spectrum as it relates to rooting for Liverpool. Greg started rooting for the club around 2008 when he lived in Los Angeles. He was always watching soccer when the World Cup came around every four years, and then he picked up the European Championships when ESPN televised that tournament in the summer of 2008. Spain was the dominant team at the time, and he fell in love with Fernando Torres for the style and class he displayed during that tournament. When Greg learned that these talented athletes actually played for a paycheck during the fall and winter months, and that those matches were televised on Fox Soccer Channel, he quickly adopted Torres' Liverpool Football Club as his favorite team.

While Greg's support for the Reds is in its infancy, Vikas has been with the club his whole life. Born and raised in East London, he actually wanted to become a West Ham United supporter. He was about five years old when he heard a neighbor singing the West Ham anthem "Forever Blowing Bubbles." He started singing at the house when he father stopped him, telling him, "If you want to be like those guys, then go live with those guys." Surely his father was not seriously considering kicking his son out of the house for singing a silly song, but a five-year-old Vikas wasn't taking that chance. His cousin lived nearby and supported Liverpool, and he wasn't getting kicked out of the house. He figured Liverpool was an acceptable club for the family. Twenty-five years later, the long-suffering Reds fan moved to America. Both Greg and Vikas came from different backgrounds in different parts of the world, yet both appeared to be the best of friends sitting at the bar moments before kickoff. It's almost surreal to think about.

The Boot Room started to fill up, with not a single seat open at the bar. Smaller groups of fans sat in the booths, watching one of the numerous big screens around the pub. Magically a small plastic shot glass filled with a gold-colored liquor appeared before my eyes. I looked around and saw Riain holding up a shot. Urging the other Kopites in a toast, he shouted, "UP THE REDS!" It would be the first of many.

The starting lineups walked onto the pitch as the stadium sang "You'll Never Walk Alone" loudly and proudly. Flags were once again flying in the Kop after a long hiatus, creating a fervent atmosphere for this important match. I had my second pint of Guinness in front of me, and was brimming with more confidence. It was definitely going to be a great day.

From the start of the match, Liverpool looked the better squad. They held the majority of possession and dangerously pushed forward on the attack. Jordan Henderson and Emre Can bossed the midfield around as though they had been playing together for years. It had been a long time since I had seen the captain take command, and my confidence continued to grow. Their dominance in the middle allowed Philippe Coutinho the freedom to roam forward with Roberto Firmino and Adam Lallana. In the first fifteen minutes, Coutinho let loose on three shots, which showed the attacking intent that had been lacking in recent weeks.

"They're all over these bastards!" was a claim I heard to my immediate left. I was so focused on the match that I didn't even notice a young English lad that had taken a seat next to me. I nodded to him in agreement, because he spoke the truth. We were all over those bastards and, quite frankly, deserved the lead. Leicester City was content to sit back and defend in hopes of catching our weakened defense on the counterattack.

It turned out that my new neighbor was Liam Coleman, a former professional footballer from Colchester, England. Liam was proud to call himself a member of the Essex Reds Supporters Club based on the east coast of England. He signed his first professional contract at the age of eighteen for Colchester United, but failed to make the first team, and was sent to Torquay United the following summer. His professional career was the prototypical journeyman career, toiling around the lower divisions hoping to catch a break. Unfortunately, injuries would end his career, as he could never gain full fitness, and he left England to become a coaching director for a youth academy in Bergen County, New Jersey. Turned out the guy knew a little about the sport. I made a mental note to listen closely to his analysis.

There was a palpable groan in the room when Origi pulled lame with a hamstring injury in the thirty-eighth minute of the match. Hamstring injuries were becoming an issue for the club, with Daniel Sturridge still shelved recovering. I know from personal experience how challenging this injury can be, having pulled my right hamstring during my college career. No matter how long you take, it never fully heals.

"This is not good," claimed Liam. "We need Origi's speed up top to keep the defense honest. Now [Klopp]'s got no choice but to bring on Benteke, and the defense can bunker down and play for the cross."

I reminded him about some of the world-class goals that Benteke had already scored for the club, but we both knew that he was probably right. Liverpool would need to change their tactics, but thankfully Klopp would have the halftime break to do just that. The whistle blew with the score knotted at 0-0.

I looked around the Boot Room at halftime and noticed a pretty good crowd had found its way to this remote hideout. Riain continued to restock everyone's beer supply while simultaneously introducing me to the other NYC Kopites in attendance. A trio of wonderful young ladies was the first to chat with me, keenly aware of my project. Sam Wood is a true Scouser from Liverpool, having relocated to New Jersey five years ago with her husband. As she put it, it was easy rooting for the Reds. Being raised in Liverpool leaves you with two choices of clubs, and there was no way she was going to root for the "blue shite."

Erin Gromen was the second young lass of the trio, but I couldn't tell immediately if she was a fan of the club or just the group's official photographer. She had the type of camera you see professionals using at a wedding, snapping great pictures to capture the atmosphere of the moment. My ego was telling me that she'd brought it specifically for this occasion, but it turned out photography was simply a convenient hobby. Erin is married to Joe Cadigan, also in attendance for the match. With Joe's full beard and red flannel shirt tied around his waist, I wasn't sure if he was in the right place before Erin introduced us. It turned out they both fell in love with the sport when they took a trip to Argentina. Football season was its peak during their trip, and the passion they witnessed had them hooked. When they got home, they discovered that the Premier League was covered significantly more on television than the Argentina Primera Liga, so they each picked a team to root for. Erin was initially embarrassed to admit that she picked the Reds simply because they were based in Liverpool, home to her beloved Beatles. I quickly assured her that was a completely legitimate reason, explaining how my own love was solidified through a Pink Floyd song. She did admit that her love for Liverpool was confirmed once she learned that the club had a guy from Slovakia on the team. Being of Slovakian descent herself, the fact that Martin Skrtel was a Red sealed the deal. Being a good husband, Joe agreed to join forces and root for the Reds as well.

The last young lady I met at halftime was Sabina Nelson. The Dallas-born pediatrician has always been a fan of the sport, and picked Liverpool because that's who her English cousins rooted for back in the day. Sabina talked about trying to create a "family culture" in the Boot Room where supporters could bring their kids on match day. She talked about having LFC-themed coloring books for the kids to work on while the adults watched the match. Admittedly, I don't have children, but I can't think of a better place to host childhood daycare. Better for the child as well as the parent! Sabina recently got married to Kevin Shevlin, a bartender at Carragher's Pub near Times Square. Kevin is from Belfast, not far from Brian's hometown in Northern Ireland. Sabina admitted that despite getting officially married by a justice of the peace, her NYC Kopite friends held their own ceremony in the Boot Room, with a small reception following. I've always been told that fans consider football a religion, so having a wedding at your football pub with your fellow supporters seemed natural.

I was enthralled to learn more about all of my new friends, and I could've talked to them for hours, but the second half was about to kick off. It was time to regain focus on the match. Liam had left my side at halftime to chat with his mates in a nearby booth, but he soon returned to the bar once play resumed.

Klopp made no changes at halftime, presumably because the Origi injury had forced him to use one of his substitutions already. Ten minutes had passed when Liam pointed out how the club was working the flanks a bit more than in the first half. We assumed this a tactical move, which eventually paid off in the sixty-third minute. Emre Can fed the ball to Firmino on the left side, as the Brazilian worked to create some space near that edge of the penalty box. He crossed over to a lunging Benteke, who was able to get significant pace from the inside of his foot past a diving Kasper Schmeichel. It was a brilliant play. It was nice to see a goal scored from Liverpool's talented new acquisitions. Firmino had been largely silent in the last month, so it was good to see him get involved in the goal.

Quite obviously, the pub erupted. I jumped out of my chair and immediately started hugging Greg to my right. I looked to my left to see Liam pounding the bar with his fist in celebration, as others behind me embraced as well. I had only met these people just over an hour ago, yet you could feel the relief of frustration that had been building up inside everyone for weeks. Suddenly all was well with the world again.

It doesn't take much to get a crowd going, and one excited fan couldn't help to increase the mood by starting a chant. "WE ARE LIVERPOOL!" he cheered loudly, followed by an entire bar full of supporters responding, "TRA LA LA LA LA!" The song continued through to the end with the line "We're the best football team in the land! YES WE ARE!"

Within seconds of that chant ending, another supporter at the end of the bar had his say by yelling, "OH, WHEN THE REDS!" which was immediately repeated back by the rest of the pub at the top of their lungs. The instigator continued, "GO MARCHING IN!" The next thing you knew, there was more singing, dancing, and clapping to the hymn "When the Saints Go Marching In." The hair on the back of my neck stood up. For a brief moment, I felt as though I was sitting in the Kop celebrating with the season ticket holders at Anfield.

After another round of shots courtesy of Riain, the mood settled back in. It's fine to be excited about taking the lead, but all too often earlier this season the club would let in a late equalizer. It feels strange to admit, but somehow this match felt different. I never felt like we were going to concede. Maybe it was the Klopp Effect, or maybe it was the mood inside the Boot Room. Whatever it was, I confidently watched the Reds defend with pride. I wasn't even upset when Benteke missed the open net in the closing seconds, vacated when Schmeichel pressed forward to aid the Leicester City attack.

The final whistle blew with Liverpool defeating the league leaders 1-0. It was an important three points for the Reds and the catalyst for what would become a great afternoon. Soon after the match finished, I received a text message from my wife, indicating that she'd arrived in Midtown and wanted to do some shopping. The clock on the wall said noon, so I advised her that we would be relocating the party to Carragher's in a few hours. And then Riain handed me another shot of gold with a fresh pint of Guinness.

Erin attempted to corral the group to a single point and get a group photo. It took some effort, but it also gave me time to meet some of the guys from the other side of the bar. Robby Lundon and his friend were over from Galway, Ireland, in town for a wedding. I asked him how he came to find the Boot Room. In a word, "Google." They were joined by countryman Mark O'Keeffe at the bar. Mark is from the small county town of Wicklow just south of Dublin and works for the Irish Red Cross. He travels across the pond every Christmas to spend the holidays with his sister. A few days earlier he was sightseeing around town and noticed an Irish and Liverpool flag hanging outside a pub on John Street. It intrigued him enough to give the Boot Room a try for the next match. In previous years he would trek up to the 11th Street Bar for the Boxing Day match. His sister lives in Staten Island and he took a morning ferry over and walked through the Financial District to the pub like I did. I wonder if we were on the same ferry earlier in the morning?

Multiple group pictures were taken, and plans were discussed. Some fans departed for home, but the core remained. We continued to sing songs, drink some pints, and celebrate the win. A tall young man handed me another pint and introduced himself to me. Russ Garton hails from Birkinhead, and is another lifelong Liverpool fan that relocated to New York City about eleven years ago. Russ works in the financial industry, and I inquired about life for the expatriate LFC fan living in the Big Apple. He replied, "I used to be a member of LFC NY and I'm still good friends with those guys. It's just that the club outgrew their pub over time. It gets too crowded, and I just want to enjoy myself watching the match. When I found this place, I knew it was a new home for me."

It was an epiphany of sorts. I was starting to understand the need for a separate club. New York City is too big for just one team in a sports league. In every major American sport, there are at least two teams that call the NYC area home. Baseball has the Yankees and Mets. Football has the Jets and Giants. Basketball has the Knicks and Nets. Hockey has the Rangers, Islanders, and Devils. Soccer has the Red Bulls, NYC FC, and the Cosmos.

It makes sense that they could get away with having two supporters clubs that serve two different types of fans.

I took another swig from the pint that Russ gave me and suddenly heard a shout that I wasn't expecting. "LAST CALL!" shouted Riain. I looked at the clock on the wall, which read two thirty, and replied, "But it's only two thirty."

"If you want to stay here, go next door. But I'm headed up to Carragher's now," he answered.

"Makes sense. Gimme one more pint of Guinness and close out my tab, please."

Riain motioned over to the computer screen. "Ken, do you see your name on this screen?" It was a simple question that only required a shake of my head. "Your drinks are on us today. Thanks for coming down."

It was overwhelming. Food and drink are more expensive in Manhattan establishments, so I don't even want to speculate what the bar tab would've been. The NYC Kopites provided me with my first "Christmas box" to celebrate Boxing Day, and I couldn't have been more flattered. I passed over a nice cash tip to Riain, thanking him again for the great day.

It wasn't until I nearly finished my final pint at the Boot Room that I saw the text message come across. It was the wife. *Done shopping. I'm at Carragher's now.*

Uh-oh. I'd figured we had enough time to get this rowdy bunch uptown before Tori was done shopping. That was three hours ago, and somehow we were still in the Boot Room. I typically find that it's better to keep my replies short and try to explain later. I typed into my phone: *Leaving now. Get a snack if you want. Be there shortly.*

We left the Boot Room and headed to the subway. Some of the patrons had left with their friends and family, but we still had about a dozen Reds taking the E train uptown to Carragher's. We were certainly the most jovial crowd waiting on the platform for the next train, singing songs for everyone to enjoy. I saw a few rolled eyes, but mostly the other people smiled and enjoyed the show. Someone even took off their Santa hats and tried to get a collection started for our efforts.

The train arrived with few seats available, so most of us stood as best we could. One of the Galway guys started the "We are Liverpool" chant, which prompted another large singalong. Most of the locals didn't appreciate our jubilation, and they relocated to another car. We didn't mind, as it opened up a few seats for us to rest our weary legs.

Somehow we made it safely to our destination without anyone getting arrested or clobbered by a local. All things considered, that was an accomplishment. Carragher's Pub is located a few short blocks from Times Square—a prime location to attract the tourist crowd on match day. Brian McLaughlin acquired the space a few years ago with an idea to create an authentic British pub in the touristy spot. He had connections with some of the folks running Jamie Carragher's charitable foundation, so he brought up the idea of forming a partnership to use the Liverpool legend's name. Much to his surprise and delight, he obtained permission.

We walked into the pub to see another crowd of Kopites singing along. I immediately bypassed the bar and found Tori sitting at a table in front of the big screen. She had a bowl of French onion soup that she had snacked on waiting for my arrival. We spoke for a few minutes as some of my new friends came over to meet my wife. Much like the reception I got walking into the Boot Room about six hours earlier, Tori was immediately embraced as one of their own. It was the camaraderie that we have come to expect as Liverpool fans.

We ordered a late lunch as I caught up with Brian. I had never met the pub owner until that moment, but corresponded enough through social media and email that I considered him a good friend. We watched Southampton dismantle Arsenal 4-0 in the late game and consumed more pints of Guinness. Brian gave us the tour of his new joint, explaining to me his future growth plans. If he can pull it together, and from what I have already seen at the Boot Room, I have no doubt that he will, then Carragher's Pub will become a destination not to be missed.

I looked at the clock. It was five eighteen p.m., and I looked around the pub. The gang was still there: Riain, Sam, Sabina and Kevin, Erin and Joe, Liam, Greg, Russ, and the Galway guys. With all of the live soccer matches done for the day, the television was showing highlights of all 186 goals scored in Steven Gerrard's Liverpool career. The Beatles were playing over the speakers. For the second time in the day, I felt almost as if I had been transported across the pond.

Never in my wildest dreams did I expect this party to last as long as it did. Tori and I had made dinner reservations for seven forty-five p.m., which in retrospect may have been a good thing. We didn't want to leave this party, but it gave us a hard out. I thought back to the first date I had with my beautiful wife in 2003, where we ended up in a Greenwich Village tavern until four a.m.. Without a concrete reason to leave Carragher's Pub, I believe we easily could've had a similar experience.

Despite numerous attempts to persuade us to stay, Tori and I say our goodbyes and departed. I couldn't have scripted a better day. From the moment I set foot into the Boot Room, I was welcomed with open arms. So many of us didn't know each other before the day began. Now we considered ourselves to be great friends. It's what I love about this sport and about this club specifically. We are Liverpool. Tra la la la la.

18 - SCAVENGERS

Wednesday, December 30
Scavengers Bar, Chatham County, NC
Premier League match #19 (vs. Sunderland)

As I'm president of the OLSC based in Raleigh, many people are surprised to discover that I actually live about an hour's drive from the pub in rural North Carolina. I moved to the state in 2007 when a work opportunity opened the door for my escape from New Jersey. Tori and I moved to an apartment in Raleigh as we searched for our new home. We eventually settled on rural Chatham County in the unincorporated town of Silk Hope. It's far enough away from civilization that we could escape from reality, yet close to enough to Raleigh that my commute was half of what it was living in New Jersey. The fact that my work colleague and new friend Tom Brewer lived in the area helped immensely. Tom helped recruit me to the area, so the fact that he lived only ten minutes away helped convince me that I'd made the right decision moving out to the country.

Tom moved to the Raleigh area in the eighties from Kentucky, a pure-bred Wildcat that lives and dies by Kentucky basketball. When he and his wife Lisa lived in the downtown area of Five Points, they became great friends with their neighbors Charles and Susan Thomas. Charles worked for years on the railroad and now plies his trade as an expert carpenter. Together they bonded and eventually formed their first garage bar, which they dubbed Scavengers.

Over time they decided it was time to leave the growing metropolis of Raleigh, and found close to forty acres of riverfront property about an hour west of town. They jumped at the opportunity and relocated to the country, building their new homes only a few hundred yards away from each other, despite having acres of space to choose from. In 2009 they decided to recreate the Scavengers experience with a new six-hundred-square-foot cabin built from scratch. Over time they were able to outfit the new bar with all of the proper amenities, including two televisions (each with their own satellite television receiver) and four beer taps. They pulled out old pictures and trinkets from the original Five Points Scavengers to authenticate the environment. After a few pints behind closed doors, it was likely you'd forget that you weren't actually in a public commercial establishment.

Scavengers became the local first choice for three sporting events: Kentucky basketball, NASCAR, and Sunday NFL Football. I remember the day that I helped turned Scavengers into a Liverpool pub as well.

For most sports fans in the Raleigh-Durham area, the early part of February is all about college basketball. That is until the third Sunday, when stock cars finally hit the track for the Great American Sports Race known as the Daytona 500. NASCAR's biggest race, it is also the start to a long season and one of the most anticipated sporting events in the southeast. NASCAR is so ingrained in the culture of rural North Carolina that it has practically become a local holiday to watch the season-opening Daytona 500 every February at Scavengers.

In February 2012, the Liverpool Football Club was still in recovery mode. Former American owners Tom Hicks and George Gillette had driven the club to the brink of bankruptcy, and were forced into selling the club after the Royal Bank of Scotland won a court battle in October of 2010. The new ownership group led by Boston Red Sox owner John Henry stepped in to acquire the club for £300m. This venture was called Fenway Sports Group (FSG), and came in with high aspirations to return to the club to glory. The success achieved in bringing the Red Sox their first World Series championship in eighty-six years after only three years of ownership gave the Liverpool faithful hope that they could duplicate the feat with the Reds.

FSG had only owned the club for a few months when they parted ways with manager Roy Hodgson. Liverpool living legend "King" Kenny Dalglish returned from the unknown to become the club caretaker as FSG developed their long-term plan. After a subpar 2010-11 campaign where Liverpool finished well below expectations, FSG retained the services of Dalglish with the hopes of giving the fans something to get excited about. The first real step in that direction was when Liverpool advanced to the League Cup final to be played at Wembley Stadium on February 26, 2012, against Cardiff City. It was Liverpool's first legitimate chance at a trophy since winning the 2006 FA Cup on penalties against West Ham. This reinvigorated my passion for the club, as now I was certain that I needed to watch this final.

At the time of this final, LFC Raleigh hadn't yet been formed. I wouldn't meet Colin Russell and Darren Bridger until the next summer. I knew that I wanted to watch this match in a pub environment with pints of draught beer as opposed to my couch. As luck would have it, the final was to kick off exactly two hours before the green flag was scheduled to fly for the Daytona 500. Clearly there would be people at Scavengers getting ready for the annual Daytona 500 party, so it would stand to reason that I should be able to watch the Capital One Cup final there before the race began. No one would really care if I watched some silly soccer match on one of the two televisions.

I arrived at Scavengers Bar that morning at eleven with my charcoal-striped long-sleeved LFC jersey, with Luis Suarez's #7 on the back. I sidled up to the bar and drew a fresh pint of Guinness, ready to watch the first Liverpool match ever televised at Scavengers. Tom is a general fan of all sports, and joined me at the bar. As a Kentucky fan dedicated to Big Blue Nation, he struggled with rooting for the team wearing red shirts that morning. Charles also joined us at the bar, and he didn't really care much about the match itself as long as his good friend (me) was happy and drinking beers. For the next few hours, the three of us sat at the bar watching the match, as I tried to explain the offside rule and other subtleties of the sport. I even got high fives from them both when Dirk Kuyt scored in extra time to take a 2-1 lead. Cardiff City would eventually equalize on a late goal by Ben Turner off a corner kick, and the cup was ultimately decided by penalty kicks. When Steven Gerrard's cousin Anthony missed his final penalty for Cardiff, the celebrations began. Captain Fantastic hoisted the trophy victoriously as Liverpool won its eighth League Cup. It would end up being the final cup that Steven Gerrard would win as captain of Liverpool Football Club.

NASCAR fans started to file their way to Scavengers as I smoked the celebratory cigar that I'd brought to the bar that afternoon. The television was switched over to the NASCAR pre-race coverage, which immediately announced a rain delay. The race would eventually be postponed until Monday night, but that didn't stop the approximately thirty patrons from partying all afternoon into the late evening. Most of them were curious to why I was wearing a Liverpool jersey and smoking a cigar, obviously happy with something that already happened earlier in the day.

The following week I was still beaming over the cup victory when I decided to buy an official LFC poster and frame to hang on the walls of Scavengers. With a full-fledged bar completely immune to local laws only ten minutes away from my home, I felt it was the right strategic move to make Scavengers adopt Liverpool as its official Premiership club. Tom struggled with the fact that they wear red uniforms, but ultimately he saw the light. He still doesn't like to wear red, but he has acquired some LFC apparel in other colors.

I would return to Scavengers quite often to watch Liverpool, as well as other sporting events. I'll never forget the moment I was watching Liverpool as Scavengers when Tom referred to the club as "we" in his halftime assessment. His wife Lisa caught his faux pas, challenging him with the question: "We?" The only reply could be a trademark Tom Brewer curse, typically reserved for that moment a Kentucky basketball game goes against the Wildcats. I could only smile with pride, as I'd finally accomplished the incredible feat of transforming normal North Carolina country folks into fans of the beautiful game played five time zones away. It was at that moment that Scavengers became the first Liverpool bar in Chatham County, North Carolina.

As I started to follow Liverpool more closely, the word "Merseyside" started popping up in the common vernacular. At first I didn't understand what it actually meant, except that it obviously referenced the River Mersey that flows just west of Liverpool. Merseyside is actually the name of the county that occupies the city of Liverpool, which is why they refer to matches against cross-town rival Everton as the Merseyside Derby. When describing geographical areas around an estuary, the English like to use the suffix "side" to describe the region. Deeside is used to describe the area surrounding towns and villages along the River Dee on the nearby border with Wales. Tyneside is used to describe the similar region surrounding the River Tyne in the northeast of England, and any match featuring Newcastle United vs. Sunderland is often referred to as the Tyneside Derby. While the residents like to simply refer to the area as "the river," I decided to take it a step further. Since Scavengers sits not far from the banks of North Carolina's Rocky River, I started calling the neighborhood Rockyside.

Many people confuse Scavengers as a public business. They've inquired about this country tavern with the great parties, and I have to tell them it's a private, invitation-only local hangout where good friends can hang out and drink a few beers while watching sports. It's really not much more than an elaborate man cave where money doesn't change hands and drinks aren't purchased. Some people bring their own beverages, while others may bring a premade snack or munchies. Common courtesy is to not come empty-handed, but even then you'll likely be able to grab a few brews on the house. You don't just accidentally stumble upon Scavengers. Every time I bring someone there for their virgin visit, I get concerned looks of fear as I turn down the gravel road. As the road narrows and dips into a tunnel of thick-leaved trees with the Rocky River flowing in the background, you might hear one joke: "Paddle faster. I hear banjoes." The truth is that the remote location just off the river is part of what makes this place special. The unrivaled hospitality of the owners and camaraderie of the patrons is the other part.

A year had passed since Liverpool won that League Cup. Brendan

Rodgers was in his first year as Liverpool manager, and the team was suffering through what would end up being another subpar season. The arrival of spring meant an increase in evening activities hosted at Scavengers. At some point, an uninvited guest started wandering into the pub. Buddy is a mid-sized, mild-mannered black and gold dog that somehow found his way to the pub. He got along with Tom's black lab, affectionately named Guinness, so no one really worried whenever Buddy would show up. At that time, no one knew his real name, so he was dubbed Black and Tan in honor of his pretty two-toned coat. It didn't take long to figure out where Buddy actually lived, and Charles left a note inviting them to come over to their property.

Noel McCabe and Angie Poole returned from dinner that night and saw the note about Buddy's adventures on Rockyside. Noel had lived in Dublin, Ireland, for the first forty-eight years of his life. He had a successful car audio installation business, married a local gal named Veronica, and raised two beautiful children. When cancer took Veronica's life, he eventually came to North Carolina to visit family and get some time away. He would ultimately meet Angie and move in with her. After reading the note, they got back in the truck and left to go meet the neighbors at Scavengers.

Noel walked into the bar unsure of what to expect. The first thing he noticed was a custom-crafted wooden bar with four taps, one of which controlled the flow of Guinness draught beer. He looked over at Tom, pointing to the Guinness tap, and asked, "Is that real?"

Tom replied, "Help yourself if you want to find out."

Looking around the bar, the first things people notice are the numerous pictures, neon signs, and generally entertaining trinkets that make Scavengers an inviting retreat. Noel caught glimpse of a large Liverpool poster hanging in the corner. Pointing at the sign, he excitedly inquired, "Is *that* real?"

After Tom acknowledged their support for the Reds, everyone laughed. Noel turned to Angie and said, "I came all the way from Dublin to the back woods of Chatham County and found Liverpool fans with fresh Guinness on tap. This must be heaven."

Noel and I immediately became great friends, sharing our love for Liverpool, golf, and Guinness. He hosted Tori and I at his house in Ireland, showing the sights of Dublin as any great host would. He accompanied me on my first pilgrimage to Anfield, where Liverpool defeated Arsenal 5-1 to begin the run that nearly earned them the 2013-14 Premiership title. Rarely does a day go by during the season when Noel and I aren't discussing something about Liverpool. If I decide to watch a match at Scavengers, Noel will almost always accompany me.

Social media has made Scavengers legendary. Facebook remained the primary means of communication for Raleigh Reds, and people started to take notice of some pictures posted of Scavengers. Tom had reluctantly joined the social media site years before, but did so incognito with the name "Scavengers Bar." He would later change it to his actual name, but people started asking about this wonderful place in Chatham County. The first person to take action was Steve Quasny. Steve had just moved his family from the Chicago area and lived just outside of Chapel Hill. I had never met him before when he asked if he could watch a Liverpool match at Scavengers. With Tom's permission, I agreed to meet Steve in town and escort him to Rockyside.

Steve pulled up to the prearranged meeting spot in a Toyota Prius, prompting me to wonder if this might be the first time a hybrid vehicle had braved the back woods and gravel roads to Scavengers. Steve became a Liverpool fan in Chicago through association with a Scouser expatriate friend. The two would venture off to watch matches at the OLSC Chicago pub, and he quickly latched on. When his wife Holly had the opportunity to relocate to the Raleigh area for work, they jumped at the chance to leave the large city and raise their daughter in the milder climate. He quickly endeared himself to the Scavengers crowd, even bringing his father-in-law Doug to a few matches. And the legend continued to grow.

Last season many of the regular London Bridge Pub patrons made the courageous decision to abandon their comfort level and drive out to Scavengers. I remember that day well, as Liverpool lost a tough match to Crystal Palace. It was an easy date to pick, since the match was scheduled for early Sunday morning. North Carolina blue laws don't apply to the private establishment, so we could enjoy a few libations that morning. About eight guys made their first trip on that visit, including London Bridge Pub owners Mike Ruiz and Darren Bridger. One of the bartenders Joey Smith even made an appearance, making me wonder who was going to be tending at the pub. The day was highlighted by the after-party of steamed oysters and great Kentucky bourbon. Everyone had a great time that day, despite Liverpool losing the match. Everyone vowed to make this an annual event.

Occasionally I will get to the London Bridge Pub for a match and someone will inquire about Scavengers. The guys that made that first trip will tell stories and others will feel left out. I remind everyone that it's a private location and you must be invited. That exclusivity just makes it more desirable for everyone else. And the legend continues to grow.

****

The first half of the season was coming to a close with a midweek clash just before the New Year holiday. Liverpool had played every club in the league at least once, with the exception of Sunderland. After a big win against league leaders Leicester City, it was imperative that Liverpool get another three points against the Black Cats. Sunderland was deep in a relegation battle, sitting nineteenth on the table with only twelve points and a goal difference of -18. Even though the match was being held at the Stadium of Light, everyone expected a Liverpool victory.

Since it was the holidays, I had the entire day off. It's only a fifteen-minute drive from my house to Scavengers, so I got there early. Tom was already drinking a Guinness when I arrived. Noel hadn't yet arrived, but he typically pulled up about a minute before kickoff. I poured myself a pint and got situated for the kickoff. True to form, Noel walked in moments before the opening.

Liverpool dominated possession in the opening fifteen minutes, but they still lacked the ability to break down the defense in the final third of the match. Sunderland manager Sam Allardyce seemed content to pack the defense and follow the blueprint that had been Liverpool's death knell against bottom-dwelling competition. Sit back and counterattack. It is a maddening philosophy that had proven exceptionally effective against Liverpool, and it nearly worked when Jermaine Defoe shot from twenty yards out was deflected over the bar by Simon Mignolet. I breathed a sigh of relief as Noel let out his trademark cry of "Jay-sus!"

The combination of Brazilian countrymen Coutinho and Firmino had been brilliant at times this season, and it nearly paid off again in the twenty-fifth minute when Firmino almost scored. He received possession and made some nifty moves to shake off the defense before blasting a right-footed shot toward goal. Sunderland's goalkeeper Vito Mannone was able to tip the ball enough off its course to keep it out of the net. It caromed off the post to safety.

Former Liverpool striker Fabio Borini nearly gave the home squad the lead in the thirty-third minute, and all things considered, he probably should have. He found himself with the ball inside the left side of the box. He moved to his right to find an opening as Dejan Lovren charged to close him down. He let loose for the far post with no obstruction, but the ball missed the post by mere inches. Mignolet had no chance, and watched it go out for a goal kick. The Italian striker should've done better, but it was a clear indication of why he wasn't successful at Liverpool during his brief tenure at Merseyside. Liverpool had sixty-six percent of the possession when the halftime whistle blew. Noel remarked about how this was going to be another grinding, tough match, the kind that great teams always find a way to win.

Brian Williams and Chris Church walked into the bar just before halftime, mildly curious about the match. Brian and Chris live in the area and frequently stop by Scavengers on the weekend. They were usually more interested in having a few beers with good friends while busting our balls, but deep down inside they have gravitated to becoming Liverpool fans, even though they may never admit it. Brian works mostly from home as account manager for Iron Mountain. He jumped on the Liverpool bandwagon during the 2013-14 season as the Reds made their title run. As a die-hard Cincinnati sports fan, he knows frustration all too well. Chris is an electrical superintendent for a local contractor, and lives across the street from me. He moved to the area from Miami not long ago. Since there is a lack of proper watering holes in the Chatham County countryside, it is fairly common for friends to visit each other and down a few beers over sports. Both Brian and Chris have their own private neighborhood bars like Scavengers named the Shady Bulldog and Blue Moon Saloon respectively, and I've done my part ensuring they all have some LFC gear hanging from the rafters.

"Does Chewbacca still play for you guys?" asked Chris. We all looked at each other, confused. Who was Chewbacca? My first thought was a big hairy player that looked somewhat like the *Star Wars* character, but I couldn't pick out a recent player to fit that description. The light bulb went on for Tom before Noel or I could inquire.

"Do you mean Luis Suarez?" Tom replied.

"Yeah, the guy that keeps biting people," answered Chris.

We all laughed and explained that our favorite Uruguayan striker had moved over to Barcelona. You could argue that we desperately needed him in the second half, because, quite frankly, it didn't look promising.

Liverpool kicked off the second half with some safe back passes and tried to build an attack. Emre Can passed over to Coutinho in the midfield, and he sent the ball laterally over to Nathaniel Clyne on the right side. Clyne played a long ground pass optimistically toward Firmino and Adam Lallana. The ball was slightly deflected by Lallana in behind the standing Sunderland defense. Christian Benteke charged the ball uncontested and shot the ball toward the far post and into the net. Only twenty-two seconds after the half had restarted and Liverpool finally had their lead.

The second half took shape much like the first half, with Liverpool dominating possession but with not much to show for it. Jordan Henderson came off in the sixtieth minute for what appeared to be another injury, and the former Sunderland product received a standing ovation from the home crowd. It was a nice moment to see.

Sunderland could no longer sit back and wait for the counterattack, and started pushing forward to get the equalizer. Their efforts were rewarded in the seventy-seventh minute with a corner kick, which always tests the nerves for the Liverpool faithful. The ball was sent in dangerously as Firmino headed the ball in an effort to clear. Mignolet came off his line, but found himself in no position to get the ball. It was a comedy of errors for the Liverpool defense, but the Black Cats simply couldn't capitalize. Any other team put the ball in the net on that play, and this just showed why Sunderland was at the bottom of the league table.

As the match entered the final minutes, Sunderland continued to attack, and left themselves vulnerable. Lucas Leiva, who'd come on as Henderson's substitute, intercepted the ball in the defensive third and passed ahead to Firmino. The Brazilian connected well with Benteke, who got a clear breakaway on goal. He shot the ball straight at Mannone, who easily kicked the ball clear to safety. Reflecting on that play now, it seems miraculous that Benteke scored that first goal forty-five minutes earlier.

Sunderland was unable to mount another attack as the final whistle blew, giving Liverpool the victory. It was an important three points, and that was all that mattered in the end. Great teams find ways to win these types of difficult matches, but there was little indication in my mind that this Liverpool squad could be considered a great team. There were clear gaps in quality throughout the roster. The January transfer window was about to open, and we were all curious to see if the club would do anything to bring in reinforcements.

****

Halfway through the Barclays Premier League season, and Liverpool sat in seventh position, nine points behind leaders Arsenal, who, strangely, were only besting Leicester City on goal differential at this point in the season. More important was the fact that Liverpool were still within five points of the top four and a return to Champions League. Despite Liverpool being the only team in the top twelve without a positive goal differential, Klopp had everyone dreaming of a return to glory.

19 - HALFWAY

Saturday, January 2
Camp Kendra
Premier League match #20 (at West Ham United)

The halfway point of the season had been reached, and Liverpool fans had much to be optimistic for the second half of the campaign. The club was still alive in all four competitions, including a top-four position in the Premier League for a much-desired return to the Champions League. The past few seasons had shown Liverpool to be a better club in the spring, and most of the matches against our traditional rivals would be played at home. With a two-match winning streak in play, the Reds traveled to Upton Park for a match against West Ham United.

This match would be the second of four straight away matches held over a ten-day stretch. Many supporters were upset about how the schedule played out, but this sort of anomaly can occur with multiple different competitions. Following this match, the club would travel to Stoke City for the first leg of their League Cup semifinal before traveling to Exeter City for their first match in the FA Cup on the following Friday. With Martin Skrtel and Divock Origi recently succumbing to hamstring injuries, the squad depth was surely to be tested in the next few days.

The other significant event going on at this time was the opening of the January transfer window. This is an opportunity for clubs to bring in reinforcements for the second half of the season. Traditionally, the January transfer window doesn't produce game-changing moves for a club, although Liverpool has had recent significant success in past Januaries acquiring Philippe Coutinho (from Inter Milan in 2013), Daniel Sturridge (from Chelsea in 2013), and Luis Suarez (from Ajax Amsterdam in 2011). Of course, the club also acquired Andy Carroll from Newcastle United for a club record fee just as the January 2011 transfer window closed, and he didn't exactly work out as Liverpool had hoped.

Before the West Ham match, Liverpool confirmed the acquisition of nineteen-year-old Serbian starlet Marko Grujic from Red Star Belgrade. As part of the transfer agreement, the winger remained in Belgrade on loan for the remainder of the season. With squad depth being called into question, many fans wondered why the club would send him back on loan. The simple answer was that Red Star Belgrade would not likely have made the transfer otherwise, as they were trying to secure the Serbian SuperLiga title and a spot in next year's Champions League themselves. This was an opportunity for Liverpool to acquire a talented prospect that would've left in the summer at a cut-rate price.

Sensing the importance of this match, Klopp fielded a strong lineup to face the Hammers. Christian Benteke was the only available striker, so he started as the lone attacker in a somewhat defensive shape.

West Ham came out firing on all cylinders, scoring ten minutes into the match when Michail Antonio hit a close-range header on a cross from Enner Valencia. It was a lead that West Ham deserved. The anemic play from the Reds was frustrating to watch, and they were lucky to only be losing by one goal headed into halftime.

Liverpool started the second half with more motivation and intensity, apparently after getting a stern lecture from Klopp in the dressing room at halftime. Coutinho had a great chance that sailed mere inches over the crossbar, and Benteke failed to connect on a fine Alberto Moreno cross. The equalizer looked to be coming.

The momentum Liverpool struggled to create disappeared in an instant. In the fifty-fifth minute of play, Mark Noble sent in a cross that was easily headed into the net by former Liverpool striker Andy Carroll to give the Hammers a 2-0 lead. The goal deflated the Reds, who would never recover. It was vindication for Carroll, who had been shipped off to West Ham on loan in August 2012. The move to Upton Park was made permanent in May 2013 for less than half of what Liverpool paid for him. He is considered one of the biggest flops in English football history, and he had just given West Ham a two-goal lead over his former club.

When the final whistle blew, it left fans scratching their hands in befuddlement. West Ham was a good squad, so nothing could be taken away from their victory. But Liverpool's inability to rise to the occasion of a big match was concerning. It had become a trend for Liverpool in recent years, one that could end up becoming Klopp's biggest challenge.

****

Three days after the difficult loss, the Reds were back in action in the

League Cup semifinals at Stoke City's Britannia Stadium. Up until this point in the competition, all matches were one-game fixtures, with the host determined as part of the random draw process. With only four teams left, the format shifted to a two-legged affair, with matches to be held at each stadium.

The chance to win silverware would not be taken lightly, so a strong lineup started against Stoke City. The advantage of playing the first leg on the road meant a good result should help take the Reds into their first cup final since 2012.

It was a cold, rainy evening in Stoke. It had already been well documented how injuries had taken its toll on Klopp's side since he took over in the fall. Freak accidents like ruptured knee ligaments are unavoidable, but one always needs to question muscle pulls and strains. Proper training and warmup should be enough to prevent muscular injuries, yet Liverpool was afflicted by these cases more than expected. One theory was that Klopp's style of fast "Gegenpressing" put enough stress on the leg muscles that the players weren't prepared and thus susceptible to injury. Kolo Toure, James Milner, Jordan Rossiter, Philippe Coutinho, Daniel Sturridge, Martin Skrtel, and Divock Origi had all been sidelined to hamstring injuries since Klopp took the helm. It'd been so prevalent that Klopp even joked in a press conference that he considered the word "hamstring" a curse word now.

It was little surprise when Coutinho came up lame holding his hamstring and had to be replaced by Jordon Ibe in the eighteenth minute of play. Disbelief turned into anger seventeen minutes later when Dejan Lovren hurt his hamstring as well. With only youngsters Connor Randall and Brad Smith on the bench, Klopp elected to bring on veteran James Milner and push Lucas Leiva back in central defense to replace the injured Croatian. Only thirty-five minutes into the match and two of Klopp's available three substitutions had to be used for injury replacements. It could be a factor later in the match if tactical changes were needed.

While no one wants to see players injured early in the match, the silver lining to this cloud was that the tactical shift in formation would make Stoke City adjust their style as well. The introduction of Ibe provided more pace down the left flank, and that caused the balance of play to shift in Liverpool's favor. The Reds dominated play up, and were rewarded with a goal in the thirty-second minute. Adam Lallana was able to cross the ball into a dangerous position, where Joe Allen cleverly diverted the ball to Ibe. The youngster fired a shot toward the far post that found the side netting to give Liverpool a 1-0 lead.

Stoke City were able to regain control of the match after Lovren's departure, but the Potters couldn't find the equalizer they needed. Klopp was forced to make a final injury substitution in the eighty-second minute when Mamadou Sakho limped off with an apparent knee injury. As if that wasn't enough, it would appear that Kolo Toure hurt his hamstring in the final minutes. Unable to be replaced, Toure soldiered on to help preserve the 1-0 victory.

It was a huge win, all things considered. Three weeks from that moment the two clubs would play at Anfield, and one would have to think Liverpool would be heavy favorites to advance forward following the away win.

****

Liverpool was hit with more bad news following the victory at Stoke City when it was announced that Mamadou Sakho would need to sit out a short spell for that minor knee injury sustained in the match. That was followed by the news that Jordon Ibe would need some rest for straining his hamstring muscle in training. Another hamstring? Are you kidding me? You can't make this stuff up. Thirteen roster players were unfit to play due to injury, seven of those injuries being hamstrings. The good news for Liverpool was that this upcoming match was an FA Cup battle against League Two minnows Exeter City. The Grecians sat seventy-six places behind the Reds in the league table, the loose equivalent of a Major League Baseball team having to play a single-A minor league club in a single-game knockout match. Liverpool shouldn't need a fully fit squad to win this game.

While Klopp wanted to take this competition seriously, he had little choice but to start mostly reserve players. Of the starting eleven, only Christian Benteke and Adam Bogdan had started for the club in a Premier League match that season. The direness of the situation was clearly visible as Jose Enrique was brought back into action for the club. The twenty-nine-year-old Spanish defender had largely been forgotten by supporters, since he hadn't played for the club in almost a year. Despite numerous attempts to move the player in the summer transfer window, Enrique refused to leave the club. He was deemed surplus to requirements and spent most of the season training with the reserves while collecting lucrative wages. He may have had more experience than most of the reserve players getting the call, but I worried about how rusty he might be.

Another player making his first start for the club was Tiago Ilori, a young Portuguese defender sent to Aston Villa on loan in the summer in hopes of earning some valuable Premier League experience. He failed to break into their lineup and never played a single minute for the Villains, so he was brought back on emergency recall. If he were to going to ride the pine, he might as well do it for Liverpool, where Klopp could assess his ability through training over the entire second half of the season. Ilori arrived two days before the match and was immediately inserted into the starting lineup.

Exeter City is a small club that formed in 1901 and has never played in England's top division. They also have the unique distinction of having its majority owner being a trust group of supporters. Initially formed in 2000, the Exeter City Supporters Trust was created to raise money for the club to sign players. When the chairman and vice-chairman were arrested in 2003 for financial irregularities, the trust was brought in to assist with the operation of the club. They have since acquired 53.6 percent ownership stake in the club and are now one of the few clubs actually owned by the fans.

The game was a rare Friday evening match, and the home crowd of 8298 filled up St. James Park for the epic encounter. Tom Nicholls is a young English striker that gave the home crowd something to cheer about in the ninth minute of play when he scored the game's first goal. The lead was short-lived, as Liverpool's young Jerome Sinclair equalized three minutes later. A fluke goal from veteran journeyman Lee Holmes would give the lead back to the League Two squad just before halftime. Holmes sent in a corner kick that was badly misjudged by backup goalkeeper Adam Bogdan and went straight into the net. Bogdan hadn't played since getting the emergency nod against Watford in December, where he fumbled an easy save, leading to an early Watford goal. For the second time in a month, Bogdan had made a horrific blunder that cost Liverpool a goal. Exeter City led Liverpool 2-1 going into halftime, to the delight of the majority of supporters in attendance.

The pitch was quite sloppy, and Exeter City started to show signs of fatigue as the second half started. Klopp brought on Sheyi Ojo as a substitute in the seventy-first minute in search of the vital equalizer. Ojo is an eighteen-year-old speedster that was loaned out to Wolverhampton in the championship in August. Despite playing in nineteen games, he only started in seven, and was brought back early. If nothing else, his return added some emergency depth at a time where Liverpool regulars seemed to be dropping out to injury on a daily basis.

The addition of Ojo made an immediate impact, as he assisted the equalizer only moments after stepping onto the pitch. He sent a shot that was initially saved by Exeter City goalkeeper Robert Olejnik, but the rebound went straight to Brad Smith, and the Australian fired home the equalizer in the seventy-third minute.

The goal deflated the home crowd, denying the small club with what could've been one of their biggest victories in their 115-year history. When the final whistle blew with scoreboard reading 2-2, it meant they had earned a replay at Anfield Stadium, to be played in a few weeks. Most of the players on the Exeter City squad would never see the top flight of English football, and the opportunity to play in one of the sport's most treasured stadiums was going to be a moment they would never forget. It also represented a significant financial windfall for the club. For Liverpool, however, it simply meant adding another fixture to an already crowded schedule. I almost wonder if the club wouldn't have been better off losing the match. I'd never root against the club, but given the circumstances, it would appear that adding another fixture to the calendar was the last thing anyone wanted. If some of the regular players didn't start healing soon, it could be a disastrous conclusion to the season..

20 - CHARLOTTE

Wednesday, January 13
Ri Ra, Charlotte, NC
Premier League match #21 (vs. Arsenal)

In October 2013, we made the decision to try and push LFC Raleigh into the fraternity of Official Liverpool Supporters Clubs. London Bridge Pub was growing in popularity, and many of the regulars started wondering about the benefits that may come with becoming an official club. The stipulations were published on the Liverpool website, and we knew that we could meet their requirements. They explicitly mentioned that all applications must be submitted by August and would be reviewed and approved soon thereafter. We had barely missed the deadline for 2013, but figured we had plenty of time to get our ducks in a row and try for official status the following year.

The club soon announced that their next summer preseason tour would be held in North America, with a match to be played in Charlotte. We all rejoiced. Liverpool would be coming to our home state! Charlotte is the largest city in North Carolina, and a two-hour drive from Raleigh. It was soon after that announcement that I got a text message from Jamie Harrison of OLSC Atlanta. He told me that the club had deviated from its policy and given official status to the Charlotte crew. This made perfect sense, because the club needed to coordinate match activities and events for any fans that planned to travel to Charlotte for that match. Jamie sensed an opportunity, and convinced me to send my completed application to the club and request early admission. At first we didn't hear back from the club, but our second effort paid dividends when they granted our request the day after that season ended.

It was a momentous time for OLSC Raleigh. We were the 210th chapter to be granted official status, meaning the club in Charlotte must've been the 209th. The match in Charlotte was three months away, and we knew that there would be hundreds of Raleigh Reds traveling for the match. To celebrate this occasion, we decided to host a lunch party in Charlotte to toast our new status.

Carlos Quevedo was the chairperson for the OLSC Charlotte group, and at the time they met for all matches at Courtyard Hooligans. Carlos is originally from Providence, Rhode Island, and is a huge fan of all New England sports. He started rooting for Liverpool after they won the Champions League in 2005, but his love for the club was solidified when the owners of his beloved Boston Red Sox acquired Liverpool in 2010. Carlos informed me that they would be sponsoring the official tailgate activities at Courtyard Hooligans. During a work trip in Charlotte, I stopped by their pub and immediately recognized the size would not be adequate for the pre-match lunch party that we were hoping to host. The bar secured space in the adjacent parking lot and arranged for a fantastic tailgate atmosphere, but we were hoping for a larger restaurant where our supporters could enjoy food and spirits hours before the match.

I found the Ri Ra Irish Pub in the busy section of uptown Charlotte only a few blocks away. Ri Ra is a franchise of Irish pubs with nine locations in the United States. The actual name translates from Gaelic to English as "mayhem" or "ruckus," but it's also possible that the secondary meaning refers to the Real Irish Republican Army (RIRA). RIRA aims to unite the Emerald Isle as the successor to the original Irish Republican Army. There's nothing at the pub to indicate that they're trying to indicate an anti-British sentiment, so I prefer to assume they intended to consider it a place for playful mayhem. Just like every other Irish pub I've been to.

Ri Ra has two floors, with enough seating to house hundreds of patrons in the process. It was the perfect setting for what we were looking for, so we booked our lunch party there. Word spread about our event, and over three hundred Liverpool supporters from across the country attended. It was a fantastic event and the perfect start to the day. We eventually found our way over to the Courtyard Hooligans tailgate party before walking to the stadium to witness Liverpool's 2-0 victory over AC Milan.

Due to personal reasons, Carlos stepped down from the leadership team at OLSC Charlotte, but we remain close friends. Since we consider the OLSC fraternity a family, it's easy for me to consider Charlotte our twin brother. We were both granted official status within weeks of each other, and share the bond of residing in the Tar Heel state. It made sense for me to make the short drive to the Queen City during a midweek match, so when I saw the Arsenal fixture scheduled on a Wednesday, I booked my visit. OLSC Charlotte would abandon Courtyard Hooligans and make Ri Ra their new home pub last season. Courtyard Hooligans is a great soccer pub, but you'd be hard-pressed to get more than fifty patrons inside comfortably to watch a match. In my opinion, a club of any significant size would need larger accommodations. They made the right move shifting to Ri Ra, and I couldn't help but feel a bit responsible for helping the pub get that business through our successful pre-match lunch party.

I walked down Tryon Street toward the pub and first noticed the Charlotte Reds banner hanging in the window by the front door. Then I noticed another banner displayed in the next window, which advertised themselves as home of the Queen City Gooners. It's not unusual for pubs to be the home of multiple supporters clubs, but this made the match a bit more interesting. How would two competing supporters clubs react at the same pub while playing each other? I couldn't wait to find out.

I walked in and noticed a few Arsenal supporters sitting in a booth. The bar was nearly empty, which I supposed would be expected for a Wednesday midafternoon. I asked the manager about the match, and he explained that they would segregate the clubs. Gooners stayed downstairs while Liverpool fans watched upstairs. I trekked up the steps just before kickoff to see the Charlotte Reds eagerly anticipating the match. Carlos was the first to greet me. His twenty-one-year-old son Aaron was with him, frantically typing on his smartphone.

There was a solid crowd beginning to form, and Carlos began making some introductions. First was Derek Rauscher, who was part of the new organizational committee for OLSC Charlotte. We started to discuss the potential of planning some joint events with OLSC Raleigh. Derek is originally from Kennesaw, Georgia, just north of Atlanta. He played soccer through high school and has been supporting Liverpool for over twenty years, mostly because he liked the kit.

Just before the match kicked off, there were about thirty Charlotte Reds in attendance. I got a pint of Guinness from a bartender they called "Bobby the Manc," a Manchester United supporter from Limerick, Ireland. There was some friendly banter between the supporters and Bobby, and everyone was having a good laugh.

NBC Sports started their coverage a few minutes early, panning the cameras around the stadium as fans sang "You'll Never Walk Alone." This particular version was electric, and actually gave me goose bumps. The last time that had happened to me was during my first visit to Anfield two years earlier. Liverpool defeated Arsenal 5-1 then, and I would gladly take a similar result today.

It was a sloppy evening at Merseyside, with a steady rainfall at kickoff. Liverpool had the first sniff at goal when Adam Lallana went down in the box in the fifth minute. Referee Mike Jones didn't call a penalty, which on replay looked like may have been the wrong decision. Four minutes later, Liverpool would get that goal off an extended play following a corner kick.

Emre Can got a pass from James Milner at the corner of the eighteen-yard box and fired a shot toward the far post. Arsenal goalkeeper Petr Cech made the initial save, but the rebound ended up at the feet of Roberto Firmino. Cech was helpless to prevent Firmino's shot from going in the net. The upstairs at Ri Ra erupted!

The lead was short-lived, as Arsenal equalized four minutes later. Costa Rican midfielder Joel Campbell gained possession and slid a nice pass behind the defense. Aaron Ramsey was able to run onto the ball and one-time it past Simon Mignolet at the near post. It was one of those goals that could've been easily prevented. Kolo Toure was poorly marking Ramsey at the time, and Mignolet should not have been caught away from his near post. Television commentator Arlo White called it a "goal from out of nowhere." It didn't matter, as the score was now 1-1.

Firmino would regain the lead for Liverpool six minutes later with an incredible shot. The Brazilian got a pass in the middle of the pitch about twenty-five yards out, shook off the defender, and sent a right-footed curling ball in the upper right corner. Cech had no chance to stop the world-class goal, and once again there was much rejoicing at Ri Ra.

Arsenal would equalize within five minutes off a corner kick, once again exposing Liverpool's weakness on set pieces. A hard in-swinging ball was whipped in toward the near post, deflected slightly by Olivier Giroud's outstretched left foot past Mignolet. The roller coaster of emotions continued. It was time for Bobby the Manc to pour me another pint. Two years earlier, I'd watched these two clubs battle it out with four goals scored in the first twenty minutes...all by Liverpool. Goals were being scored at the same frequency this time, but sadly, the match was tied 2-2.

That goal seemed to charge the Arsenal attack. They were dominating possession and breaking down the Liverpool defense with ease. Giroud should've given them the lead when Theo Walcott passed the ball across the six-yard line. The French striker mishit the ball in front of an open net, and Mignolet was able to get the ball to safety with his back heel as he fell to the ground. It was a lucky save, and the score remained knotted at halftime.

I received a text message at halftime from my childhood best friend Jon Hamblett, a staunch Arsenal supporter. He'd just started a new job and was in the process of relocating his family to Washington, D.C., from the Phoenix area. He was too busy to get in front of a television, so I gave him the rundown via text. Liverpool had the edge in possession with fifty-four percent, and both teams had seven shots and four shots on target. Statistically, it was an even match. Liverpool scored two goals that couldn't have been saved by any goalkeeper, while Arsenal scored two goals that could have been prevented by better defending.

I got my second pint and noticed a familiar face by the stairwell. Anish

Mirani is a young banker that used to be a regular at the London Bridge Pub in Raleigh. Apparently his employer moved him to their Charlotte headquarters in July, and it didn't take him long to discover the new home of OSLC Charlotte. It was nice to see another friendly face from the past.

I had the chance to talk with many of the Charlotte Reds at halftime. Levi Anthes is a cabinetmaker that looks eerily similar to baseball player Manny Ramirez, including the dreadlocks. Scott Daniels is a network engineer working for the city. Both of these guys picked up the Liverpool bug when the club came for their preseason match two summers earlier. Both of them said that they picked up on Liverpool during the end of the 2014 season. It was already announced that the Reds were coming to Charlotte, and the remarkable title run got everyone excited about the club. That weekend in the Queen City was epic, as the Liverpool faithful took over the uptown area. Over sixty thousand fans attended the match against AC Milan, and I estimate that the majority of ticketholders supported Liverpool. It was easy to jump on the bandwagon. Becoming part of the supporters club is what keeps them on.

Most everyone was nervous heading into the second half. While Liverpool dominated the early portion of the first half, the tide shifted considerably once Arsenal equalized for the second time. Had it not been for a missed Giroud sitter, we'd be fighting an uphill battle. Giroud would make up for that miss in the fifty-fourth minute of play.

Hector Bellerin got the ball for Arsenal near midfield and charged forward. Milner had the chance to tackle the young Spaniard and failed, allowing Bellerin to run freely down the right-hand side. He passed back to Campbell, running into the penalty box, who touched past a falling Mamadou Sakho. Giroud received the ball near the penalty spot and easily one-timed it inside the far post. Mignolet had no chance on this one, and Arsenal had the lead they deserved.

Klopp brought on Christian Benteke to replace Milner in the sixty-fifth minute, a clear offensive move in an effort to find the equalizer. In two of the last three league matches, the Belgian forward was able to find the score sheet, so I was hopeful that he could bring some magic into this game. Almost immediately the club started showing some life, as Firmino's header was deflected out. Alberto Moreno fired a long shot on the ensuing corner kick that was also deflected wide. They were started to create chances, but could they finish any of them?

I was starting to get restless watching the match with the other nervous fans. I decided to head downstairs to sneak a peek at how the Queen City Gooners were managing. I was amazed at what I saw when I walked into their space. Five fans sat in a line at a table watching the television in front of them, barely taking their eyes off the match. I looked around to see if anyone else was tucked away in a corner booth, but there was no one. One of the best teams in the league fighting for their first league title since 2004, and their fans couldn't be bothered to get off work for a huge match against a rival club. It occurred to me that possibly their fan club wasn't as large as the Charlotte Reds, and I sauntered back upstairs to watch the rest of the match.

Joe Allen came on as a substitute for Emre Can in the eighty-second minute, and the team continued to push forward. Jordon Ibe had a few efforts down the flank, but he simply wasn't able to get past his defender. It prompted one of the Charlotte Reds to cry, "Jordon Ibe couldn't beat my grandmother one on one, and she's dead!" Harsh words for the young midfielder, but the point was valid. So many Liverpool attacks failed once the ball was played to his side. Why bother?

Desperation began to set in late when Klopp brought on newly acquired Steven Caulker for Adam Lallana in the eighty-seventh minute. Due to the rash of recent injuries at the center-back position, Caulker was brought in on loan from Queens Park Rangers to help provide much-needed depth. It was a short-term fix until guys like Martin Skrtel and Dejan Lovren could return to fitness. In this situation, he was coming on in the final minutes against one of the top teams in the league and asked to play forward.

The steady rain at Anfield had turned to a light snow as the match moved into the night. Liverpool got a late free kick from twenty-five yards out after a Laurent Koscielny foul. Moreno fired an attempt straight into the defensive wall of Arsenal. Another wasted set piece, I thought. Jordan Henderson collected the ball and sent a hopeful ball into the box. Benteke leapt over the defense able to get his head on the ball to send it back across the goalmouth. Out of nowhere the five-foot-six Joe Allen crashed forward undetected to first-time the ball past Cech. Seemingly out of nowhere, Liverpool had snatched a point. It would appear as though perhaps Arsenal defenders just didn't think Allen much a threat, and how could you? He had only scored twice before in the Premier League since Liverpool acquired his services in the summer of 2012. Yet on this day, wee Joe Allen would be the toast of the Liverpool faithful. For the second straight season, Liverpool stole a point off Arsenal in the waning moments of the match.

I ordered another pint of Guinness to continue celebrating with the Charlotte Reds. Some of the fans bid adieu, but others stayed for a pint to relive the late heroics. I noticed that one fan that I hadn't yet spoken with was wearing a Guinness top. After I complimented him on the great jacket, he explained that he was the local Guinness sales rep, and he was getting ready to host an evening event at another Irish pub down the street. James Hurst graduated from UNC-Chapel Hill with a degree in broadcast journalism in 2000, but he wasn't happy in that industry, and somehow lucked into the greatest sales job ever.

James was living in Charleston and simply became a Liverpool fan to be a dick. His little brother started watching soccer before him, and initially picked Everton as his favorite team because they had American stars Tim Howard and Landon Donovan at the time. He learned that Everton's bitter rival was Liverpool, so that was how he picked his allegiance. As the sport gained popularity, he got more involved and started going to matches with the OLSC South Carolina gang at the Madra Rua pub in North Charleston. After relocating to Charlotte for the Guinness job, he'd quickly transformed into a Charlotte Red.

James invited me to join him at Connolly's on Fifth, another Irish pub just a short walk from the Ri Ra. He was setting up for an event with the Guinness Club, where fans of the beverage gathered together to drink the black gold. I had no idea that such a club even existed, but who was I to argue? The bar provided some chicken wing appetizers while James opened up a tab. Free chicken wings and Guinness? Yes please.

I didn't want to be a pest, as clearly James was working, so I situated myself at the far end of the bar. Since it was a private event, not much else was happening. The bartender came over to me and struck up a conversation. Owen Duffy came over to the States from Ireland to attend Catawba College in Salisbury, North Carolina. Their soccer coach was Irish, so he used his connections to bring over the talented Irish kids. After graduation, Owen decided to stay, and has been tending bar in Charlotte since. Owen is a Leeds United fan, the rare person that still admits that fact. I felt like an outsider to the Guinness Club as James worked the room like any good salesperson does, but Owen kept good company ensuring that I always had a fresh pint in front of me. Owen shared some stories and we recapped the earlier match as James held Guinness trivia giving away free gear for the winners. It hadn't even occurred to me that the bar was near closing time!

I thanked James for the invitation and wonderful evening. I had stopped drinking hours earlier to ensure my sobriety level was below the legal limit, and found my way to my hotel. I was starting to see a trend developing. It wasn't the first time that I had walked into a pub to watch Liverpool with people I'd never met, only to have the evening extend well beyond the final whistle. I'm pretty sure it won't be the last time either. It's what I love about being part of the Liverpool family.

21 – A SOBERING DEFEAT

Sunday, January 17
London Bridge Pub
Premier League match #22 (vs. Manchester United)

For the second time in a week, Liverpool was hosting a rival club in an important Premier League match. After the dramatic 3-3 draw with Arsenal came the most anticipated match of the season, when Manchester United came to Anfield.

Normally this fixture carried significance in the standings, as both clubs would be fighting for position on the table. Liverpool had continued its slow climb up the ladder, and any goal of finishing in the top four for Champions League qualification would likely include leapfrogging Manchester United. Liverpool sat in ninth place, but a victory would see them move up to sixth, equal in points with Manchester United and only five points shy of the coveted Champions League berth.

This was an intriguing battle of foreign managers on different career path trajectories. While Jürgen Klopp seemed to have revitalized the Liverpool spirit, trending the club upward, Manchester United's Dutch manager Louis van Gaal was constantly the subject to exit rumors fueled by an increasingly impatient fan base. There is an old adage in sports that is universal. No matter how poorly a season is going, all will be well in your world if you beat the hated rival. Van Gaal could earn some much-needed credibility with a victory at Anfield.

Another interesting parallel was how both teams had participated in dramatic 3-3 draws during the previous midweek match. While Joe Allen was rescuing a point against Arsenal on Wednesday, Manchester United dropped two points at Newcastle United when they allowed Paul Dummett to equalize in the ninetieth minute.

When two heated rivals are facing in other on the pitch, the FA likes to move kickoff up to the earliest possible starting time. A two p.m. kickoff time minimizes the number of hours supporters can spend in their local pub raising their blood alcohol content, thus reducing the risk of intoxicated rival fans clashing with each other. While that theory makes perfect sense to support the safety of fans at the stadium, it does introduce the American inconvenience of having these important fixtures start at nine a.m. EST on a Sunday. Normally that would be reason enough for me to watch this match at Scavengers or on my couch, but any match against Manchester United is certainly best experienced at the pub. So I got in the car and drove down to Raleigh to meet my friends.

It was a good crowd for a Sunday morning match, once again dominated in numbers by the Raleigh Reds. A few Manchester United fans were in attendance, but as per the norm, they remained silently hiding amongst the crowd. Most of them wore plain clothes to the pub, but a few brave guys proudly donned their Manchester United jerseys. Both sets of fans were supremely confident of their chances, but they both were nervously afraid their club would fail to deliver. It's an intriguing balance of emotions that can be difficult to manage.

By the time the match kicked off, there were about eighty patrons at the pub drinking water or soda. Liverpool was still absent some key players like Coutinho to injury, but I felt like there was enough quality in the lineup to get the victory. The majority of the first half was played in the middle third of the pitch, with Liverpool controlling most of the possession. Neither team could penetrate the other's defense effectively, which raised the question if both teams were tactically playing it safe. Adam Lallana managed the half's only shot on target, a weak header off a Lucas Leiva pass that was easily saved by David de Gea. The overall play was abysmally boring. It had all of the signs of being an overhyped match failing to reach expectations, resulting in a drab 0-0 draw. Maybe it just was easier to identify with eighty sober supporters nervously watching from the pub.

Liverpool took control of the second half and started to generate some offense. Every time the Reds looked to be mounting a scoring chance, the play would break down. Sometimes it was a shot from distance that would miss the target; other times it would be a brilliant save from de Gea. Having watched the Spanish goalkeeper's heroics over the previous three matches against Liverpool, it was no surprise to me every time he denied Liverpool a goal.

Twenty minutes into the second half, Liverpool should've had a lead. The nerves started becoming more painful, as my fingernails were now in danger of being completely annihilated by my teeth. Standing in the back corner of the pub, I turned to someone and said, "I have a bad feeling about this. We should be capitalizing, and it's going to cost us points."

Unfortunately, my words came to fruition moments later when Manchester United snatched a goal in the seventy-eighth minute. The Red Devils earned a corner kick, which was taken quickly to Juan Mata on a short pass. Mata crossed the ball into the box, where Belgian giant Marouane Fellaini was able to head the ball toward the goal. The ball caromed off the crossbar straight to an unmarked Wayne Rooney on the far post. Rooney smashed home the goal to give United the 1-0 lead.

The reaction at the pub was like the bell curve of emotions. There were a few elated United supporters that wildly celebrated the goal, and a few extremely passionate Liverpool supporters loudly cursing the club's inability to defend set pieces. The vast majority of us stood in silence, dejectedly wondering how this was possible. The fact that the goal was scored by Wayne Rooney made it even worse. Rooney was born and raised in Liverpool, but joined the Everton academy at age nine. He made his Premier League debut with the Toffees at sixteen, scoring a game-winning goal against Arsenal to become the youngest goal scorer in league history (a record that he no longer holds). After two seasons with Everton, he handed in a transfer request and the eighteen-year-old was sold to Manchester United for £25.6 million. He has been one of the more vocal players in the past decade, never denying how much he hated Liverpool Football Club. Watching him celebrate his goal by the corner flag at Anfield made me slightly nauseated. Anyone but Rooney.

The pub settled back in for the final ten minutes of play. Klopp brought on Benteke, hoping he could replicate some of his previous late-game heroics. Manchester United tightened up the defense and Liverpool couldn't generate another scoring opportunity. For the fourth straight time, Liverpool would lose to their hated rivals. We outshot them 19-7 overall, and 4-1 with shots on target. We held the majority of possession. We dominated almost every statistical category possible, except for the only one that matters. Instead of drawing level on points, we were now six points behind Manchester United. It was a severe setback in the drive for a top-four finish, with many supporters at the pub throwing in the towel on the Premier League season. I knew that there were sixteen matches to go in the league—plenty of time to rebound and make a late run. But we were utterly gutted with the loss, and those negative thoughts buried themselves into my mind as I sat at the pub watching the few United supporters celebrate. As Liverpool fans, we have come to expect disappointment throughout the season. It never gets easy, but at least we had each other. I walked over to Darren, who looked at me with a sly grin. "Cheer up, mate," he said to me. "It's only an hour until noon!"

****

The FA Cup is the oldest football tournament in the world, first played in the 1871-72 season. Years ago it was considered a major competition that teams never took for granted. Before televising sports was common, the FA Cup Final was one of the few matches televised in England and considered as big to the English as the Super Bowl is to Americans. The influx of money injected into the sport through the Champions League has since shifted priority for some of the bigger clubs, who oftentimes use these matches as a chance to rest their star players and get younger players some first-team experience. Clubs still want to win the FA Cup, but not at the expense of the more lucrative competitions.

An interesting nuance to this competition is how they manage tied matches. The matchups and locations are determined by random draw, but if the first match can't be settled on the pitch then the two clubs will replay the match at the away team's stadium to settle the score. It's probably the fairest way to run the competition, but it also piles on additional wear and tear to the players' bodies throughout an already grueling season.

Liverpool's inability to defeat Exeter City two weeks earlier meant the two clubs would need to face each other at Anfield to see which club advanced to the next round. This would be Liverpool's seventh match in twenty-two days, with two more games scheduled in the next six days. Much like the first match against Exeter City, Klopp elected to play mostly reserve players against the League Two side. With the second leg of the League Cup semifinal to be played the following Tuesday, Klopp needed to give some players a break. Joe Allen and Jordon Ibe joined Christian Benteke as the only veteran players in the young lineup.

Simon Mignolet also got the start at goalkeeper. Adam Bogdan apparently had played his last game for Liverpool, following his blunder against Exeter City in the first leg. Earlier the club had recalled the loan of nineteen-year-old goalkeeper Danny Ward from Aberdeen in the Scottish Premier League. It was a bold move, since the teenager was gaining valuable match experience and playing well, but clearly Klopp had lost faith in Bogdan.

Everyone expected Liverpool to win this match. Cinderella stories are quite rare in the FA Cup, and Exeter City had had their chance with a late 2-1 lead when the clubs met at St. James Park two weeks earlier. While Liverpool still had players with lingering injuries, the inclusion of more experience in the lineup for a home match should be sufficient to see this match through.

As anticipated, Liverpool controlled the early possession and outclassed the Grecians. Even though most fans expected to advance, it was important that the club score early to help settle the nerves. Joe Allen delivered that early goal in the tenth minute of play from a Brad Smith cross. Exeter City would never recover.

It took over an hour of play for Liverpool to double their lead, as Sheyi Ojo scored his first goal for the club with a left-footed curler into the top corner. It was a beautiful strike in the seventy-fifth minute by the eighteen-year-old, and hopefully a sign of great things to come from the prospect. Joao Carlos Teixeira sealed the match seven minutes later with his first goal for the club. The goal was assisted by Benteke, who unselfishly played Teixeira in on target.

The final whistle blew with Liverpool earning the 3-0 victory. Their reward would be yet another January fixture against West Ham United in the next round. At least that match would be played at Anfield.

Most of the post-match discussion was regarding the recent slumping form of Christian Benteke. The Belgian striker registered eight shots against the League Two side, three of which were on target and saved. He squandered a few sitters, including two close-range headers that completely missed the target. He was losing confidence by the minute. After playing 180 minutes of football against a significantly weaker side and with no goals to show for it, the £32 million striker started looking like a bigger bust for Liverpool than Andy Carroll. He had scored some brilliant goals early in the season, and netted game winners in consecutive 1-0 victories only three weeks earlier. Yet everyone could clearly see his confidence was shattering. With Daniel Sturridge, Divock Origi, and Philippe Coutinho coming back to full fitness, you could envision a long stretch with Benteke becoming football's most expensive substitute.

In the days following the victory, rumors about a possible transfer started gaining serious momentum. Liverpool scouts were reportedly taking a close look at attacking midfielder Alex Teixeira from Ukrainian side Shakhtar Donetsk. The Brazilian had made public his desire to join countrymen Coutinho and Roberto Firmino at Liverpool, and his club stated their asking price to acquire the talent would be no less than €50 million (approximately £38 million). It was the first real signal from the club that they were looking to provide player support for Klopp, but I wasn't sure this would be the best move. While it's usually a good problem to have multiple attacking options to choose from, it takes new players time to adjust to a new environment and style of play. Acquiring Teixeira in January would not guarantee offensive success, while other players like Origi and Sturridge were known threats coming back to fitness. Still, it was good to hear that players were being seriously looked at as the January transfer window came to a close.

22 - DENVER

Perhaps the most fascinating trait amongst football fans is one's dedication to the cause. Nowhere is this more evident than seeing the lengths that supporters will go to watch their club when the times are not most convenient. When the initial schedule is released in the summer, all matches in the Premier League are scheduled for three p.m. English time (GMT). Not every game will actually kick off at that time. Certain matches are moved to varying time slots in order to accommodate television contracts. One Saturday match is usually moved up to twelve forty-five p.m. for the first game of the weekend, and another match is pushed back to five thirty p.m. A few other matches will be moved to Sunday and Monday as well. Unfortunately, the decision to shift these matches isn't typically made until about two months prior, and this sometimes makes it difficult for the traveling fan to make long-term travel commitments.

I experienced this challenge during my first pilgrimage to Anfield in February of 2014. Planning this trip in advance assumed some travel risks. Tori and I had booked travel to Dublin and were going to fly into Liverpool on the morning of the match. The match was moved up to the twelve forty-five p.m. kickoff, which didn't leave much room for error with our scheduled Saturday morning arrival at Liverpool's John Lennon Airport. Thankfully, it wasn't an issue, as the flight arrived on time.

Living on the East Coast, these matches kick off at seven forty-five a.m. For big matches, this doesn't adversely affect pub attendance, but it does present a challenge when the club isn't playing particularly well and the match isn't as sexy as a derby. Mired in mid-table, having earned only one

154

point from the past three matches, Liverpool's upcoming away fixture versus Norwich City would test the loyalty of any passionate supporter.

One of my favorite quotes about the football fan's dedication comes from British expatriate pundit Roger Bennett, cohost of the NBC Sports television show and podcast *Men In Blazers*. Paraphrasing Bennett from his show: "If you're sitting at a pub drinking at seven in the morning, you have a drinking problem. But if you're sitting at that same pub drinking a pint at seven a.m. and there's a football match on the television, you're a football fan." Nowhere is this more evident than for West Coast football fans. Games can start as early as four forty-five a.m. in places like California.

Ask any general football fan that's been to Denver and they'll tell you that the Three Lions Pub is the place to watch most European football matches. While that English pub has earned its reputation by hosting fans from all clubs for years now, it's difficult to distinguish your club from the masses. There will typically be large crowds massed together watching a myriad of matches. Another great option is the British Bulldog Pub, located in the lower downtown area known as "LoDo." Both of these pubs pride themselves as being home to the English Premier League, but obviously they can't claim exclusivity to the sport. OLSC Denver had once called both pubs home. When the club first formed in 2010, they started meeting at the British Bulldog before migrating to the Three Lions. It wasn't until two die-hard LFC supporters, Glen Eastwood and Andrew Cudden, reached out to the club with an offer of exclusivity that OLSC Denver relocated to the Abbey Tavern for all matches.

The Abbey Tavern is the current home pub for OLSC Denver, located a few miles east of downtown. Irish expatriates Eastwood and Cudden opened the bar and restaurant about two years ago. The former managers of other Denver Irish pubs decided it was time to venture on their own, and the Abbey Tavern was born. It was a similar story for Darren Bridger and Mike Ruiz when they decided to open the London Bridge Pub in Raleigh after working at someone else's pub for years. As Eastwood explains, "There's no illuminated shamrocks; there's no leprechauns on the walls. I wanted to get away from that. It's more about the Irish hospitality, the Irish way of comfort." After seeing the place for the first time, I'd say he accomplished his mission.

Having a place to call your own is essential for any supporters club that wants to thrive. The local branch for Chelsea supporters was growing tired of sharing space at the other Denver football pubs, so they reached out to the Abbey Tavern and inquired about moving their club viewing parties there. It would've been easy to accept the additional revenue stream from Chelsea fans, but the ownership group held true to their word to OLSC Denver and denied the request. It helped that the owners are lifelong Liverpool fans as well. The ownership pair takes pride in their Liverpool support, so much that they've reserved a page on their website promoting their association with the Colorado Reds. You won't find anything like that on the websites for Three Lions Pub or the British Bulldog. Those two pubs may claim to be a home for the Barclays Premier League, but the Abbey Tavern remains home to Liverpool Football Club.

The clock read five thirty-five a.m. when my cab arrived at the Abbey Tavern parking lot. Kickoff would be in ten minutes, but there wasn't a single car parked in the lot. I was a bit concerned that I didn't have the right address, but the lights were on and the outside of the pub looked like the picture I saw on their website. It was cold outside, as one would expect for any January morning in Denver. I was reluctant to pay the cab fare and exit the warm car until I was convinced they would be playing the match live. Another car pulled into the lot and parked. Once I saw the driver get out and walk into the front door of the pub, I knew I had the right place.

I walked into the pub and grabbed a seat at the bar. There were only two other patrons inside at the time. A tall man was removing the multiple layers of clothing, including a nice red LFC Seattle scarf, as he situated himself next to me at the bar. A nice gal named Tara was tending bar, and delivered us both cups of hot coffee to start the morning. My new neighbor introduced himself as Arliss Merrell, an energy performance contractor from Rochester, New York. As I'm from upstate New York myself, we immediately made a connection. After graduating from college, Arliss moved out to Seattle for work. Not originally a soccer fan, he became enamored with the sport through the efforts of the Seattle Sounders in Major League Soccer. With one of the most passionate fan bases for any professional sports franchise in North America, the Sounders set the bar extremely high for fan experience. They create an incredible atmosphere that endears itself to most neutral fans. Arliss was one of these neutrals not long ago. He didn't have many friends as a new resident of Seattle, so some of his coworkers invited him to join them at the St. Andrew's pub, the home of OLSC Seattle. The passion that he saw from Liverpool fans mirrored his own experiences with the live matches of the Seattle Sounders. It was that simple.

A few more people wandered into the pub, including current OLSC Denver president Eben Dennis. Some of the fans were middle-aged men bringing their children for an early breakfast, while others appeared hung over from a Friday night of partying at clubs that only had closed a few hours earlier. About a dozen patrons found their spots at the bar as the match kicked off. Tara served up the coffee as some folks ordered breakfast from the kitchen. I thought about grabbing a pint of Guinness, mostly because it's not often one can make the claim that they were drinking the black gold watching Liverpool so early in the morning. I was informed that Colorado also has some of its own weird laws regarding the consumption of alcohol. No booze until seven a.m. You can legally smoke marijuana anywhere in the state at any time of day, yet try getting a pint of Guinness before seven at a pub. Damn it, man! There's a football match on television. I don't have a drinking problem, I'm just a football fan!

Eben Dennis moved to Denver from Dallas in 2010. He'd played the sport his entire life and became a Liverpool supporter because of his admiration for Robbie Fowler. He was a former member of the Dallas supporters club, but when he moved to Colorado for his career, he discovered the need to create a new club. They started watching at the British Bulldog and slowly began to grow in numbers. He initially expressed disappointment for me that they likely wouldn't get as large a group for an early match against a weaker opponent. "You should've been here for the Manchester United match a few weeks earlier," he said. "This place was packed." I knew he was right, but then again, every LFC pub would've been packed for that match. While watching big matches with big crowds is always fun, I also know that only the truly passionate fans will get up before six on Saturday to watch Liverpool play Norwich City.

The Canaries came into this match on the heels of a three-match losing streak, where they had been outscored 9-1. Norwich City began the week in sixteenth position on the table, only two points off the relegation zone. If they couldn't pick up their current form, they would surely be in a fight to survive at the end of the season.

Since Norwich City reclaimed their status as a regular in the Premier League, Liverpool had found an opponent against whom they enjoy consistently remarkable success. The Reds had outscored the Canaries 23-7 over seven league matches, with Liverpool winning five of those matches and drawing the other two. All of those matches had been with Luis Suarez, whose scoring record against the Canaries is nothing short of remarkable, playing striker for Liverpool,. The Uruguayan scored twelve of the twenty-three goals against Norwich City with three hat tricks. That being said, the Reds would only net one goal in September's 1-1 draw at Anfield against the East Anglian side.

Liverpool would be the first to score in the eighteenth minute of play. Referee Lee Mason awarded a free kick near midfield, from which the Reds made thirteen consecutive passes over the next forty-five seconds. Only Simon Mignolet and Jordan Henderson didn't touch the ball before Roberto Firmino was able to put it in the net. Alberto Moreno had possession along the left touchline when he found James Milner with a lateral pass. The Norwich defense moved up in an effort to play the offside trap, allowing Firmino space to move into the box unmarked. Milner timed his pass perfectly so the Brazilian remained onside due to the late movement from Norwich defender Robert Brady. Firmino got to the ball and released a shot toward the far post. It wasn't a terribly powerful strike, but placed well enough to beat goalkeeper Declan Rudd. The ball trickled off the far post into the net to give Liverpool a 1-0 lead. It was a much-needed goal to kick-start the Reds, but it also helped awaken the dozen supporters at the Abbey Tavern that were still eating their breakfast.

Milner nearly made it a two-goal lead a few minutes later when he inexplicably got a breakaway following a Norwich miscue about forty yards from goal. This time Brady was able to recover well to catch Milner on the break and time a tackle from behind. It was a gutsy play for the young Irish defender, as he risked a possible penalty and red card in the process, but he played it perfectly and saved a potential goal.

Norwich would find the equalizer and eventually take the lead late in the first half with consecutive goals scored off corner kicks. Both goals were conceded by Liverpool's failure to properly clear the ball out of danger. The first goal occurred in the twenty-eighth minute and actually ended up being an incredibly clever finish by Congolese striker Dieumerci Mbokani. When Mamadou Sakho stumbled in his attempt to clear, the Norwich striker gained possession with his back toward goal. He blindly powered a back-heel shot past Mignolet, who didn't see it coming.

While credit must be given for the clever goal to equalize, the second goal really took the steam out of Liverpool fans. With only a few minutes remaining in the first half, Liverpool failed to clear another Norwich corner kick. The Canaries possessed the ball on their right side as four Liverpool players converged on the ball, allowing Steven Naismith a path into the box unmarked. Naismith had only recently been acquired by Norwich from Liverpool's cross-town rival Everton the week before. The Scottish midfielder fired a low, hard shot from a difficult angle that found its way past Mignolet into the side net. It was a particularly tough one to concede for so many reasons, but none more than the fact that it appeared to be a goal that should've been saved.

By halftime, the Abbey Tavern crowd had doubled in size, with more patrons slowly making their way in. The atmosphere was still somewhat subdued based on the scoreboard, but there was a sense of optimism. One of the fans sitting near me was Christina Walls, who married into her support for the club. Married at Anfield Stadium in 2012, Christina actually made English history by being part of the first-ever same-sex marriage held at a Premier League stadium. She's since divorced, but her love for Liverpool never left. Christina was hanging out with John Mrovka, a relatively new fan that picked the club for no other reason than they always appeared to be on television. He loved the Beatles, who were from Liverpool, so he started rooting for the Reds as well. Good thing he didn't know at the time that most of the band supported Everton.

The second half commenced with Norwich intent on extending their lead. The newly acquired Naismith was wreaking havoc down the right side,

exposing the weak defensive skills on that flank. The former Toffee player
again snuck in behind the defense and collected a pass as he charged into
the penalty box. Alberto Moreno was out of position and retreated to
defend. He made a rash challenge as Naismith moved along the end line.
Naismith went down in what appeared to be a clear penalty, but Lee Mason
didn't blow the whistle. It appeared as though the Spanish defender had
gotten away with the foul, as Naismith stood up and continued to try to
move forward. Before he could proceed, he was hacked again from behind
Moreno and went back to the ground. This time Mason whistled for the
foul, giving Norwich a penalty. Watching the replay, I couldn't tell if the
referee was simply allowing Naismith to "play on" with the first foul, but
there was no mistake that the correct call was made. Wes Houlihan stepped
up for the Canaries and drilled home the penalty kick to give them a 3-1
lead in the fifty-third minute. The Abbey Tavern remained silent until one
passionate fan yelled, "What the fuck?" at the top of his lungs as Norwich
players completed their celebrations.

I looked at the clock and noticed it was a few minutes before seven.
Tara was diligently accepting pint requests as opportunity knocked. There's
no better time to get drink orders from a football fan than after a goal is
scored. I gladly obliged, and ordered a pint of Guinness.

As Tara served up the pints to various fans, few of us actually noticed
Liverpool had cut the deficit in half. Thirty seconds after the kickoff,
Nathaniel Clyne charged with the ball down the right side of the pitch. He
sent a cross into the box, slightly redirected by Firmino over toward
Henderson. The Liverpool captain one-timed the shot with perfect
placement inside the left post. The score was 3-2 with plenty of time for
more goals. After all, it was noted by the NBC Sports commentator that all
five shots on target had gone in the goal. Not a single save was made by
either goalkeeper.

Klopp went ahead in the fifty-eighth minute with a substitution that
proved to be game-changing for Liverpool. Adam Lallana replaced Jordon
Ibe, and the move almost immediately paid dividends. A few minutes after
coming onto the pitch, Milner played the ball from midfield down the left
flank to a rushing Lallana. He was immediately chased by three Norwich
City defenders as the ball moved toward the far edge of the penalty box.
This opened a large vacant space in the middle of the pitch for Firmino to
charge in unmarked. Lallana got the ball first and immediately recognized
the oncoming pressure of defenders. He sent the ball into the box with his
first touch to a wide-open Firmino near the penalty kick spot. Firmino
deftly brought the ball down with his first touch, and easily passed past the
charging goalkeeper into the net. Just like that, Liverpool had equalized.
This time the pub erupted with more fervor than previous goals. The
Colorado Reds seemed to be livelier at seven ten a.m. with pints of

Guinness in hand then at six with coffee.

Liverpool would regain the lead in the seventy-fourth minute with what could only be considered a gift goal. Russell Martin collected the ball for Norwich City at the midfield stripe as they looked to regroup for another attack. He turned and played the ball backward to his goal. It wasn't clear if he thought there was another defender behind him or if he simply didn't put enough power on a pass back to the keeper. In either case, the only player near the ball was James Milner. For the second time in the match, Milner found himself on a breakaway from forty yards out with nothing standing in between him and the target. This time the Englishman was able to avoid déjà vu, as he faked left before shifting to his right and passing into the open net. Liverpool took a 4-3 lead, and there was much rejoicing. There may have only been a few dozen people watching at the Abbey Tavern, but it felt like hundreds with the decibel levels achieved after that goal.

The match went into injury time with Liverpool playing well enough defensively that Norwich didn't look to equalize. Klopp had brought on Christian Benteke late in the half, and he was played offside with only a few minutes remaining. The free kick was seventy-five yards from goal, but allowed Martin an opportunity to launch a long, desperate pass toward the Liverpool goal. The ball caromed off Sakho's leg near the top of the penalty box straight to Sebastien Bassong. The French defender hadn't scored a goal for Norwich in three years, but he found himself in the right place at the right time. His left-footed shot through a sea of seven Red defenders found its way into the net. Mignolet was late to see the ball through the screen of players, and just like that, Norwich City had equalized. Four goals conceded on four set pieces, albeit one of those was a penalty kick. The inability to defend set pieces had been an issue for years, and it was clearly the impetus for allowing four goals in this match.

As soon as the ball entered the net, I heard a loud bang to my left. I looked over and noticed that this was the same guy that earlier said, "What the fuck?" after Norwich took the 3-1 lead. The young fan was Aaron Nilson, a student from Chicago currently attending graduate school in Denver. Aaron hammered the bar with his fist in frustration after Liverpool conceded a weak goal so late in the match. Aaron is a millennial that acquired his love for soccer like many fans in his generation, through the FIFA-sponsored video game. He watched the 2006 World Cup and loved watching Steven Gerrard, so he started playing Liverpool on his console. As he grew older and was able to legally consume, he started watching matches from the LFC pub. Clearly Aaron was upset with this goal, and he had every right to be. We all were pissed.

The television camera panned to the despondent Liverpool supporters in the crowd, and it quite matched what I saw at the Abbey Tavern so early in the morning. I had seen that look only twenty minutes earlier after Norwich City fans saw their club concede three unanswered goals to waste a second-half lead. At that moment we all sat speechless, yet desperately hopeful Liverpool could do something before the final whistle.

Klopp seemed to be livid on the sidelines, yelling at his club, presumably in an effort to keep them fighting. The look on his face could best be described as the look one gets they see a casual friend throwing up on the new white sofa in the living room following a night of drinking red wine. It was a look of pure anger.

Clearly you could see the players step up and react as though they didn't want to let him down. I had never seen that from these same players under Rodgers. There was still time. Klopp knew it. The players knew it. The fans at the Abbey Tavern weren't so sure.

Liverpool took the ensuing kickoff and pushed forward. Emre Can gained possession on the left side and sent a hopeful cross toward Benteke in the box. All players were attacking forward as Benteke was able to get a touch on the ball. Stephen Caulker, a tall central defender brought on by Klopp to protect the earlier 4-3 lead, found a chance to fire a shot toward goal. A Norwich City defender blocked that shot, which rebounded in the air back toward Caulker. Another shot was cleared with a looping header that found empty space in the box. Lallana charged toward the ball and hammered a left-footed shot off the ground into the side net past Rudd. The moment was surreal and unexpected, and it almost seemed like we were witnessing the play live in slow motion. As Lallana took off his shirt, running to celebrate the game winner, he charged up the field to find Klopp. The two met near the sideline and Lallana leapt into the manager's arms. It was a moment of vindication for Lallana, often criticized by both fans and media for underperforming since moving to Liverpool from Southampton in the summer of 2014. Klopp seemed to rejuvenate his early Liverpool career with this goal, a rebirth for the Englishman.

Every player on the pitch soon joined in the celebration with Klopp and Lallana. It was later revealed that Christian Benteke's arm accidentally broke the trademark eyeglasses off Klopp's face. At the Abbey Tavern, fans were hugging each other with delight after watching such an incredible conclusion. The final whistle blew with Liverpool winning the match 5-4. The NBC Sports commentator said it best: "What a match! This is going to take some drinking in." It wasn't even eight a.m. in Denver, and we already were.

It took some time for heartbeats to return to normal. It wasn't a big result against a strong squad, but still, it was the type of match where we were used to seeing the club drop points.

Two young fans that stuck around were Vlad Dobra and his companion Shannon Rivas. Vlad is a Romanian-born fan that moved to the Denver area from Phoenix in January of 2015. He adopted Liverpool as his favorite club during his childhood growing up in Eastern Europe. I ordered another pint as Arliss came over to say goodbye. He offered to exchange scarves, which I gladly accepted. It wasn't an OLSC Denver scarf, but I was touched by his gesture to ensure I had a piece of memorabilia from my trip to the Colorado capital.

As the last few fans found their way to the exit, I thanked Tara for a great morning. It's one thing to be a passionate supporter and show up at five thirty a.m. to watch a soccer match, but a completely different thing to come to work and serve those fans. I ensured that she had a good tip for exceptional service. It was a great day and a great result.

23 - WINTER PARK

Tuesday, January 26
Doc's Roadhouse, Winter Park, CO
League Cup Semifinal, Leg #2 (vs. Stoke City)

It was certainly going to be hard following up the Norwich City match, but three days later Liverpool would be back in action for the second leg of the League Cup semifinal. Three weeks earlier the Reds traveled to Britannia Stadium and defeated Stoke City 1-0 to take the aggregate lead. If they could avoid defeat at home in this match, they would advance to their first cup final in four years.

Following the previous match in Denver, I spent the next few days on a snowboarding vacation at Winter Park Resort. This short vacation was booked long before Liverpool's passage to the League Cup semifinals, but thankfully the match was scheduled for Tuesday. With my return flight home scheduled for Wednesday afternoon, I would be able to watch the semifinal leg in its entirety. Exactly where I watched was to be determined.

As much as the sport has grown across the country over the past few decades, soccer pubs haven't quite reached Colorado Rocky Mountain ski country yet. All that I really needed was a bar that carried the BEINSport network and discipline to ensure I was seated there for Tuesday one p.m. MST. My first choice was Randi's Irish Pub in town. I stopped there on the first day for breakfast, and immediately confirmed that their satellite feed included BEINSport. With fresh Guinness on tap, this could likely be my viewing spot.

The only concern that I had with Randi's was that the location isn't exactly on the mountain. This meant I would have to complete my day early and catch the shuttle bus back into town in order to ensure I was sitting at the bar for kickoff. I decided to conduct a secondary reconnaissance mission at the resort to see if any of their watering holes had the right television network. Doc's Roadhouse is one of the bars located at the base of Winter Park Resort, so I stopped there for a beer after spending Monday on the slopes. A quick search confirmed that they also carried BEINSport, so I was able to watch the match there. This was a huge benefit, since I could extend my morning runs through lunch and simply walk into the tavern before kickoff. That was exactly what I did.

I sidled up to the bar just before one and took a spot in front of the sixty-inch television. Eric Wacker was tending the bar, just like he did during happy hour the day before. He recalled how I wanted to watch this match, so it was no surprise when I asked him to change the channel. Eric is a middle-aged bartender originally from Orlando that works at the resort so he can snowboard for free on his off days. There wasn't a single other person in the bar, so clearly it wouldn't be an issue. Sadly, they didn't have Guinness on tap, but with New Belgium Brewing Company the official brewer of the resort, I could settle for the local favorite Fat Tire. Eric served my pint just before kickoff.

The first half was relatively uneventful until the very end, when Stoke City scored a goal that should never have counted. Stoke City midfielder Bojan Krkic slid a pass across to a wide-open Marko Arnautovic. The Austrian striker, who clearly wants to emulate Zlatan Ibrahimovich in both skill and looks, scored with a side-footed shot despite replays confirming he was in an offside position. The goal counted despite Liverpool's objection, and the clubs went into the break deadlocked at 1-1 on aggregate.

Resort guests slowly started making their way into Doc's Roadhouse following a nice day on the mountain, and for the most part they were interested in relaxing with a cool alcoholic beverage. It was impossible to avoid the television screen broadcasting, so some of the guests inquired about the match. Word spread about a single Liverpool supporter sitting at the bar watching a live soccer match by himself while drinking pints of Fat Tire. With every close call, people could see my emotions. At first a small group of kids from Dallas asked me about the match, and they started rooting for Liverpool. Another man wearing a Boston Red Sox hat joined me at the bar and starting asking questions about the match. I suggested that he should root for Liverpool, since they shared ownership groups with his beloved Red Sox. He was unaware of that fact, and nodded in agreement. Clearly these folks were all sports fans, but hadn't yet been bitten by the soccer bug. They were intrigued about a live soccer match being played so early in the afternoon on a Tuesday.

The second half was also uneventful, and the match went into extra time. As the teams prepared for more football, I overheard a lady behind tell her husband that she was headed back to the room. He replied, "Go ahead. I'll meet you there later. I want to see if Liverpool can pull this out."

Without looking back, I smiled. Was I converting these people into football fans? An even better question was whether or not they were becoming Liverpool fans.

No one was able to find the back of the net in the thirty minutes of extra time, and the finalist would be determined by penalty shootout. It was frustrating that this club couldn't figure out how to penetrate past the Stoke City defense and score the much-needed goal. Clearly they were capable, but they just laid an egg. Luckily they were still alive, and could win in the penalty shootout, something they had already done once in this competition, against Carlisle United.

I looked around Doc's Roadhouse and noticed about a dozen people sitting at their table watching the match. It was surreal for me to think that I had found a spot in a somewhat remote tavern at the base of a popular Colorado ski resort and temporarily turned it into a soccer pub. I didn't think a single person there was interested in seeing Stoke City win, either.

The shootout went into sudden death, with both teams converting four of five penalties. After both clubs converted their sixth attempt, Mignolet made a nice save on Stoke City defender Marc Muniesa's shot. The door was open for Liverpool to advance, and up stepped Joe Allen to take the kick. The Welshman calmly slotted home the winner as I jumped off my chair in glee. A few people gave me high fives, while others patted me on the back and congratulated me as though I had accomplished some great feat.

One of the guys from Dallas turned and asked me, "So what does this mean now?"

"It means we play in the finals at Wembley Stadium," I replied.

I looked over at Eric, who was pouring shots of some golden liquor into one-ounce glasses. "It means much more than that," Eric replied as he handed over a dozen shots to the group of us. "It means victory shots!"

I couldn't help but feel like this exact moment was being re-created at the London Bridge Pub as they poured celebratory shots to the Raleigh Reds. I grabbed my shot glass and raised it in the air victoriously. I thought I should probably say something poignant to signal the momentous victory, but I was speechless in this surreal moment. One of the guys from Dallas took over and shouted, "To Liverpool!" We all repeated the toast and clinked our shot glasses together.

As I let this moment sink in, I could only laugh to myself. Never in a million years would I have predicted that I would be drinking celebratory shots with a dozen random strangers that likely had never watched a soccer match on television before…at a bar at the base of a Colorado ski resort. As I sat back and reflected on the journey that began five months earlier, I couldn't help but think what may become of my new friends. I envisioned them sitting at a pub years from now watching Liverpool play on the television. As someone approached them asking why they chose to root for the Reds, the reply would be something like: "I was on this ski trip to Winter Park Resort a few years ago, and we stopped at this bar for a quick beer and met this guy from North Carolina that was watching Liverpool play in the League Cup semifinals…" Knowing how that story ends puts a smile on my face. I thought I may have just given birth to some new additions to the Liverpool family.

****

For the ninth time this month, Liverpool had to play a match. They were still alive in all four competitions that they'd entered this season, but Jürgen Klopp was starting to feel the pressure of managing English club football. This would be the club's thirty-seventh match in 175 days, or a match every 4.7 days. It was Klopp's twenty-seventh game at the helm of Liverpool in only 106 days, roughly equivalent to one match every four days. Most players had already spent considerable time sidelined with injury, and some were still recovering. With the Europa League knockout stage on the horizon and the League Cup final in a few weeks, many reserve players were given the opportunity to show Klopp what they could do.

West Ham United came to Anfield full of confidence, having beaten the Reds in both league matches this campaign. They'd only been defeated once in the month of January, so this would not be an easy match.

The last thing anyone wanted to see was another match added to the fixture list, but that was exactly what would happen. It was one of those drab matches that give the sport a black eye, with not much to report. West Ham never really threatened to score and Liverpool missed out on some decent chances. Christian Benteke, losing confidence by the second like a tire loses air after running over a bed of nails, missed another sitter from six yards out. Fans started wondering if perhaps the Belgian striker had turned into a bigger flop than Andy Carroll.

I wondered if the club would be better off had they been eliminated. Injuries had taken their toll in recent weeks, with many key players finally coming back to fitness. The final whistle blew with the score knotted 0-0, and a replay would be added to the schedule for a midweek trip to London in less than two weeks.

24 - TURBULENT TIMES

Tuesday, February 2
London Bridge Pub
Premier League match #24 (at Leicester City)

A trip to league leaders Leicester City was next on the schedule only three days after the weekend's FA Cup draw. Having lost to Tottenham in the FA Cup a few weeks earlier, Leicester City had only Premier League matches left. Many people, myself included, felt that it would be difficult for the Foxes to sustain the high level of performance through the rest of the season. Over the holidays I had even bet Dan Franklin a pint of Guinness that they wouldn't even qualify for the Champions League. I carelessly assumed that some richer clubs may offer the club large sums of cash to buy their talent in the January transfer window. That deadline had passed a few days earlier with their squad intact.

Liverpool had made a late effort before the window closed to bring Brazilian attacker Alex Teixeira to the club from Shakhtar Donetsk, but the Ukrainians refused to budge from their asking price of £38 million. I wasn't convinced that he was a player that would fill a necessary void for Liverpool, so the failure to acquire his services did not bother me as much as it did other fans. He would ultimately get shipped off to Jiangsu Suning, as the Chinese club met the high price tag.

It was another midweek match for Liverpool, and that meant another trip to London Bridge Pub for me. The usual suspects were already consuming their first pints when I walked in just before kickoff. There were about twenty Raleigh Reds in attendance, a far cry from the atmosphere we would enjoy for a midweek encounter two years earlier.

Dejan Lovren and Nathaniel Clyne had both returned to the lineup following injuries. Lovren was starting to find his place in the lineup, forming a solid partnership with Mamadou Sakho in central defense. It was no secret that I held a soft spot for the Croatian, and I was happy to see him rebound from a dismal first season at Liverpool.

Even though the season was barely past the midway point, Jamie Vardy had already caught the eye of the world as the best story of the year. The English striker began his career in the youth academy of Sheffield Wednesday, but was released at the age of sixteen. He picked up with the non-league outfit Stocksbridge Park Steels before joining FC Halifax Town at twenty-three. He scored twenty-six goals for the Northern Premier League club, seven divisions below the Premier League. His success earned him a transfer to Fleetwood Town of the Conference Premier, the fifth level of English football. Vardy would score thirty-one times that season, catching the eyes of many clubs in the process. He would sign for Leicester City in the Football League Championship for a non-league record transfer fee of £1 million in 2012. Two seasons later, he scored sixteen goals to help Leicester City earn promotion to the Premier League.

Still a relative unknown talent to most of the world, Vardy would announce his presence with authority in November by breaking the Premier League record of consecutive games scoring a goal. Manchester United's Ruud Van Nistelrooy previously held the record of ten straight games, so it was fitting that Vardy broke the record at home with a goal in his eleventh match in a row, a 1-1 draw against the Red Devils.

The first match left little to be excited about for Liverpool. It was maddening to see our boys being dominated by a club that only a year ago had barely escaped relegation. Claudio Ranieri was proving his worth as a world-class manager as Leicester City continued to prove skeptics like myself wrong. The match was knotted scoreless at halftime.

Vardy would score twice in the second half to give the home squad a 2-0 victory over Liverpool. It was the opening goal of the match in the sixtieth minute that would spark the biggest debate at the pub that afternoon. The outstanding young Algerian midfielder Riyadh Mahrez had possession only ten yards ahead of their penalty box when he sent a fifty-yard pass beyond the Liverpool defense on the right side. Vardy was already behind Sakho, sprinting ahead past the slower Lovren toward the ball. The ball bounced only ten yards from our penalty box when Vardy looked up to see Simon Mignolet a few yards off his line. With the precision of a military sniper, Vardy one-timed a right-footed volley over Mignolet into the back of the net. The crowd at the King Power Stadium erupted as Vardy ran to the corner flag in celebration. Everyone at the pub was stunned.

Immediate blame was cast on Mignolet for being so far off his line when Vardy struck the ball. The moment the play started the ball was about eighty or ninety yards away from our goal. Four seconds later, Vardy took the shot. Two seconds after that, it was in the net. It was the sort of play that left you speechless with your jaw dropped, paralyzed in awe of what you'd just witnessed. The goal would earn the title "goal of the year" from the media, and rightfully so. I defended Mignolet at the pub, explaining that not every goal requires a scapegoat. People immediately look for blame after every goal, and sometimes it is easy to spot. In this case you could only tip your cap to Vardy for having the moxie to take the shot and the skill to execute it. It was a world-class finish and one of the greatest strikes I had seen in a long time.

Minutes later, Vardy would score a second goal to put the game out of reach. Leicester City earned another valuable three points on their march to the title. For me, the realization hit on how much I'd underestimated the Foxes. I could only hope that these three points dropped would help Leicester City win the league ahead of teams like Arsenal, Tottenham, or Manchester City. As I walked out of the pub in defeat, I had another somewhat painful realization. I would soon owe Dan Franklin a pint for losing that bet, as this Leicester City team was clearly going to finish in the top four at the end of the season.

****

The following Saturday was a home match against Sunderland. Earlier in the week Fenway Sports Group had announced a new ticket pricing plan in which overall prices increased in an effort to drive revenue. As an American sports fan, the increase didn't seem to be too egregious. We are used to seeing ticket prices escalate to the point where most professional sports games are simply too expensive for the average fan. In England they still have many affordable tickets that offer great views of the match.

Liverpool fans seemed to fixate on the significant price increase of the most expensive ticket. While it only represented about two percent of the capacity, some fans would be forced to pay £78 for a match. Fans in England were outraged, calling it a move of pure greed. Everyone seemed to offer an opinion, and it dominated the discussions all week. Personally, I offered nothing in terms of a voice, simply because it was not my battle to have. The price of a match ticket at Anfield was something that didn't affect my life. The cost of airfare and lodging would far outweigh the ticket price to make an impact for me.

Plans were made by supporters groups in Liverpool to stage a protest at the Sunderland match. Fans decided to walk out on the match in the seventy-eighth minute in an effort to voice their displeasure with the club. If nothing else, the move might add some late theatrics to a match against an otherwise dull opponent.

One of the requirements for being an official club with LFC is to have an annual general meeting where all members have the opportunity to have their say with the leadership. Many clubs take this responsibility very seriously, but for LFC Raleigh it is nothing more than a checkbox on the annual renewal process. We don't charge a large fee to join, nor do we have a large bank account to manage. We simply like to come together at the pub to enjoy a good Liverpool match. If you care to donate to the cause, we'll take your money. But no one will be refused admission at the door. The AGM is always scheduled about thirty minutes before kickoff of a Liverpool match, and lasts about ten. This year was no different. With unanimous approval, the club remained on track.

The biggest news before the match was that Klopp was too ill to attend, so his chief assistant Zeljko Buvac was put in charge. With talk about the ticket price protest and Klopp's illness dominating the conversations at the pub, we hardly noticed Daniel Sturridge had made the bench for the first time in about two months. His fitness was going to be a critical component for Liverpool to have any success the rest of the season.

The first half was another dull affair, mostly due to Liverpool's inability to break down the bunkered defense deployed by Sunderland manager Sam Allardyce. Liverpool dominated with seventy-one percent of the possession, but had nothing to show for it in a scoreless first half.

Roberto Firmino opened the scoring in the fifty-ninth minute with a simple header to the far post off a James Milner cross. Ten minutes later, Firmino assisted Adam Lallana with a deft pass to double the Liverpool lead. Life was good and the pub crowd seemed to relax. Sunderland showed little offense all match, so it would seem that three points were in the books for Liverpool.

Then the seventy-eighth minute came. True to their word, over ten thousand fans got up and left the grounds. The television cameras did a great job covering the mass exodus, and it turned out to be a significant moment in the match. Four minutes later, Adam Johnson, who was playing in his final match before going to prison following a statutory rape conviction, scored on a free kick goal from about twenty yards out. It was a goal that Mignolet should've saved easily. Just like that, the deficit was cut in half. Nerves descended upon the rest of the faithful at Anfield, and at the pub as well.

With only a few minutes remaining in the match, Jermain Defoe would break our hearts with a left-footed shot from the center of the box past Mignolet. Sunderland had no business getting to this position in the match, yet here we were deadlocked at two when the final whistle blew.

It was another frustrating result, and I couldn't help but wonder if the walkout affected the outcome. On the surface you'd think that was crazy to think that the fan activity would affect their play. But perhaps there was enough distraction to take away Liverpool's focus enough and allow Sunderland back into the match. The aftermath didn't help, as it was later revealed that Liverpool legend Jamie Carragher had joined the fans in the walkout. Former manager Roy Evans urged the owners to listen to the fans, while Klopp himself agreed that the club needed to find a solution. The message was received, as days later Fenway Sports Group would recant their plan and announce a two-year freeze on all ticket prices. It was considered to be a major victory for the fans. The unprecedented move made headlines globally, getting press on American mainstream sports programs. Now if only the players could score a few more victories down the road, all would be well with the world again.

****

The FA Cup replay against West Ham was scheduled for Tuesday afternoon at Upton Park, so another midweek clash with the pub regulars was in the cards. Klopp had had his appendix removed three days earlier, but was back in good health, and looked recharged on the sidelines. Klopp continued to play many reserves in this match, choosing to give his mainstays a little rest. Tiago Ilori, Kevin Stewart, Pedro Chirivella, Joao Carlos Teixeira, and Brad Smith all returned to the starting lineup and were able to hold their own throughout the match.

West Ham's Michail Antonio would give the home team the lead just before halftime, but Coutinho equalized in the opening minutes of the second half with some trickery on a free kick. Instead of trying to curl the shot around the wall, our little Brazilian magician anticipated the West Ham wall's leap in the air. He fired a low shot that went under the wall, past a shocked Darren Randolph in goal. It was either exceptional scouting to know that the West Ham wall would leap on contact, or blind luck for Coutinho. Either way, the score was tied at one goal apiece.

The match was quite exciting, with both teams going end to end. Despite the lack of star power for both lineups, the players made the most of the moment and entertained us. The match went into extra time for another thirty minutes of football. As the play continued, you could see the toll that the early frantic pace had taken on the players. They were knackered, and it showed. In the final minute, West Ham earned a free kick from a dangerous position. It seemed that Liverpool only need to survive one final attack before the match would be decided on penalties. Gus Payet crossed the ball into the box, where Angelo Ogbonna was able to head home the winner.

Just like that, Liverpool was finally eliminated from their first competition. At the pub, there was disappointment, but no one seemed really bothered at the time. There were much more important fixtures on the horizon, like the Europa League knockout stage before a trip to Wembley Stadium for the League Cup Final. Before we looked ahead to those matches, there was one more match to be played on Sunday, at league bottom dweller Aston Villa.

****

Prior to this season, Aston Villa was one of the few teams to have never been relegated since the creation of the Premier League in 1992. They were well on their way to taking their name off that list. The week earlier they'd defeated Norwich City 2-0 for only their third victory of the season, and sat firmly in last place on the table. This game was being played on Valentine's Day, and Liverpool fans were hopeful that they could perform their own massacre at Villa Park. With the eighty-thirty kickoff on Sunday morning, I elected to watch this match at the house instead of trekking down to the pub.

Sturridge returned to the starting lineup, making this only the fourth time all season that he and Coutinho had started together. The injury history from Sturridge had been well documented, and with some important fixtures ahead, it would be critical for him to get fully fit and firing on all cylinders. It didn't take long against the woeful Aston Villa defense. In the fifteenth minute, Coutinho sent a cross from the left flank to the unmarked striker eight yards from goal. It was a perfect cross and an easy header into the net to give Liverpool the early lead.

James Milner would double the lead nine minutes later when his in-swinging free kick went untouched by everyone. It fooled goalkeeper Mark Bunn and ended up in the back of the net. Liverpool spent much of the first half dominating play, with sixty-two of the possession and a 6-1 advantage on shots. Home fans were distraught, booing the team as they walked down the tunnel. Fans held signs that read, "Proud History. What Future?" Unfortunately, the immediate future of the next forty-five minutes of football would not be pleasing to their eyes.

Emre Can scored in the fifty-seventh minute on a counterattack after a nice pass from Firmino to make the score 3-0. That cushion gave Klopp the opportunity to give Sturridge a little rest, so he brought on the other talented striker recovering from a recent injury. Divock Origi came onto the pitch to replace Sturridge in the sixty-first minute, and immediately made an impact. Jordan Henderson got possession deep in the defense and dribbled out of danger. He passed up to Coutinho, who sent Origi on the breakaway. Origi is one of the fastest players in the league, and got behind the defense for a one vs. one against the goalkeeper. The Belgian slotted the ball inside the left post to give Liverpool a 4-0 lead on his first action in the match. Notable about this goal was the celebration, as Origi streaked toward the traveling Kop and leapt into the stands. He was immediately hugged by one amorous fan that grabbed his head to kiss his cheek. I chuckled and said to myself, "Happy Valentine's Day, Divock."

Defenders Nathaniel Clyne and Kolo Toure would add the final insults to injury to make the final score 6-0. By the time Toure was celebrating on the sidelines, dancing with Mamadou Sakho after his seventy-first-minute goal, the vast majority of Aston Villa fans had left the building like Elvis. It was an embarrassing display of sport for the home crowd. The best analogy to the misery that is Aston Villa Football Club at the moment is the Cleveland Browns in the NFL. Decades away from the good years, with darker days seemingly ahead, it should be no surprise that both teams share a common denominator. Both teams are owned by Randy Lerner. I think it's time for the American investor to find a new hobby, because clearly being a team owner is not working out.

Finally, Liverpool had some momentum as they headed into an important stretch of their season. By virtue of the Reds crashing out of the FA Cup, the next weekend was now open, with no match to be played. That left Liverpool's next three matches to be a two-legged playoff match in the Europa League round of thirty-two against FC Augsburg, followed by the League Cup final. We all hoped that this offensive burst of six goals would carry forward for this critical stretch.

25 - AUSTIN

The moment had finally come when Liverpool began the arduous task of trying to win another European trophy. Having taken first place in their group of the Europa League, Liverpool had earned a top seed in the draw. It made perfect sense that the club were to face FC Augsburg from the German Bundesliga. Why wouldn't Liverpool's new German coach be sent home?

Augsburg is a relatively small town in Bavarian Germany, about an hour's drive from Munich. I actually had the pleasure of visit this town of about 250,000 people in the summer of 2006. Tori and I were winding down our summer vacation during Germany's World Cup and headed up the Romantic Road to Frankfurt. Established originally as a trade route that connected Germany to Southern Europe during the Romantic Era, this has largely been marketed as a themed route for travelers to enjoy some of the finest German scenery. It connects the castle town of Füssen along the Austrian border with the town of Würzburg. We picked up the Romantic Road from the university town of Augsburg.

FC Augsburg was promoted to the Bundesliga for the first time after the 2010-11 season, and had made the most of that experience, slowly improving their league finish annually. In 2014-15 they finished in fifth place in the Bundesliga, earning the club's first ever entry into European competition, with qualification to the Europa League.

Augsburg defeated Serbian club FK Partizan Belgrade in the final group match to finish second place and earn a spot in the knockout round, a tremendous achievement for the small club. They were struggling to

174

perform in the Bundesliga, only one point above the relegation zone at the time, but their fans were rewarded with an important affair against one of the most storied clubs in the sport's history.

Much like the League Cup semifinals, the format for this stage of the competition was to play ninety minutes at each club's home stadium and use the aggregate score to determine the winner. The first match was held at WWK Arena in Augsburg. Conventional wisdom is that playing the first match away is an advantage. With the away goals tiebreaker, it frees up the visiting squad to try and attack while the home team tends to tighten up in a preventive defense mode, like an NFL team does to protect a lead late in the fourth quarter.

For the first time in thirty matches of Klopp's reign, the starting eleven players remained unchanged from the previous match. When your team goes on the road and defeats a Premier League squad 6-0, there is good reason to keep the lineup consistent.

I watched the first leg at the London Bridge Pub, and there wasn't much to report. There was a decent crowd at the pub, but the opponent didn't seem to scare up any fear for Reds fans. As a result, there was an apathetic feeling toward this match. Expectation was Liverpool would win handsomely in Germany and then be afforded the luxury of completing their advancement to the next round without worry. Many supporters chose not to cash in a work excuse for this particular fixture.

Both clubs had decent chances to score, but no one could break through, and the final score was 0-0. It was a rather dull affair. That was the sort of result we'd come to expect under Brendan Rodgers, but this was Klopp's team now. This was the same team that had scored six goals over the weekend, and it was frustrating to see them struggle. Luckily for Liverpool, their weekend Premier League clash with Chelsea would be postponed, since the Blues had a conflict in the FA Cup. This open weekend would allow Klopp a full week to evaluate and prepare for the return leg against Augsburg. While it would've been nice to rest some players in advance of the League Cup final on the following Sunday, failing to advance against a potentially relegated German squad would be devastating for the club's confidence. It wasn't the worst result, but not scoring the away goal meant Thursday's match at Anfield was a must-win for the Reds.

****

Fado's is a popular Irish pub franchise with fifteen locations spread all across major cities in America. The Irish term "fado" is typically used to start a story, much like how we would say "once upon a time." As the old adage goes, great stories rarely begin with the phrase "I was eating this great salad." Great stories usually begin with a pint, so why not name your Irish pub "Fado's"?

I had been to Fado's in both Washington, D.C., and Denver before, so I was quite familiar with the franchise. With all due respect, it is difficult to distinguish one great Irish pub from another. They all have Guinness on tap, and that matters most to me. Many supporters clubs tend to meet in Irish pubs, so it was no surprise to finally locate a club that met at a Fado's pub.

Austin had long been a city that I wanted to visit. The state capital of Texas has a great reputation for music, drink, and food. It is also the home to an old high school friend that I hadn't seen in over twenty years, so it was an easy choice to visit.

I grew up playing soccer with Tony Giannetti, a classmate that lived just up the street in the small town of Apalachin, New York. While I chose to attend the U.S. Coast Guard Academy after graduation, Tony elected to continue his education at the U.S. Military Academy in West Point. We lost touch soon after high school graduation, but reconnected thanks to social media. He left the Army from Fort Hood and settled down in Austin. Before he married and had kids, Tony used to frequent Fado's in downtown Austin, and highly recommended it. Even though he is a Chelsea supporter, I trusted his judgment in pubs.

I arrived in downtown Austin a bit early and walked down to Fado's well ahead of kickoff. I noticed a small crowd of four or five other degenerates waiting for the pub to open its doors at eleven fifteen a.m., some of whom were donning Liverpool kits like I was. Kickoff was scheduled for noon local time, since Austin is in the Central time zone, so I had enough time to order lunch and a pint of Guinness.

With only a few people filing into the pub, the staff was still getting things ready for a big day of football. I spoke with Eric the manager, who explained that Fado's was the home pub for both the local Liverpool and Manchester United supporters clubs. They were expecting a decent crowd, since both clubs were in action that afternoon. Liverpool kicked off at noon, with Manchester United playing two hours later.

The pub itself was set up much like you would expect, with several small rooms and nooks for patrons to hide with their pints. With the English clubs kicking off at separate times, there would be no conflict over which match would occupy most television sets in the pub. Eric informed me that both Liverpool and Manchester United fans would be able to watch their matches from the main viewing room with the sixty-inch projector television. After finishing my corned beef sandwich, I gladly relocated to enjoy the match with the other Liverpool fans.

Chris Delcros was the first Austin Red to greet me, extending an invitation to join him at his spot on the bar. Chris hails from County

Kildare in Ireland, and moved to Austin about five years ago. He works as a real estate agent in the suburbs, which gives him the flexibility to attend many midweek fixtures at the pub. For Chris to become a Liverpool supporter wasn't as much a choice as it was a family obligation. He told me the story of his seven-year-old nephew that bravely announced to the family that he chose to support Chelsea. It didn't sit well with his brother-in-law, so they arranged a field trip to Anfield so his son could witness his first live football match. That was the last time he son spoke of a Chelsea allegiance, and order was restored to the clan.

Chris was chatting with Steve Wilson, a youngish-looking, fit lad that you could tell still laced up the boots. Steve was an Air Force brat as a child, living in all parts of the country. He graduated from Goldsboro High School outside of Raleigh while his father was stationed at Seymour Johnson Air Force Base. He started following Liverpool because of their beautiful attacking style of play in the mid-1990s. As owner of a steel-fabrication business, he also rarely misses a match at Fado's. We started chatting, and learned that we shared a common friend in Brian McLaughlin from New York. Brian and Steve played together in the Legends match, where fans get to play against some of the Liverpool legends.

Everyone was mildly confident that Liverpool would win the match, but you could sense nervousness amongst many of the fans at the pub. Some of the discussion at the pub focused on the upcoming League Cup final against Manchester City, considering this particular match almost as an afterthought. I hoped the players weren't doing the same thing.

French referee Clement Turpin got the match started, and it didn't take long for him to get called into action with a tough decision. Liverpool earned a corner kick from the right side in the third minute of play. James Milner passed short back to Jordan Henderson, who drove the cross hard across into the goal box. Mamadou Sakho was the target man, but he was well marked going into the challenge. The ball was seemingly cleared behind the far post and out for another corner kick. Instead of pointing to the corner flag, Turpin pointed to the spot, signaling for a Liverpool penalty kick.

No one in the pub could understand the call, although no one was complaining about it either. Most of us thought the foul was for impeding Sakho's attempt to make a play, which would've been a weak decision. Replays confirmed that the ball was handled by Augsburg defender Dominik Kohr. It looked like their tall Brazilian striker Caiuby was in perfect position to make the play, but Kohr clumsily got himself in the way trying to jump at the ball as well. His arms flung in the air and solidly struck the ball as Caiuby moved his head in. It was a "bang-bang" play that was difficult to discern on live television. Turpin was positioned perfectly to see the infraction, and got it right. Milner stepped up to the spot and kicked a low, hard shot to the right post. Even though the Augsburg goalkeeper guessed correctly, he couldn't make a play, and the ball went into the back of the net. Liverpool took the early 1-0 lead.

Despite this, it was imperative for Liverpool to score another goal and provide a cushion. A goal from Augsburg would equalize the match and give them the outright series by virtue of the precious away goal. Liverpool's defense had been less than impressive for most of the season, so it was too much to expect another clean sheet.

Phillippe Coutinho nearly doubled the Liverpool lead in the twenty-first minute when he received a brilliant pass from Daniel Sturridge in the box. The Brazilian could only manage a quick shot straight to Augsburg goalkeeper Marwin Hitz, who made an easy save. There were hints of frustration at the effort in the pub, but no one seemed worried. Liverpool were in complete control of the play for the first quarter of the match.

Knowing that they needed to score a goal to get back into the match, the German squad picked up their attack and created some nervy moments for us. In the twenty-fourth minute of play, Greek wide man Kostas Stafylidis sent a hard shot toward goal, requiring Simon Mignolet to make a diving safe to his left and preserve the lead.

Mignolet would be tested again ten minutes later when Lucas Leiva sent a weak pass back toward goal that was easily intercepted by Caiuby on the left flank. Mignolet came off his line to cut down the angle and force the Brazilian further wide. The striker got off a weak attempt toward an empty goal. Sakho was able to retreat and prevent the ball from crossing the goal line, although replays confirmed it was going to be wide of target. As bad as Augsburg's attack may have been most of the season, you still couldn't count them out from equalizing due to Liverpool's propensity to concede scoring chances. The halftime whistle came with Liverpool clinging to a tenuous one-goal advantage. Both Sturridge and Roberto Firmino had good chances on target, but Hitz was up to the task, making the saves.

Most of the Austin supporters took the opportunity to head outside to the patio and enjoy some sunlight away from the dark pub. It was there I met Jeff Cleveland, a student at the University of Texas getting his master's degree in music. Jeff grew up in Dallas and moved to Austin after graduating from Illinois State. He was always a soccer fan growing up in Dallas, but picked up Liverpool through his international travels with the bugle corps. He'd made many friends abroad, one English friend in particular that strongly supported Liverpool. While studying in England, Jeff fell in love with the Reds and has followed them since. Jeff was talking with Jake Harding, a manager in the golf department at Dick's Sporting Goods. Jake was born and raised in Austin. He attended boarding school as a child with nothing to do one day in May of 2005. Flipping through the television that afternoon, he came across a soccer match where Liverpool would end up winning the Champions League. Not knowing anything else about the sport, he saw the Liverpool faithful on television in Istanbul help will their club to victory. As with many fans that I'd already met on this journey, Jake's allegiance to Liverpool Football Club was birthed on that day.

The second half began, and Liverpool started to look like the dominating presence we'd expected. There were more chances created early, but Augsburg defenders continued to get in the way, or a nice save was made by Hitz. Fans started getting a little restless looking for that second goal, but OLSC Austin social media chairperson Justin Dohr started some chants to keep the mood positive. It's hard to describe, but Justin just looked like someone that would be living in Austin. That starving musician look with a trendy hat was further confirmed when I saw him rolling his own cigarettes. "We love you, Liverpool, we do!" he would scream, and the rest of the crew joined in.

Seventy minutes into the match and Liverpool was still clinging to the one-goal lead. Lucas Leiva sent a difficult pass toward Milner near midfield that was intercepted by an Augsburg player. A dangerous through-ball was played forward to Tobias Werner, the bald German thirty-year-old with a striking resemblance to American national team player Michael Bradley. Mignolet sprinted forward to retrieve the ball, preventing a dangerous scoring threat. The television camera focused on the frustrated Werner, prompting Justin to start chanting, "You're just a shit, Michael Bradley!" We all gladly joined, chanting something that I was quite sure only we were singing anywhere in the world.

As the minutes kept ticking, we just knew that Augsburg would get more chances. I had that same feeling I used to get with Liverpool when you just knew the team would regret putting the game away earlier. The fact that Augsburg had a long-throw specialist made me feel even more uncomfortable anytime Liverpool cleared the ball from their defensive third. The clear had to be kept in play or Augsburg could launch the ball into the box from a throw-in.

The Germans threatened again in the eightieth minute when Caiuby got possession near the left end line and sent a dangerous cross into the six-yard box. Alberto Moreno did a good job tracking his mark on the play, preventing an easy tap-in goal as Lucas was able to clear the ball from danger.

Clearly momentum was shifting away from Liverpool, and the tension continued to build inside the pub. I looked around to see about thirty fans nervously focused on the big-screen television. No one could believe that this match was still in question. All it took was one mistake and Liverpool could be eliminated from this competition. Lucas nearly made that mistake in the eighty-eighth minute with a reckless, unnecessary foul on Caiuby just outside the box. Without specifics to back up this claim, it seems to me that Lucas often makes an ill-timed challenge late in the game to give the opponents a late chance at goal.

The ball was spotted about twenty yards from goal in the center of the pitch. Mignolet set up the wall with about six Liverpool players, hoping to create enough obstruction to reduce the sight on target. Stafylidis lined up to shoot with his left foot and fired a shot that appeared to go in the goal. It was a funny angle from the camera, because the shot actually missed wide by mere inches. That didn't stop someone from loudly cursing at the pub. Once it was evident that the ball had missed, we all breathed a sigh of relief.

The final whistle blew and Liverpool was through to the next round. It had the feeling of an NCAA college basketball tournament game when the top seed sneaks by the heavy underdog after they miss the potential game-winning basket at the buzzer. It never should've been that close. Augsburg was outclassed throughout, but somehow the Reds couldn't find the target against the Germans. It took a difficult-to-spot penalty call to give Liverpool the scoring chance they needed. No one was particularly happy with how it went down, but all that mattered was we got the result with the 1-0 victory on aggregate. Survive and advance to the next round.

****

Slowly most Liverpool fans started vacating the pub. With no plans for the rest of the afternoon, I hung around with Steve and a few other Reds to watch the Manchester United match. They had lost their first leg 2-1 on the road against Midtjylland from Denmark, but were still favored to advance at home. I earlier recalled how Eric the manager informed me that the Manchester United supporters club also called Fado's their home pub, and he expected another large crowd for their match. I looked around and spotted exactly one United fan. I could only shake my head at this perceived lack of support.

Joining Steve and I for another pint was Albert Padilla, an IT manager looking sharp in a nice suit. Albert is actually from San Antonio, and one of the founding members of the OLSC San Antonio club. Six months earlier he'd relocated to Austin, and only recently started coming to Fado's on match day. He started watching the Premier League back when it formed in the early nineties, and admitted first rooting for Manchester United. He credited David Beckham and the fact that he married a Spice Girl as the sole impetus for going to the dark side, but after watching the passion of Liverpool fans in the Kop on match day, he saw the light and changed his allegiance. Albert had spent most of the match talking with Leo Martinez. Both were original club members from San Antonio that had recently relocated to the state capital. It was easy to see what Leo did for a living, as he was still wearing the all-brown uniform donned by drivers of UPS. I refrained from asking if he was simply on an extended delivery stop. He left soon after the final whistle.

Brent Barner also hung around for another pint, and as an accounts manager for the Internal Revenue Service, I couldn't blame him for not wanting to go back to the office. Together the four of us grabbed pints and wandered over to harass the lonely United fan at his table.

Having already punched our ticket to the next round, it was easy to start talking shit to him. He had a few friends sitting with him, but they were quick to dismiss themselves as neutrals. Maybe they feared repercussions from being outnumbered by fans from the archrival club, but there really wasn't any animosity.

Brenton Trammell was the lone supporter, and he was wearing a white Manchester United kit. He'd picked up the sport through the FIFA video game about ten years ago. The only reason he'd picked Manchester United was because they were good on the video game. In other words, he was another admitted glory hunter.

Things got interesting in the match when Pione Sisto scored in the twenty-sixth minute to give the Danish club a 3-1 aggregate lead. We laughed loudly at our rival's current misfortunes. If only Justin hadn't left, I was certain that he'd lead us in a fine rendition of our great chant, "Who the fuck are Man United?"

Midtjylland would put the ball in the net again five minutes later, but this time it was an own goal by Nikolay Bodurov. Still, the match went to halftime with Manchester United losing 3-2 on aggregate. Much was posted how they'd closed some sections of Old Trafford since they couldn't sell out this match, but about fifty-eight thousand supporters were still in attendance and shocked that they were still behind in this leg. I know there was one particular fan sitting in an Austin pub that shared that sentiment.

The second half began and you could simply see the class of Manchester United on the pitch. We all knew it was only a matter of time before they saw this through. Young Marcus Rashford gave them the lead with goals in the sixty-third and seventy-fifth minutes, and the match was put away when Ander Herrera converted a penalty in the eighty-seventh minute. Memphis Depay provided the icing on the cake with an insurance goal to make the final score 5-1 on the day. Manchester United would advance with a 6-3 aggregate victory. In the end, both Liverpool and United had struggled against inferior competition, but they'd advanced to the round of sixteen, which was all that really mattered.

It was a fun day for everyone as we enjoyed more pints. We didn't know it at the time, but fate would intervene on this party the following day, as Liverpool and Manchester United would be drawn to play each other in the next round. I really had nowhere to be until dinner plans with my friend

Tony later that evening. It had been a long day, and I felt like a nap was calling my name. I finished my final pint of Guinness before closing out the tab. This was a good victory for Liverpool, but it was expected. The next match would certainly be a more challenging task against Manchester City. It was a cup final at Wembley against one of the best teams in the league. And I couldn't wait.

26 - SAN ANTONIO

Sunday, February 28
Sherlock's Baker Street Pub, San Antonio, TX
League Cup Final (Manchester City)

The last time Liverpool appeared in a cup final was the 2012 Football League Cup, then sponsored by beer maker Carling. It was a memorable shootout victory over Cardiff City that I watched live at Scavengers. It also marked the only silverware won by the club since Fenway Sports Group bought the club in 2010. With the spark of newly appointed Jürgen Klopp at the helm, this current squad had found themselves back in the cup final of the same competition. In only five short months Klopp had taken a squad assembled by Brendan Rodgers to a cup final, something Rodgers himself had never done in three years at the helm.

Many supporters judge success over a season with silverware. Every club is entered into three different competitions, and for most of them, the league title is not a realistic target. Both the Football League Cup and FA Cup are real opportunities for clubs to give their fans a chance at glory. What makes this possible is that each round matchup and host location is determined by random draw. With a little luck, a mid-table club can make a deep run into the knockout competition by getting to face inferior squads early. People rarely remember the route a team took on the way to a cup final.

In the 2011-12 competition, Cardiff City was competing in the second tier of English football, also known as the Championship. They went on the road to defeat Oxford United 3-1 in extra time. Oxford United had finished ninth in League Two that season, the seventy-seventh best football team in the land. Their next three matches were all held at their home stadium against Huddersfield Town (playing in League One at the time), Leicester

City, and Burnley (both playing in the second tier of English football at the time). They advanced to the quarterfinals without having to face a top club. They dispatched Blackburn Rovers at home in the quarterfinals before taking out Crystal Palace in penalty kicks to earn a trip to the final. Four of their five matches were played at home against teams at their level or below, yet they got to play in a cup final at Wembley Stadium.

Meanwhile, Liverpool entered that competition in the second round and had four successive road matches through the luck of the draw. They had to defeat League One side Exeter City 3-1, Championship squad Brighton and Hove Albion 2-1, Premier League rivals Stoke City 2-1, and Chelsea 2-0 to get to the semifinals. It then took a 3-2 aggregate victory over Manchester City to advance to the finals. Suffice it to say that Liverpool had a much more challenging run that season. Many fans remember winning that trophy, but few of them remember how difficult that competition was for the Reds, despite playing the smaller Welsh club in the final.

In this year's competition, I've already documented Liverpool's run to the cup final with victories over Carlisle United, Bournemouth, Southampton, and Stoke City. On the other side, Manchester City had to defeat Sunderland, Crystal Palace, Hull City, and Everton en route to Wembley. Three of those teams played in the Premier League, while Hull City was in contention for promotion to the top flight, hovering in the top four of the Championship. Clearly Manchester City had the more difficult run, but none of that mattered. Regardless of who won the final, few would remember how each team got there.

Most Liverpool fans were disappointed that Manchester City had defeated Everton in the semifinals. While it is always special to watch your club in a cup final, it is something extremely special to play your cross-town rival. Not only was Everton perceived to be the weaker opponent, but the last time that Everton and Liverpool played in a cup final against each other was in 1989. Sadly, the Toffees couldn't seal the deal in the semifinals. Manchester City would make for an exciting match regardless, and Liverpool would fancy their chances, having already beaten them 4-1 at the Etihad Stadium in November. It would give Liverpool supporters great pleasure to defeat the Citizens and have midfielder Raheem Sterling watch his former club celebrate on the pitch.

****

OLSC San Antonio is another new club to the Liverpool family that was made official in October 2014. They were a fledgling satellite club for OLSC Austin for many years before finally taking the steps required to form their own club. Steve Scheck was the man credited with taking that club to the Promised Land, but family and work obligations made it difficult for him to continue as their chairperson. Enter Conrad Hinojosa.

Like many club presidents, Conrad is a young adult with time and ambition. He was introduced to Liverpool Football Club in 2009 by a close friend. Conrad was working in Austin at the time, living in his friend's spare bedroom during the week before returning to San Antonio for the weekend. One weekend he decided to stick around, and joined his friend to watch a soccer match at Fado's at six on a Saturday morning. Conrad played soccer as a child and still liked the sport, but didn't have a rooting interest at the time. He enjoyed the match and started paying more attention to how Liverpool was performing. Then he watched a video of the Kop singing "You'll Never Walk Alone" before their semifinal victory over Chelsea in the 2005 Champions League. It gave him goose bumps, and his allegiance was sealed.

Kickoff for the final was set for ten thirty a.m. local time, so Conrad invited me over to his friend's house for a pre-match party. Jason Roach lived about a mile from the club's home pub, so it made sense to get an early start to the day at his home. Jason used to work with Conrad but had left to become a real estate agent three months before. He grew up playing soccer as a child in Nebraska, but had just started following Liverpool a few months ago. Once he moved down the street from the pub, Conrad started dragging him to matches, and Jason quickly adopted the club as his own.

It usually takes me a few minutes to figure out which of my numerous Liverpool jerseys to wear for a particular match. It's not a decision to be taken lightly. As I noted earlier, it had been four years since Liverpool played in a cup final. I remember that day well, wearing my long-sleeved 2011-12 charcoal Luis Suarez jersey while smoking a post-match victory cigar at Scavengers. I knew that I had to wear that same jersey in an effort to re-create that mojo. I even brought a nice victory cigar for after the match. Once I was properly outfitted, I headed up toward the northern San Antonio suburbs to meet my new friends.

I was a little nervous that Sunday morning. Up until that point, this was the most important match of the season for Liverpool. It was a chance at redemption for the past eighteen months of mediocrity suffered under Brendan Rodgers. But I was also nervous driving to the house of a man I'd never met in a town I'd never been to before. It's one thing to meet new friends at a public establishment, quite a different story to meet at a strange house in a quiet neighborhood. Conrad met me outside.

Any fears I might've had were quickly washed away when I saw mimosas and bags full of breakfast burritos on the kitchen counter. Conrad introduced me to the crew and made me a mimosa with ruby-red grapefruit juice instead of the traditional orange juice. It was an intriguing beverage selection at the time, but quite tasty, and went down way too easily. I learned that San Antonio does Sunday brunch a bit differently than what

I'm used to, but I loved it.

Sitting on the couch was Conrad's younger brother Joaquin, who was keeping tabs on the Tottenham vs. Swansea City match playing on the television. Joaquin lived four hours away in McAllen near the Mexican border, but drove up for the big match. He had always been a soccer fan, but became a large Liverpool fan simply because his big brother rooted for them. As a younger brother myself, it was a somewhat foreign concept to select your favorite club based on what Big Bro says. It worked quite opposite for NFL allegiances in my family, as I picked the Eagles because they were rivals of my brother's beloved Redskins. It made sense at the time. Later in life, when we both discovered that we rooted for Liverpool, there was a brief debate as to who would own the family rights to support the Reds. Thankfully, we were adults when this happened. While we still were capable of acting childishly, we ultimately called a truce and accepted each other's allegiance to Liverpool.

The fourth man sitting in the living room was Joe Valdez, another newcomer to the Liverpool family thanks to Conrad. Joe works with Conrad at Labatt Food Services, and he started going to watch matches at the pub after the epic 2013-14 title run. The atmosphere and camaraderie at the pub kept him coming back, and now he's hooked.

As soon as the final whistle blew for Tottenham's 2-1 victory over Swansea City, Jason closed up shop and we all left for the pub. OLSC San Antonio's official pub was Sherlock's Baker Street Pub. Normally closed on Sunday morning, they always opened for Liverpool matches and were opening at ten a.m. for this cup final. About twenty fans were already waiting for the doors to open when we pulled into the parking lot. The first to greet us was Jeremy Barker, another coworker of Conrad's that supported Liverpool. Unlike Joe and Jason, however, Jeremy had been supporting the club since 2004 after studying abroad in Spain. His love for the Spanish national team carried over to Liverpool when they had players like Xabi Alonso and Fernando Torres.

When San Antonio's Liverpool fans first started gathering to watch matches, they went to the Lion & Rose British Restaurant and Pub in downtown. That pub is known as a soccer pub, and invites fans from all clubs to watch matches. The LFC club wasn't that large at the time, but as they slowly started to grow, it became clear that they needed a new home…a home of their own.

Brian Clark has been a Liverpool fan since the late seventies, when he played youth soccer in Oklahoma. His youth coach was a huge Liverpool fan from Vietnam. That love transferred over to Brian and never left. Brian is the general manager at Sherlock's Baker Street Pub, a British pub themed around Sherlock Holmes. There are currently six locations across Texas, and Brian has been running the San Antonio pub for a few years.

San Antonio is a thriving soccer community. The city built Toyota Field, a soccer-specific stadium for their minor league franchise, down the road a few miles from Sherlock's. Fans would stop into the pub after San Antonio Scorpion matches before heading home, and word spread about the soccer-friendly atmosphere at a British-themed pub. Brian learned that some of the LFC fans in San Antonio were looking for a new home, and he made some concessions to attract the fans of his favorite club. The pub was normally open on Sunday, but Brian agreed to open for all LFC matches and allowed fans to decorate the pub with scarves and banners. Finally, the San Antonio crew had found a home.

The match started innocently enough, with not much action to note. Both clubs seemed to be taking their time settling in, but Liverpool seemed to have the better of the play in the early stages. About ten minutes into the match, I looked around and estimated about seventy-five supporters had found their way to the pub. There was a huge buildup for this event, and every LFC pub around the country was filled. I counted eight different televisions hanging throughout the tavern playing the match as the commentary blared over the stereo speakers.

The first significant moment of the match came in the fifteenth minute when Emre Can and Mamadou Sakho collided heads going after the same ball. The impact seemed to affect Sakho, as he appeared a bit lost. A few minutes had passed by when Sakho stumbled to allow Sergio Aguero get away a clean shot on target. The shot was brilliantly saved by Simon Mignolet, who was able to tip the ball barely deflecting it off course. It hit the post and was cleared away to preserve the 0-0 score line. The poor defending on the play alerted Klopp that a change was needed. Using a substitute in the twenty-third minute of a match for injury puts you at a distinct disadvantage in a cup final, but Sakho did not appear to be capable to continue at a hundred percent, so he was replaced by Kolo Toure.

Sakho adamantly wanted to remain on the pitch, and you could see his frustration when he appeared to throw a water bottle at the bench. Competitors don't want to be removed from a huge match, and I love Sakho for his passion, but everyone knew that Klopp had to make this change.

The remainder of the first half was relatively uneventful, as the players went to their locker rooms deadlocked at nil-nil. As is the uniform practice at every sports bar in America, halftime signified the mad rush to get the bartender's attention for your next pint. Lindy was an attractive young blond gal tending bar, and she diligently served drinks without missing a beat. Brian later told me that she was one of his servers who was hoping to become a bartender, so he suggested that she get some experience by working the match, since his regular staff expected to be off on Sunday. She worked the bar like an experienced veteran, and I had my next Guinness within a few minutes.

A large bleach-blond male wearing an earring came up to the bar next to me and got Lindy's attention. With a thick Australian accent, he ordered an IPA. Lindy explained that they had two different brands on tap, to which he replied, "Give me the stronger one." It made me chuckle a bit, as I liked his style.

Tom Denny is from Adelaide, Australia, and comes to San Antonio for work three or four times a year. As a member of the OLSC Adelaide group, he got to fly with the club around the island continent during their preseason tour last summer. I asked him if he missed Australia having to be in Texas so often. He explained that two of his favorite things in the world are guns and fast cars, so I think he was getting along quite well in the Lone Star State.

I only knew one other Liverpool fan from Australia, a passionate forty-six-year-old named Sean McGerty. Sean was at first a huge baseball fan, and loved the Boston Red Sox. It wasn't until FSG bought Liverpool that he started to follow the sport, so he naturally looked to Liverpool. Sean loved statistical analysis and was always trying to dissect the club in a quantifiable way. It's one of the reasons I loved chatting with him. Sean started a podcast he called *Big Red LFC*, which grew to over five thousand subscribers in a few years. He mostly hosted with my friend Nick Coughlin from OLSC Washington D.C., but was often joined by other North American compadres as well. We connected via social media and communicated often in spite of the fifteen-hour time difference. As last summer's preseason was coming to a close, Sean invited me to host one of his podcasts to discuss Liverpool and plug this book project. Sadly, I would never get that opportunity, as he had a massive heart attack playing soccer with his son and passed away on August 13, 2015. Although I never had the pleasure of meeting Sean in person, I was deeply saddened by his loss and felt like a true friend had departed my life way too soon.

I told Tom the story about Sean, and he put his arm around my shoulder. "Give me your phone, mate," he said. I handed over the phone and he opened my Facebook app. He punched in some letters and returned the phone. I looked down at his Facebook profile as he continued, "I just sent myself a friend request for you. I'd be honored to take Sean's place as your Australian Liverpool brother." I won't lie: I had to fight back a tear after he said that.

I returned to the table with Conrad, Joaquin, and Joe. I thought it was interesting how new their club seemed to reflect many newer fans of Liverpool. For me it was an interesting parallel that confirmed the growth of both the sport and brand. Then Conrad introduced me to two gentlemen sitting at the adjacent table, which blew that theory out of the water.

A.J. Singh is an older gentleman from Singapore that immigrated to the

United States in 1995. He was joined by Shashi Pinheiro, a slightly younger man that Conrad calls "the Godfather" of OLSC San Antonio. Shashi left his home country of Kuwait in 1987 to attend college at the University of Texas. It was there he met his wife and settled down in San Antonio. They were married just after Liverpool's last league title in 1990, a fact he continually needs to remind his bride. For his marriage's sake, I hope that he is not as superstitious as I am and asks for a divorce just to see Liverpool win title #19. Although it wouldn't bother me if he did. It's only weird if it doesn't work, right?

Both men were of Indian descent and joined by younger children at their table. Every one of them wore this year's solid black third jersey in an obvious show of family solidarity. Throughout the first half, no one in the pub showed more passion and exuberance than A.J. When I asked them how they came to root for Liverpool having been raised so far away from England, they explained that the globalization of the sport hadn't yet been realized to its full potential. If you were a fan of soccer in their respective home countries in the seventies or eighties, you either rooted for Liverpool or Manchester United. There was no third choice.

The second half kicked off, and it didn't take long for Manchester City to find the net. Four minutes into the half, Fernandinho got a free look at the goal from a difficult angle on the right side of the penalty box. The shot moved quickly toward the near post and found its way under the diving body of Mignolet into the back of the net. It was a decent shot, but clearly one that any decent goalkeeper should be expected to make. Instantly the wind got knocked out of our sails, and the fan frustration was unmistakable.

"Good thing we signed him to a long-term contract," came one sarcastic reply.

Another irate supporter screamed, "A high school keeper could've made that save!"

I didn't necessarily agree with either of those statements, but the team was playing too well to lose the final in such a disappointing manner. As frustrated as I was personally, I reminded myself that there was still forty minutes of football to be played. Under Rodgers, the team would've dropped their heads and struggled to continue positively. However, this team under Klopp proved that they wouldn't quit, and were capable of finding the equalizer. Since Klopp took over as manager, Liverpool had come back to win or draw in eight of sixteen matches after falling behind. This resiliency was something rarely seen in recent Liverpool squads. There was renewed optimism that we could come back from this deficit.

The goal seemed to inject life into the Manchester City squad, who pushed on the attack to put the game away. Sterling missed an easy goal from eight yards out in the fifty-ninth minute, prompting many cheers from the pub. Three minutes later, Aguero broke free on a pass from Yaya Toure and was brought down in the penalty box by a careless tackle from Alberto Moreno. Replays confirmed it probably should've been called a penalty, but referee Michael Oliver motioned to play on.

In a bold attacking move, Adam Lallana was brought in for Moreno as Liverpool pushed forward for the equalizer. James Milner was pushed back into the defense, and his lack of speed caused me to worry about the counterattack.

Sterling had yet another opportunity to extend the City lead in the seventy-ninth minute, but his shot ran wide, to the delight of everyone in the pub. A few shouts of "greedy wanker!" were heard in the background. Liverpool regrouped and continued to press forward. Their efforts were finally rewarded in the eighty-third minute.

Daniel Sturridge crossed the ball from the left side of the pitch, where it found Lallana. His shot ricocheted off the post. The capacity crowd of close to a hundred fans groaned collectively for a brief moment, but then Phillippe Coutinho collected the rebound and fired the ball into the net. It was a "shot heard around the world" as Liverpool leveled the match 1-1. Social media would eventually be filled with video clips of pub celebrations around the world, including one from Indianapolis, where the exuberant celebrations caused enough vibration for a ceiling light fixture to fall to the floor.

The final minutes of regulation proved to be gut-wrenching, as City attacked for the game winner. Mignolet made a save late in the match as Lucas Leiva swept away the rebound. With two minutes left, Mignolet made another fantastic save off a City corner kick. Not many high school keepers would've made those two stops in the final minutes, and our faith in the Belgian was restored. You could hear the Liverpool faithful drowning Wembley with the chorus of "You'll Never Walk Alone" as the final whistle blew. It was exhilarating, and my heart was pounding a mile a minute.

The action wouldn't stop through the two fifteen-minute periods of extra time. Late in the first period of extra time, Aguero found himself with the kind of breakaway that the Argentine stud striker usually put away. He was again denied by Mignolet. The pub started singing proudly to the tune of "The Lion Sleeps Tonight":

> *"He's our keeper,*
> *Our Belgian keeper!*
> *He's Simon Mignolet!"*

The second period began as furiously as the first one. Divock Origi, a late second-half substitute, headed toward target from five yards out, only to be saved by City goalkeeper Wilfredo Caballero. The Argentine backup keeper came up huge again with another Origi shot moments later. Players from both teams were giving a hundred percent effort, and after 120 minutes, it was obvious that they were knackered. This cup final was destined to be decided in a penalty shootout. Twice this season Liverpool had advanced in this competition through a successful penalty shootout, and we'd last won this competition four years earlier in the same way. I liked our chances.

The penalty shootout has been hotly debated for deciding who advances in knockout competitions, or in this case who would be crowned champions. The first shootout in English professional football was held in the 1970 Watney Cup semifinal match between Hull City and Manchester United. It seems like an unfair way to determine a victor, akin to deciding the winner of a baseball game with a homerun derby or a basketball game by shooting free throws. Personally, I would love to see the return of the "golden goal," where the first team to score wins the match. Much like the National Hockey League does in their playoffs, teams continue to play full periods until a goal is scored. Be that as it may, my opinion doesn't matter.

Each team gets five chances to score on a penalty kick, and whichever team scores the most wins. Great penalty kick takers should score over ninety percent of the time. It takes great guesswork and better skill for a goalkeeper to make a save. All the shooter needs to do is hit the target with power and accuracy and the chances of scoring are high.

Liverpool were first to take their kick, and it was Emre Can stepping up to the spot. As he made his run-up to the ball, Caballero dove early to his left, hoping that was where the ball would be. Can connected with a soft chip down the middle to a wide-open net to give the Reds the first goal. It was a cheeky attempt that carried a lot of risk if the goalie didn't move early, but it worked.

Fernandinho was first to take a kick for Manchester City, and his shot caromed off the left post for no goal. If only his shot in the forty-ninth minute hit the post instead of scoring, perhaps we would already be celebrating. Still, there was much rejoicing in the pub as Liverpool took the advantage.

Cheers turned to groans when Caballero saved the next shot from Lucas. City were back on even terms when Jesus Navas scored shooting to his left. Mignolet guessed correctly but simply couldn't make the save.

It was all downhill from there, as Coutinho failed to fire home from the spot. He tried the stutter-step move made popular by Cristiano Ronaldo—the sudden move frequently forces the keeper to tip his hand as to what direction he's planning to dive. I prefer to see players simply pick a corner, fire a low, hard shot, and hope that the keeper guesses wrong or that it's placed so perfectly that he can't save it. The move backfired on Coutinho as Caballero held his ground, possibly due to being embarrassed when Emre Can scored so easily on the first kick. Coutinho fired weakly to his right and it was easily saved.

Sergio Aguero stepped up to the spot and everyone knew he was going to score. He did, to give City the edge. Mignolet would have to come up big if Liverpool were to win the cup. Adam Lallana stepped up and fired toward the side net, but again Caballero guessed right and extended to make a brilliant save. Once Yaya Toure fired into the side net, the match was over. Manchester City had won the League Cup.

It was a devastating defeat for Liverpool fans. Everyone in the pub was utterly gutted and silent. Some fans exited in disgust, while others just blankly stared at the television. It wasn't supposed to end this way. As Manchester City celebrated on the television, fans started closing out their tabs. I was left sitting next to two guys named Patrick and Dorien. Together they played in a Sunday adult soccer league, and had come to the pub to enjoy the match. While not officially fans of any Premier League club, you could sense that they felt the love of the Liverpool family and would soon be joining the club.

I closed out my tab and started gathering my things as the final patrons departed the pub. Brian and Lindy were frantically cleaning and trying to close up. One young fan named Jon remained pacing across the room in despair. He looked at me in disbelief I didn't exactly know how old he was or how long he was following the club, but you could feel his pain just by being in his presence.

"Why wasn't Milner taking penalties? Why not Sturridge? What about our captain Jordan Henderson? Where were they?" he asked me.

It was a great question that I couldn't answer. It's unfair to Jordan Henderson to make this comparison, but I'm certain that Steven Gerrard would've stepped up to the spot. Yet they all stood on the midfield line watching. I don't know if Klopp made the decision or if the players just didn't feel it. As a fan, it left me wondering what could've been.

Eventually Jon collected himself and left the pub. I thanked both Lindy and Brian for their hospitality and complimented them on their atmosphere. It was a disappointing result, but still a great day. I left Sherlock's Baker Street Pub with a smile, and couldn't help but think to myself that I'd be back soon.

27 - ON THE REBOUND

Wednesday, March 2
London Bridge Pub
Premier League match #27 (vs. Manchester City)

For the second time in three days, Liverpool would have to play Manchester City. It was heartbreaking to lose the League Cup final in a penalty shootout, but fate would give the Reds an opportunity to exact some revenge with the scheduled Premier League match.

I was able to conclude my business early enough to get to the pub just before kickoff. The usual suspects were in attendance, but I noticed a few fresh faces in the crowd for this match. I was especially glad to see Ty Harrell make an appearance. Perhaps the most positive and genuine man that I have ever met, Ty knows exactly how to say the right things to put a smile on your face. It was a craft he'd likely acquired through years of public service as a North Carolina state assemblyman. He left the world of politics not long ago for family reasons, and now runs a thriving mortgage business. I hadn't seen Ty in a while, so I immediately knew it was going to be a good day.

Both teams set up with strong lineups. Liverpool was desperate to push up the table, while Manchester City had a tenuous hold on a top four spot. It had already been announced that Manuel Pellegrini would not have his contract renewed at the end of the season. It's hard to fathom a guy being considered "underperforming" after winning three trophies in three seasons, including a Premier League title at the expense of a Steven Gerrard slip. Yet that was precisely the reason the Middle Eastern owners felt compelled to bring in Pep Guardiola to manage next season. Manchester City still had much to play for, yet their manager was already a lame duck.

The most interesting change to the Liverpool lineup was the inclusion of young Jon Flanagan in the defense. Flanagan had last started in a Premier

League match in May of 2014 before suffering a series of debilitating knee injuries. Any concerns about his knee were answered in the opening minute with his hard tackle on former teammate Raheem Sterling. It was a jarring hit that caused everyone at the pub to cheer. Jürgen Klopp would later admit in his post-match interview that the only word he could think of to describe that play was "Boom!" That sound bite would get much play amongst Liverpool fans.

Both teams shared possession in the first thirty minutes, with no real great chances on goal. Divock Origi got the nod at striker as Christian Benteke continued to ride the pine, suffering from a lack of confidence. Origi had added another dimension to the Liverpool attack with his speed and game sense, but it was Adam Lallana who would give Liverpool the lead with a surreal goal that looked like was moving in slow motion. As he pushed forward with the ball, the defense retreated, letting him proceed. Lallana fired a shot to Joe Hart's left, and it was hardly a screamer. It was perfectly placed past the outstretched arms of the English goalkeeper, caromed off the post, and dribbled over the line into the net. At the time I wasn't exactly sure what had happened or if the ball had actually gone into the net. We looked around at each other in the pub, shrugged, and cheered as the Liverpool players celebrated the goal.

Seven minutes later, Lallana would start the next goal with a nifty back heel to Roberto Firmino. The Brazilian would find a streaking James Milner, who charged into the penalty box to fire home the game's second goal. It was nice to see Milner score against his former club, and this time there was no doubt about the goal. Liverpool would take the two-goal lead into the locker room at halftime.

Manchester City seemed to capitulate in the second half as Liverpool continued to dominate. Lallana would secure man-of-the-match honors in the fifty-eighth minute with a nice assist. Driving forward on the attack, Lallana slotted a pass to Firmino for an easy goal. With more than thirty minutes to play, it was clear that Manchester City were defeated. They were listless, with no attacking threat. Liverpool made it look easy. All that I could ask myself was, "Where was this on Sunday?" It was difficult to determine if this result was due more to Liverpool kicking it up a notch or Manchester City still suffering from a League Cup hangover. Most likely, it was a combination of both. Sadly, we could only ponder what could've been, taking the three points in the process. I couldn't really say that revenge was sweet. They were still cup champions. But it felt good to beat one of the league's better teams twice in the same season.

Another weekend trip to London was on the agenda for Liverpool, but instead of going to Wembley, they would be headed to play a league match at Crystal Palace. The London-based team had become a decent club since promotion a few years ago, and it would be no easy task to get a good result. I was concerned that the club may be looking ahead at the next Europa League encounter with Manchester United. It was another early Sunday morning kickoff, which meant I would remain at home to watch from my couch.

Joe Ledley would give Crystal Palace the lead in the forty-eighth minute, and matters were made worse when James Milner was rightfully sent off for his second yellow card in the sixty-second minute. Liverpool was down a goal, down a man, playing on the road. Things looked bleak. It would take a ghastly mistake from the Palace goalkeeper to let the Reds back into the match. Backup goalkeeper Alex McCarthy slipped trying a routine clearance with no pressure. Instead of sailing into the Liverpool half, the ball went straight to Roberto Firmino only a few yards outside the penalty box. Firmino collected the ball and calmly put the ball into the open net for the equalizer. It was undeserved, but sometimes you need to have a little luck on your side.

Crystal Palace had had an anemic offense for much of the season, and their inability to sustain a consistent attack would cost them. Despite carrying a man advantage, the Eagles just never could get anything past Simon Mignolet. The game went into the final minutes of stoppage time looking like both teams would earn a point. Then Damien Delaney got a little too close to Christian Benteke inside the penalty box and the Belgian striker went down easily. Television replays confirmed that there was contact, but the theatrics were quite over the top. Referee Andre Marriner didn't whistle for the foul immediately, but the linesman flagged and convinced him to award the penalty kick. Benteke converted the goal and Liverpool earned a surprising three points.

Manager Alan Pardew was not happy with the final play, calling out Benteke for diving and ruining the integrity of the sport. I would've been pissed off myself had the tables been turned. It's a sad fact that embellishment has crept its way into the sport like it has. It was an extremely difficult call, and I wouldn't have been upset had Marriner not made it. I think that Pardew went a little overboard with his comments. It's likely that his frustration was directed at his team's inability to protect a slim lead at home against a shorthanded squad.

For Liverpool it was another three points. More importantly, it added to the momentum for the club as they headed into the biggest match of the year. Next Thursday would be the next round of the Europa League knockout stage. For the first time in history, Liverpool would be playing archrivals Manchester United in a European competition. I couldn't wait. If only there was a fast-forward button in life. It simply didn't get much better than this.

28 - A EUROPEAN FIRST

Thursday, March 10
London Bridge Pub, Raleigh, NC
Europa League Round of 16, First Leg (vs. Manchester United)

Without question, the two most storied clubs in English football history are Liverpool and Manchester United. Their historic rivalry is arguably the most bitter in all of English sports, and considered one of the fiercest rivalries in global football. As of 2016 the two clubs have combined to win thirty-eight domestic league titles and eight European Cups. The first meeting of the two clubs was held in 1894, only two years after Liverpool Football Club was formed. Back then Manchester United were known as Newton Heath LYR Football Club, changing their name to the current form in 1902, and they had just finished dead last of sixteen teams in England's First Division. Liverpool had just completed an undefeated season, running away with the Second Division. Instead of automatic promotion and relegation for the two clubs, as would be the case today, the clubs had to play off for the right to play in the next season's First Division. The match was held on April 28 at Ewood Park in Blackburn with Liverpool victorious 2-0, and as a result, the Reds were promoted while the soon-to-become Manchester United Football Club was relegated.

The two clubs had met in official competition 194 more times since that initial encounter in the nineteenth century, with Manchester United holding the advantage, winning seventy-nine times versus Liverpool's sixty-five (including that first victory in 1894). Of those matches, twenty-eight were held in domestic cup competitions. Yet somehow these two clubs had never faced each other in European competition before.

The first European Cup competition was held in the 1955-56 season when sixteen clubs from different countries played in a knockout-style tournament. Oddly enough, the competition was the brainchild of two French journalists. Jacques Ferran was a writer for the French sports publication *L'Equipe*. He traveled to Santiago, Chile in the late forties to cover a South American club competition that would eventually be come to known as the Copa Libertadores. Upon his return to France, he became fascinated with this continental club competition, and collaborated with his editor Gabriel Hanot. Together they started forming proposals for UEFA, and eventually the competition was approved by the governing body in March 1955. Chelsea was initially invited to participate as one of the sixteen clubs, but the Football Association barred their participation, as they felt this tournament would only distract from the more important domestic league competition. Real Madrid went on to win that inaugural tournament with a come-from-behind 4-3 victory over French club Stade de Reims.

Manchester United was invited to participate in the 1956-57 European Cup competition, which they did despite the Football Association's continued objection. Twenty-one clubs were represented in that competition, which saw Manchester United eliminated in the semifinals by eventual champion Real Madrid. Liverpool's first entry into the competition was in the 1964-65 season, when they lost in the semifinals to Italy's Internazionale of Milan. This competition remained an exclusive tournament for domestic league champions until the 1997-98 season, when multiple clubs from the continent's larger countries were invited in an effort to bolster the competitiveness of the tournament.

Another European knockout competition was introduced in the mid-1950s and called the Inter-Cities Fair Cup. Organizational control was taken over by UEFA in 1971 and it was renamed the UEFA Cup. This competition initially invited the runners-up from domestic leagues, but later included all European domestic cup winners when the competition absorbed the separate UEFA Cup Winners' Cup in 1999.

UEFA rebranded this competition the Europa League for the 2009-10 season. With multiple ways to earn a berth into the UEFA Cup, this was the only way that two clubs from England could face each other in a European competition before 1997-98. Both Manchester United and Liverpool were winning the majority of those league titles in that time period, so it was highly unlikely that they would ever play in the same European competition until the expansion of the Champions League.

From the introduction of the UEFA Cup and its predecessor in 1955 through 1997, Manchester United had participated in the competition nine times to Liverpool's eight. Only once in that period did both clubs participate in the same tournament with a chance to play against each other in European competition. That was in the 1995-96 competition, but Manchester United would lose in the first round to Russian club Rotor Volgograd on the away goals tiebreaker.

The European Cup was rebranded the Champions League in 1992, but it remained the same competition. The competition was expanded to allow league runners-up in 1997, and now up to four English clubs typically compete in it.

In the eighteen subsequent seasons, Liverpool and Manchester United participated in the same European competition nine times, including the current season. UEFA rules prohibit clubs from the same country playing until the latter stages of each competition, so unless both clubs were having particularly good tournaments, they likely wouldn't face each other.

After the 1995-96 UEFA Cup, the first opportunity for the clubs to play was in the 2001-02 Champions League. Both clubs advanced to the knockout stage, but Liverpool was defeated in the quarterfinals against German club Bayer Leverkusen 4-3 on aggregate. Liverpool won the opening leg at Anfield 1-0 that year, but couldn't complete the deal on the return trip to Germany. Had Liverpool held on, they would've faced Manchester United in the semifinals for their first ever European match against each other.

The next opportunity came in the 2006-07, when Liverpool and Manchester United joined Chelsea in the Champions League semifinals. Liverpool defeated Chelsea in a penalty shootout, but United lost to AC Milan in their semifinal (which set up a rematch of the 2005 Champions League final, this time won by the Italian squad 2-1 in Athens). The following season saw a similar semifinal situation, where Liverpool, Manchester United, and Chelsea represented three-quarters of the participants. This time Chelsea exacted their revenge against the Reds with an extra-time victory, while Manchester United defeated Barcelona to reach the final. The Red Devils ultimately won the final in Moscow with their own penalty shootout victory after John Terry slipped on the slick turf and sent his effort high and wide.

The final chance to meet for the clubs was the next season, when Liverpool lost again to Chelsea, this time in the quarterfinals. Manchester United eventually lost to Barcelona in the finals that season.

At first glance, it would seem to be a statistical improbability that Liverpool and Manchester United had never faced each other in a European competition. Five times prior to this season, Manchester United had played another English club with European silverware on the line. Each time the Red Devils were victorious. Liverpool also played English opponents five times in Europe, but the two recent losses versus Chelsea kept their record at 3-2 against fellow English clubs.

Reviewing this history got me thinking about the statistical odds of Liverpool and Manchester United avoiding each other in European competition this long. UEFA prevents clubs from the same country from playing each other in the round of sixteen, so the first chance that they could play each other would be the quarterfinals. With a truly random draw, Liverpool has a six-out-of-seven chance (85.7 percent) to avoid drawing Manchester United in a quarterfinal match and a two-out-of-three chance to avoid them in a semifinal (66.7 percent).

There were only six possible times when both clubs progressed far enough to draw each other in the competition: 2001-02 quarterfinals (85.7 percent chance to avoid each other), 2006-07 quarterfinals (85.7 percent) and semifinals (66.7 percent), 2007-08 quarterfinals (85.7 percent) and semifinals (66.7 percent), and 2008-09 quarterfinals (85.7 percent). If you multiply those odds to avoid each other through each of the six draws, you'll come up with the fact that there has been only a twenty-four-percent chance that these two giant English clubs had yet to play in a European competition.

Manchester United had qualified for this year's Champions League by virtue of their fourth-place finish in last year's Premier League table. They were placed into a relatively easy group with Dutch club PSV Eindhoven, Wolfsburg of Germany, and CSKA Moscow from Russia. They only managed to finish third place in that group, which was not enough to advance to the knockout stage. However, UEFA does have a provision where finishing third place in Champions League group play drops directly you into the Europa League knockout stage with the twenty-four qualifiers from that competition's group play. It's an intriguing crossover rule that makes these competitions unique. Start in the Champions League, underperform, go directly to the knockout stage of an entirely different competition.

Both Liverpool and Manchester United entered the Europa League round of thirty-two together, but wouldn't be allowed to face each other. As Liverpool were scraping by FC Augsburg 1-0 on aggregate, Manchester United needed to come from behind Danish club FC Midtjylland at Old Trafford to win 6-3 on aggregate. Both English clubs didn't have time to celebrate their victories before UEFA randomly drew them as opponents in the next round. There was a 6.7 percent chance that they could face each other. Six times earlier the two clubs had avoided each other in a draw that could've pitted the giants against each other. The seventh time was apparently a charm.

****

The first leg was scheduled for three p.m. on Thursday, March 10 at Anfield. I cleared my calendar, as there would be no doubt where I would watch this historic match. I spent the morning in my office trying to get work done, but I was completely useless by one p.m. I even texted Colin telling him that I was done "pretending to work" and that I would head downtown to the pub for an early start to the match. He replied that he was already there.

I pulled up to the parking area on Blount Street and saw spot #178 was open. I flashed back to the Arsenal and Bournemouth games in August, when Liverpool had good results after I parked my car in this spot. I felt that the parking gods had taken control of my steering wheel and guided my car to its rightful spot. I paid the meter and walked into the pub. Most of the regulars were already there, even though kickoff was about an hour away.

There was a serious buzz to this match, and Darren was sitting next to Mike at the bar, each with a fresh pint. I grabbed a seat in between the two owners and ordered a Guinness. I immediately joined the group conversation about the importance of this match and tried to settle myself down. It wasn't working. The nerves were taking over, and I feared that my fingernails didn't stand a chance.

The "away goals" rule was introduced by UEFA in 1965 as a method to break aggregate draws in knockout competition. Simply put, the team that scored more goals "away from home" would advance over their opponent if the aggregate score ended in a draw. It would seem like an arbitrary way to settle a match, but not much more so than a penalty shootout. Hosting the first leg of a two-legged tie was considered a disadvantage of sorts. Not only did you need to win the match, but it was imperative that you kept a clean sheet and avoided conceding the dreaded away goal. With the first leg randomly selected to be at Anfield, we were cautiously optimistic about getting a result. But could we keep a clean sheet?

Early talk at the pub was focused on the UEFA appointment of Spanish referee Carlos Velasco Carballo. He'd been in control of twenty-six matches to date this season, and was already responsible for issuing ten red cards. He was also averaging about five yellow cards issued per match. There weren't many matchups in the world today that pitted such hated rivals against each other in a match that carried such importance. Pub patrons worried whether the referee's book would end up playing a more significant part in the result than the players.

The match kicked off with about thirty fans in the pub. I sat next to Darren and barely had time to get settled before Manchester United nearly scored in the opening seconds. Marcus Rashford mishit a golden chance on a cross from their left flank and Alberto Moreno mistimed his attempt to clear. Two minutes later, Carballo pulled out his yellow card against Jordan Henderson for an ill-timed tackle on a loose ball at knee level with the sole of his foot. It was a debatable call at any point in the match, but perhaps the Spaniard was intending to send a message to both clubs not to fuck around. He knew the animus that existed between these clubs, and an early message may have been needed to keep control. Henderson was simply the guinea pig that took the early bait. There was great concern in the pub about the potential impact that would have on his play for the rest of the match.

Fifteen minutes passed and neither club appeared to be taking control. Manchester United had the better opportunities, but nothing that really threatened the scoreboard. It wasn't until the eighteenth minute that Liverpool got the breakthrough they were looking for. Dejan Lovren got possession on the right side of the field and played a simple ball to the touchline for Nathaniel Clyne. The former Southampton defender played the ball across to Henderson before streaking toward the goal loosely marked. Henderson one-timed the ball back to Roberto Firmino, who had already spotted Clyne's run toward the goal. Firmino sent the ball into the box, where Manchester United's Memphis Depay was clearly beaten. The Dutch player fouled Clyne, who easily went down inside the penalty box. Carballo hesitated at first, but eventually whistled a foul and pointed to the spot, signaling for a penalty kick. Replays would create a debate as to whether initial contact from Depay was made inside or outside the penalty box. It was close, but the debate was pointless, as the call was not going to be reversed. Daniel Sturridge stepped up to take the penalty kick. Sturridge took a long stride and stuttered his step before firing a shot to his left. It wasn't a great line to the target, and goalkeeper David De Gea guessed correctly and got a hand on the ball. But the velocity of the shot was too much for the Spanish goalkeeper and the ball hit the back of the net. Liverpool had an early 1-0 lead.

The goal was a great relief for the pub dwellers, but hardly the celebration I had expected for the first Liverpool goal scored against United in a European competition. It was almost like we'd expected to score early and often. I knew that United were not in the best of form, but this was still a talented football club that could score at any moment. We needed insurance, but more importantly, we needed to keep them from scoring that away goal.

Five minutes after opening the scoring, Sturridge nearly assisted a second goal with an incredibly deft cross. As he moved into the right side of the box, the entire United defense collapsed toward him, and he sent a hopeful ball towards the goal. It found its way to the far post, where an unmarked Phillippe Coutinho stared at nothing but net from four yards out. The Brazilian fumbled the moment and weakly shot toward target with his right foot. De Gea recovered nicely to make the save, which looked fantastic in real time. Replays confirmed that Coutinho should have slammed home the game's second goal with ease, but his mistake allowed De Gea to keep United in the match.

Liverpool had yet another chance in the thirtieth minute when Chris Smalling mistimed his diving header clearance, allowing the ball to drop into Sturridge's possession with nothing in between he and the United goalkeeper. He fired from ten yards out, but De Gea flared out to make the save. The score remained 1-0.

Late in the first half, Adam Lallana had another chance to double the Liverpool lead with a one-time effort off a Firmino cross. Unfortunately, the quick shot went straight to De Gea for an easy save. It was by no means an easy play, and Lallana should be credited with the effort to get a shot on target, but once again Liverpool were looking at a Spanish goalkeeper as the only thing keeping them from dominating their bitter rivals.

The halftime whistle blew with Liverpool deservedly leading the match 1-0. Statistically they'd dominated the match with sixty-nine percent possession, outshooting their opponents 6-3 in the process. Had it not been for David De Gea and his three incredible saves, Liverpool could be leading 4-0 at halftime. The pub was growing in confidence. Surprisingly, there weren't many Manchester United fans in the pub for this match. Their recent form had left something to be desired for a club that expected so much more, so perhaps their fans couldn't bear the thought of being outnumbered at a Liverpool pub as their bitter rivals dominated. If that was truly the case, they were wise in their assessment.

Pub owner Darren Bridger spent the entire first half sitting next to me anxiously in his seat. It appeared as though he had consumed a few pints already, so his creative juices were at full potential. He decided it was time to come up with a new chant at the half. It was something that would later be called the official OLSC Raleigh chant, because it was appropriate for any match regardless of opponent. The chant is simple but effective:

"We're better than you!
We're better than YOU!
We're SOOOO much better...
We're better than you!"

As the second half began, the crowd had grown to about forty strong, and everyone joined us in singing the new OLSC Raleigh fight song. Manchester United manager Louis van Gaal, whom I have dubbed "Butthead" because of his bizarre similarity his appearance to the MTV cartoon character, brought on defensive-minded Michael Carrick to help lock down the midfield. We presumed this was a move to try and keep the deficit at 1-0 as opposed to attacking for that all-important away goal. It didn't work.

The first fifteen minutes of the second half were quite chippy. Marouane Fellaini was thugging about all over the pitch, elbowing a Liverpool player with every head-ball opportunity. Despite numerous fouls, it took sixty minutes before the Spanish referee had enough of the Belgian midfielder's antics and issued a yellow card.

Jordan Henderson had the first real chance to double the lead in the second half in the sixty-fifth minute, when Adam Lallana took possession off a press. He looked up calmly and spotted the captain running unmarked into the box. The pass was perfect, but the shot was off target by a few feet. The entire pub collectively gasped in despair at the miss.

"Fuck off, Hendo!" came one shout from the back of the pub. I echoed his sentiments but was less vocal, as I calmly said to Darren, "That's why he's not my captain. Gerrard puts that in the back of the net."

"Comparing Henderson to Gerrard to Henderson is a bit unfair, don't you think?" replied Darren. One of my favorite sports movie quotes is from *Miracle*, with Kurt Russell as 1980 U.S. Olympic hockey coach Herb Brooks. As he lectures his young hockey team in the locker room during the legendary game against the Soviet Union, he says a line that I'll never forget and was completely applicable at this moment.

"Great moments are made from great opportunities, Darren. Henderson won't get much greater opportunities than that one."

Much of the frustration stemmed from the fact that Liverpool were in complete control of the match and dominating their rivals. Yet they were only leading 1-0 on the scoreboard with another ninety minutes at Old Trafford scheduled for a week later. No one would feel comfortable headed into that return leg only leading by one goal.

Ten minutes passed before Liverpool finally got the break they were looking for in the seventy-second minute. Liverpool had possession in their defensive third as Manchester United started gaining confidence with their press. Clyne found Lallana on the right sideline as he started moving forward on the attack. Henderson made the overlapping run down the flank and Lallana sent his English countryman the ball down the line. Henderson was almost offside on the play, but he appeared to time the run perfectly when the replay was shown. Henderson played a simple ball into the box that should've been easily cleared away by United. Carrick weakly flailed at the ball, which ended up back in Lallana's possession. The Liverpool midfielder attacked the near post to draw the defender and laid the ball back to a wide-open Firmino. The Brazilian one-timed the ball into the back of the net to give Liverpool a 2-0 lead.

The pub erupted in jubilation. The play had occurred so quickly that no one really expected to see the ball in the back of the net. I was still firmly seated on my barstool but jumped off the chair to find someone to hug. The goal may have been caused by a dreadful Manchester United mistake, but the beautiful precision from Lallana and Firmino still warranted our adulation.

Liverpool was clearly the better team on the night, and even Manchester United fans would agree with that assessment. I didn't notice at the time, but it was later reported that some United fans started chanting, "Murderers!" in the stands as their club was outclassed on the pitch. For years Liverpool fans had been blamed for overcrowding the Hillsborough Stadium during the 1989 FA Cup semifinal, which resulted in the death of ninety-six Liverpool supporters. The story has been well documented to be anything but the fault of the Liverpool fans, yet rival fans continue to pour salt into that wound.

Every team has bad supporters, and sometimes the knuckleheads are the ones that draw the most attention. Liverpool fans have been known to sing about the Munich air disaster, when twenty-three people perished when British European Airways flight 609 crashed attempting take-off from Munich-Reim airport. The plane was carrying the Manchester United squad along with some journalists and supporters. Both clubs have been hit with tragedies that have taken innocent lives, yet the level of hatred between some of these supporters is so enormous that some fans get pleasure poking their rivals. The audio recording from the telecast was clear enough that Manchester United officially condemned the chants and apologized in a released statement. With another match to play at Old Trafford in a week, I feared that this story was not finished.

The final whistle blew with Liverpool victorious 2-0. Ninety minutes of football were played, but we were only halfway done. A week later Liverpool would travel to Old Trafford in front of eighty thousand fans in hopes of protecting this delicate two-goal lead. The good news was that Manchester United had failed to score an away goal, meaning that any Liverpool goal next week would force the Red Devils to score four total goals to advance to the quarterfinals.

29 - MAKING HISTORY

Thursday, March 17
London Bridge Pub, Raleigh, NC
Europa League Round of 16, Second Leg (at Manchester United)

St. Patrick's Day is a huge day for any pub in a downtown city. When you put the second leg of the first ever European confrontation between Liverpool and Manchester United on the same day, you can expect an event at any soccer pub.

The city of Raleigh decided to host its annual St. Patrick's Day parade on the Saturday in between this epic football clash between English giants. The wife and I attended with friends, so that gave me another opportunity to head to the London Bridge Pub to gloat with friends over the result from two days earlier. Noel McCabe also made the journey in from Chatham County to celebrate his home country's heritage with many friends and family. We talked about how much we were looking forward to the football match on Thursday, which was the primary reason Noel had volunteered to be the designated driver for the parade. If he let his beautiful bride Angie drink on Saturday, then she would return the favor on March 17 when Noel returned to the pub to watch Liverpool put the final nail into the Manchester United coffin.

Due to conflicting daylight savings time schedules between the U.S. and U.K., the match kicked off an hour later than most midweek matches. This game was originally scheduled to start two hours earlier, but UEFA granted both clubs' requests to start later due to traffic and general safety concerns. I walked into the pub at about three forty-five p.m. and eagerly anticipated the start. Noel was the first person to greet me with a pint of Guinness in hand.

Every seat at the bar had already been taken, so I grabbed a spot next to the Walken Fridge. If you've ever been to the London Bridge Pub, you know exactly what I mean. Near the back of the pub by the courtyard entrance is a walk-in refrigerator covered with hundreds of pictures of actor Christopher Walken from all stages of his career. The "Christopher Walken Fridge" doubles as an homage and functional storage for cool beverages.

As people continued to pile into the pub, you could immediately tell their purpose by looking at the color of their shirt. Those that were wearing green made their way past the televisions and into the courtyard patio area to celebrate St. Paddy's Day. People wearing red found a spot inside near a television to watch the Reds play the Red Devils.

It was critical for Liverpool to get off to a good start. I told myself to separate the match into ten-minute segments. Keep the match scoreless through the first ten minutes, then focus on the next ten. The longer we could keep United off the scoreboard, the more desperate they would become on the attack. That would create opportunities for Liverpool to counterattack and hopefully score a critical away goal.

UEFA had assigned refereeing duties to Milorad Mazic from Serbia, whom I had read was one of the lowest-rated referees that saw action in the 2014 World Cup. As important as this fixture was to an entire region of England, I feared that a critical decision might make the difference. Specifically, I was worried about someone getting sent off.

Fellaini got the start for Manchester United in midfield, and if anyone would earn a straight red card, it would likely be him. There were reports that he could've been issued a suspension for a blatant elbow on Emre Can near the end of the previous match. The play was missed by the referee, which by rule allows the governing body to issue retroactive punishment. As vicious as the foul appeared to be, Emre Can dismissed the intent and thought nothing of the play. Personally I was hoping that Fellaini *wouldn't* get suspended, mostly because I don't rate his ability to create offensive chances. As long as he remained on the pitch, that was one less threat on goal against Liverpool. In the ninth minute of play he avoided another card with a striking elbow blow to Firmino's head as they both challenged for a ball in the air. Why a six-four midfielder needs to swing his elbow to defend himself against a five-ten opponent is beyond me, yet he does it practically every time. Mazic whistled for the foul and verbally cautioned Fellaini, but no card was issued on the play.

Liverpool made it through the first ten minutes without conceding, and I breathed a quick sigh of relief. Eighty more minutes to go. Just take it ten minutes at a time.

Manchester United would get the first great chance on target in the eighteenth minute, when Marcos Rojo crossed from their left flank over the defense toward the far post. James Milner was caught ball-watching as Jesse Lingard snapped a header toward the near post. Mignolet spotted the shot and dove to his right, parrying the ball away from the net and out for a corner kick. The few Manchester United fans in attendance groaned at the missed opportunity as about sixty Raleigh Reds exhaled. Juan Mata had a great chance to score on the ensuing corner kick, but mishit the shot wide of target. Twenty minutes had passed with no score. The plan was working.

Coutinho had the first good Liverpool chance in the twenty-seventh minute when he rushed onto a loose ball at the top of the penalty box. He tried blasting a shot to the right corner, but didn't appear to get good contact with the ball. Still, De Gea's view was obstructed slightly by his defenders, so it wasn't an easy save, yet he made it look so. There was another gasp from the majority of the patrons in attendance. Thirty minutes had passed and Liverpool was holding firm. *Just make it to halftime*, I thought. Almost immediately after thinking that, the walls came crashing down.

Rojo intercepted the ball while pressing for United in the offensive third of the pitch. He passed over to a wide-open Juan Mata in the center. Mata passed to the left side of the box, where Tony Martial cut inside the box with possession. He easily juked past Nathaniel Clyne, who clumsily fouled the striker inside the box. It was a clear penalty, and everyone in the pub knew it. A week earlier Clyne had made a nice attacking run to earn the penalty kick, and now he'd returned the favor with poor defending.

Martial easily converted to give Manchester United the 1-0 lead. As Old Trafford madly celebrated, two courageous fans in the pub hugged each other in joy amongst dozens of quietly cursing Liverpool fans. As much as I kept telling myself to relax, that we still held a one-goal edge in the aggregate score, I couldn't. I could only shake my head in disbelief, making eye contact with strangers who clearly felt my pain. Words needn't be spoken at that point.

The goal seemed to have awakened the players a bit, as a minute later Liverpool were awarded a free kick just outside the right side of the box. Sturridge stepped up and struck a beautiful ball over the wall and past the outstretched arms of De Gea, but the ball caromed off the crossbar and off to safety.

In the fortieth minute, Jordan Henderson made a nice, long give-and-go connection with Coutinho, and he moved unmarked into the box for a perfect ball from the Brazilian. With only the goalkeeper standing in between the ball and the target, Henderson missed the mark from twelve yards out and shot wide. Reaching the pinnacle of frustration, I uncharacteristically yelled to no one in particular, "YOU'RE NOT MY CAPTAIN!"

A few people glanced over at me, concerned that a normally reserved fan was publicly crying out his frustrations, but mostly I noticed some casual nods in agreement. "Gerrard would never miss that," I continued. It was an unfair comment to make about the current Liverpool captain, because ninety percent of the players on the pitch couldn't live up to the reputation earned by our former leader. Still, I reminded myself of Henderson's horrible miss from last week's match, and the comment that I'd made then. I don't dislike Henderson and I think he is a great player for the club. I simply miss the goal-scoring talents of Steven Gerrard.

Manchester United continued to gain more confidence on the pitch, and everyone could see it. Only a few minutes remained in the half when Coutinho carelessly fouled near the penalty box and was cautioned by the Serbian ref. Sakho was able to clear the initial cross to safety, but Daley Blind collected the ball from about forty yards and looped a long pass toward the end line. It looked as though the Liverpool defense assumed the ball was going out, as they lollygagged their way back into position. Fellaini showed great hustle in running down the ball before it crossed over the line, and he passed over to a wide-open Rojo only a few yards from goal. Rojo one-timed the shot but missed wide left. It was a bang-bang play and Liverpool was helpless. Rojo probably should've scored their second goal of the match, which would've been devastating for Liverpool to concede just before halftime. Groans had turned to audible curses after the miss. There was genuine worry at the pub.

Earlier I mentioned that great moments are made from great opportunities. Sometimes those moments become legendary. It can build up over time, or can happen in an instance, and it can happen to anyone at any time. With about thirty seconds left before halftime, Simon Mignolet collected an innocent long pass and distributed the ball to James Milner on the left. Milner passed it over the Emre Can in the middle of the pitch running toward the left sideline. Looking up the field, Can noticed acres of open space down the left flank. Coutinho was unmarked in the general region. The German midfielder passed the ball into the clear space as the Brazilian ran onto the ball. This time it was the Manchester United defense lollygagging back into position.

As Coutinho dribbled into the box, people started to take notice of the developing situation. Those that were sitting down suddenly found themselves standing up. People in the back crept forward a few steps. You could see the eyes of every fan suddenly open up as though they'd just opened their first Christmas present. I only heard one comment, loudly shouted by my Irish friend Noel: "USE IT, YOU FECKING SQUAD PLAYER!" He was referring to the long-running joke from two years earlier. As Liverpool made the title challenge in the 2013-14 season, Noel insisted that the club's success would bring in enough talent that he predicted Coutinho would end up being nothing more than a decent squad player. Whenever the Brazilian scores a magical goal, we jokingly call him the "greatest squad player in history."

As Coutinho moved into the penalty box, I noticed that there was no central defender recovering to support. If Coutinho could somehow get past Uruguayan defender Guillermo Varelas, he would have a shot on target. With a quick glance to his right, Coutinho dipped his right shoulder, signifying a possible move in that direction. Varelas bit and barely flinched to block the path. That split-second flinch was all that Coutinho would need, as he burst forward to the left, continuing his run toward the near post. Varelas was now out of position and could either foul the Brazilian for a sure penalty and possible red card, or watch and pray that his goalkeeper would bail out the Manchester United defense for the umpteenth time.

De Gea saw that Coutinho had broken free and only had time to make one guess at where the ball was headed. As De Gea lunged to his left, hoping to block the play, Coutinho masterfully dinked the ball over the goalkeeper's right shoulder into the back of the net.

At that singular moment, the London Bridge Pub erupted more than I had ever witnessed. Grown men of all sizes and shapes hugged and cried in unison. I never checked officially, but I wouldn't have been surprised if that moment had registered on the Richter scale with the U.S. Geological Society.

Play didn't resume after that, as the teams went into the locker room for halftime. I spent the next few minutes hunched over, trying to catch my breath. I think I was hyperventilating and struggling to breathe. I was reminded of the quote from former Liverpool manager Bill Shankly: "Some people think football is a matter of life and death. I assure you it's much more important than that." Could I possibly be having a near-death experience from the adrenaline rush of watching a goal scored in a football match? Thankfully, I was able to catch my breath and smile. I walked over to Noel for a hug, celebrating a great goal from the great "squad player."

The goal was a magnificent move of brilliance. Officially Emre Can got the assist, but it was all Coutinho. It only took fifteen seconds from the time Mignolet collected the ball to the moment that ball was in the back of the net. No one at the pub saw it coming. Certainly none of the eighty thousand fans at Old Trafford could see it. In an instant, the match was turned upside down. With Liverpool scoring that precious away goal, Manchester United would need to score three times in the second half to advance. It wouldn't happen.

For the next forty-five minutes of football, everyone at the pub relaxed and enjoyed themselves again. Maybe if United would find a way to get another goal, then we would tighten up our focus. But that never happened. I couldn't remember the last time I had enjoyed an entire half of Liverpool football as I did that afternoon. I didn't care that no one was scoring goals. I simply savored the atmosphere with my pint of Guinness and good friends. We watched Liverpool's European dream continue as Manchester

United's nightmare began.

The final whistle blew with the official result being a 1-1 draw, but Liverpool advanced 3-1 on aggregate. Liverpool advanced to the quarterfinals and inched a step closer to glory. For the first time in history, an English club would eliminate Manchester United from European competition. It seemed fitting to have Liverpool be that club.

In the days following the epic victory for Liverpool, it was revealed that UEFA was going to sanction both clubs for their fans' behavior at the matches. Initially it was reported that only Liverpool fans were to blame for singing about the Munich air disaster. These initial reports were maddening, since you could clearly hear Manchester United fans also singing about Hillsborough. After further investigation, it was determined that both clubs were equally at fault, and they were hit with fines of €20,000 and two years of probation. It was an afterthought by deplorable fans whose actions will mostly likely never cease.

Most importantly, though, Liverpool kept the Europa League dream alive. The fact that Liverpool were now unbeaten against Manchester United in European competition was the proverbial cherry on top of the sundae. It's a bragging right that we can hold on to forever. I know that there will come a time in the future where Manchester United will be able to exact revenge on this loss, but the fact will always remain that we won the first European head-to-head match against them. That's history that will never be rewritten.

30 - CHARLESTON

Sunday, March 20
Madra Rua Irish Pub, Charleston, SC
Premier Match #29 (at Southampton)

I first met Nicki Ace in the summer of 2014 during Liverpool's North America preseason tour. Liverpool had decided to include Charlotte among the cities on their preseason tour that summer. We were all excited that our beloved Reds would be playing so close to home, but it was also a fantastic networking opportunity for all newly born OLSC branches located in the southeastern United States. Raleigh, Charlotte, and South Carolina were among the new branches made official by LFC within the past twelve months, and we all had numerous members making the trip to the Queen City. In preparation for that epic weekend we had been corresponding with each other over email, so when we actually met face to face, we felt like we had already known each other.

Nicki is the proud secretary for OLSC South Carolina, a title that she takes extremely seriously. It's easy to pinpoint why she devotes her loyalty to Liverpool. She married into it. Her husband Jim Lynch was raised in Derry, Northern Ireland, where he picked up his love for Liverpool, as many other kids do growing up on the Emerald Isle. Jim moved to Charleston in 1994, the same year that Nicki prematurely gave birth to her youngest son Johnathan in upstate New York. Back then he had few options to get coverage of Liverpool in the States, so he would try to listen to the BBC on a shortwave radio. It was an arduous challenge for Jim to get his weekly Liverpool fix back then.

Nicki would eventually get divorced and relocate to Charleston. She met Jim a few years later and has been with him since. When Johnathan was about eight years old, Jim would take him to the pub to watch Liverpool games. At the time, Johnathan was a huge baseball fan and loved the Atlanta Braves. The Premier League was starting to get better television coverage, so Jim found a local pub that would allow him to bring the young child to watch the Liverpool match. Nicki didn't mind having her son get out of the house on a Saturday morning, and slowly Johnathan lost interest in the Braves and baseball in favor of Liverpool and English football.

In March of 2003, three Irish lads living in Charleston decided there was a need to open an Irish pub. Jason Weber, Robert Spencer (a.k.a. "Spence"), and Steve O'Connor pooled their resources and found prime real estate north of downtown in the Park Circle area of Charleston. They spent time designing the pub properly with décor that invoked the feeling of being in Ireland. They named their new pub "Madra Rua," which is Gaelic for "red fox." I was curious what the significance of "red fox" had to do with Ireland, but it turned out that they agreed it was simply a really cool name for a pub.

Over the years Jim had met some other Liverpool fans, and they started going to watch matches at the Madra Rua in 2007. The pub gained a reputation as being the only place to watch live soccer matches on television, so pockets of supporters from all clubs would find their way to the Park Circle pub for matches. These small fan groups started growing in size along with the overall popularity of the sport, and many of these clubs felt like they needed their own place as a home pub. Since the owners of Madra Rua are all Liverpool supporters, Jim and his friends never saw the need to change venues.

When you first walk into the pub, you must decide whether to go to the room on the left of the bar or to the room on the right. The room on the left is filled with Liverpool fan gear and reserved for the club on all match days, with no exceptions. Fans of every other club can watch their matches in the other room. Even though the Madra Rua officially only hosts the Liverpool and Tottenham clubs, fans from most clubs will show up on match day to enjoy the great atmosphere. The pub's popularity grew so much that they opened a second franchise in the northern suburb of Summerville.

It was a cold and rainy Sunday morning when I made my way over to the pub. The pub is located in a somewhat trendy section known as Park Circle. As you exit the interstate and drive along the perimeter fence line of a riverside military base, you pull into what appears to be a manufactured village that doesn't belong in its surroundings. The Olde Village or Park Circle is part of a major revitalization project which includes many shops and eateries, including a nice Irish pub on the main drag. The match was scheduled to kick off at nine thirty a.m., so I arrived a few minutes ahead of kickoff. Soon after I parked my car, I saw Nicki and Jim pull up in their minivan with Johnathan.

I walked in and immediately noticed some fans were bellied up to the bar drinking Guinness. Apparently South Carolina had decided they didn't need to pass laws to prevent fans from drinking alcohol before noon on Sundays. I had assumed that most states in the Bible Belt of southeastern America had laws restricting alcohol consumption on Sundays. I was wrong. The states directly north and south of my home each allow people to go to their local pub on a Sunday morning and grab a pint to watch the match on television with. What a novel concept.

Nicki took the first few minutes to have an informal roll call, walking around to see which of her club members had made the journey to the pub. She has embraced the administrative role and admits to be more interested in the social aspect of the club than the sport itself. Everyone benefits from her efforts, including the OLSC branch network of North America, as she created a master document of pubs across the continent Liverpool supporters have been known to frequent for matches. This document is immensely helpful for fans that must travel away from home and still want to enjoy the pub atmosphere for a match. A copy is included as an appendix to this book.

I settled down in a booth with a good view of the television and ordered a pint of Guinness. Nicki took time to introduce me to some of the regular crew, including the owner Jason, who was tending bar and pouring my pint. There were about thirty people inside the Madra Rua at kickoff, most of them sitting on a barstool at the bar. Fans started discussing the lineup decisions announced earlier. Most surprising was the debut of Jon Flanagan as first team captain. It was a popular move amongst the fan faithful, since Flanagan was born and raised in Liverpool. James Milner was suspended following his two yellow cards against Crystal Palace, and Jordan Henderson was unfit to start due to illness.

Southampton is never an easy place to play, as it is one of the longer trips within England. The team itself was comprised of talented players and had an exciting, successful Dutch coach, Ronald Koeman, leading them on their chase toward a top-six league finish. Recently Liverpool had been accused of poaching Southampton's talent during the offseason, acquiring players Adam Lallana, Dejan Lovren, and Nathaniel Clyne in the past few summers. These moves were the reason some fans called the southern club Liverhampton.

The match kicked off with Liverpool controlling the early play. They struck first in the sixteenth minute. Philippe Coutinho received the ball along the left sideline, looking up to find a passing target. Not finding anything to his liking, he cut back to the inside. He took a few steps with the ball before noticing a crack in the Southampton defense. From twenty-five yards out, Coutinho ripped his trademarked right-footed curling shot into the far corner of the net. Southampton goalkeeper Fraser Forster was caught flat-footed on the play, perhaps not expecting the Brazilian to unleash his fury from so far out. In this same fixture just over a year ago, Coutinho had scored against Forster on a near-replica strike from close to the same spot on the pitch. It was a fantastic goal to give Liverpool the 1-0 lead.

Just as fans were celebrating the first goal, Liverpool looked to double the lead. Southampton's Serbian midfielder Dusan Tadic was dispossessed deep in the offensive third by the pressing combination of Nathaniel Clyne and Mamadou Sakho. Clyne passed up the field to Coutinho, who sent the ball up to Divock Origi on the midfield line. The Belgian striker is one of the fastest players in the Premier League, so he took the ball and jetted forward toward goal. Daniel Sturridge moved forward in an onside position to create a two-versus-two attacking situation. Origi passed over to Sturridge in the box, who drew both attackers to try and block his shooting lanes. Sturridge faked a shot, which created a small opening. It was big enough for the Englishman to fire a left-footed shot to the far corner of the goal. Forster had no chance to make the save, and the Reds were firmly in control with an early two-goal lead.

There was great atmosphere in the quaint pub as fans gave each other high fives and fist bumps. I looked around and noticed one person even doing his own version of the Sturridge dance to celebrate the striker's prowess. It was a great start to the morning.

Joe Allen appeared to have given Liverpool their third goal in the thirty-second minute with a twelve-yard shot off a corner kick that found its way into the back of the net. The players celebrated a rare goal from the wee Welshman while the Madra Rua patrons did the same. Nicki turned to me and said, "If this keeps up, we won't let you leave!" I can't think of many places I would rather be held captive than Charleston, South Carolina. It was an unnecessary threat, because the linesman flagged late to signal offside. The referee disallowed the goal, as replays confirmed that Sakho didn't retreat quickly enough as Southampton pushed out, and was left in an offside position when Allen struck the ball. Whether Sakho affected the play or the goalkeeper's ability to make a play was certainly debatable, but Liverpool had had their fair share of offside calls going their way this season, so it was hard to be upset about this one.

While Allen was denied that goal, he had no excuse for missing the target moments later. The Welsh midfielder stole the ball in the middle third and passed up to Coutinho. The ball was played ahead to Adam Lallana and then Emre Can, who played a luscious pass to a streaking Allen in on goal uncontested. With an entire net in front of him and only Forster to defend the goal, the ball was shot straight at the goalkeeper for an easy save. If his corner kick goal was wrongly disallowed, Allen had no excuse for not scoring this attempt.

The halftime whistle blew with Liverpool leading on the road 2-0. Still, I couldn't help but be concerned. A two-goal lead can be treacherous at times. Once a team scores to cut the deficit in half, the momentum seems to shift. Liverpool had squandered a few chances to extend their lead in the first half, and I worried that those misses would come back to haunt the club.

The mood at the pub in general was confident. Southampton looked inferior against our boys, and I couldn't see how they would get back into this match. I sat down with Nicki and Jim to discuss the first half over a pint, and we all agreed that Liverpool should have a bigger cushion. Yet we all figured it wouldn't matter, either.

Southampton manager Ronald Koeman would certainly make necessary adjustments to improve their anemic attack in the second half. The Dutch gaffer brought on Sadio Mane and Victor Wanyama to help bolster the midfield. Jürgen Klopp brought on Martin Skrtel for Dejan Lovren in central defense. It was the Slovakian's first action since December 20, so the move was questioned by many at the pub. I could find nothing on social media about a possible injury to Lovren, so it was assumed that Klopp felt comfortable enough to give Skrtel some minutes. It would prove disastrous.

Only three minutes into the second half, the impact of the changes was evident. Skrtel was beaten in the box by Graziano Pelle and immediately called for a penalty. Looking at the replay, it appeared that both players were tugging at each other's shirts, but Skrtel had earned a reputation for this maneuver for years now, and it was an easy call for the referee. Mane stepped up to take the penalty and fired to his left. Simon Mignolet guessed correctly to make the diving save and preserve the clean sheet for the moment.

It took another defensive miscue from Liverpool to give Southampton their next scoring chance in the sixty-third minute. Flanagan gave the ball away poorly in the defensive third as Pelle took possession. He played the ball up forward to Mane, who juked Sakho badly and opened up a moment to fire a left-footed shot toward the goal. This time Mignolet couldn't stop the Senegalese striker. Just like that, the lead was back to one.

With Southampton pushing forward trying to equalize, Lallana intercepted in the seventy-fourth minute and started to counterattack. He found Christian Benteke, who'd come on minutes earlier as a sub for Sturridge. Benteke looked up to see nothing but Forster between himself and the goal. He tried to place a shot inside the far post, but it missed just inches wide. The frustration was evident at the pub. He had been suffering a cataclysmic lack of confidence lately, and his offensive ineptitude started transforming our confidence into concern at the pub. There were genuine questions about his future at the club, as he most likely would be shipped off to another club in the summer.

With only a one-goal lead to protect late in the match, there was serious concern about dropping points. This was confirmed in the eighty-third minute when Skrtel failed to clear a header over Pelle. The ball fell to a Southampton attacker and eventually back to Pelle, who had lost Skrtel in the process. The Italian was now wide open and able to curl a left-footed shot in the top corner of the net to equalize the match.

Two minutes later, our fate was sealed with another comical set of defensive errors. Flanagan was pressured by Southampton and calmly laid a safe back pass to Mignolet. Instead of firing the ball to midfield, Mignolet mishit the ball and popped it straight up in the air. Skrtel mistimed his effort to head the ball and missed it completely. Joe Allen came over to make a play but failed to win his tackle, and the ball found itself at the feet of Pelle once again. He passed up to Mane, who was loosely marked by Sakho. Mane fired another beauty past Mignolet to give the Saints the 3-2 lead and eventual victory. At the pub we could only shake our heads in disbelief. For the second time this season, Sadio Mane broke our hearts with a late goal. For the first time, Klopp got the tactics wrong and was beaten on the day by his counterpart. While Koeman made the right moves to bolster the attack, Klopp's decision to bring in Skrtel proved to be the death knell for this match.

Fans were still hanging at the pub in disbelief at what had just transpired. I grabbed another pint of Guinness and sat down at a table with Jim and Nicki. While some Liverpool fans departed, other fans drifted into the pub in anticipation of the Manchester derby that was scheduled to kick off at noon. One particular City fan took off his jacket while sitting at the bar, revealing the light blue Raheem Sterling #7 kit on his back. Jim clearly recognized the guy, calling out to him, "For fuck's sake, mate. I thought I told you to burn that shirt already!"

The man chuckled and replied, "You won't say that about him when he scores to beat United today." It was the typical friendly banter between fans of opposing clubs that makes this atmosphere appealing. Jim explained to me that Manchester United fans used to come to the Madra Rua to watch matches, but they found another hangout, probably because of the strong numbers of Liverpool supporters that would frequent the pub. In fact, some of the United supporters in the area tried to recruit Nicki over to the dark side. Clearly her administrative skills had earned her recognition, but as Jim quickly pointed out, "She's no fucking Michael Owen, I tell ya that much."

Nicki and her husband are season ticket holders for the city's local soccer team the Charleston Battery, which competes in the United Soccer League. She is always organizing events for the supporters in Charleston, and has even extended the reach of their OLSC to beyond her hometown.

A few years ago she caught wind that a bunch of Liverpool fans living in the state capital of Columbia needed to find a refuge to watch matches. It started with two Liverpudlians living in Columbia watching at the British Bulldog, slowly growing into a force of about twenty supporters. Jim and Nicki decided to make the hour-long drive up to Columbia to check them out, eventually bringing them into the family. Their inclusion helped OLSC South Carolina get the required numbers to obtain their official status with LFC in 2013 after a four-year wait. Since that time, a third city has joined the family. Fans in the Greenville-Spartanburg area of upstate South Carolina formally named Gringos Cantina as their place to watch all Liverpool matches.

Johnathan remained seated at the bar as Nicki, Jim, and I continued to chat at the back table. I finished my pint in time to see Marcus Rashford score the opening goal for Manchester United as they took a 1-0 lead into halftime. I decided it was time for me to leave, with a four-hour drive home ahead of me. As disappointing as the Liverpool loss was, I didn't think I could've taken the mental overload of witnessing a United victory immediately after.

The upcoming international break meant it would be two more weeks before Liverpool could get the chance at redemption. It also meant the disappointment would marinate a bit longer. In November we had seen Liverpool follow an epic 4-1 road victory at Manchester City with a disappointing loss to Crystal Palace before that international break hit. It's a bitter feeling having to wait two weeks before the next shot at redemption.

It just goes to show you how fickle this game can be. Only three days earlier we were on cloud nine, having eliminated Manchester United in the Europa League. Then we sat and watched our team take firm control of a match that we ultimately let slip away. Such is the unpredictability of the storm that seemingly follows every Liverpool fan.

Through thirty-one games of the season, Liverpool had faded back to ninth place on the table, well behind league leaders Leicester City, who were holding on to a five-point lead over Tottenham. Liverpool still had two games in hand to play against Everton and Chelsea later in the season, matches postponed due to advancement in the cup competition. Winning those two matches would get them within four points of the top four, a near-monumental feat to overcome in only seven matches.

31 - BLIND FAITH

Following the tough defeat at Southampton was the brutal week off for a FIFA-mandated international break. These breaks are designated years in advance by the sport's governing body, and each league strictly adheres to that schedule. The interruption to the calendar is frustrating for fans, especially when it falls so late in the regular season.

It is considered a great honor to be called to action for your national team, especially when the matches are critical toward qualification to a major tournament. I don't have a problem when Philippe Coutinho flies across the pond to his home country of Brazil for World Cup qualifiers, even if it's only for twenty-three minutes as a substitute in a 2-2 draw with Uruguay. I do get nervous watching Liverpool's starters playing meaningless international friendly matches. While Coutinho had to spend the equivalent of a full day on airplanes traveling back and forth to Brazil's matches, six other Liverpool starters remained for England's exhibition match against Germany. Thankfully, all Liverpool players returned unscathed.

With the final break behind us, seven weeks remained before this season concluded. Leicester City remained the most surprising story in the Premier League, with a five-point cushion at the top of the table. Almost as surprising was the fact that the club chasing them down for that coveted title was Tottenham. Spurs had only finished high enough in the league standings to qualify for Champions League twice in the relatively short history of that competition. Seeing these two clubs battle for the league title was a conundrum for all fans. I was not sure if this parity was a result of improvement of certain clubs or the dilution of talent from the traditional giants. I tended to believe it was a combination of both, and the overall mediocrity of the league was a further indictment of how disappointing Liverpool's league campaign had been thus far. Tottenham came to Anfield hoping to narrow their deficit with Leicester City to two points. With the Foxes not playing until the day after, it would be crucial for Spurs to keep pressure on the leaders.

It was a beautiful spring afternoon in Raleigh, and the twelve thirty p.m. kickoff was a perfect way to start the weekend. I headed down to the pub hoping to see a good crowd revitalized for the final stretch. I wasn't disappointed, with about fifty fans packing the pub. I grabbed a pint of Guinness and joined my friends in the usual corner spot next to the Walken Fridge.

Liverpool jumped out on the front foot, attacking the Tottenham end early and often in the first half, but Spurs goalkeeper Hugo Lloris made numerous great saves to keep the score deadlocked through halftime. It wasn't until the opening minutes of the second half that Liverpool opened the scoring. Coutinho played a nice give-and-go pass with Daniel Sturridge that easily sliced passed the Spurs defense, as our little Brazilian magician delicately placed his shot past Lloris. The pro-Liverpool crowd at the pub erupted in joy, singing the praises of the goal scorer: "Ca-TEEN-ya, oh, oh, oh!"

The crowd had barely settled down after that goal when Coutinho nearly returned the favor with a nice cross, but Sturridge's header barely skimmed over the crossbar for a goal kick. Even with the brilliant attacking play from Liverpool, the defense remained vulnerable, and kept the fans from getting overconfident.

As Liverpool tried to shore up the midfield, Tottenham regained control to get back into the match. Spurs were desperate to win all three points, and I was hopeful that their offensive play would open the door for a late counterattacking strike. Unfortunately, Harry Kane turned the tide in the sixty-third minute when he equalized following a clever pass from Denmark international Christian Eriksen. The goal deflated Liverpool and left the fans clinging to the hope of salvaging a result.

For the final thirty minutes, Tottenham was clearly the better team. They looked like a club fighting for three points to stay in the title hunt, while Liverpool played on their back heel, praying not to concede. Play turned sloppy toward the end as both teams frenetically ran around the pitch trying to find an attack. Neither was successful, as the match ended up being a 1-1 draw.

Coupled with the loss at Southampton, the draw seemed to put more distance between Liverpool and a top-four finish. Consensus at the pub following the match was to put maximum effort into the Europa League, as that would be the best chance to earn a Champions League berth next season. I laughed at the notion that Klopp would do anything but play his best squad on Thursday. He was returning to the city that he'd called home for seven full seasons, strategizing against players he had managed less than a year ago, trying to defeat one of the strongest teams in all of Europe. It was going to be a highly emotional, anticipated affair, something that every football fan would be paying attention to. And I couldn't wait for it to begin.

****

Following the historic victory over Manchester United in the previous round of the Europa League, Liverpool would be one of eight clubs remaining in the competition. Just like in the other cup competitions, Liverpool's next opponent would be determined by random draw. The other clubs still in the competition were defending champion Sevilla (Spain), Villareal (Spain), Athletic Bilbao (Spain), Shakhtar Donetsk (Ukraine), Braga (Portugal), Sparta Prague (Czech Republic), and Borussia Dortmund (Germany).

On paper, the strongest team in the competition would be Borussia Dortmund, the team that Jürgen Klopp was managing only a year ago. They were the only team still capable of catching Bayern Munich for the Bundesliga title, and only three years removed from playing in the Champions League final. They were the bookmakers' clear favorite to win this competition. Defeating them in a two-legged affair would not be easy for anyone. One lesson that I'd learned following this season so closely was that Liverpool didn't do easy. It was little surprise when the quarterfinal was announced as Liverpool vs. Borussia Dortmund.

There is a deep connection between these two clubs, and fans share a mutual respect. Both clubs consider "You'll Never Walk Alone" as their anthem, as fans serenade their players with the tune before and after every match. In the aftermath of the Hillsborough tragedy, the Dortmund fans were amongst the first clubs to show support in the families' struggle for justice. Liverpool fans have never forgotten that fact, so it was no surprise to learn that many Red fans would publicly support "die Schwarzgelben" (translated from German as "the black and gold").

The first leg would be played at Westfalenstadion, the largest stadium in Germany with a capacity of 81,359. That's larger than every NFL stadium with the exception of MetLife Stadium outside New York City. The only stadium in England that comes close to holding that many supporters is Old Trafford, yet there is a stark contrast to the atmosphere created by the Dortmund fans. Watching the thousands of flags and banners waved fervently before the match is a sight to behold. It's an experience that has made its way onto my bucket list. Jürgen Klopp was named their manager in July of 2008 after the club finished in thirteenth place, struggling to avoid relegation. Three years later, he had them crowned champions of Germany despite a vastly inferior payroll to Bayern Munich. Dortmund fans hold a special place in their heart for Klopp, so they would surely provide a warm welcome for his return, even if he was with the opposing team.

Dortmund was in incredible form since returning from their winter break, having not lost a single match in fifteen. Their three top goal scorers (Pierre-Emerick Aubameyang, Marco Reus, and Henrikh Mkhitaryan) had amassed seventy-five goals to date, more than Liverpool had scored as a club altogether. Even though everyone thought that Dortmund would advance easily to the next stage of the competition, the fact that Klopp was intimately familiar with the players would help Liverpool. He knew their strengths and weaknesses, and was hopefully able to deploy a strategy that would see Liverpool through.

I'm reminded of a quote that I heard in the 2014 HBO music documentary *Sonic Highways* about the rock band Foo Fighters. The docuseries followed the band through eight American cities steeped in musical history as they sought inspiration for their next album. During an episode in Nashville, music producer Tony Brown was referring to aspiring songwriters coming to the city when he said, "You need to have blind faith. And no false hope. But you have to have blind faith." It was a quote that the band later used as a lyric in their song "Congregation" on the ensuing album. It's a quote that applied to Liverpool fans as well. To have any confidence against a stronger club like Dortmund, they would need to have blind faith in Klopp. When Brendan Rodgers led the club into important matches as the underdog, we would have false hope. But with Klopp we had that blind faith that we'd get the result.

The match was scheduled for a three p.m. kickoff on the first day of my family vacation in the Florida Keys. We arrived on Wednesday night, and the first thing I did was ensure that the cable package at the house rental carried Fox Sports One. My plan for Thursday was clear. I would relax in the confines of the rental, enjoy the Florida sunshine by the pool, and relocate to the couch in time for kickoff.

Klopp was already limited in his attacking options, which made it even more surprising to see him name young Divock Origi in the starting lineup over experienced goal scorer Daniel Sturridge. While some people criticized the move publicly, I kept my blind faith.

When the game finally kicked off, I quickly noticed that the best lineup change wasn't made by either manager. It was made by Fox Sports, replacing the often-criticized Alexi Lalas as color commentator with former Liverpool and American national goalkeeper Brad Friedel. Lalas had gained a reputation for being opinionated and pompous. There was even an online petition signed by thousands of American soccer fans pleading with Fox to keep him off their telecasts. Personally I was done with him after he exclaimed, "I love it!" following Tony Martial's penalty goal for Manchester United in the last Europa League match to cut Liverpool's lead to one. The substitution of Brad Friedel was a pleasant surprise. The American joined Liverpool in 1997 and would ultimately make twenty-five appearances for the club before moving to Blackburn Rovers after three seasons in Merseyside. The jury was still out on his skills in the booth, but surely he would be an improvement over Lalas. The warm Florida sun beat down outside, cold beer was in my hand, and Liverpool were playing Dortmund on the television with no Alexi Lalas. Life was good.

The match was quite even, but as expected, it was Dortmund that generated the first few chances on target. Mamadou Sakho came up huge with a leg block on Mkhitaryan's shot toward goal in the seventeenth minute. The defense held firm throughout the first half. The center defense pairing of Sakho and Dejan Lovren had formed a great partnership under Klopp, and their efforts were keeping Liverpool in the match, preventing the vaunted Dortmund attack from scoring.

Liverpool would shock the home crowd in the thirty-sixth minute. Following a long, high pass from Alberto Moreno on the left side, James Milner was able to flick the ball forward with his head to a streaking Origi. With a single touch to control possession, the Belgian national struck a well-placed ball to the left post past Roman Weidenfuller to give Liverpool the lead and a precious away goal. I jumped off the couch and shouted in jubilation. The crowd was stunned as Liverpool fans celebrated.

Origi nearly doubled the lead just before halftime with a counterattacking break started by Philippe Coutinho, but his effort on target was brilliantly saved by Weidenfuller. That goal would've been huge for Liverpool just before halftime.

Dortmund was creating chances, and I knew that they'd come out firing in the second half to find the equalizer. It only took a few minutes for them to accomplish that feat. Instead of the goal coming from one of their big three scorers, it would be Liverpool's anemic set piece defending that created the opportunity. On a short pass from a corner kick, defender Mats Hummels was able to break free from him mark and sky over Adam Lallana to head the cross into the back of the net. Simon Mignolet made a nice effort to get a hand on the ball, but the powerful header was too much. Dortmund had found their equalizer.

The next forty minutes were nerve-racking. Both clubs had decent chances to score, and the only thing I could do was drink cold beer and eat my fingernails. When the final whistle blew with no more goals, I let out a huge sigh of relief. Even had Dortmund scored a second goal, the fact that Liverpool got the away goal was going to give them mountains of confidence for the return leg at Anfield. Had any Liverpool fan been given the choice to accept a 1-1 draw before kickoff of this match, I would've bet my house that they'd take it. It was a great way to start my vacation.

The stage was now set for another great European night at Anfield. I'd be returning from Florida a few days prior to that match, so I made sure that my calendar was blocked off for that match. Barring an emergency, there was no way I was going to miss being at the pub for that match.

****

Riding high from the result in Germany, Liverpool returned to Anfield to play Stoke City for the fourth time this season. It seemed like a lifetime ago when Coutinho's late strike rocketed into the net to give Liverpool the 1-0 victory in the opening match of the season. I had almost forgotten that it was at the expense of Stoke City that Liverpool advanced to League Cup final in January. Now the Potters returned to Merseyside to try and exact some revenge for earlier results.

Klopp rightfully decided to rest many key players for this match. The second leg of the Dortmund match would be held on Thursday, and it was clear to everyone what was most important for the club. Martin Skrtel and Kolo Toure would return to the starting lineup along with regular reserve players Kevin Stewart and Sheyi Ojo. Most fans were apathetic toward this match, with their sights clearly focused on Thursday's game, but it was still a great opportunity for some of these players to showcase their talents in front of the home crowd.

It only took eight minutes for Liverpool to open the scoring when Alberto Moreno fired a left-footed shot into the far corner from about twenty yards out. Stoke City would equalize in the twenty-second minute against the run of play. Swiss international Xherdan Shaqiri curled a free kick dangerously into the box, targeting former Liverpool striker Peter Crouch. The defense collapsed on the tall attacker as the ball eluded everyone and went straight to one of the shortest men on the pitch, Bojan Krkic, who easily headed the ball into the net. It was the first attempt on target for Stoke City, a disturbing trend for the Reds.

Liverpool would restore the lead before halftime when Ojo burst past Shaqiri on the left side and laid a perfect cross to the far post. Sturridge got to the ball and headed it into the net for the 2-1 lead.

Divock Origi made a substitute appearance in the second half, replacing Ojo, and he would extend Liverpool's lead to two goals in the first few minutes on the pitch, heading in a cross from James Milner. Fifteen minutes later, Origi would find the score sheet again when his curling shot was placed perfectly into the side net. I couldn't tell if Origi's ball was actually intended to be a pass to Sturridge running on to the far post. Regardless of his intentions, the goal put the game out of reach, as

Liverpool would go on to defeat the Potters 4-1. It was a tasty appetizer to the main course of football that would arrive at Merseyside later in the week. While Dortmund was back in Germany also resting players in a match against local rivals Schalke, Liverpool seemed to be gathering some confidence in the attack. With both Sturridge and Origi finding the target in recent weeks, I thought that we would need to find goals if we were to advance in the Europa League. While a 0-0 draw would be enough to advance based on the away goals tiebreaker, I was skeptical that we were keeping a clean sheet against the strong Dortmund attack. Regardless, it felt good to be looking forward to important European matches once again.

32 - A NEW MIRACLE

Having returned from vacation the day before this match, my day was going to be spent catching up on work. It didn't matter how much got accomplished—I knew that I was leaving the office for the pub with plenty of time to catch the opening kickoff of this incredibly important match. My boss understood completely.

Before the first leg was played, Dortmund was the clear favorite to advance over Liverpool. Their attacking threat was one of the best in all of Europe, so many people were still predicting the German club would advance despite being held to a 1-1 draw the week before. I walked into the pub about fifteen minutes before kickoff to find the establishment was, surprisingly, at about half capacity. If this were a Champions League quarterfinal then perhaps more fans would be drawn to leave work early, but it was clear that many Raleigh Reds were still unconvinced of their chances.

The significance of this match went far beyond a simple competition. As luck would have it, Liverpool was drawn to host this leg on the day before the twenty-seventh anniversary of the Hillsborough tragedy. Liverpool Football Club hadn't played a match on that date since the ninety-six fans were lost almost three decades before. It was an emotional time for the city, and you couldn't have asked for a more fitting opponent to be played on this date.

All throughout the day there were videos and pictures on social media of the two sets of supporters eagerly mingling before the match. Fans wearing the red colors of Liverpool hugged, drank, and sang alongside fans wearing the black-and-gold garb of their opponent. Even though I was thousands of miles away on another continent, the emotions of this spectacle caught up with me. I eagerly anticipated the biggest match to be played at Anfield in a long time. Even though the Europa League is considered the lesser of the two European competitions, this had the feel of those epic Champions League matches seen not long ago.

The regular midweek crowd had already assembled in their normal bar positions, and I greeted all of my friends as I walked toward the back of the pub. Sam was pouring my first pint of Guinness as soon as he saw me.

Early discussion at the pub focused on the slight advantage Liverpool carried into the match, having scored an away goal in Germany. I was less than convinced that our weakened defense could keep a clean sheet against the highly rated Dortmund offense, so I tried to temper my enthusiasm. The nerves were pinging at an all-time high, and it felt good to experience that tension once again.

With fans still filing into the pub, the starting lineups made their way onto the pitch. The pub went silent as the bar's stereo system raised its volume for the ceremonial playing of "You'll Never Walk Alone." It was perhaps the most anticipated moment of the day. As the voice of Gerry Mardsen blasted throughout Anfield, the only words you could hear him sing were the first few opening words. The 42,894 fans took over from there. The electricity and passion of the moment gave me goose bumps. It was a moment I won't soon forget.

The match kicked off as I took position, hiding in the back of the pub. You could sense the tension, and I could only imagine how it felt at Anfield. Liverpool clearly looked the more nervous of the two clubs from the outset, but they still looked to assert control of the match. Slowly they possessed the ball and tried to move into the attacking third of the pitch.

Philippe Coutinho got the ball and was immediately pressed by the Dortmund defense. It was the sort of press that Klopp was trying to bring to Liverpool, players pestering the opposition like a swarm of gnats on a hot and humid North Carolina evening. Coutinho looked around and saw Alberto Moreno behind him unmarked. There was a bit of miscommunication as Moreno burst forward to attack just as a simple pass back was played. The ball rolled into empty space and was taken by Henrikh Mkhitaryan, who moved on the counterattack. As the Armenian midfielder dribbled forward, Moreno tried to track back on defense, but remained a few steps behind. The ball was played ahead to Pierre-Emerick Aubameyang inside the box, and he fired a shot from close range on target. The initial shot was saved by Simon Mignolet, but the rebound could not be controlled, as Mkhitaryan followed the play with a simple shot into the back of the net. Four minutes into the match and Dortmund had taken the lead. And just like that, Liverpool's precious away goal advantage was nullified.

The pub fell silent as everyone watched the Dortmund players celebrate their early fortune. It was hard to pin the blame for the goal solely on the defense. It was simply a fine goal created by superior midfield play on the counterattack. It was a stark reminder that our opponent was a stronger club and victory would not come easy.

I remained silent in the back of the pub, but there were a few choice words overheard from other supporters in near proximity. I tried to calm myself down, reminding myself of the fact that I'd never expected this team to keep a clean sheet. For Liverpool to advance would require an attacking threat that we had seen a few times earlier in the season. *Just get into a groove and play your game*, I thought.

Four minutes later, Dortmund struck again with another stellar counterattack. This time it was the great German stud Marcos Reus that stole the ball from his own defensive third and dribbled out of danger toward the Kop end of the pitch. Aubameyang was streaking forward unmarked as Liverpool's defense struggled to get back into position. Reus expertly passed the ball behind Mamadou Sakho and straight to his Gabonese teammate, who one-timed a shot past Mignolet in front of a shocked Liverpool crowd. Less than ten minutes into the match and the German outfit had taken a comfortable 2-0 lead on the road. The goal also gave Dortmund the away-goal tiebreaker, meaning that Liverpool would have to score three unanswered goals to advance to the semifinals. The panic button had clearly been hit.

There were more than a few expletives shouted amongst the approximately fifty supporters watching at the London Bridge Pub. I could only shake my head in despair, preparing myself for the potential of an embarrassing onslaught with over eighty minutes of football remaining. It wasn't a pretty moment.

After that second Dortmund goal, the play started shifting toward Liverpool's favor. I knew that it would be a tall order to score three goals against this great team. As much as I wanted Liverpool to score before halftime, I was simply hoping to apply a tourniquet on the defense and keep the deficit to two before halftime. Much to my delight, the Reds picked up their play. On more than one occasion they worked the ball into the attack and generated legitimate scoring chances. Divock Origi, playing in the biggest match of his young career, had three chances on target that failed to connect, while Roberto Firmino missed wide on his own head-ball attempt toward goal. Later on in the half, Adam Lallana missed a chance in front of the goal. It was encouraging to see the club manufacture some decent attacks, and it gave me some hope heading into halftime down 0-2.

I grabbed a seat at the booth next to Colin Russell, who was clearly as dismayed with the result as the rest of us. "I can't believe they failed to show up for the biggest match of the year," he said in disgust.

"I seem to recall not long ago when Liverpool had to score three goals in the second half to help win an important match," I reminded him. Of course I was referring to the 2005 Champions League final at Istanbul. AC Milan took a 3-0 lead at halftime in the most important game of that year. Then Liverpool fired home three goals in the opening fifteen minutes of the second half before eventually winning their fifth European Cup in a penalty shootout. I even texted this comment to Noel McCabe, who was watching the match from the comfort of his living room couch. Noel answered that he'd made the same comment to his Irish friends watching from across the pond.

"Yeah, but I can't see our defense keeping Dortmund from scoring another goal," Colin replied.

"Then we'll just have to score four," I confidently answered. It was the blind faith talking, with a little help from my good friend Sir Arthur Guinness.

Needing a change of scenery for the second half, I relocated to the front of the pub next to Sean Dotzauer. "If we can just score in the first few minutes, I think we can do this," he said to me. I confidently nodded in agreement. There was still a lot of football to be played.

Two minutes later, our hope was restored. With Dortmund looking to ice the match, the ball was played in toward our end. Thirty yards from our goal, Sakho cleared the ball forward with his head over to Moreno, who quickly passed up to Emre Can near the center circle. A quick give-and-go between Can and James Milner began a Liverpool counterattack. Can then found Firmino with another one-two pass, and suddenly the home team was slicing through the midfield with ease. Dortmund's defense set up with a high line, hoping to keep Liverpool's attack from settling in. This created space behind the defense for Origi to sprint ahead. Can passed forward into the open space as Origi's perfectly timed run put him in position. The Belgian took one touch to settle the ball before poking the ball past the Dortmund goalkeeper into the back of the net. The pub erupted as the deficit was cut to one.

Sean and I briefly hugged as other supporters made their way over to congratulate each other on the great goal. It was a beautiful goal created by the Liverpool attack, much like the goals scored by Dortmund that couldn't be blamed on a defensive error. Game on!

Play quickly resumed, and the realization hit that we were still two goals shy of advancing against a much better club. I thought that another quick goal was needed before we started building that confidence.

Belief started creeping back into the fans at the pub. Every call that went against Liverpool was met with screams of disagreement. Every time Liverpool lost possession, it resulted in another cry of despair from a random fan. It only took ten minutes of play for all air of hope to get deflated. Dortmund defender Mats Hummels received the ball near midfield and pushed forward down the left flank. Nathaniel Clyne moved forward to halt the play, opening up space in the left corner of the defense. It was there that Hummels passed to a wide-open Reus, who calmly slotted the ball past Mignolet into the far corner, giving Dortmund the two-goal cushion once again. I bowed my head in disgust and could only hear the television announcer declare, "SEALS IT!" As Reus ran to the corner of the pitch celebrating in front of the traveling Dortmund supporters, the entire pub stood in a deafening silence.

I tried to think positive thoughts, reminding myself that there was still thirty minutes of football to be played. Sean looked over at me, clearly recognizing the direness of the situation. "We just need to get one goal every ten minutes," he calmly said. "It's not over yet."

It was as though he'd turned on the light bulb. "You know what? You're right!" I replied. "We can do this! We just need to get it back. We need to score one before we can score three." I can't explain the feeling of confidence that was suddenly injected into my body. It wasn't false hope. It was that blind faith.

A few moments after Reus restored the seemingly insurmountable advantage, Klopp made the move to bring on Daniel Sturridge and Joe Allen. Firmino and Lallana got off the pitch, which changed the Liverpool formation. Two natural strikers now sat up at the top as Allen pushed into the midfield to shore up possession. It was a move that had to be made in order to bolster the Liverpool attack.

Dortmund recognized the change and shifted to a slightly more defensive posture, allowing Liverpool to control the midfield. They had seen this club struggle to break down a bunkered defense in the Premier League, so this tactical change seemed logical.

The shift in both formations seemed to have immediate gains for Liverpool, as suddenly it created more space for the midfield. In the sixty-fifth minute, Emre Can played a simple pass over to Allen, who found Moreno near the left sideline. As the Spaniard moved toward the center of the pitch, he slid the ball up to Coutinho. Looking to attack and penetrate into the attack, he passed forward to Milner, who had no option but to play back to Coutinho. Somehow the Brazilian found enough space to collect the pass and fire from about twenty yards out. We had seen Coutinho score some masterful goals from this distance with rockets off his right foot, but this wasn't exactly like those other goals. It still surprised Roman Weidenfeller in the goal and found the back of the net. No one saw it coming, even the staunch supporters at the pub. Once again the pub erupted. The Dortmund lead was now 3-2. We were right back in the thick of it! The celebrations were quickly tempered with the realization that two more goals were needed. But as Sean reminded me once again, we still had twenty minutes to play. "Just get another goal in the next ten minutes," he said.

Watching replays of the goal on the television, you could see Coutinho waving his arms to the crowd, trying to pump up the volume. It was reminiscent of Steven Gerrard's goal in that Champions League final at Istanbul, reminding everyone that there was still a fight in this club.

Play soon continued with Liverpool pressing on the attack. Origi fired from distance but narrowly missed the target. Three minutes later, Liverpool played a quick free quick that caught Dortmund by surprise, and Hummels pulled back on Origi inside the box. At first glance it looked like it could've been a penalty, but I would later concede that could've been a harsh call had it been made. That didn't stop the pub dwellers from screaming at the television after it happened.

As the clock continued to roll, it seemed inevitable that Liverpool would find the equalizer. That happened in the seventy-fifth minute off a James Milner corner kick. The ball was played in low toward the near post. Nine times out of ten, that ball is met by a defender and easily cleared to safety. Somehow the ball eluded all Dortmund players and bounced inside the box to a dangerous position only a few yards from goal. Mamadou Sakho found a brief opening in that space when the ball magically arrived to meet him. He redirected easily into the back of the net. The score was now level at 3-3. Bedlam ensued at the pub.

I couldn't believe what was happening. There was simply no tempering this celebration. Dortmund was still in position to advance to the next round, but somehow the Liverpool squad kept fighting and found themselves only a goal away from creating their own miracle. Sean reminded me once again, "Just one more goal in the next ten minutes."

The tension at the pub was palpable. It was as nervous as I had ever been watching a match. And it excited the hell out of me. Every time Liverpool gained possession, you could feel the collective anticipation rise in the pub. When that play was thwarted, the groan was amplified. Before you knew it, the clock hit the eighty-ninth minute. For the most part the patrons were silent. Over the loudspeakers from the telecast you could hear the Anfield faithful belting out "You'll Never Walk Alone." The commentators smartly went silent, letting the moment sink in for the viewers. Without missing a beat, everyone at the pub joined in as if we were sitting in the Kop ourselves. Some even hoisted their LFC scarves in the air. Time was running out, but we were doing our part at the pub, trying to will the club to one more goal from an entirely different continent. I knew that we weren't alone. Every Liverpool pub around the world was surely joining in this global chorus.

Just as the clock went into extra time, the fourth referee signaled for four additional minutes. That was all that remained for Dortmund to defend and advance. Two-hundred and forty seconds, give or take a few.

The ball was played from midfield over to Clyne on the right side of the pitch. Melner Schmelzer rashly challenged the Liverpool player, who coughed up possession in the process. The ref whistled for a foul and promptly showed Schmelzer a yellow card. Liverpool players pushed forward, but could only advance as far as the high line established by the Dortmund defense at the top of the box. Friedel commented before the kick that the defense was holding a really high line, potentially exposing them. The camera showed Liverpool players collecting near the box, where I noticed Daniel Sturridge pointing toward the near corner of empty space. It was clear that he was communicating to Milner to play him the ball into that space, which he promptly did.

Sturridge received the ball with a suspect first touch, drawing two defenders to his position. Aubameyang stayed with the ball, failing to see Milner follow the play with a bursting run from midfield unmarked. Somehow Sturridge was able to collect the ball and play it into the box to Milner. His first touch appeared to be a bit heavy, and the ball rolled toward the end line looking like it would cross over for a goal kick. Somehow Milner found another gear and was able to get there just in time to cross the ball before it went out of play.

Moments like this are hard to imagine in real time, but I honestly felt like the play was moving in slow motion. Milner's cross sailed to the far post, where multiple players from both teams struggled to get in position. I grabbed Sean by the shoulders, knowing that this had to be the moment we had been waiting for. Dejan Lovren leapt at the far post over the defense and headed the ball toward the far post. There was no denying this destiny as the ball caromed slightly off the post into the back of the net. Liverpool took a 4-3 lead in the match, 5-4 on aggregate, and put themselves in position to advance. Of all people, the much-maligned Dejan Lovren had just cemented his place in Liverpool history with perhaps one of the biggest goals ever scored at Anfield.

Words can't describe the feelings that ensued at that moment. I don't actually recall much of what went on at that moment other than dozens of fans massing together in the largest group hug I've ever had the pleasure of being part of. I do recall Chris Valentine coming up to me with the comment: "It had to be Lovren!" For the better part of two seasons I'd felt like I was on an island supporting the Croatian defender, and it was Chris that was the first to join me on that island. I had always known that he would somehow come good for the club; I just could never have predicted it would be like this.

Even so, there were a few minutes more to be played, and the slight fear of losing this lead at the death was brought to life with another late foul by

Lucas Leiva near the Liverpool goal. Tension returned as Ilkay Gündoğan lined up the free kick from just outside the penalty box. The television flashed over to Klopp on the sidelines, who had a look that said, "We can't lose it like this, can we?" I was sure I was not alone, as a quick prayer was relayed in my mind to the football gods. A curling shot was fired over the Liverpool wall that missed the near post by a few feet, and the final whistle blew immediately after. Liverpool won the match and advanced to the Europa League semifinals.

It was one of the most incredible moments I had ever experienced as a fan. Darren Bridger had spent most of the match standing by the bar silently, but he made his way over to me and Sean. There were tears in his eyes as he softly asked, "What just happened?"

I hugged him and smiled. "They fucking did it!" And then I felt the tears building up in my eyes. In all of my life I had never before cried watching a sporting event. Until now.

It was only a quarterfinal match of the Europa League, but it felt like so much more than that. It was a changing of the guard. Under Brendan Rodgers, this team would've capitulated after eight minutes. If not then, for sure they would've quit after Reus made it 3-1. The same players under Klopp would not relent. They gave complete effort and they made us proud. I could only imagine what it must've been like at Anfield, on the eve of the Hillsborough anniversary, to watch what could be the biggest victory in that stadium's storied history. I wanted to be there. Since I couldn't, I was quite happy with being with my mates at the pub to celebrate.

Once the dust settled and we caught our breath, I looked around at the Raleigh Reds, unsure of what to do next. Darren found time to gather himself, and made his way behind the bar to start fixing victory shots. I can't recall exactly what he poured, and it really didn't matter. He could've put a dishwater and urine cocktail in front of me and I would've gladly downed the shot with him. At one point, Mike Ruiz came up to me and jokingly asked if I knew who won the Liverpool match.

It was an incredible day, and a reminder of the possibilities with Klopp leading this club. To this day I get goose bumps thinking about that afternoon. For the rest of my life I will always remember where I was on this day and how Liverpool dug deep to find a way to win this match.

33 - THE (NOT-SO) FRIENDLY DERBY

Sunday, April 17
Camp Kendra
Premier League match #32 (at Bournemouth)

It would be difficult for anything to follow the extreme drama against Dortmund on Thursday. Yet three days later the club would travel to the southern shores of England to play Bournemouth. Originally scheduled for a normal Saturday ten a.m. kickoff, this match was moved to Sunday morning at seven. Jürgen Klopp was rightfully disappointed and confused by the start time. At over three hundred miles away, Bournemouth was one of the cities furthest from Liverpool in the Premier League, so the squad would be forced to travel by air. Surely no one slept following the Thursday night victory, and the early Sunday kickoff would put the team at a severe disadvantage.

Liverpool sat in eighth place on the table with a game in hand, but the fact that eleven points separated them from the top four meant it would be an uphill challenge to overcome. Europa League was clearly the club priority, and only a semifinal victory over Spanish squad Villareal stood in the way of another cup final for Liverpool. As expected, the circumstances dictated major changes in the lineup.

Klopp made ten changes to the starting lineup from Thursday, including handing twenty-two-year-old Welsh goalkeeper Danny Ward his Liverpool. Ward spent the first half of the season on loan with Aberdeen in the Scottish Premier League, but was recalled in January after Klopp lost faith in Adam Bogdan as a backup to Simon Mignolet. Ward would be the only reason I was interested to watch.

As you can imagine, there was no chance that I would be going anywhere for this match. I would be lucky enough to get out of bed before the match kicked off. All day Friday, the social media accounts from OLSC clubs across North America were loaded with comments about opening up pubs for this match. There is an obvious cost associated with opening an establishment, and pub owners rely on the match-day revenue from the supporters to help justify their return on that investment. This game carried absolutely no significance, and few fans were expected to turn out. Even Mike and Darren struggled with the idea of opening London Bridge Pub that morning, but ultimately their fandom overwrote common sense and they opened anyway. Despite the inability to legally consume alcohol, about a dozen Raleigh Reds showed up to the pub. Personally, I was content with the living room couch and fresh cup of coffee.

At the beginning of the season, Bournemouth was a popular pick to be one of the three relegated teams. The newly promoted club would be playing their first ever season in England's top flight since being formed in 1890, so it was an easy prediction to make. Yet with five games remaining, the Cherries were eleven points clear of the relegation zone in thirteenth place. It would take a colossal collapse for them to get relegated, so there would appear to be little motivation for the players.

As expected, the match was a bit of a bore. Danny Ward impressed early with a commanding presence in the back, but the real highlight of the first half was Daniel Sturridge. Late in the first half, the Englishman found himself about six yards from goal with possession and his back to the target. Instead of passing it off, Sturridge tried a cheeky shot with his back heel. The shot mustered more power than expected, and forced Polish goalkeeper Artur Boruc into making a difficult save. The ball rebounded straight to Roberto Firmino, had the easiest of goals, tapping into an empty net.

Minutes later, Sturridge would find the back of the net himself. Jordon Ibe took a free kick from the left wing that found Sturridge minimally marked by the Bournemouth defense. He headed it on target to double the Liverpool lead.

There was little excitement in the second half, as Liverpool controlled possession and the mostly reserve squad continued to hold their own. As the match went into the final minutes of extra time, everyone was waiting for the final whistle so we could go on with the rest of our day. Before that would happen, Joshua King would ruin the moment with a fine long-range effort that beat Ward to the far post. Partially obstructed by the defense, Ward got a late jump on the shot, and the goal cut the Liverpool lead down to one. It was a shame, since Ward had played extremely well in his debut, deserving of the clean sheet. He would have to settle for the victory, and Liverpool would close out the match as 2-1 winners.

****

It's a surreal thing to see the Merseyside derby on the calendar and think so little of its importance. The rivalry is akin to that of the New York Yankees and New York Mets in major league baseball. While one team has all of the history and championships to revel in, the other has nothing more than pride and a desire to gain local bragging rights, if only for a few months.

The Merseyside derby is one of the most unique rivalries in the sport. Whenever there is a city with two major clubs to choose from, your loyalties are predetermined at birth. No self-respecting Yankee fan would ever tolerate a son swearing allegiance to the Mets. Yet for some reason, the line that divides Everton and Liverpool fans has been blurred across family lines so much that red and blue have become purple. You'll find families with split loyalties, houses that have been divided across Merseyside for multiple generations.

The best depiction of the great rivalry was made by former Liverpool skipper Bill Shankly. It's the same quote about football being much more important than life or death, which was actually taken a bit out of context. The full quote was his view of the relationship between Liverpool and Everton supporters throughout the city. According to the website LFCHistory.net, Shankly said, "I've seen supporters on Merseyside going to the ground together, one wearing red and white and the other blue and white, which is unusual elsewhere. You get families in Liverpool in which half support Liverpool and the other half Everton. They support rival teams but they have the same temperament and they know each other. They are unique in the sense that their rivalry is so great, but there is no real aggro between them. This is quite amazing. I am not saying they love each other. Oh, no. Football is not a matter of life and death. It's much more important than that. And it's more important to them than that. But I've never seen a fight at a (Merseyside) derby game. Shouting and bawling…yes. But they don't fight each other. And that says a lot for them."

Everton Football Club was founded in 1878 as St. Domingo's so that the parishioners at the local Methodist church could play sport year-round. It was renamed Everton a year later to include non-parishioners. Everton was one of the founding members of the Football League in 1888, winning the title in 1889. At that time all of their matches were played at Anfield, which was owned by club chairman John Houlding. Politics separated him from the majority of board members at the club, so he was constantly at odds with them. The acrimony reached a crescendo in 1892 when the board voted to leave Anfield, acquiring the new ground at Goodison Park in the process. Houlding responded by forming Liverpool Football Club, and remained at Anfield.

The Merseyside derby is the longest-running rivalry in the sport's top flight. The clubs have played each other 225 times prior, with Liverpool winning eighty-eight times against Everton's sixty-six. They have tied seventy-one times. It remains one of the few local derbies where fan segregation isn't enforced at the ground, so you'll often see blue and red shirts sitting side by side regardless of which ground is being used. While it has been dubbed the "friendly derby" by some people, the actions by the players don't live up to that moniker. Since the formation of the Premier League, this fixture has resulted in more red cards being issued than any other match.

Fans were still riding on cloud nine less than a week removed from the miracle at Anfield in the Europa League. Attendance at the pub on match day is always higher when the team is playing well, so there would be an expected spike at the London Bridge Pub. Some fans couldn't be bothered to watch Liverpool play the lesser half of town, but it was a good crowd for a midweek clash.

Klopp fielded a stronger squad than he did at Bournemouth, so it wasn't going to be an easy task for Everton. Roberto Martinez started his best squad, despite the temptation to rest players in advance of the weekend FA Cup semifinal match against Manchester United at Wembley Stadium. There was growing speculation that the Spanish manager's job was already in jeopardy. In an interesting twist of fate, Martinez nearly became Liverpool manager four years earlier. He was a leading candidate for the post eventually given to Brendan Rodgers, and there is still some debate as to whether he was offered the job. Instead he ended up at Everton to replace David Moyes, who had left Merseyside to take on the difficult task of following Sir Alex Ferguson at Manchester United. Under Moyes, the Toffees consistently challenged for a European berth in the top half of the table. While Martinez had led the club to a fifth-place finish in the 2013-14 season and entry into the Europa League, the club suffered the following season, finishing eleventh on the table with twenty-five fewer points. This was supposed to be a rebounding season for them, yet they hovered around the same standard. These results were unacceptable to the board, but a convincing win over their cross-town rivals just might save his job.

Liverpool dominated play from the outset as Everton struggled to find positive play. It wasn't until the forty-third minute that the Reds would finally get on the board with a Divock Origi header from newly crowned "king of crosses" James Milner. The lead was doubled just before the break on another header from a Milner cross, this time by way of Mamadou Sakho.

It went from bad to worse for Everton when the second half started. Four minutes had passed when Everton defender Ramiro Funes Mori stamped harshly on the ankle of Divock Origi. He was immediately shown the red card and stormed off the field in disgust. He petulantly grabbed the Everton badge in pride as Origi lay on the ground in pain. It was a play that was widely criticized, including by Everton supporters. Origi would be stretchered off and substituted as Liverpool fans worried about the young striker's immediate future. But having Daniel Sturridge come on as your substitute is not a drop in class, and now the Reds would be playing the final forty minutes with a man advantage.

It didn't take Sturridge long to hit the mark, scoring in the sixty-first minute with a left-footed shot to the upper corner. Philippe Coutinho would round out the scoring with another long-range beauty in the seventy-sixth minute.

The 4-0 victory for Liverpool was easily the most lopsided affair of the season. They possessed the ball sixty-seven percent of time and outshot Everton 37-3 (shots on target was 13-0). Despite the dominating performance, I still couldn't help but remain pissed off at the injury to Origi. The Belgian striker had become a key component to the recent upswing in form for the club. It's moderately easier to accept when a player misses time to an injury like a pulled muscle. When you can squarely point the finger at an opposing player as the sole reason for a serious injury, it's a bitter pill to swallow.

For the rest of the evening, I couldn't get that image out of my head. Not the image of a goal celebration, nor the sight of Origi being stretchered off—the sight of Funes Mori grabbing the Everton badge on his jersey, as though he was proud of what just happened. Injuring an opponent is never something to be publicly celebrated. Up until this match I had reserved most of my hatred for Everton's Kevin Mirallas, who had intentionally spiked Luis Suarez with his cleat in the November 2013 match. Mirallas wasn't shown the red card for his rash challenge, but the despicable display had earned him the title of my most hated player. The Argentine may have stolen that title from his teammate.

Origi would eventually be diagnosed with a serious ankle injury and be sidelined for four to six weeks. If Liverpool were to have success in the remainder of this season, it would likely be without the services of Divock Origi.

34 - WASHINGTON, D.C.

Saturday, April 23
The Queen Vic, Washington, D.C.
Premier League match #34 (vs. Newcastle United)

As the popularity of the sport grew, so did access to information. I remember getting SiriusXM satellite radio installed in my car in 2005, and there was a weekly broadcast aptly named *The Football Show*, with New York Cosmo legend and personal idol Giorgio Chinaglia. Eventually other shows followed, like Steven Cohen and Nick Geber's *World Soccer Daily*. As I drove in my car I would eagerly await one of these shows to get a daily fix on soccer. These shows didn't focus on one particular team; rather, they would discuss the details of whatever hot topic was on the caller's minds. The more I would listen, the more I would crave discussions about Liverpool. Enter the podcast.

Soccer podcasts are an integral form of entertainment and information for every fan. They can also be quite frustrating. The best way I can describe a soccer podcast is that you're eavesdropping on a conversation a few strangers are having at the pub without the ability to interrupt with your own opinion. Every morning I choose a particular episode from a variety of options, and *Big Red LFC* used to be one of my preferred choices.

Nick Coughlin was one of the voices of the podcast he cohosted with my late Australian friend Sean McGerty. After Sean tragically passed away last summer, the podcast abruptly came to an end. Through this podcast I would learn that Nick was also the chairman of OLSC Washington, one of our closest neighbors in the OLSC family. I first met Nick in August 2014 when Liverpool came to Charlotte. I had been in contact with him about hosting a joint celebration before the match. We became good friends, and we often collaborate on issues dealing with the OLSC network. Going to visit Nick and the Washington crew was a no-brainer.

As the season waned to a close, my opportunities to travel for Liverpool matches started to dwindle. With only a few weekends left on the fixture list, the Newcastle match was the only chance I could get to Washington. Unfortunately, it was a weekend where Nick had prior family obligations and couldn't meet me at the pub.

OLSC Washington is another one of those wide geographic areas that requires multiple pubs to support its members. Since many of the supporters actually live in Northern Virginia, they have aligned themselves with the Courthaus Social in Arlington. Serving the downtown District of Columbia is the original home pub, the Queen Vic, which is where I decided to watch the match.

****

Jon Hamblett is my absolute best friend on the planet. We grew up on the same street and have been friends since third grade. After college graduation, Jon got a job with Motorola and relocated to the Phoenix area. He met his first wife, who gave birth to three fantastic children, got divorced, and eventually remarried. For twenty years I maintained a close friendship with Jon while living on opposite sides of the country. Then all of a sudden an incredible business opportunity came his way, requiring a permanent move to the nation's capital. He accepted it, bringing him back to the East Coast.

I had the pleasure of taking Jon to his first Liverpool match in 2012. He was at a work conference in Boston the same time that Liverpool was scheduled to play AS Roma at Fenway Park. He was gracious enough to allow my brother and I to crash at his corporate hotel, while in return I brought him to Fenway for the match. Jon claims to support Arsenal, only because he heard about them through work colleagues in the mid-nineties and thought that was a really cool name for a sports team. He asked me if he could wear an Arsenal shirt to the Liverpool match, to which I calmly replied, "Not if you want to hang out with us." He acquiesced and purchase a red Kopite shirt solely to wear at the match.

One of the reasons that I picked the Newcastle match for my trip to D.C. was that Jon was scheduled to be in town. He had just closed on a new home in Chevy Chase on the outskirts of the district. His family wouldn't be relocating east until after the school year was over, so it was just me and him. Once again I had the opportunity to use my best friend for free lodging while I was traveling to watch Liverpool.

Even though Washington is well connected, with an excellent subway system, we decided to venture downtown through the use of the car service Uber. The pub was planning to open at nine thirty a.m., but our Uber driver dropped us off about fifteen minutes early. There was a light rain that morning, so we tucked away in the small covered entrance, hoping that a nice bartender would let us in a few minutes early. They did not.

As we patiently waited and tried to stay dry, a young lady walked up and joined us. Courtney Menard was all decked out in Liverpool gear, right down to the shoes. It was quite impressive how much Liverpool gear one was willing to wear out in public. I learned a lot about her in the few minutes we shared under the covered space, including the fact that she loves Liverpool because of Michael Owen. The more I thought about it, the more I realized that she possibly wasn't even a teenager the last time Owen donned the Liverpool jersey. It's impressive to see someone pick up the passion at such an early stage in life and then maintain it.

Owen had just been offered and accepted an ambassador role with Liverpool a few days earlier. It was a move that was met with great disdain from most Liverpool fans. The first time that I watched Liverpool play live was one of the last times that Michael Owen wore the Liverpool jersey in a match. It was preseason in the summer of 2004, and Liverpool played a match at the original Giants Stadium in East Rutherford, NJ. I was watching the Kop end as Owen scored a brilliant goal to equalize the match. A week later, he left for Real Madrid and his career went downhill from there.

Owen eventually returned to the Premier League, playing for Newcastle United, which didn't bother most fans. It was his move to Manchester United in July 2009 that irked every Liverpool fan worldwide. Pictures of Owen and Sir Alex Ferguson evoked images of Emperor Palpatine recruiting Anakin Skywalker during the Star Wars prequels. Considering that both Owen and Skywalker left the forces of good to ply their trade for the evil empire makes it the perfect analogy.

Being a traitor didn't sway Courtney from her love of Michael Owen. When I asked her what she thought about fans being irate over our new club ambassador, she curtly replied, "Get over it." That's easier said than done for most, including myself.

The bar finally opened its front door, and we walked into the old-style English pub. Jon and I bellied up to the bar and ordered a pint. The bartender was named Josh, and he started attempts to draw our first pint. His struggle with the Guinness tap was obvious. There was no pressure in the downstairs bar. Thinking on his feet, Josh cautioned us not to fret, and trotted to the upstairs bar to fetch our pint from another tap. The smart barman was working his way to a great tip.

Most of the pregame chatter at the pub was geared around the announcement that Mamadou Sakho had been removed for the roster under suspicion of failing a drug test. It seemed awfully bizarre, since Sakho isn't the bulkiest player on the squad. Rumors were all over social media, and the substance appeared to be a "fat burner" ingredient on the banned list. It was a mutual decision by club and player to keep him out of the lineup. To be clear, he wasn't suspended by the sport's governing body, so some people were curious why he was being kept out. With this late-breaking story on his mind, I had to believe that his focus might suffer, and it was probably in the club's best interest. Kolo Toure would replace the Frenchman in the starting lineup.

The other side note to this match was Rafa Benitez's return to Anfield. The Spaniard had led Liverpool from 2004 to 2010, including the 2005 Champions League crown. He is still revered by Liverpool fans and was rumored to replace Brendan Rodgers after his dismissal. Following his departure from the club in 2010, Benitez made the rounds across continental Europe, coaching Inter Milan, Napoli, and most recently Real Madrid. There was also an interim stint at Chelsea in 2013. Following his dismissal from Real Madrid in January of this year, he was brought in to try and save Newcastle United from relegation in March. It would be a daunting task on short notice.

The bar was slowly filling up as kickoff approached. Strangely enough, we sat next to an Aston Villa fan, who ensured that one of the available televisions was broadcasting their match. Looking behind the bar, I noticed a small Aston Villa banner, declaring this to be an official Aston Villa Supporters Club home pub. I have to give credit for the dedication, since Aston Villa had already been mathematically relegated with their dismal season. I assumed better days would see better numbers at the pub for their club.

It only took Liverpool sixty-eight seconds to get on the board, with a Daniel Sturridge strike from an Alberto Moreno cross. I turned to my left, where a middle-aged man sat wearing a nice Hawaiian shirt. I saw him make a fist pump after the goal, so I offered a high five that he accepted. After the game resumed with Liverpool leading 1-0, I struck up a conversation with the man. Don McKinnon is from Western Massachusetts and works in town for his local congressman. He didn't appear to be your typical fan, since he wore nothing to show his allegiance. Don was actually born in the London area to young English parents. They were so young that they gave him up for adoption to a nice couple from New England. He was raised as an American, and grew up loving the Boston Red Sox. When he learned that his birth parents were from England, he did some research and learned that not only were his birth parents still together, but that they had borne another son. He flew out to England and arranged to meet his brother for the first time, and it turned out that his brother loved Liverpool Football Club. For over twenty years the two men had stayed in contact, and frequently made arrangements to meet. For Don's fiftieth birthday his brother arranged to get his seats in the Kop to watch the Reds play against

West Ham United. When the owners of his beloved Red Sox acquired Liverpool Football Club, his allegiance was sealed.

Liverpool continued to dominate the first half of play as my friend Jon decided to order breakfast. Josh the bartender continued to work the upstairs tap to keep my Guinness pint filled, and his tip increased with every trip. He'd just served my next glass when Adam Lallana fired a left-footed shot from outside the penalty box into the top left corner. Just like that, Liverpool had a 2-0 advantage.

Halftime came with Liverpool comfortably leading. I walked over to the other end of the bar, where the lovely Courtney was sitting next to her good friend. She introduced me to Patty Granados, a young gal from El Salvador. Patty became a fan because of Fernando Torres and the Hispanic influence that was forming around the club. We talked about the first half and how the club was playing. Patty and Courtney were two of the most knowledgeable fans I had ever met at a pub, and we had a great discussion about tactics. We all felt comfortable with how the first half had transpired, but I cautioned them how the two-goal lead was the toughest to maintain. Just ask Borussia Dortmund.

A few minutes had passed when a cute, short Irish girl approached me. Her name was Maureen, but I was told that she went by Little Mo Danish. She was joined by her husband Jonny, who was born in Brooklyn and raised in the Washington area. Little Mo was raised properly in Dublin by Liverpool fans, so there wasn't much choice for her football allegiance. In 2010 she traveled to Washington on holiday, where she met Jonny. They two started a long-distance relationship that resulted in her moving to the States and then getting married. Jonny reluctantly admitted that he was a Manchester City fan, but he joined his bride at the pub for every Liverpool match, so he was okay by me.

The second half kicked off with people still getting settled back in. There were about thirty Liverpool supporters in the pub, but the atmosphere was a little subdued. Most fans had already given up on the hopes of finishing in the top four, and the clear focus was on winning the Europa League.

My concerns about the dangerous two-goal lead were confirmed a few minutes in. Papiss Demba Cisse scored on a header from a nice cross by Vurnon Anita. For the first forty-five minutes of the match, Liverpool were riding high, cruising to another victory. Now Newcastle had found some life and started to gain confidence. The problem with protecting a two-goal lead is that teams tend to shift their game plan to a more defensive posture, ignoring the tactics that gave them that lead to begin with. Once the first goal is scored, doom is destined to follow.

Jack Colback fulfilled this prophecy in the sixty-sixth minute with a left-footed shot that found the back of the net following a short pass from

Georginio Wijnaldum. Heads were shaking all across the pub, as Liverpool had inconceivably let the relegation-bound team back in the match. I was worried that they'd give up the lead.

The final twenty minutes couldn't produce another goal, and the match ended in a 2-2 draw. Clearly a disappointing setback for Liverpool, it virtually assured that their only path to the Champions League next season would be to win the Europa League.

Jon and I settled up our tab and wished our new friends well. The rain was subsiding, and it was turning out to be a beautiful day in the nation's capital. As we waited for the next Uber driver to pick us up on the street, I couldn't help but feel apathetic about the loss. This is what it has come to mean being a Liverpool supporter late in the season. Expect disappointment and enjoy the rare occasion of being pleasantly surprised. I did believe that Klopp would turn it around, just sooner rather than later. I kept reminding myself that he still hadn't had a full summer to acquire the players that he needed to play in his system.

All it took to change my attitude from apathy to anger was a simple question that Jon asked as we waited for our ride. With a sly smirk on his face, my best friend inquired, "What time is the Arsenal match?"

35 - THE DREAM CONTINUES

Thursday, April 28
London Bridge Pub, Raleigh, NC
Europa League Semifinal, First Leg (at Villareal)

One of the most challenging concepts that new American fans to the sport face is the structure of European football. While every major American team sport functions similarly, with a regular season and playoffs to determine a singular champion, European football is a mesh of multiple competitions played simultaneously across the entirety of the season. Most American fans are attracted to the sport innocently enough for a variety of reasons, but sometimes the complexity and compression of the schedule will test the new fan. If you're an American that acquired this passion as a secondary sports love, then you know exactly what I am talking about.

Most fans quickly adapt to the simplicity of domestic cup competitions, but trying to understand the nuances of European competition can be a challenge. As the season progresses through the winter, priorities may change. Make no mistake about it: every club enters every competition with the intention of winning.

There are variables throughout the season that cannot be predicted that may end up shifting the focus for both club and supporters. This was the case this season for Liverpool. As the season progressed, it became clear that winning the Europa League would be Liverpool's best chance to get back into the Champions League.

Many of my friends understand the rules of the sport and enjoy watching matches with me, but sometimes they struggle to comprehend the magnitude of the European competitions. The best analogy that I have come up with is college basketball in America. A total of 351 schools from thirty-four different conferences competed in the 2015-16 college basketball season, each with the objective of earning one of sixty-eight berths into the NCAA tournament. While each conference champion is represented in the field, the best teams that advance to compete for the title tend to come from one of the top conferences, like the Big Ten, Southeastern Conference, or the Atlantic Coast Conference. When the final field of sixty-eight is announced, many schools are left out. As a consolation prize, these "second best" schools may get invited to play in the National Invitational Tournament (NIT). This alternative tournament is clearly not as popular as the NCAA tournament, but for thirty-two schools it is an opportunity for fans to watch their favorite players compete in a few more games at the end of the season.

European football competitions have a similar feel. There are currently fifty-four football associations that belong to UEFA. With the exception of the tiny principality of Liechtenstein, all have their own domestic league (all professional clubs in Liechtenstein play in the Swiss leagues). Approximately seven hundred football clubs participate in the top flight of the fifty-three domestic leagues across Europe. Some domestic leagues are small, like Andorra's Primera Divisio, where only four clubs participate at the highest level. Others, like the English Premier League or Spanish La Liga, have as many as twenty teams. Regardless of size or quality, when your club wins the domestic league crown, you are invited to play in the next season's Champions League.

At the beginning of this season, a total of seventy-eight clubs were invited to play in the Champions League. Fifty-three of these clubs were automatic qualifiers, like the Lincoln Red Imps, winners of the Gibraltar Premier League. These clubs are analogous to the NCAA field when smaller schools like Kennesaw State from lesser-known conferences like the Atlantic Sun secure an automatic spot in the field. No one expects them to be in contention, but the invitation to the dance is the carrot that keeps them competing. The twenty-five non-champion clubs invited to the Champions League are like your "at large" schools in the NCAA tournament. Teams that finish second or third place of the major leagues like England or Spain earn an automatic spot in the Champions League. While not technically a "champion" of their country, their inclusion makes for a more interesting competition that will attract ratings and advertising dollars.

Conversely, the Europa League is like the NIT, a competition meant to be a reward for clubs that fell just short of making the Champions League. This competition begins with 158 clubs that have automatically qualified via winning a domestic cup (e.g. the FA Cup) or finishing high enough in the final league table to earn an "at large" invitation. Every season there are typically four English clubs playing the Champions League, with an additional three in the Europa League. As a general rule of thumb, the previous season's top seven teams in England get rewarded with a chance to win a European tournament the next season. The obvious exception to this rule is when a weaker club wins one of the domestic cups, like when Wigan Athletic won the 2013 FA Cup. Despite being relegated out of the Premier League the following season, Wigan Athletic were invited and participated in the 2013-14 Europa League, where they were quickly eliminated after finishing last place in their group.

Both competitions begin in July with a series of play-in games to narrow the field to a more manageable number. Teams like the Lincoln Red Imps play against champions from other small associations for the right to advance and play against the larger clubs. Of the seventy-eight clubs in the Champions League, only twenty-two are automatically placed into the group stage. The remaining fifty-six teams participate in these play-in games, where only ten advance to the group stage.

As noted earlier, there are 158 clubs that start in the Europa League, but that number grows as the season progresses. Up to twenty-five clubs that fail to advance to the Champions League group stage will drop down into the Europa League as a consolation prize. This increases the number of competitors to 183. Through a series of similar play-in games held in the summer, the Europa League field is narrowed to forty-eight for the group stage.

Taking a broader look, you'll see that 236 clubs from a pool of about seven hundred have qualified for European competition. That's roughly one-third of all clubs. Using the NCAA analogy, they have a hundred schools qualifying for their two big post-season tournaments from a field of 351, also roughly one-third. The only difference being that the most prestigious European football competition has fewer competitors, while the secondary tournament has nearly double their number in the beginning.

Before UEFA added the carrot of Champions League football for winning the Europa League in 2015, few people cared about it. Even some supporters from teams that advanced to the later stages couldn't be bothered, as it was still considered a consolation prize to most. In that respect, it was exactly like the NIT. But imagine a world in college basketball where the NCAA declared that the winner of the NIT would be automatically entered into the next season's primary tournament. All of a sudden, that consolation prize becomes more lucrative and would garner more attention from both fans and media. It was a brilliant move by UEFA, and was giving Liverpool a second breath of life this season.

Ask any fan of a big English club about their priorities in the beginning of the season and you'll likely get one of two answers. Either win the Premier League or win the Champions League. Technically speaking, there are twenty clubs eligible to win the Premier League when the season begins in August. At most, only five of those clubs will be entered into the

Champions League. It's an extremely prestigious and lucrative competition that dates back to 1955. The extra revenue earned for simply qualifying for Champions League gives the club a financial advantage over domestic rivals when competing for the signatures of the best available talent. It's a case of the "rich getting richer," and creates desperation for every club to earn one of the four or five spots.

In the 2014-15 season, each club was entitled to a minimum payment of €8.6M for participation in the Champions League, with added incentives for getting results and advancing to the later stages. Additional revenue is earned from what UEFA calls the "market pool," where, according to the UEFA website, money is "divided according to the proportional value of the national television market allocated to each individual club, among other factors." Liverpool qualified for the 2014-15 Champions League and failed to progress out of the group stage. They still earned €33.6M in bonus payments just for playing dismally, not including the match revenue realized from hosting three matches. That's a lot of money simply for participating. Eventual champions FC Barcelona earned approximately €61.0M from UEFA. This proverbial pot of gold is the reason every club aspires to get to the end of that rainbow.

It used to be that only the top four clubs that finished in the Premier League would qualify for the next season's Champions League. With the additional berth going to the winner of the Europa League now, it opened a new door down a path to the prosperity of Champions League. Following Liverpool's disappointing 2-2 draw with Newcastle, the Reds sat in seventh place on the table, nine points behind fourth place, with only four games remaining. While technically not impossible to achieve, the more likely path to Champions League football next season was to win the Europa League and earn the automatic spot. After defeating Borussia Dortmund in the quarterfinals in such dramatic fashion, all fan focus shifted from the Premier League to the Europa League. Not only was it our last chance at winning a trophy, but it was our last chance at glory. Villareal now stood in our way. The Spanish club was firmly fixed into fourth place of La Liga. Regardless of how they performed in the rest of their regular season, they were headed back to the Champions League next season. Defeating them would not be an easy task, but since when did Liverpool do easy?

****

Villareal is a club based in the province of Castellon along the Spanish eastern shore of the Mediterranean Sea. They earned the nickname "Yellow Submarine" due to the color of their home kit, and are a smaller club that perennially punches above its weight class. It was somewhat apropos that Liverpool would play a club whose nickname was derived from a Beatles song. This would be the first time that these two clubs had faced each other in competition, although they did play each other in a 2008 preseason friendly. The first leg was to be played in Spain at the Estadio El Madrigal.

I was pleased to see a large crowd at the pub when I arrived about fifteen minutes prior to kickoff. The magic of the Dortmund result in the last round got supporters excited about Liverpool Football Club once again. It is funny how there is a direct correlation to club success on the pitch and fan attendance at the pub. All of the regulars were there, and some others that I hadn't seen since the 2013-14 season.

The big talk in the pre-match was how Klopp elected to keep fully fit Daniel Sturridge on the bench despite losing Divock Origi to injury a week earlier. Instead, Klopp put Roberto Firmino up top as a makeshift striker, indicating a less attacking mindset. This would be the fourth straight European match that Sturridge wouldn't start, despite scoring four goals in the previous five matches.

There was also concern about losing Mamadou Sakho for the failed drug test, which was now officially a suspension after he'd refused to prolong the process and appeal earlier in the week. Veteran defender Kolo Toure was the preferred choice to partner with Dejan Lovren in the center of the defense, and that was perceived to be another weakness for Liverpool.

Joe Allen was a surprise starter in the midfield, making his first start in the competition since the group stage, and he nearly put the Reds on top in the fifth minute, redirecting an Adam Lallana cross. Unfortunately, the shot went straight to goalkeeper Sergio Assenjo. Neither team threatened the target much in the first half, but former Spurs striker Roberto Soldado fired a few near-misses toward Mignolet late in the half.

Concern at the pub was inflated once we learned that Jordon Ibe was coming on for Philippe Coutinho at halftime. There was no real explanation from the commentators, so fans at the pub frantically scrolled through their Twitter feeds to see if was an injury or simply a bizarre tactical move by our German manager. Colin Russell was first to announce that Coutinho was feeling unwell and couldn't compete at a hundred percent, so he was replaced. He'd read it on the Internet, so we all knew it to be true.

As the clock continued to wind down, there was a growing confidence at the pub. Nervously waiting out the final moments, the pub remained mostly silent, hoping to hear that final whistle. Mignolet made a nice save off a long-range effort by Cedric Bakambu a few minutes from time, and the crowd clapped in approval.

The fourth referee signaled for three additional minutes of time to be added, and I recall thinking, *Just get out of here unscathed and we'll take them down at Anfield.* I wasn't alone. Someone belted out at the top of their lungs, "Come on, you Redmen!" I'm pretty sure it was Colin, but I was too fixated on the television screen to know for sure.

Christian Benteke substituted for Firmino with only a few minutes left, presumably to serve as a large target man and assist on defensive headers. He managed to get off a mild shot with his head off a Lallana cross, but the effort innocently drifted wide of target. Then disaster struck on the final play of the match. Villareal's young Spanish midfielder Denis Suarez got possession and easily ran past a knackered Kolo Toure down the right side. Defensive help was nonexistent. I held my breath with great concern, instantly knowing danger lurked. Suarez slid the ball over to an unmarked Adrian Lopez, who easily slotted the ball past Mignolet to give the Yellow Submarine a 1-0 victory. The goal came far too easily, and bewildered everyone at the pub. I don't recall cursing out loud, but there were some choice words floating about my mind.

The players celebrated on the pitch as though Villareal had just won the cup. I shook my head in disgust watching the replay. You could see the looks of despair on both the players and fans as the cameras panned over to the Liverpool faithful in the stands. It was the same look we all had inside the London Bridge Pub: disbelief. I can't recall for certain, but I'm sure that there was a curse or six blurted out in the pub. One thing that I do recall was Darren speaking up to anyone around him that would listen: "It's all right, guys. They still have to come to our place next week." As devastating as it was to watch the boys lose so late in an important match, he was absolutely right. My anguish quickly turned to anticipation. There was no way that the club was going to go down without a fight, not after the incredible miracle against Dortmund in the quarterfinals.

Heads started coming up, and the vibe completely transformed as soon as Gerry and the Pacemakers were played on the loudspeakers. Scarves that were hanging around the neck were thrust into the sky as the immortal words began.

As the song concluded, I started making my way to the exit. I looked up at the television screen to see the Villareal players still celebrating their dramatic win. I don't know if I was talking to my friends at the bar or the players celebrating on TV when I quietly muttered, "See you next week."

36 - OLSC NEW YORK CITY

Sunday, May 1
11th Street Bar, New York, NY
Premier League match #35 (at Swansea City)

Over the holidays I had made the choice to watch Liverpool's Boxing Day encounter with Leicester City at the Boot Room. That decision was made primarily out of convenience, since that pub is located within walking distance of the Staten Island ferry terminal near Battery Park. While the Boot Room has a fantastic atmosphere and is loaded with Liverpool memorabilia that would make any fan jealous, it is not the home of New York City's Official Liverpool Supporters Club. Their home pub is the 11th Street Bar in the lower East Village. When I returned to the New York to visit family, I decided to watch Sunday's Liverpool match versus Swansea City there.

Founded at the start of the 1995-96 season, OLSC New York is the oldest active supporters club in North America. Their initial days of watching the club required early kickoffs, reliable satellite systems, and trustworthy bar owners. They started meeting at Cleary's Pub near Madison Square Garden. To quote their website, "The match day experience usually involved loud, boorish cockneys and ten-a-penny non-manc mancs." I'm not exactly sure what that means, other than there were a bunch of British fans in attendance.

Daragh Kennedy took on the role of club president in that inaugural year, a role he maintained until last year after relocating to Charlotte. I first met Daragh during the 2014 summer preseason tour, when the club organized an OLSC focus group session before Liverpool's preseason match with Manchester City at Yankee Stadium. Sean Dotzauer and I decided to fly up to New York for the match while crashing at my brother's house in Connecticut. Sean and I took the train into the city early that morning so that we could attend an OLSC focus group meeting with our club liaison Jane Phillipson. That trip was my first visit to the 11th Street Bar, and turned out to be an epic journey in its own right. We met with leadership from branches all across the country and discussed matters pertaining to the North American OLSC network. Of course, we consumed a few pints in the process.

Immediately following the meeting at the pub, Sean and I ended up on a double-decker bus touring Manhattan with other Liverpool supporters. Roy Yates from Florida set it up for us, and we were joined by Jamie Harrison and Stuart Brennan from LFC Atlanta. As the bus drove around the city, we drank beers and sang songs until our bodies couldn't take it much longer. I recall fondly riding through Times Square on the rooftop of the bus singing songs about Liverpool as hundreds of random strangers on the street gleefully took pictures of us. It was quite the surreal moment. At some point, we made it to the stadium for a football match as well.

Daragh hails from the Dublin suburb of Dundrum, and picked up Liverpool as his favorite club as a child. He immigrated to the United States, where he settled in the northern parts of New Jersey. Our love for Liverpool isn't the only connection we have, as we both uprooted our family and moved from New Jersey to the great state of North Carolina.

With Daragh leaving the city, he transferred the duties of LFC NY president to Nathan Smith. Unfortunately, Nathan was not going to be available to meet at the pub, as he continued working on a second home in the Catskills, but he entrusted my hospitality to club treasurer Chris Andrade. She wasn't always a huge sports fan, but Chris had lived about three blocks away from the 11th Street Bar for almost twenty years. Her friends started going to the bar to watch Liverpool play, and she followed suit, mostly to be social. Eventually the virus caught and cemented her love for Liverpool. Since she lives so close to the bar, she's in attendance at almost every match.

The 11th Street Bar has been home to OLSC New York since the turn of the century. The group left Clancy's Pub and had wandered around various pubs in the city before eventually finding home in the lower East Village. The owner is a Liverpool fan from Ireland who once famously bounced actor Daniel Craig. The British actor and Liverpool supporter is best known for playing James Bond in recent movies, and lives in the same neighborhood as the pub. He wanted to watch a big match at the pub and showed up at kickoff. Unfortunately for the actor, the bar had reached capacity, and the owner turned away one of the most famous Liverpool fans in the world. Rules are rules, even for celebrities.

A city as large as New York will have numerous fans, and as a result requires more options to watch amongst friends. If the 11th Street Bar is filled to capacity, people can wander down to the Grafton, only a short walk away. Other boroughs of the city are well represented, as The Monro (Brooklyn) and the Celli House (Queens) maintain official allegiance with the club. The Prost Grill and Garten on Long Island and The Cottage Bar in Teaneck, New Jersey stretch their reach beyond the borders of the city. Plus, there are the unofficial pubs that show soccer on a regular basis, like Nevada Smith's, the Boot Room, and Carragher's. It's safe to say that a soccer fan should be able to find a great place to enjoy any match when visiting the New York City area.

The other significant moment that plugged me into the strength of OLSC New York was the day that former radio and television personality Stephen Cohen stepped away from the booth. A lifelong Chelsea fan from London, Cohen moved to the United States and eventually started an Internet radio show called *World Soccer Daily*. Initially the show was cohosted with Liverpool supporter Nick Geber, and it was eventually picked up by Sirius. When I transitioned my drive-time listening habits from terrestrial radio to satellite in 2005, I soon discovered their program. The show entertained for me for years and helped educate me about other clubs and players worldwide. Eventually Geber would depart and get replaced, but it was Cohen that remained the anchor of the show.

I will never forget the moment in April of 2009 that would end up being the death knell for both Cohen and his radio show. It was the twentieth anniversary of the Hillsborough tragedy, an epic moment that would turn the tide of public opinion when Liverpool fans convinced local politician Andy Burnham to take on their case for justice. What I heard on that radio show that day was shocking. I had always heard the cries of "Justice for the ninety-six" and understood the significance of the event. It didn't matter to me that these fans were Liverpool fans. I was sixteen years old at the time of the Hillsborough tragedy, and had attended numerous sporting events at that age. Had I been raised in Liverpool, that easily could've been me among the victims. Yet that afternoon I listened in disgust as Stephen Cohen blamed ticketless Liverpool fans as the root cause for overcrowding the turnstiles and causing the crush.

His growing popularity in the American soccer culture had reached Liverpool Football Club, who took exception to his comments and referred him to the facts as stated in the Lord Justice Taylor report, where ticketless fans did not contribute. Instead of taking the smart road by apologizing and moving on with his burgeoning career, Cohen refused to give in, and insisted that Liverpool fans should accept some of the blame.

I heard these comments live on the radio, and they bothered me. When word reached the leadership of OLSC New York, it incensed them and drew them to action. The group orchestrated a boycott of Cohen and all of his enterprises. They targeted the sponsors that paid for time on his show, wielding the power of Liverpool supporters worldwide. The campaign stretched across the continent and slowly started making positive impact. Sponsors started pulling the plug, and eventually his radio show was dropped by Sirius. As a fan of the sport, I was disappointed that his show was pulled off the air, but I was more outraged that he refused to admit defeat. Despite all of the revelations made by the Hillsborough Independent Panel, Cohen still refused to acknowledge that he might be wrong, and partially blamed Liverpool supporters for that tragedy. The sport that spawned the man's career now wanted nothing to do with him.

This was the first match on British soil after the inquest ruled that all ninety-six supporters that perished in the Hillsborough incident were killed unlawfully. I watched Swansea City captain Ashley Williams and Liverpool skipper Martin Skrtel take a wreath of flowers and lay it in front of the traveling Liverpool supporters. Members of the Hillsborough Justice Campaign were present to receive the gesture from Swansea City, and the thought crossed my mind as to whether Cohen regretted his stubbornness on the issue that cost him a career. I quickly shrugged off that thought, not wanting to waste much time thinking about it. He dug his own grave with his refusal to admit wrong, and we had the leadership of OLSC New York to thank for helping to ensure that grave was backfilled properly.

Liverpool's advancement to the Europa League semifinals had put a kink in this week's match. With the first leg against Villareal held the previous Thursday, the upcoming match against Swansea City was moved to Sunday. Normally that wouldn't be a huge issue, but for some strange reason, kickoff was pushed up to noon local time. That equated to a seven a.m. kickoff for us in New York on a Sunday. The change in kickoff time sparked a huge social media blitz. Much like the Bournemouth match two weeks earlier, many other clubs were questioning the value of opening up their pubs. I knew that Darren would be opening London Bridge Pub for a few dedicated fans, but many other cities left their fans in the dark.

I couldn't blame most of these pubs for not opening. Sandwiched by the more important legs of the Europa League semifinal, this Liverpool squad was destined to be loaded with reserve players and it wouldn't be the most exciting match. Most of these establishments have to bring in staff to wait on the customers, and that means they have to pay those employees. If only a handful people showed up for the match, then the pub would lose money. I made sure that the 11th Street Bar would be open before driving over the Verrazano-Narrows and Manhattan Bridges to the lower East Village. I quickly noticed one advantage of such an early Sunday kickoff: finding adequate street parking. It's normally a challenge to find a parking spot in the city, but that day I located a prime spot only a hundred yards from the bar.

The bartender introduced himself as Drew as I walked into the pub. He brewed a fresh pot of coffee and served it up free of charge, which I gladly accepted. There were seven people including myself when I walked in about fifteen minutes prior to kickoff. It was hard to tell if most of the people were just getting up or hadn't yet fallen asleep from an excellent Saturday night in the city that never sleeps. Nonetheless, I took a seat at the bar and got settled in.

"What time can you start serving beer on Sunday?" I asked Drew.

He shrugged. "I don't know. I think eight. No one has really told us either way."

"Well, as soon as you feel legally able to pour, please get me a pint of Guinness." I replied. "No need to rush on my behalf. Coffee will do fine for now."

The 11th Street Bar is a fine establishment set up like a traditional shotgun-style apartment. About thirty feet separates the side walls, as the length of the bar extends to over a hundred feet from the front door to the back wall. The foyer area has one television hanging on the wall, while the main bar has two screens behind the counter. There is a backroom with a full-screen projector, and I imagine it fills to capacity during important matches. The walls are covered in brick, which greatly enhances the décor, as various Liverpool-themed pictures and other artwork hang from the wall.

I looked behind the bar to see the chalkboard of beer selections at my disposal for later and noticed a sign that advertised sausage rolls. The mere thought of greasy sausage wrapped in dough so early in the morning made my stomach growl, so I knew I needed to have one. I called out to Drew to place an order with my coffee. He informed me that their minimum order on rolls was fifty, and they couldn't justify placing an order for a match when they knew they'd never sell out. Sensing my disappointment, Drew suggested that I walk to the corner bagel store at halftime. He even offered to save my seat at the bar, a generous offer for the pub filled to about five percent of its capacity.

As expected, Klopp went with a team loaded with reserves, including Danny Ward at goalkeeper. Martin Skrtel made his return to the lineup, along with Australian Brad Smith. In all, eight changes were made from last Thursday's match in Spain. Swansea City started a relatively strong squad, but they were also left with little to play for, since their European dreams had faded months earlier.

Swansea got on the board first with a short-range header by Andre Ayew. It was no shock to anyone that the goal was scored off another set piece, this time a corner kick from Iceland national midfielder Gylfi Sigurdsson in the twentieth minute. That lead was doubled thirteen minutes later as Jack Cork fired from outside the penalty box to the top right corner.

I left the bar at halftime to get breakfast with Liverpool trailing 2-0. Taking Drew's advice, I stopped into the bagel store and ordered an everything bagel toasted with butter. I got a few strange looks from the locals, as clearly cream cheese is the spread of choice in the city. You don't put cream cheese on your dinner roll, do you? So why put it on your breakfast roll? But I digress. I grabbed my bagel and returned to the 11th Street Bar, where magically a pint of Guinness had appeared at my spot. I looked up at Drew, who winked with a grin. It must be close enough to eight o'clock.

By this time the bar had increased its patron count substantially, including two young gentlemen seated to my immediate right. Both were drinking beer and looked like they had just woken up from a nap. I tried to ignore their conversation, but it was difficult when the two guys started Skyping one of their buddies from the bar. Once I realized that they weren't speaking English, it became impossible.

Joffrey Favretto looks like he just graduated from college, so you can imagine my surprise when I learned he worked as a corporate lawyer for the Nestle Corporation in France. His buddy with him was Nicolas Durousseau, who works as a financial advisor. Both are active members of the Official Supporters Club in Paris, one of the largest branches in the network outside of the United Kingdom and Ireland. I learned that they were Skyping with their buddies who were also watching the match live from their home pub, the Rush Bar in Paris. Joffrey and Nicolas were in town for ten days on holiday, visiting a childhood friend that had relocated to New York a few years earlier. Their buddy was still sleeping in the apartment, so they left him and decided to visit the home of OLSC New York. It's amazing to see how the globalization of the sport has taken a new twist with the growth of social media. Two guys from Paris decide to spend some time in a foreign country, yet have no trouble finding a friendly pub to watch a Liverpool match with other fans.

Joffrey and Nicolas are originally from Marseille in the south of France. They are lifelong supporters of Olympique de Marseille from the French Ligue Une. They absolutely hate Paris-St. Germain, possibly more than I hate Manchester United (although that would be difficult to comprehend). They started rooting for Liverpool as kids because the French league teams were never really competitive in European competitions. When they moved to Paris, they discovered the supporters club and fell in love with the atmosphere. They both readily admitted rooting for Olympique when the clubs met in the 2007 Champions League. Marseille will always be their first love.

The three of us quickly became friends, telling stories about our experiences rooting for Liverpool. Both had finally made their first visit to watch the Reds play at Anfield earlier this season, only to watch Manchester United win 1-0. Wayne Rooney scored that game winner and celebrated right in front of their section. Recalling the moment vividly, Nicolas shook his head and muttered, "I fucking hate Rooney." I couldn't agree more.

We continued our conversation with fresh pints served by Drew, barely noticing Christian Benteke's ninth goal of the season off a corner kick header to cut the deficit to 2-1. We celebrated with some high fives before that moment was tempered with Ayew's second goal of the match only two minutes later. The final score would be 3-1 in favor of Swansea City.

As the post-match show played on the televisions, more people started wandering in from the street. The more important match of the day for most was Leicester City vs. Manchester United. At this stage in the competition, it was Leicester City's title to lose. A year earlier the club was fighting to avoid relegation, and now they were about to win their first top division league crown in club history. We were all pulling for them to beat United that morning, but then again, when wouldn't we?

I looked over to see Joffrey scheming something with Drew, immediately thinking that this couldn't be good. My two new French friends could easily hail a taxi back to the apartment, but I needed to remain sober for the drive home. To my dismay, I learned that they were concocting a French favorite cocktail, and somehow Drew had all of the necessary ingredients. Ricard is an anise and licorice-flavored aperitif created in Marseille in the 1930s, and I soon learned that it is mostly served one of four ways. The Original is served with water and ice. The Tomate is served with grenadine syrup and water. The Mauresque is served with orgeat syrup and water. The Perroquet is served with menthe. Don't ask me to name which drink we sampled that morning—possibly all of them. I tempered my intake, ensuring my sobriety for the drive home.

I stayed around the bar long enough to see Leicester City draw with Manchester United 1-1, moving another step closer to their first league crown. Eventually Joffrey and Nicolas were joined by their friend, who finally appeared to join the party. The three of them got another round of drinks and continued to celebrate life. It got me thinking about how far we have come as a supporters network. You can travel to every continent on this planet and visit practically every country. Chances are you will be able to find a place to watch Liverpool with like-minded fans. Three French guys sitting in a lower East Village neighborhood watering hole are proof of that reality.

I settled my tab with Drew and bid adieu to my new friends. I thanked Chris for the club's hospitality and headed for home. It wasn't the result we were hoping for, and certainly wasn't the best time to visit the home pub of the largest and oldest OLSC in North America. It was a wonderful experience, and they make every visiting Liverpool fan feel at home. I was quite certain this would not be the last time I watched a match at the 11th Street Bar.

37 - A FINAL HURDLE

Thursday, May 5
London Bridge Pub
Europa League Semifinal, Second Leg (vs. Villareal)

I had been looking forward to this day all week. Liverpool had faced adversity many times this season, and not always were they successful. This day was going to be different. I had a feeling in my gut that I couldn't explain. I woke up at my normal time and went through my routine on the way to work, but all day long I was eagerly anticipating kickoff. Liverpool needed to overcome the 0-1 deficit to advance to the Europa League final.

The day seemed to drag on, and I found myself to be quite unproductive after lunch. I wrapped up early and headed down to the pub. Normally they wouldn't open the pub until about thirty minutes prior to kickoff, but I had been texting with Darren about the match, and he divulged that he had already opened the doors to the pub.

I arrived about an hour early, thinking I'd be the first Raleigh Red at the bar. I was wrong. Colin was sitting at a table scrolling through the Twitter feed on his phone in search of the starting lineup, which was usually announced around this time. Jeff Carroll was standing in the back talking to Chris Valentine. Apparently I wasn't the only person with the idea to get to the pub early.

Earlier that day I had received a message from Eben Dennis, head of the OLSC Denver crew, whom I had met over three months earlier. Eben happened to be in Raleigh for a work convention and was looking to skip out early in order to catch the match. I assured him that I would be there. That's one of the advantages of having a strong network amongst other supporters clubs. There's no need to miss such an important match just because your job gets in the way. In most major cities you will have no problem finding a place with other friendly Liverpool supporters to enjoy the match. While the Reds take pride that they "never walk alone," the strength of our network helps traveling fans with the fact that they "never watch alone" either.

I grabbed my first pint of Guinness and sat down next to Colin to discuss the starting lineup. Daniel Sturridge started up front alongside Firmino, a clear sign from Klopp that Liverpool would be on the attack. Sturridge was a healthy scratch from the starting eleven in the first leg, and Klopp was grilled by the Friday-morning quarterback journalists as a result. He was not making the same mistake. While it was nice to see the offensive tactic being deployed, I was more concerned with the defense. Conceding a goal against Villareal would require Liverpool to score three in order to advance. The defensive players forced into the lineup didn't exactly instill confidence in keeping a clean sheet.

The biggest news was confirmation that Emre Can was healthy enough to start. The German center defensive midfielder had stepped up to be a stud this season, and his inclusion in the lineup was critical to helping the defense take proper shape. Three weeks earlier Can had sprained his ankle against Dortmund on the corner kick with which Mamadou Sakho equalized the match. At the time, speculation was that he could be out for the rest of the season. He'd returned to training earlier in the week, but no one was really certain that he was at full fitness. Someone at the pub expressed concern about him not being at hundred percent or possibly incurring permanent damage. Was it really worth it? Of course it was. Can is a better player than the alternative, and it was critical to shore up the center of the pitch, with both Lovren and Toure as perceived weaknesses that Villareal could look to exploit. As for the injury, I can't recall many players suffering career-ending ankle injuries before. In my opinion, the reward of getting to the Europa League final was worth that risk.

Fans had been pouring into the pub all afternoon. Eben walked in just before kickoff, and I proceeded to order him a pint courtesy of OLSC Raleigh. Liverpool's success in this competition had helped revive interest late in the season, and there weren't any available seats at kickoff. I took my regular spot next to the Walken Fridge behind most every other fan.

Having won the European Cup five times, more than any other English club, gives the Anfield faithful extreme pride. As the players took the pitch, flags and banners were flying all across the Anfield stands declaring Liverpool to be "European Royalty." With the winner of the match headed to the final in Basel, this was the last important match of the season to be played at Anfield. The rest of the football world was watching, and Liverpool fans used this opportunity to stake their claim as the greatest fan base in the sport. As the final words to "You'll Never Walk Alone" played over the loudspeakers, we were only moments away from the start.

It was critical for Liverpool to have a strong opening fifteen minutes to this match. My heart couldn't handle a repeat of the Dortmund quarterfinal, when the Reds were down two before you could blink.

Liverpool broke through in the seventh minute of play with the first legitimate attack of the game. Roberto Firmino crossed the ball across the goalmouth into a dangerous position from the left side of the box. Daniel Sturridge lunged at the ball to try and deflect it in the net, but he was milliseconds late. Fortunately for us, the ball struck Villareal's midfielder Bruno and was redirected into the back of the net. Before anyone could get settled into position at the pub, Liverpool had taken control of the affair and leveled the scores.

Celebrating an own goal is somewhat awkward. It wasn't like a Liverpool player did anything special. Most times you are celebrating the misfortunes of an opposing player, but this was an important goal and no one cared. It helped ease the tension a bit. I tried to remind myself that any Villareal goal would be devastating and to not get carried away with the early fortune.

The goal seemed to energize the Anfield crowd more than the pub. As play restarted, you could hear "The Fields of Anfield Road" being sung by over forty thousand spectators. I couldn't help myself as the crowd belted out, "As we watched the King Kenny play." In unison with everyone at Anfield, I raised my arms to form the victorious V and screamed, "AND COULD HE PLAY!" I wasn't the only one at the pub to do so.

There were some positive moments as the first half came to a close, with both Adam Lallana and Philippe Coutinho coming close to target on some shots. At the end of the first half, it became clear that Villareal had lost confidence and were playing for the shootout. In retrospect, it was their only hope.

At halftime I grabbed a seat next to Eben at the bar to catch up. I had only known him for three months, but it seemed like we had a lot of catching up to do. Before we realized it, the teams were back on the pitch, getting ready to start play back up. I thought about returning to the spot by the fridge that had helped Liverpool to the early lead, but decided a change of scenery would do some good for the team. I remained at the bar next to Eben.

The second half started with more dominating play from Liverpool's midfield, but nothing to show for it early. Villareal patiently waited for a moment, and nearly had one in the fifty-sixth minute. Against the run of play, they earned a free kick deep along the touchline of Liverpool's end. Jonathan dos Santos crossed the ball into danger, where it was met by former Tottenham striker Roberto Soldado. His header barely missed the top right corner in what would've been a devastating moment in the game for Liverpool. It prompted me to laugh. I looked over at Eben, who looked at me, slightly startled. "Fucking Spurs reject," I explained to him. It got the chuckle it deserved.

Liverpool regained their composure and took control of the match in the sixty-third minute, when Firmino was able to collect possession inside the box and pass through the defense to Sturridge, who did well to keep himself in an onside position. Sturridge composed himself well on the ball and played a simple pass through goalkeeper Alphonse Areola's legs. The ball changed directions ever so slightly and caromed off the right post, but crossed over the line for a goal. Liverpool had the lead in both the match and aggregate.

Immediately after seeing the ball hit the back, I looked up at the television to watch Sturridge sprinting to the corner flag. With all of the Sturridge goal celebrations I had witnessed these past few years, this one stood out above all others. Never before had I seen such joy and excitement in the Englishman after scoring a goal for Liverpool. It wasn't a look of spite, as if to tell Klopp that he shouldn't have been benched in the first leg. It was a look of accomplishment, helping the team to advance in the competition with what he immediately knew was the most important goal of his Liverpool career. It made me smile to see such joy from a player that had had such a tumultuous past few seasons. It showed that he wanted to win as badly as we did.

Of course, the pub went berserk after the goal. As I sat on the barstool, my shoulders would get grabbed and shaken vigorously by random unknown fans. There was an element of relief in the celebration, because up until this point Liverpool had been the clearly dominant team. Villareal hardly looked threatening to score, yet now they would be forced to try. As it stood at that moment, Liverpool would be through to the final.

Even with the 2-0 lead in the match and the appearance of complete control, it was still critical to maintain composure defensively. Any mistake that would lead to a Villareal goal would give them the advantage with the away-goals tiebreaker, and Liverpool was certainly prone to the occasional defensive lapse. A third goal would be needed before anyone could let down their guard.

I had finished my pint of Guinness and needed to use the bathroom. It's always a difficult choice to pick the right moment for using the toilet, because you don't want to miss anything, and you certainly don't want to change the complexion of the match with a sudden, unexplained position relocation. Sort of like the old beer commercial where the guy runs to the basement to get a case of beer just before his team scores a touchdown. He takes one for the team and stays in the dark basement for the rest of the game. We've used this same tactic at Scavengers in the past. One time Brian Williams was outside the bar socializing with friends when his return to the bar preceded a Liverpool goal. Clearly the shift in fan location over 3700 miles away had a sudden impact on the position of the planet, just enough to make the ball redirect slightly and end up in the back of the net. It's a tactic we still use today. When Brian Williams is watching Liverpool at the bar and they're are desperate to score a goal, we'll order him to leave the bar and return within a few minutes. And he will happily oblige our silly superstition. The point is that you don't want to get stuck in the can when a Liverpool goal is scored, because you may just have to remain there for the good of the team. I don't care how many intoxicated bastards need to take a piss, there are multiple bathrooms at the pub for this very reason. Well, maybe not that very reason, but you get the point. It's only weird if it doesn't work, right?

I took a chance and quickly used the bathroom. Liverpool didn't score, so I could safely return to the bar to watch the rest of the match on a mostly empty bladder. I noticed that the bartender was on the left side of the bar helping out some other patrons. I didn't usually hang out on this side of the pub, since it is so close to the entrance, but there wasn't much activity on this side, and it was clearly the quickest route to my next pint of Guinness.

Akshay Nadkarni is a millennial from the Raleigh suburbs that was sitting by himself watching the match on that side of the bar. The NC State graduate of Indian descent is usually watching with his friends, but found himself alone for this particular match. I stood behind his shoulder and ordered my next pint with the bartender.

Just as I was handed my beverage, I looked up at the screen to see another Liverpool attack. It was just after the eighty-minute mark of the match when Coutinho passed to Firmino on the left flank. The Brazilian went on the attack into the corner of the box, facing the Villareal defender one on one. With a shoulder juke to his right, Firmino beat his man to the left. As the play developed, I was immediately envisioning Coutinho's goal at Old Trafford in this same competition less than two months earlier. Instead of going for the shot like his countryman did against Manchester United, Firmino cut the ball back to an onrushing Sturridge in the middle of the box. Sturridge appeared to flub the shot toward target, where Adam Lallana was able to redirect it into the back of the net.

At first glance Lallana looked to be clearly in an offside position, so I was reasonably certain that the goal wouldn't stand. Yet Lallana rushed over to the corner flag to celebrate with his teammates as the linesman's flag remained down. The goal would count, and Liverpool would have that much-needed insurance. Replays confirmed that Lallana was indeed onside, but only because Villareal's Mateo Musacchio was on the ground in the field of play after he slid out of bounds trying to block Firmino's initial pass. Had he lifted his hand quickly enough, the goal would've been disallowed.

At this point the pub was clearly in a euphoric state, and it looked certain that we would add one more game to the fixture list. I celebrated briefly with Akshay and apologized in advance. He looked at me with bewilderment as I explained that there would be no way I was relocating my position after watching that play develop from over his right shoulder. For the final ten minutes plus stoppage time, I was planted in position to ensure Liverpool would remain victorious. He understood completely. These efforts were rewarded with a final score of 3-0, and Liverpool was going to their second cup final of the season.

Immediately after the final whistle blew, I got a text message from Tori: *Be careful tonight. Don't be stupid. Great win.* She was right to send that message. She knew the importance of the match and knew that there would be celebratory shots and free drinks. At that point, I had two choices. I could leave the bar immediately and try to beat Raleigh rush-hour traffic home from downtown, or I could sit around with my friends to soak in the momentous victory. Guess which option I took? Let's just say there was a Foreigner singalong in my near future.

****

Watford was the next opponent to visit Anfield for a late Sunday morning kickoff. With a huge gathering planned at Scavengers the night before, the early plan was to enjoy Bloody Marys and a home-cooked Irish breakfast courtesy of Tom Brewer. Both were delicious.

The game was not expected to be an exciting one, as Watford had recently secured their Premiership survival, while Liverpool fans were still recovering from their Europa League hangover. Klopp used many reserve players, so there wasn't much appeal going into the match. It took Liverpool thirty-five minutes to open the scoring on a Joe Allen one-timer from a Christian Benteke header. Firmino would double the lead midway through the second half on an assist by Sheyi Ojo. The match would end with Liverpool victorious 2-0. On the table after the weekend, Liverpool was still in contention to earn another Europa League spot with two more victories in their final two league games. Yet no one cared. Victory over Sevilla in the Europa League on May 18 would secure passage back to the Champions League, and that was all that the fan base cared about.

The Chelsea match at Anfield would follow during midweek. This was rescheduled from earlier in the season due to Chelsea's advancement in the FA Cup. Normally I would find myself down at the pub for a midweek fixture, especially when one of the big clubs was the opponent. Still, it was hard to get excited about this particular match. Chelsea had had a miserable campaign, falling well behind their lofty expectations for the season, and Liverpool's season would be judged by the result in Basel a week later. I decided to skip the pub and stay in the office that Wednesday afternoon. I would ultimately watch this match from my iPad at my desk.

Eden Hazard scored in the first half to give Chelsea the lead, and they probably should've won the match by that same 1-0 score. A gaffe from goalkeeper Asmir Begovic in the second minute of stoppage time allowed Benteke an easy open net, which he converted with the rare chest ball. The match would end 1-1.

No one seemed too bothered by the result. Those few Chelsea fans that were still watching them play matches in that abysmal season were just happy that the season was one game away from closure. Liverpool fans couldn't have cared less about the result either. I would later hear from the guys at the pub that turnout was extremely low, further validating my initial decision. I'm sure they weren't worried, because the biggest crowd of the season was expected the following Wednesday for the cup final. If only life had a fast-forward button. I couldn't wait a full week.

38 - BOSTON

As I planned the travel schedule for this project out, I thought it would be fitting to conclude the season in the city where my introduction to the OLSC world began. I foolishly thought the club wouldn't be able to rise and earn another cup final after the Premier League concluded, but that was a pleasant surprise.

Four years earlier I was fortunate enough to find a booth at the now-closed An Tua Nua pub near Fenway Park, where eventually Colin Russell and Darren Bridger would settle in for the afternoon. Liverpool was set to play a preseason friendly against Italian club AS Roma on a Wednesday in late July. The match didn't kick off until six p.m., but my brother and I arrived at the pub when it opened at noon.

For my entire life I'd held a sibling rivalry with my brother; we always rooted against the other's favorite team in every sport. When we both declared our love for Liverpool for different reasons, it was a challenge to accept. Luckily, our stubbornness lost out to maturity as we agreed that it would be nice to have commonality in one sport. When the club announced a preseason tour in North America for 2012 with a match in Boston, we knew that would be the perfect opportunity for us to meet up and watch the club we love together.

My brother Kevin is a few years older and I followed him to the U.S. Coast Guard Academy mostly so I could play on the same pitch with him. One of his best friends from college is Michael Collins, himself a lifelong Liverpool fan that he inherited from his Irish ancestors. Michael now lives just north of Boston in the small town of Andover. He introduced Kevin to the world of Liverpool, inviting him along to attend the Merseyside Derby years ago on tickets he had won in an OLSC Boston raffle.

We arrived in Boston the day before the match and were able to secure attendance to a few pre-match events. We attended a meet-and-greet session with legendary strikers Ian Rush and Robbie Fowler, where I was able to get Fowler to autograph some custom photographs I had made of his infamous "line-sniffing" goal celebration against Everton in April of 1999. While my brother attended live training at Fenway Park later that afternoon through tickets he got from Michael's son Declan, I waited for him inside the great Bleacher Bar to enjoy some libations and revel in my newly-acquired signed photographs. It was there that I met and befriended Bernie Allen, a Liverpool fan that lives only a few hundred yards from Anfield. Michael joined us there later that evening after getting off from work.

We were only in Boston for a few days, but the activities sponsored by OLSC Boston opened my eyes to the many benefits that come with being part of an official supporters club. That feeling was seconded by both Colin and Darren as we drank a few pints hours before kickoff. It was then that OLSC Raleigh was born.

One of the reasons I was able to plan a weekend getaway to Boston for the final match is that you know exactly when the match will kick off months in advance. While the other thirty-seven matches during the regular season may shift start times due to television contracts, all ten matches on the final week are kicked off simultaneously to protect the integrity of each match. I could safely make travel plans knowing that the match would be played on Sunday at ten a.m. EST.

Tim Treacy is the chairman of OLSC Boston, a post that he has kept for many years. I first met Tim during that wonderful 2012 summer in Boston, and he was a big help as we worked hard to get LFC Raleigh up and running. Tim is a lifelong Liverpool fan from County Kildare, Ireland. Unfortunately, he'd made family plans for that Sunday, so I wouldn't be able to reconnect with my good friend. Much like every other Liverpool fan, he was saving himself for the Europa League final on Wednesday.

Tori and I spent a glorious spring weekend in downtown Boston and took the subway train to Cambridge on Sunday morning. OLSC Boston claims the Phoenix Landing as their home pub, a short walk from the subway station. I was worried that there wouldn't be a great turnout for the match. Most Liverpool fans were clearly looking ahead to Wednesday's Europa League final, and a weaker squad was expected to start for the Reds. It turned out not to be the case for the crew at OLSC Boston.

The pub looks innocent enough from the outside along the bustling Massachusetts Avenue in the town that Harvard University calls home. Then we walked inside to a near-capacity crowd. Thankfully, we found a table near one of the nine television screens.

The pub was a little quainter than I expected, with about the same footprint as the London Bridge Pub in Raleigh, if not slightly smaller. Much like our home pub, there was no doubt that this place was home to a Liverpool supporters club. Behind the bar hangs a sign that reads "This is AnPhoenix," an homage to the "This is Anfield" sign hanging at the stadium. Signed jerseys from King Kenny Dalglish and Luis Suarez were framed and hanging near the entry. If felt like home.

About fifty patrons were already at the pub, the vast majority of which were ready to watch Liverpool take on West Bromwich Albion. A small group of Arsenal supporters occupied the near corner next to our table watching their final match against Aston Villa, but mostly everyone was there to watch the Reds.

For the most part, all of next year's European spots were accounted for. There was a small chance that Manchester United could nick the final Champions League spot from Manchester City, but their final match against Bournemouth was ultimately postponed due to a bomb scare. City could secure fourth place in the league with only a draw over Swansea, so one television remained fixed on that match. Other than those two matches, every television was playing Liverpool against West Bromwich Albion.

As expected, Klopp rested many key players in advance of the Europa League final. Most of the expected starters for Wednesday wouldn't even dress for the match. With Danny Ward sidelined to injury, it would mark the last game Adam Bogdan would likely ever play as Liverpool first-team goalkeeper. The squad was filled with youngsters like Brad Smith, Jon Flanagan, Kevin Stewart, Cameron Brannagan, and Sheyi Ojo. Technically Liverpool could still claim seventh place in the league with a tiny hope of getting that final Europa League spot should they lose to Sevilla, but they would need Southampton or West Ham to drop points for that to happen. Clearly all of next year's European eggs were being put into Wednesday's basket.

Most of the tables at the pub were occupied by Liverpool fans enjoying a fine Sunday breakfast. I immediately noticed not a single pint of beer being consumed at any table, prompting me to inquire about the Sunday drinking laws in the state of Massachusetts. Not until eleven, I was sadly informed, so I started off with a cup of coffee.

It didn't take long for the Baggies to take the early lead. In the thirteenth minute of the match, seventeen-year-old Jonathan Leko passed off to Salomon Rondon, who would beat Bogdan to the bottom right corner of the net to put the home team up 1-0. Normally I would expect to hear a loud chorus of groans from a pro-Liverpool crowd, but the somewhat apathetic group seemed hardly bothered by the early deficit.

Ten minutes later, Liverpool would equalize thanks to the misfortune of former Manchester United defender Jonny Evans, who slipped trying to stop a pass from Flanagan to Jordon Ibe. The young winger sped down the right side and fired home with a left-footed shot into the corner. There was a tempered cheer from the Liverpool fans at the pub.

The match entered the second half as I placed an order for my first pint of Guinness to arrive at the table when legally allowable. It wasn't exactly an exciting match for what ended up being a relatively boring final week of Premier League football. The most exciting moments came when Andre Ayew scored for Swansea City just before halftime to draw level with Manchester City. A single Manchester United fan erupted with the hopes that the Swans could snatch a victory and open the door for United to leapfrog their cross-town rivals. It wasn't until that goal was scored that I realized the plain-clothed man was actually a Manchester United fan afraid to don his colors in a Liverpool pub.

As the second-half minutes ticked off the clock, I found myself watching more Manchester City than Liverpool. With both Southampton and West Ham securing their positions ahead of Liverpool on the table, I was mostly hoping to enjoy the Schadenfreude of seeing Manchester United eliminated from next season's Champions League. I would not be disappointed, as Manchester City secured fourth place in the league with a 1-1 draw.

Meanwhile, a few late Arsenal goals had their fans singing and dancing as they eased past Aston Villa 4-0. Arsenal had already secured third place, but their hated North London rival Tottenham Hotspur were in the process of a massive fall on the road against Newcastle United. Tottenham hadn't finished above Arsenal in the table since 1995, and weeks ago they'd seemed like a team that might actually win the league. They would only earn two draws in the three most recent matches, followed by a 5-1 loss to a club already relegated. Their final month of the season capped one of the club's biggest capitulations in their long history. And the dozen Arsenal fans at the Phoenix Landing loved every minute of it.

The loudest cheer of the day came in the sixty-third minute of the Liverpool match when Danny Ings entered the match as a substitute. Ings had suffered a major knee ligament injury on the first day he trained with Klopp at the helm. It was widely suspected that he would be out for the season, a disappointing setback for the striker in his first season at the club. He'd worked diligently throughout the season to speed his recovery and earned the respect of the entire club. His entry signified a just reward for the hard work, and every Liverpool fan appreciated it. The cheer was so loud at the pub that a neighboring Arsenal fan asked me who had just scored for the Reds. His surprise was genuine when I told him that Danny Ings was entering as a sub. "Good for him," the Boston Gooner said.

When I made plans to watch this final league match in Boston, I had envisioned a grand event with everything on the line for Liverpool. I expected it to be one of the greater occasions on my tour. I absolutely loved the Phoenix Landing, an intimate pub that would easily be packed for big matches. One of the benefits of being a member of OLSC Boston is the right of admission for the free match. During the League Cup final against Manchester City, they had a bouncer at the door, ensuring that only club members in good standing would be allowed to enter. Other fans were directed to nearby pubs for the expected overflow. The maximum capacity at the Phoenix Landing allowable by law couldn't be far off from about a hundred fans.

I was hoping to meet an old friend who would hopefully introduce me to new friends. I hadn't had a problem meeting fans in other cities, but I wasn't in the mood to interrupt the Sunday brunch of strangers. With my wife by my side, we simply enjoyed the atmosphere.

Boston is a great city that holds a special place in my heart. Both of my parents were born and raised in the area, and I've spent many summers in the suburbs visiting relatives. My uncle took me to my first baseball game at Fenway Park when I was nine years old, and all of my cousins root for their sports teams. Boston has it all: history, great food, breweries, atmosphere, and great people. I made a promise to both my wife and OLSC Boston chairman Tim Treacy that we would return in the very near future. That was an easy promise to make.

Liverpool would end up drawing their final match against West Bromwich Albion 1-1, finishing eighth on the table. That wouldn't be good enough to earn a spot in next year's Europa League campaign, which was certainly disappointing. A small consolation prize was finishing ten points ahead of Chelsea, who ended up tenth on the table. And unlike Chelsea, our season wasn't over.

It was the end of a weird season for the Reds. There was so much optimism at the beginning following two wins and a road draw at Arsenal, but soon the season went south. Brendan Rodgers would get the sack before the end of September as the new era with Jürgen Klopp began. Klopp was able to take the team and inject life back into the club. Despite a season filled with injuries, we'd lost a cup final at Wembley in a penalty shootout. We saw one of the most incredible comebacks of the season, beating German juggernaut Borussia Dortmund. We finished the league in eighth position, only seven points shy of finishing in the top four, hardly an improvement from the previous season. And while the majority of the league started their summer vacation, Liverpool had one more match to be played. The Europa League final would be played in Basel, Switzerland in three days, with a spot in the Champions League at stake for both clubs.

39 - MAKE US DREAM AGAIN

Wednesday, May 18
London Bridge Pub, Raleigh, NC
Europa League Final (vs. Sevilla)

It's not often that Liverpool finish the season with a game that actually matters. Unlike all major American sports, the Premier League title is determined by the team that has the best overall finish after all regular season games have concluded. When the club performs well in a cup competition and gets to play in a final, like they did against Manchester City earlier this season, it's a nice distraction. Winning the League Cup would've guaranteed a spot in next year's Europa League, something they didn't earn by virtue of their eighth-place league finish this season. At the time, no one was really bothered by that fact, and it could be argued that the bigger fish to be fried was winning the Europa League anyway.

The Europa League and its predecessor the UEFA Cup had always been a fun competition but rarely taken seriously by major clubs. It was a nice carrot dangled in front of the clubs that offered a small glimpse of glory. Occasionally a small Cinderella club would get to play on the big stage for a rare chance at stardom, like Fulham experienced playing in the 2010 Europa League final. UEFA had increased the size of that carrot, offering an automatic berth into the Champions League for the 2014-15 season. It was smart move that kept the light shining at the end of the tunnel for Liverpool this season. As fourth place in the Premier League drifted out of sight, Jürgen Klopp could focus on the Europa League title with a chance to win silverware while simultaneously catapulting the club into the upper echelon of European football next season. It had been a long time since we saw a match that carried more importance than this Europa League final. The reward for victory in a single match had not been this great since the two recent Champions League finals.

In October, Klopp had inherited a squad of decent players, but they weren't exactly the players he'd picked. A few weeks after the season would conclude, Klopp and the Liverpool transfer committee would commence a flurry of activity to improve the squad with players that Klopp could use to shape a team he believed could be successful. Recruiting talent is not as easy as it once was. The best players want to play on the biggest stage, and there is no bigger stage in football than the UEFA Champions League. Despite finishing mid-table, Liverpool had a chance to sneak into that competition with a victory in the Europa League, ultimately making the prospects of signing major talent much easier.

American sports fans are used to having finality in their seasons. As the regular season concludes, a team only needs to perform well enough to make the playoffs for a chance at ultimate glory. The 2006 St. Louis Cardinals finished the regular season with an 83-79 record, barely winning more games than they lost. Yet they managed to sneak into the playoffs and negotiate their way to winning the World Series title. At the end of the day, fans don't care how many games they won that season. Both the New York Mets and New York Yankees won ninety-seven regular-season games that season, yet their fans had to watch a supposedly inferior club celebrate the championship.

There was a similar sense of finality to this cup final being played in Basel, Switzerland. Standing in Liverpool's way was two-time defending Europa League champions Sevilla. Much like Liverpool, this was a season of disappointment for the Sevillistas. They had lost their final three league matches earlier in the month to finish seventh place in the La Liga table. They also needed a win in this match to ensure advancement to next season's Champions League.

Sevilla would be playing in their third straight Europa League final. The previous season they had defeated Ukrainian club Dnipro Dnipropetrovsk 3-2 in Warsaw in a match that also awarded them a spot in the Champions League (Sevilla finished fifth in that season's La Liga table, falling just short of automatic qualification). The year before they'd hoisted the cup by virtue of a penalty shootout victory over Portuguese side Benfica. Sevilla had been there before, and were going to be a formidable opponent.

****

The last time Liverpool had played their final match of the season with such significance was nine years earlier, with the 2007 Champions League final. That year Liverpool traveled to Athens, Greece to play against Italian rivals AC Milan for the coveted European Cup. It was a rematch of the final from two years earlier, when Liverpool miraculously defeated the

Rossoneri with three second-half goals. Milan defeated Liverpool 2-1 in the rematch winning their seventh European Cup while denying the Reds their sixth continental title. While this upcoming match against Sevilla didn't carry the same level of significance, it was still the last chance at glory for a team of supporters starving for success.

A large crowd was expected at the pub for this midweek match, and the Raleigh Reds didn't disappoint. As soon as Liverpool cemented their advancement to the final, I had cleared my schedule for the final and took the day off. Even if I wanted to try to get work done for my regular job, I knew that my mind would be elsewhere all day long. Even Tori wanted to be involved, and she agreed to be the designated driver for a day that would ultimately involve the consumption of multiple pints of Guinness.

Days before the match I had discussed my plans with Tom Brewer, who was trying to figure out the logistics of attending this important match at the pub. I offered to pick up his wife Lisa at the house and bring her to the pub to make life easier, an offer that he quickly accepted. Not only did it give his wife transportation, it gave his neighbor Charles Thomas the chance to tag along as well. The other owner of Scavengers had grown to love Liverpool as much as the next guy, but mostly Charles was a fan of enjoying great sporting events with his friends and some cold beers. This was an event he didn't want to miss, and I was happy to ensure he didn't.

I headed down to the river to pick up Lisa and Charles, and proceeded to get Tori at her office. Together we drove down to the pub. We walked in a solid hour before kickoff, and already the pub was packed with Red fans. It was reminiscent of the 2013-14 title run late in the season, when fans started piling into the pub as the team continued winning matches. Meaningful football in May was something that we hadn't experienced recently as Liverpool fans, and I made certain to enjoy it.

Many regulars that have been previously mentioned in this book were already present, and others were on the way. I expected to see some others show their face, as this game was far too important to let life get in the way. The first one I noticed was Beau Jimmerson, a computer engineer working not far from my office in Morrisville. He was quick to point out that Liverpool had never lost a match that he watched from the pub, which obviously raised the question why he wasn't attending more matches. Beau is a sarcastic smartass that always looks to get a good laugh at most every situation. I liked him as soon as I met him. He became a fan of Liverpool through his work travels, which took him to London in 2005. He knew that his English colleagues were big soccer fans, but he hadn't latched on to a club at the time. They were huge Liverpool fans, and took him to a pub to watch the Champions League final that season. The dramatic victory led to an epic night of celebrations all over London. Eventually he ended up in a bed and got some sleep before returning to work the next day. As he recalled the story with a smile, he pointed out, "How could I ever root for another team after that?"

Not every Raleigh Red was expected to be in attendance at the pub for this match. A few had made the trip across the pond to Switzerland to try and witness a piece of Liverpool history in person. Max Chiswick was one such fan. Raised in the East London suburb of Ilford, Max relocated to North Carolina years ago. She remains a season ticket holder of Liverpool and wasn't about to miss out on this opportunity. She would be one of the approximately forty thousand fans sitting at St. Jakob Park in Basel to watch this epic match.

I grabbed pints of Guinness for both myself and Tori and took notice of the attendance. Darren was diligently working behind the bar, trying to stay busy in the final hour before kickoff to take his mind off the match. Of all the Raleigh Reds that I have had the honor to call my friends, Darren has invested the most time into his fandom. Born and raised in England, he supported the club through great times and bad. There was no denying his love for Liverpool, and it was because of him that we had a pub to call our own in Raleigh. He was the first person I hugged after dramatically defeating Dortmund a month earlier, with the most genuine tears I have ever seen coming from a grown man watching a sporting event. He clearly couldn't be bothered by the pre-match hype, and desperately tried to keep his mind occupied with anything other than football.

For all intents and purposes, this was quite an improbable run for Liverpool. The team had experienced its share of adversity throughout the season. Mamadou Sakho had been an integral part of the defense, but remained suspended by UEFA for suspicions of a failed drug test. He had been admirably replaced by Kolo Toure, who was starting his fourth match in defense following Sakho's suspension. Both Emre Can and Divock Origi had experienced serious ankle injuries late in the season that threatened their involvement, but both had recovered enough to be part of the squad. Yet despite all of this late adversity, Liverpool still appeared to be the team of destiny heading into this final.

The game kicked off on time with well over a hundred supporters packing the London Bridge Pub. It reminded me of the 2014 World Cup, when the United States advanced to the knockout stage. That summer they experienced record numbers of American Outlaws suffering through unbearable North Carolina summer heat in a packed pub to watch a soccer match. The tension was palpable, and everyone was eagerly anticipating the match.

Liverpool came out firing on all cylinders, and had the first real chance early on through an Emre Can shot that was saved by Sevilla goalkeeper David Soria. Daniel Sturridge had two chances as well, but couldn't capitalize either. Sevilla looked to settle the play as best they could, but

Sturridge wouldn't be denied in the thirty-third minute with a magnificent effort. He received the ball inside the box and curled a shot with the outside of his left foot; it beat Soria to the far post and perfectly hit the side netting. It was a goal worthy of any highlight reel, and gave Liverpool the 1-0 lead.

To say that bedlam ensued might be an understatement. I'm quite certain that the reaction from the pub was felt by local downtown Raleigh establishments blocks away from the London Bridge Pub. The resulting impact on the Richter scale hadn't even peaked at that moment, because five minutes later, Liverpool found the goal again. This time it was Dejan Lovren that headed the ball into the back of the net. Unfortunately for Liverpool, the assistant referee had waved his flag for offside and the goal was disallowed. It was the first of many dubious calls made by the referees in the match. Apparently the claim was made that Sturridge made an attempt to flick the shot from an offside position, but I couldn't disagree more with that decision. Nonetheless, the goal didn't count, and the Liverpool lead remained one.

On three separate occasions, Sevilla players had apparently handled the ball inside the box, but not once did Swedish referee Jonas Eriksson whistle for the penalty. In isolation, the referee's vantage point and perception of each incident could be debated, but it was almost unfathomable that Eriksson did not point to the spot for at least one of the infractions. While the lead could've been three of four heading into the break, it should've been at least two. Instead Liverpool went into halftime only leading by a single goal.

The mood at the pub was positive but nervy. If we'd learned anything about the club this season, it was that we didn't do anything easily. Millions of fans worldwide were on the edge of the seat wondering why this game was still in question. Instead of having a comfortable lead that would force Sevilla to open up their formation, Liverpool would be forced to hang on to a slim lead.

Any signs of optimism quickly disappeared eighteen seconds into the second half when Sevilla equalized. Brazilian defender Mariano made his way past two Liverpool players and squared a simple pass to Kevin Gameiro, who easily scored from about five yards out. Just like that, the score was level at one. It should be noted that much-maligned defender Alberto Moreno failed to adequately clear the ball on the initial cross before getting beaten by Mariano, and could be considered at fault for the goal. Liverpool had acquired the young Spanish defender in August 2014 from Sevilla for £12 million, which made it slightly ironic that he was one of the contributing factors on that goal.

The Sevilla goal instantly stole the air from the pub before most fans had a chance to get settled in from halftime. There were a few loud expletives shouted throughout the pub, but for the most part the patrons stood in collective shocked silence. Forty-five minutes of positive play had been negated by eighteen seconds of terror.

The goal transformed the match in Sevilla's favor, and they began to dominate the play. Gameiro had a golden opportunity thwarted by Toure two minutes later, and Simon Mignolet saved another Gameiro effort in the sixtieth minute. Liverpool was hanging on by a thread. That thread finally broke four minutes later when Coke blasted a first-time shot from the edge of the penalty box past Mignolet. It was a quick play that was difficult to defend, and a brilliant goal, but that didn't help ease the sting of losing the lead.

Despite losing the lead so quickly in the second half, the Raleigh Reds began to rally. After all, this had to be a team of destiny, hadn't it? Twenty-five minutes remained, more than enough time to find an equalizer. This could be an opportunity for someone to cement their legacy at the club and etch their moment in history. All that was needed was a moment of sheer brilliance, and we all thought it was coming.

Sadly, the Sevillistas never let that moment come. Five minutes after giving his club the lead, Coke found the back of the net again. It was a simple finish off a pass that took two deflections off Liverpool defenders Lovren and Moreno. Unmarked with a clear shot on target, Coke gave the defending champions a two-goal cushion.

There were no loud expletives this time. There was only desperation. I looked around at the sad faces at the pub, even noting one unknown fan praying to his God for help. Klopp showed his own desperation, calling for Christian Benteke and Divock Origi to make late substitutions in search of any offense to get back into the match. It was all for naught. As the final seconds ticked off the clock, defeat was inevitable. When the final whistle blew, it felt like a dagger being sent straight into the heart.

****

As Sevilla celebrated their third consecutive Europa League title, Liverpool players and fans watched in dismay. It wasn't supposed to end this way. We were supposed to be the ones celebrating our ninth European trophy, announcing our return to the European elite with authority. Instead it was yet another Bill Buckner moment of misery. In 1986, the much-maligned and cursed Boston Red Sox were one out away from winning their first World Series championship in sixty-eight years when Buckner failed to collect a simple ground ball at first base. His error opened the door for the Mets to make a miraculous comeback, and added to the misery of Red Sox fans around the world. While the Buckner error was more analogous to the Steven Gerrard slip against Chelsea in 2014, this loss was yet another unfortunate moment in recent Liverpool history.

Most fans stuck around for one final pint to help drown the sorrow of the defeat. The pub blasted Gerry and the Pacemakers one final time as the pub sang "You'll Never Walk Alone" in unison. It was a bittersweet moment. As I have noted numerous times already, Liverpool don't do easy. North Carolinians will attest that "the Storm" is never predictable. Just when you think you are safe, the conditions shift and it takes a turn for the worst. You can never let down your guard or you will pay the price.

An hour later I found myself still hanging at the pub with my friends. Many had left for home, but most of the regulars remained. We simply didn't want the ride to end. Liverpool wouldn't play another meaningful game for three months, and most of us wouldn't see each other again until then.

While we all were disappointed, the overall mood shifted from disappointment to optimism. Instead of reflecting on what could've been, we started thinking about what was to come. Under Klopp, this club had progressed further than any of us could imagine. Soon the transfer window would open and the makeup of the squad would change dramatically. It would be Klopp's first real opportunity to put his mark on the player pool. He'd had most of a full season to assess the squad, and he could implement his plan to improve the way he wanted.

"The Storm" is a fickle beast. Getting through it is never easy, and I have learned to accept that I don't want it to be. Throughout the season I traveled to many places and met many new friends. We have all found Liverpool through different paths. In the end, there is no denying that we all share the same struggles. And we will all share the same glory. "The Storm" will always be a test, but in Klopp I believe we have found the right man to captain our ship. He has provided the juice to make us dream again. It's not false hope. It's blind faith. As he negotiates the journey safely through the tempest, I look forward to seeing that golden sky at the end of the journey. And when that happens, I look forward to celebrating the arrival of that beautiful scene at the only place I would want to be…at the pub with my Liverpool family trying to keep the tears from spilling into my pint of Guinness.

APPENDIX ONE

Throughout the course of this book, you have undoubtedly discovered the recurring theme of finding pleasure watching the beautiful game amongst likeminded supporters. The sport's popularity continues to grow in North America, as does the likeliness of finding pubs where fans congregate to watch the game. One of the other themes scattered throughout this book is the concept of being part of an Official Liverpool Supporters Club (OLSC). What exactly does that mean? According to the club website, the "Official Supporters Clubs provide a valuable service to loyal Liverpool Football Club supporters living in the local area. The Supporters Clubs also provide an excellent way of meeting fellow supporters who are devoted to following Liverpool Football Club, wherever they live in the World. Official Supporter Clubs are closely affiliated to Liverpool Football Club and enjoy a close working relationship with the Club."

If you can't locate an official club near you, then you can do what we did in Raleigh four years ago and form your own club with the aspirations of becoming official. Guidelines are subject to change and can be found on the website, but as of the publishing date a local needed at least fifty members with fifteen of them having joined LFC as official membership holders. If you and some friends find yourself seeking guidance towards the path of becoming an official club, I offer the following basic plan:

1. **Find a pub to call home**. Seek out the ownership and make your intentions known. While most of the pubs that broadcast the sport on their televisions will be happy to accommodate you, it is this relationship between pub and club that is most important. Matches will be scheduled at inconvenient times, and the ownership may not want to open their doors for the early Sunday

morning kickoff. Ultimately your strength in numbers will be enough motivation for the pub to open, but it will take time to get there. Additionally, it's important for your club to maintain consistency about where to watch matches. Word will spread about supporters that watch the matches at a specific pub, so your club can grow organically as long as they know where to meet.

2. **Create a social media campaign**. Do an extensive search of Facebook, Twitter, and Instagram to locate other likeminded supporters in your region. If there isn't already an established network, create one.

3. **Seek out support from your neighbors**. One of the great things about the OLSC network is how other clubs are willing to help your cause. They can help boost participation on your respective social media accounts, getting the word out in the process. You can also get some lessons learned from the people that were in your shoes not that long ago.

4. **Form an Organizational Committee**. As your numbers grow, activity will need to be managed. While it all starts with the love of watching football, people keep coming back for the camaraderie. They want to watch the big games with the other fans while perhaps enjoying a pint. You'll need to have an organizational structure in place to help plan events, work with the pub, and take advantage of the benefits that come with being associated with the parent club.

5. **Reach out to the Club**. Once you feel like you have met the requirements established for official status, inform the club of your intentions. It may take time for it to happen, but ultimately the club is interested in growing their network as much as you want to be a part of it. They will help you get there.

Having gone through this process already, I know that there is an extensive network already in place. Below is a state-by-state list of North America's **LFC Supporters Clubs (official and unofficial)** along with the pubs they go to for matches should you be traveling. This list was compiled following a thorough search of social media and internet websites and may be subject to change. You are encouraged to conduct your own search and contact the home pubs to verify that the local Liverpool supporters club still congregates at this specific location. Pubs that have the designation "Official" next to them in the below list indicate that they are already associated with an OLSC, but not necessarily as the only pub for that group. Many clubs have multiple taverns where their members may congregate to watch a Liverpool match.

In addition to the list of pubs, I have included current state law restrictions regarding the sale of on-premises alcoholic beverages which is effective as of publishing date. This information is intended to educate you for those early morning matches should you decide to partake in a libation. Note that this list is based on internet research at the time of publishing and subject to change. If you do choose to indulge, please drink responsibly always.

Alabama: Currently no known home LFC pubs in this state.

Current state alcohol restrictions include: Prohibited between 6 AM and 12 PM on Sundays in some counties. Private clubs, which require a membership fee and a membership card, have no day or time restrictions.

Alaska: Currently no known home LFC pubs in this state.

Current state alcohol restrictions include: Allowed daily from 8 AM–5 AM

Arizona:
- **Phoenix (Official):** Rose and Crown, 628 E Adams St, Phoenix, AZ 85004

Current state alcohol restrictions include: Consumption is allowed 6 AM–2 AM seven days a week.

Arkansas: Currently no known home LFC pubs in this state.

Current state alcohol restrictions include: Prohibited Sundays. Consumption not allowed between the hours of 1 AM-7 AM on all days, as well as the hour between Sunday midnight and 1 AM Monday morning.

California:
- **Culver City (Official):** Joxer Daly's (Home Pub), 11168 Washington Blvd, Culver City, CA 90232
- **Millbrae (Official):** Fiddler's Green, 333 El Camino Real, Millbrae, CA 94030
- **Pasadena (Official):** Lucky Baldwin's, 17 S Raymond Ave, Old Town Pasadena, CA 91105
- **Fresno:** Strummer's, 833 E Fern Ave, Fresno, CA 93728 (Tower Arts District)
- **Tustin, Orange County (Official):** The Auld Dubliner, 2497 Park Ave, Tustin, CA 92782
- **Sacramento:** de Vere's Irish Pub, 1521 L St, Sacramento, CA

- **San Diego (Official):** The Princess Pub, 1665 India St, San Diego, CA 92101 (Little Italy)
- **San Francisco (Official):** Kezar Pub, 770 Stanyan St, San Francisco, CA 94117
- **Sunnyvale (Official):** Fibbar MaGees, 156 S Murphy Ave, Sunnyvale, CA 94086

Current state alcohol restrictions include: Consumption is allowed 6 AM–2 AM daily

Colorado:

- **Denver (Official):** Abbey Tavern, 5151 E Colfax Ave, Denver, CO 80220

Current state alcohol restrictions include: Consumption is allowed 7 AM–2 AM daily

Connecticut:

- **Collinsville:** Wilson's Pub, 3 River Street, Collinsville, CT 06019
- **New Haven (Official):** The Trinity Bar & Restaurant, 157 Orange Street, New Haven, CT 06510
- **New Haven:** Anna Liffey's, 17 Whitney Ave, New Haven, CT 06510

Current state alcohol restrictions include: Consumption is allowed 9 AM–1 AM (Mon–Thurs), 9 AM–2 AM (Fri–Sat), and 11 AM–1 AM (Sunday only).

Delaware:

- **Wilmington:** Catherine Rooney's Irish Pub, 1616 Delaware Avenue, Wilmington, DE 19806

Current state alcohol restrictions include: Consumption is allowed daily 9 AM–1 AM

District of Columbia:

- **Washington D.C. (Official):** The Queen Vic, 1206 H St NE, Washington, DC 20002

Current alcohol restrictions include: Consumption is allowed 8 AM–2 AM (Sun–Thurs), and 8 AM–3 AM (Fri–Sat)

Florida:

- **Fort Lauderdale (Official):** Fox & Hounds (Oakland Park), 4812 N Dixie Hwy, Oakland Park, Fort Lauderdale, FL 33334
- **Lake Worth:** Brogues DownUnder, 621 Lake Ave, Lake Worth, FL 33460
- **Miami:** Fado Irish Pub, Mary Brickell Village, 900 South Miami Ave, Miami, FL 33130
- **Miami:** Churchill's Pub, 5501 NE 2nd Ave, Miami, FL 33137
- **Miami Beach:** Playwright Irish Pub, 1265 Washington Avenue, Miami Beach, FL 33139
- **Orlando (Official):** Harp & Celt (Harp side), 25 S Magnolia Ave, Orlando, FL 32801
- **Tampa (Official):** Four Green Fields, 205 W Platt St, Tampa, FL 33606

Current state alcohol restrictions include: Prohibited between 1 AM-7 AM unless the county decides to change the operating hours.

Georgia:

- **Atlanta (Official):** Meehan's Public House, 200 Peachtree St, Atlanta, GA 30303

Current state alcohol restrictions include: varies by local government rules

Hawaii: Currently no known home LFC pubs in this state.

Current state alcohol restrictions include: Bars and restaurants stop serving alcohol at 2 AM, but some hold a special 'cabaret license' that allows them to continue serving alcohol until 4 AM.

Idaho: Currently no home LFC pubs in this state.

Current state alcohol restrictions include: Consumption is allowed 6 AM-2 AM, 7 AM-1 AM in some counties

Illinois:

- **Chicago (Official):** AJ Hudson's Public House, 3801 N Ashland Ave, Chicago, IL 60613

Current state alcohol restrictions include: Consumption is allowed 6 AM-4 AM

Indiana:
- **Indianapolis (Official):** Union Jack Pub, 924 Broad Ripple Ave, Indianapolis, IN 46220

Current state alcohol restrictions include: Consumption is allowed daily 7 AM–3 AM

Iowa: Currently no known home LFC pubs in this state.

Current state alcohol restrictions include: Consumption is allowed 6 AM–2 AM (Mon–Sat) and only 8 AM–2 AM on Sunday

Kansas:
- **Kansas City (Official):** The Dubliner Irish Ale House & Pub, 170 E 14th St, Kansas City, MO 64105

Current state alcohol restrictions include: Consumption is allowed 9 AM - 2 AM, however some dry counties do not allow on-premises sales at all.

Kentucky:
- **Covington (Official):** Molly Malone's, 112 E 4th St, Covington, KY 41011
- **Lexington (Official):** The Paddock Bar and Patio, 319 S Limestone # B, Lexington, KY 40508
- **Louisville (Official):** Molly Malone's Highlands, 933 Baxter Ave, KY 40204

Current state alcohol restrictions include: Allowed 6 AM-4 AM on Monday through Saturday. No on-premises drinking on Sundays.

Louisiana:
- **Baton Rouge:** The Londoner Grill, 4215 S Sherwood Forest Blvd, Baton Rouge, LA 70816
- **New Orleans:** Finn McCool's Irish Pub, 3701 Banks St, LA 70119

Current state alcohol restrictions include: None

Maine: Currently no known home LFC pubs in this state.

Current state alcohol restrictions include: Consumption is allowed 6 AM-1 AM (Mon–Sat), 9 AM-1 AM (Sun)

Maryland:

- **Baltimore (Official):** Smaltimore, 2522 Fait Ave, Canton, Baltimore, MD 21224

Current state alcohol restrictions include: varies by local government rules

Massachusetts:

- **Boston (Official):** The Phoenix Landing, 512 Massachusetts Ave, Central Square, Cambridge, MA 02139
- **Oxford (Official):** Whistle Stop Bar & Grill, 85 Main St, Oxford, MA 01540
- **Worcester (Official):** Funky Murphy's, 305 Shrewsbury St, Worcester, MA 01604

Current state alcohol restrictions include: Allowed 8 AM–2 AM by state law, although individual cities and towns may prohibit sales before 11 AM and after 11 PM. No on-premises drinking is allowed before 11 AM on Sunday.

Michigan:

- **Detroit (Official):** Thomas Magee's Whiskey Bar, 1408 E Fisher Fwy, Detroit, MI 48207

Current state alcohol restrictions include: Consumption is allowed 7 AM–2 AM (Mon-Sat), noon-2 AM (Sunday

Minnesota:

- **Minneapolis (Official):** Brit's Pub, 1110 Nicollet Mall, Minneapolis, MN 55403

Current state alcohol restrictions include: Consumption is allowed daily 8 AM–2 AM

Mississippi: Currently no known home LFC pubs in this state.

Current state alcohol restrictions include: varies by local government rules

Missouri:

- **Clayton:** Barrister's, 7923 Forsyth Blvd, Clayton, MO 63105
- **St. Louis (Official):** Amsterdam Tavern, 3175 Morganford, St. Louis, MO 63116

Current state alcohol restrictions include: Consumption is allowed 6 AM–1:30 AM (Mon-Sat), 9 AM–Midnight on Sunday.

Montana: Currently no known home LFC pubs in this state.

Current state alcohol restrictions include: Consumption is allowed until 2 AM daily

Nebraska:
- **Omaha (Official):** St. Andrews Pub, 6102 Maple St, Omaha, NE 68104

Current state alcohol restrictions include: Consumption is allowed 6 AM–1 AM daily

Nevada:
- **Henderson:** Shakespeare's Grille & Pub, 790 Coronado Center Dr Suite 130, Henderson, NV 89052
- **Las Vegas:** Rí Rá Las Vegas, The Shoppes at Mandalay Bay Place, 3930 Las Vegas Blvd South, Las Vegas, NV 89119

Current state alcohol restrictions include: None

New Hampshire: Currently no known home LFC pubs in this state.

Current state alcohol restrictions include: Consumption is allowed 6 AM–1 AM daily

New Jersey:
- **Teaneck:** The Cottage Bar, 178 Cedar Lane, Teaneck, NJ 07666

Current state alcohol restrictions include: varies by local government rules

New Mexico: Currently no known home LFC pubs in this state.

Current state alcohol restrictions include: Consumption is allowed 7 AM–2 AM, except Sundays where it is prohibited.

New York:
- **Buffalo:** Mes Que, 1420 Hertel Ave, Buffalo, NY 14216
- **New York City (Official):**
  - 11th Street Bar (New York – Home Pub), 510 East 11th St,

New York, NY 10009
- The Grafton, 126 First Ave, New York, NY 10009
- The Monro (Brooklyn), 481 5th Ave, Brooklyn, NY 11215
- The Ceili Bar (Queens), 6956 Grand Ave, Maspeth, NY 11378
- Prost (Long Island), 652 Franklin Ave, Garden City, NY 11530
- **New York City (Unofficial):**
  - The Boot Room NYC, 17 John St, New York, NY 10038
  - Carragher's, 228 West 39th St, New York, NY 10018 (between 7th and 8th)

Current state alcohol restrictions include: Consumption is allowed 8 AM–4 AM (Mon-Sat), Noon-4 AM (Sun)

North Carolina:
- **Charlotte:** Ri Ra Irish Pub, 208 N Tryon St, Charlotte, NC 28202
- **Charlotte (Official):** Valhalla Pub & Eatery, 317 S Church St, Charlotte, NC 28202
- **Raleigh (Official):** The London Bridge Pub, 110 E Hargett St, Raleigh, NC 27601

Current state alcohol restrictions include: Consumption is allowed 7 AM-2 AM (Mon-Sat), Noon-2 AM (Sun)

North Dakota: Currently no known home LFC pubs in this state.

Current state alcohol restrictions include: Consumption is allowed 8 AM-2 AM (Mon-Sat), Noon-2 AM (Sun)

Ohio:
- **Cincinnati (Official):** Rhinehaus, 119 East 12th Street, Cincinnati, OH 45202
- **Columbus:** Fado Irish Pub, Easton Town Center, 4022 Townsfair Way, Columbus, OH 43219
- **Columbus:** The Three Legged Mare, 401 N Front St #150, Columbus, OH 43215
- **Columbus:** Fourth Street Bar and Grill, 1810 N Fourth St, Columbus, OH 43201

Current state alcohol restrictions include: Consumption is allowed 5:30 AM-2:30 AM daily

Oklahoma: Currently no known home LFC pubs in this state.

Current state alcohol restrictions include: Consumption is allowed 6 AM-2 AM daily

Oregon:
- **Portland:** 4-4-2 Soccer Bar, 1739 SE Hawthorne Blvd, Portland, OR 97214

Current state alcohol restrictions include: Consumption is allowed 7 AM-2:30 AM daily

Pennsylvania:
- **Philadelphia:** Iron Abbey Pub (Horsham area), 680 North Easton Rd, Horsham, PA 19044
- **Philadelphia:** Victoria Free House, 10 South Front Street, Philadelphia, PA 19106
- **Philadelphia:** Jose Pistola's, 263 South 15th St, Philadelphia, PA 19102
- **Pittsburgh (Official):** Cain's Saloon, 3239 West Liberty Avenue, Dormont, Pittsburgh, PA 15216
- **Pittsburgh:** Piper's Pub, 1828 E Carson St, Pittsburgh, PA 15203

Current state alcohol restrictions include: Consumption is allowed 7 AM-2 AM (Mon-Sat), 11 AM-2 AM (Sun)

Rhode Island:
- **Providence:** Murphy's, 100 Fountain Street, Providence, RI 02909

Current state alcohol restrictions include: Consumption is allowed 9 AM-1 AM (Mon-Sat), Noon-1 AM (Sun)

South Carolina:
- **Charleston (Official):** Madra Rua-Park Circle (N. Charleston-Home pub), 1034 E Montague Ave, Park Circle, N Charleston, SC 29405
- **Columbia (Official):** The British Bulldog, 1220 Bower Parkway E-10, Columbia, SC 29212
- **Greenville (Official):** Gringos Cantina, 11 W Camperdown Way (11 Falls Park Dr), Greenville, SC 29601
- **Myrtle Beach (Official):** McCann's Pub & Eatery (The Old Bull

and Bush), 4700 US Highway 17 Bypass South, Myrtle Beach, SC
- **Summerville (Official)**: Madra Rua, 2066 N Main St, Summerville, SC 29483

Current state alcohol restrictions include: Consumption is allowed 10 AM-2 AM daily.

South Dakota: Currently no known home LFC pubs in this state.

Current state alcohol restrictions include: Consumption is allowed 7 AM-2 AM daily.

Tennessee:
- **Chattanooga:** The Feed Table and Tavern, 201 W Main St, Chattanooga, TN 37408
- **Knoxville:** Hops and Hollers, 937 N Central St, Knoxville, TN 37917
- **Knoxville:** The Casual Pint, 143 Brooklawn St, Farragut, TN 37934
- **Memphis:** Celtic Crossing, 903 S Cooper St, Memphis, TN 38104
- **Nashville:** Franklin Abbey, 9200 Carothers Parkway, Franklin, TN 37067

Current state alcohol restrictions include: Consumption is allowed 8 AM-3 AM (Mon-Sat), Noon-3 AM (Sun)

Texas:
- **Austin (Official):** Bull McCabe's, 714 Red River St, Austin, TX 78701 *(Saturday matches only)*
- **Austin (Official):** Fado Irish Pub, 214 W 4th St, Austin, TX 78701
- **Colleyville:** The Londoner, 5150 Colleyville Blvd, Colleyville, TX 76034
- **Dallas (Official):** The Londoner, 14930 Midway Rd, Addison, TX 75001
- **Houston (Official):** The Gorgeous Gael, Rice Village, 5555 Morningside Dr, Houston, TX 77005
- **Houston (Official):** Ron's Pub, 1826 Fountain View Dr, Houston, TX 77057
- **San Antonio (Official):** Sherlocks Baker St. Pub, Park Oaks

Center, 16620 US-281, San Antonio, TX 78232
- **San Antonio:** The Lion & Rose, 17627 La Cantera Pkwy, San Antonio, TX 78257

Current state alcohol restrictions include: Consumption is allowed 7 AM-Midnight (Mon-Fri), 7 AM-1 AM (Sat), Noon-Midnight (Sun).

Utah: Currently no known home LFC pubs in this state.

Current state alcohol restrictions include: Consumption is allowed noon to midnight for liquor daily, 10AM-1AM for beer.

Vermont:
- **Burlington:** Rí Rá Irish Pub, 123 Church St, Burlington, VT 05401

Current state alcohol restrictions include: Consumption is allowed 8 AM–2 AM daily

Virginia:
- **Arlington (part of OLSC Washington):** Courthaus Social, 2300 Clarendon Blvd, Arlington, VA 22201
- **Richmond (Official):** Penny Lane Pub, 421 E Franklin St, Richmond, VA 23219

Current state alcohol restrictions include: Consumption is allowed 6 AM–2 AM daily

Washington:
- **Seattle (Official):** St. Andrews Bar and Grill, 7406 Aurora Avene North, Seattle, WA 98103
- **Tacoma (Official):** Doyle's Public House, 208 Saint Helens Ave, South Tacoma, WA 98402

Current state alcohol restrictions include: Consumption is allowed 6 AM–2 AM daily

West Virginia: Currently no known home LFC pubs in this state.

Current state alcohol restrictions include: Beer and wine consumption is allowed 7AM-2PM (Mon-Sat), 1PM-2AM (Sun). Same times apply for liquor except that it is prohibited on Sunday.

Wisconsin:

- **Madison:** The Wise Restaurant & Bar, 1501 Monroe St, Madison, WI 53711
- **Milwaukee (Official):** Three Lions Pub, 4515 N Oakland Ave, Milwaukee, WI 53211

Current state alcohol restrictions include: Consumption is allowed 6 AM–2 AM (Sun–Thurs). On Friday and Saturday, the closing time is extended to 2:30 AM.

Wyoming: Currently no known home LFC pubs in this state.

Current state alcohol restrictions include: Consumption is allowed 6 AM–2 AM daily.

Canada:

- **Calgary (Official):** The Cat 'n Fiddle, 540 16th Ave NW, Calgary, T2M 0J4
- **Durham Region (Official):** The Courtyard Restaurant (Courtice), 1437 King Street E, Courtice, L1E 2J6
- **Montreal:** Kellys Pub, 88 Donegani, Pointe Claire, Montreal, H9R 2V4
- **Ottawa:** The Georgetown, 1159 Bank St, Ottawa, K1S 3X7
- **Toronto (Official):** Scallywags, 11 St Clair Avenue West, Toronto, M4V 1K6
- **Vancouver (Official):** The Butcher & Bullock Pub, 911 W Pender St, Vancouver, V6J 1W9
- **Victoria:** Irish Times Pub, 1200 Government Street, Victoria, V8W 1Y2
- **Winnipeg:** The Pint Winnipeg

Barbados:
- **Barbados (Official):** Wendy's Sports Bar, Risk Road, Fitts Village, Saint James, Bridgetown
Bermuda:
- **Bermuda (Official):** Docksider Pub & Restaurant, 121 Front Street, Hamilton HM 19, Bermuda

ABOUT THE AUTHOR

Kenneth J. Kendra is a lifelong fan of the beautiful game since the age of six when he started playing as a child. Not quite a great player for Vestal High School in upstate New York, he was good enough to play through four years at the U.S. Coast Guard Academy as an outside midfielder. After serving six years on active duty, he eventually settled down in North Carolina where he helped start the Official Liverpool FC Supporters Club in Raleigh. He has blogged numerous times about all things Liverpool on the LFC Raleigh official website. He lives with his wife Tori and their blue heeler Dakota in the Pittsboro area west of Raleigh. This is his first book.

He can be reached via his website at **kjkendra.com** or through social media: Facebook (**@kennethjkendra**) and Twitter (**@kjkendra11**).